American government in Ireland, 1790–1913

American government in Ireland, 1790–1913

A history of the US consular service

BERNADETTE WHELAN

Manchester University Press

Copyright © Bernadette Whelan 2010

The right of Bernadette Whelan to be identified as the author of this work has been asserted by her in accordance with the Copyright, Designs and Patents Act 1988.

Published by Manchester University Press
Altrincham Street, Manchester M1 7JA, UK
www.manchesteruniversitypress.co.uk

British Library Cataloguing-in-Publication Data is available

Library of Congress Cataloging-in-Publication Data is available

ISBN 978 1 7849 9377 1 *paperback*

First published by Manchester University Press in hardback 2010

This edition first published 2016

The publisher has no responsibility for the persistence or accuracy of URLs for any external or third-party internet websites referred to in this book, and does not guarantee that any content on such websites is, or will remain, accurate or appropriate.

Printed by Lightning Source

Contents

List of tables	*page* vii
List of appendices	viii
List of terms and usages	ix
Preface	xi

1 The United States consular service in Ireland: appointments and conditions, 1790–1906   1
    Establishing the United States foreign service in Ireland: recruitment and terms of employment, 1790–1856
    Bribery, corruption and consular reform
    Reform regains momentum

2 'Oh Lord, not in my district, Amen': consular work in Ireland, 1790–1907   54
    Protecting American citizens
    Reporting the famine, 1845–51
    Developing trade and commerce

3 Protecting the Union: the American Civil War, 1861–5   105
    Combating Confederate navy-building and blockade-running
    Recruiting Union soldiers and labour

4 'Our Guardian Angel abroad': American foreign policy and Irish nationalism, 1865–70   157
    1865: the 'year of action'
    1866: the suspension of *habeas corpus*
    1867: the year of the rising

5 Building the Union, 1865–1913: the immigration process   210
    Pace of emigration
    The departures of the 'very bone and sinew of the land'
    Implementing the legislation

6 Conclusion 261

   Appendices 267
   Bibliography 275
   Index 289

List of tables

1.1	Salary scales for some consular posts under the 1856 legislation	*page* 30
2.1	Exports of domestic merchandise, 1860–1903	103
3.1	Number of overseas emigrants from Ireland to the United States, 1851–65	129
5.1	Number of Irish immigrants in the United States, 1820–1940	212
5.2	Number of overseas emigrants from Ireland to the United States, 1865–70	212
5.3	Emigrants from Queenstown, February, March 1879 and 1880	219
5.4	Number of overseas emigrants from Ireland to the United States of America, 1875–85	225
5.5	Number of emigrants who embarked at Queenstown for the United States during the twelve months ended 30 September 1882–5	234
5.6	Number of overseas emigrants from Ireland to the United States, 1886–90	235
5.7	Number of overseas emigrants from Ireland to the United States, 1891–1914	237
5.8	Number of emigrants embarked from Ireland by the aid of HMS *Barberer, Britomart, Seahorse, Orwell*, 20 March–20 May 1883	250

List of appendices

1.1 US consular officers in Ireland, 1790–1913
4.1 Table of prisoners claiming to be American citizens on 20 April 1866 (following September 1865 round-up)

Terms and usage

Boards of Guardians. The Poor Relief Act 1838 divided Ireland into districts or 'unions' and 'guardians' were elected by ratepayers to administer to the needs of paupers particularly in workhouses.
County is an administrative unit, of which there are thirty-two. There are four 'provinces' – Connacht, Leinster, Munster, Ulster – comprising counties.
Cove, county Cork, is used until 1849 when the town was renamed 'Queenstown' in honour of a visit from Queen Victoria and reverted to 'Cobh' in 1922. Cove/Cobh/Queenstown/Cork are used interchangeably.
Currency: £=pound, *s.*=shilling, *d.*=pence. The sterling currency system applied to Ireland and Britain during this period. In US currency, $=dollar, *c.*=cent.
Dublin/Dublin Castle government refers to the seat of British administration in Ireland until 1922. As well as a military garrison, the chief secretary of Ireland and lord lieutenant of Ireland had offices there.
Dún Laoghaire, county Dublin, was named 'Kingstown' in 1821 in honour of a visit from George IV and reverted to Dún Laoghaire in 1921.
Exequatur: a recognition by a head of state of a foreign country's consul.
HMS: His/Her Majesty's Service.
Ireland is used to describe the thirty-two county island. The Act of Union in 1800 removed Ireland's legislative independence.
Londonderry was established in 1613 and is pre-dated by the term Derry.
PS: Paddle Steamer. **SS:** Screw Steamer.
Royal Irish Constabulary known as the Irish Constabulary until 1868, was the police force located throughout Ireland from 1822 to 1922.
Sinn Féin ('Ourselves' or 'Ourselves Alone'), a political group formed in 1905 to end the link between Ireland and Britain.
Union/Northern/Federal and **Confederate/Southern** are used interchangeably.

Preface

This book examines the development, role and influence of the United States consular service in Ireland in the period 1790 to 1913. It is a history of America's official presence in Ireland (see appendix 1.1). The existence of this consular network has been largely ignored in the historiography of US foreign policy and US–Ireland relations, except for Francis Carroll's recent study of US–Ulster diplomatic relations and occasional references to US consuls in studies on other themes.[1] Yet, the consular presence represents a continuity of contact and an official link that still exists, although somewhat altered in status. The Belfast consulate was upgraded to a consulate general in 1923 while its Dublin counterpart became a legation in 1927 and a full embassy in 1950.[2] These changes reflected the political realities of twentieth-century Ireland as it moved towards independence just as the establishment of the consular offices reflected the same process in the American colonies in the late eighteenth century. The consular presence represented, to use Carroll's words in the context of the Belfast consulate, a 'bridge linking two worlds' day in and day out and year in and year out.[3] This study is also a history of the men who filled posts as consuls, vice consuls, deputy consuls and consular agents. It reveals their identities, how they interpreted and implemented US foreign policy, it uses their words to examine their outsider perspective

---

1 Francis M. Carroll, *The American presence in Ulster: a diplomatic history, 1796–1996* (Washington, DC, 2005), vii. For works where consular reports were used as one source see Kerby Miller, *Emigrants and exiles: Ireland and the Irish exodus to North America* (Oxford, 1985); Susannah Ural Bruce, *The harp and the eagle: Irish-American volunteers and the Union army, 1861–1865* (New York, 2006); Deirdre M. Mageean, 'Emigration from Irish ports', *Journal of American Ethnic History*, 13:1 (1993), 6–30; A. C. Davies, 'Roofing Belfast and Dublin, 1896–98: American penetration of the Irish market for Welsh slate', *Irish Economic and Social History*, 4 (1977), 26–35.
2 See Bernadette Whelan, *US foreign policy and Ireland, 1913–29: from empire to independence* (Dublin, 2006).
3 Carroll, *The American presence*, vii.

on seminal events in both Ireland and America and, it examines their contribution to the expanding transatlantic relationship.

There were many differences between Britain's Irish and American colonies, but in the period 1760 to 1800, at the very least a shared history underpinned by transatlantic migration and the imperial context, existed.[4] Political subjugation from London was matched by an economic equivalent whereby the economic development of both regions was aligned with English needs. Up to 1775, these political and economic concerns linked Irish and American patriots albeit in a fitful way.

During the revolutionary period, Ireland's usefulness to the American leaders was three fold; as a source of propaganda to convince opponents of the revolution of its merits, as a source of skilled labour and for trading and commercial opportunities. But the impact of the American Revolution on Ireland remains problematic with Morley concluding that similarities of interest should not imply direct American influence in Ireland. However, there is an acknowledgement that the example of the revolution combined to the international war hastened the process of change in Ireland.[5] In the interim, Britain's counter-revolutionary strategy that condemned the 1798 insurrection to failure, extended to removing Ireland's parliamentary independence.

When the American colonists' insurrection turned into a continental-wide revolution, many thought of themselves as American and part of an independent nation. The war to win that status lasted until 1781 by which time key foreign policy concepts had developed along with the machinery and leadership of the new state. Although interpretations of the birth of the nation's foreign policy remains a matter for debate and discussion, the themes of democracy, free trade and independence had emerged.[6] Twenty years after gaining independence, America found itself

---

4 Homer L. Calkin, 'American influence in Ireland, 1760 to 1800', *Pennsylvania Magazine of History and Biography*, 71 (April, 1947), 103–20; Kerby A. Miller, Arnold Schrier, Bruce D. Bolling, David N. Doyle (eds), *Irish immigrants in the land of Canaan: letters and memoirs from colonial and revolutionary America, 1675–1815* (Oxford, 2003), 5; Maurice Bric, *Ireland, Philadelphia and the re-invention of America, 1760–1800* (Dublin, 2008); Vincent Morley, *Irish opinion and the American revolution, 1760–1783* (Cambridge, 2002), 330. See also Miller et al (eds), *Irish immigrants*, 4; David Fitzpatrick, *Irish emigration 1801–1921: studies in Irish economic and social history 1* (Dundalk, 1984); David T. Gleeson, *The Irish in the South, 1815–1877* (Chapel Hill and London, 2001), 11, 12; Patrick J. Blessing, 'The Irish' in Stephan Thernstrom (ed.), *The Harvard encyclopedia of American ethnic history* (Cambridge, 1980), 524–45; Kerby A. Miller, *Ireland and Irish America culture, class and transatlantic migration* (Dublin, 2008).
5 Morley, *Irish opinion*, 95, 331.
6 Mary A. Giunta (contributing ed.), 'The diplomacy of the American Revolution' in

Preface

surrounded by British, French and Spanish colonies and, therefore, was keenly interested in bilateral diplomacy and European inter-state rivalries.[7] However, America's defeat of the British in New Orleans in 1815 which ended the War of 1812 combined with the collapse of the Spanish empire in central and southern America in the 1820s initiated a period of expansion of its authority and growing aloofness from European political affairs. Trade, military force and treaty-making were all used to expand the country and protect its interests. For much of the nineteenth century, US governments concentrated on creating a continental sphere of influence and an overseas commercial empire of modest territorial ambitions, all the while enjoying protection from a generally friendly British navy.[8] The Spanish–American war of 1898 which brought the country's imperial intentions to the fore, represents for some scholars of late nineteenth-century US foreign relations, the emergence of America as a 'Great Power' with an overseas empire.[9]

Protecting and pursuing these interests necessitated having representatives and posts abroad. Even though discussion of the foreign service often focuses on the diplomatic service, the consular service was a distinct unit. Indeed Steiner suggests that within republican America, prejudices existed against the concept of professional diplomacy but consuls were regarded as appropriate representatives for a nation whose interest in the wider world was largely commercial.[10] By the time the American Revolution broke out, the tradition of a country with significant commercial and maritime interests, supported by a consular service was well established. Ireland as part of the British empire would be graced by the presence of American consuls while American diplomats would be resident in London.

The shared history of the US and Ireland, economic links and formal and informal political ties did not always account for specific appointments. Against the background of American state-building and the expanding foreign service, a focus is placed on the individual consul's motives for seeking a post in Ireland. In order to identify their path

---

Robert L. Beisner (ed.) *American foreign relations since 1600: a guide to literature* (Santa Barbara, 2003), 142–57.

7 Hugh De Santis and Waldo Heinrichs, 'The Department of State and American foreign policy' in Zara Steiner (ed.), *The Times survey of foreign ministries of the world* (Westport, 1982), 576.

8 Quoted in LaFeber, *The American age*, xx.

9 Edward P. Crapol, 'Coming to terms with empire: the historiography of late-nineteenth century American foreign relations', *Diplomatic History*, 16:4 (autumn, 1992), 573–97.

10 Zara Steiner, 'Introduction' in Steiner (ed.), *The Times*, 22–4.

to consular office, the lives of individual consuls is reconstructed and the process through which they obtained the post. The manner of their appointment by individual presidents and congresses reveals much about the evolution of the US political system, how patronage and clientèlism worked and uncovers another avenue through which Irish immigrants and their descendants could enter the US polity. Uncovering the 'spoils system' that existed within that political system reveals some unsuitable appointments and improper consular practices along with the response of congress and the executive. The consular service in Ireland was not free from weaknesses: some consuls engaged in bribery, corruption and other nefarious practices.

Many were hard-working, however. American sailors, masters and passengers looked for assistance and advice arising from accidents or incidents such as impressment. Death from natural causes of American citizens resident in Ireland or those with Irish connections in America, involved the consul in testamentary work while the loss of life during American wars brought the additional duty of securing and dispensing pensions for wives and parents of soldiers and sailors. Beyond the duty of protecting US citizens, consuls had to avail themselves of every opportunity to expand American trade and commerce, not least during the calamity of the 1845–51 famine.

Although often thought of as a derided commercial functionary located abroad, the consul was more than that. The consul had sufficient political skills and connections in the US to get the job, and in Ireland, at least, his world included not just merchants and businessmen but members of the civil service, the judiciary, police, military and the public. Throughout the nineteenth century, these skills were tested. Some consuls conducted their work within the wider diplomatic framework. Protecting American national interests in Ireland brought defining events such as the War of 1812 and the American Civil War to their door. The presence of the US minister and consul general in London meant that at times the consul's work in Ireland attained a political, diplomatic and intelligence complexion. Ireland's strategic location and transatlantic ties gave it an importance during the impressment controversy of the early nineteenth century and to both the Confederate and Federal sides in the American Civil War. Consuls engaged in intelligence, recruiting and propaganda work during the 1861–5 period. An additional theme, namely the challenge of Fenianism, brings into focus Ireland's role in the American–British relationship. At these times of crisis, the minutiae of the individual consul's daily work elucidates the interconnectedness of America's foreign interests, Irish nationalism and British imperialism. The routine and reactive nature of their work in Ireland involved consuls

Preface

in political upheavals, risings, wars, economic and social events and the unexpected, such as famine, maritime accidents and incidents.

Yet, all the while they supervised and managed the flow of emigrants from Ireland to the US. Consular work arising from the transatlantic migration underpinned the US–Ireland relationship. Keeping American interests to the fore, consuls commented on the circumstances surrounding departures, implemented the growing body of immigration legislation and noted the consequences of departure throughout the nineteenth and into the early twentieth centuries.

Writing a book relies on many people and offers a welcome opportunity to acknowledge the assistance of colleagues, friends and family. The staff in the following libraries and archives were always helpful and courteous: Mary Immaculate College, Limerick; National Archives and Records Administration, Washington; National Archives of Ireland; National Library of Ireland; the National Archives, London; the National Maritime Museum, Ireland; Sanford Museum, Sanford, Florida; The Queen's University of Belfast; Trinity College Dublin; University College Dublin; Yale University Manuscripts and Archives Department. The assistance of Alicia Clarke in the Sanford Museum and Rebecca Hatcher in the Sterling Memorial Library, Yale University, is noted. As always special mention must go to Anne Butler and Carmel Ryan in the inter-library loan section of the Glucksman Library, University of Limerick, for their efficiency and courtesy. Gobnait O'Riordan, Director, Glucksman Library, facilitated the use of research materials. The early stages of this research could not have been completed without financial assistance from the Irish Research Council for the Humanities and Social Sciences in 2005, 2007 and 2008 and from the Gilder Lehrman Institute for American History, New York in 2007. Finalising the manuscript in 2008–9 was facilitated by Dr Ruán O'Donnell, Head, Department of History, University of Limerick and Professor Pat O'Connor, Dean, Faculty Arts, Humanities and Social Sciences, University of Limerick. Thanks to Joyce Harrison and Professor Ann Heiss of Kent State University Press for their interest in the work. Research collaborations with Professor Gerardine Meaney (University College Dublin) and Professor Mary O'Dowd (The Queen's University, Belfast) have led to new ways of thinking about the research themes. Professor Joe Lee, Glucksman Ireland House, New York University, US, has been a constant source of encouragement. Friends and colleagues in the Department of History, University of Limerick and Department of History, Mary Immaculate College, Limerick, deserve thanks for their support. Current and former graduate students – Odette Clarke, Theresa Hereward-Ryan, Declan Jackson, Alexandra McCarthy, Mary

McCarthy, Pat McMahon, Catherine O'Connor, Conor Reidy, Gavin Wilk – always expressed an interest in the work.

Thanks to friends for their words of encouragement, particularly Máirin Barry, Catherine Bird, John Brennan, Jean Cónacher, Sally Fossitt, Dymphna Hill, Treasa Landers, Nuala McDermott, Pádraig Lenihan, Susan Mulcahy, Anne Marie O'Donnnell, Mary O'Donoghue and Oonagh Walshe. David Fleming and John Logan generously gave their time to read a draft. I cannot adequately express my gratitude to Brendan and Mary O'Malley, Pat and Deirdre Whelan and John and Paula Whelan and their families for their support. Paddy Whelan and Sophie Wallace arrived towards the end of this project and their smiles give much joy to all. Finally, I acknowledge the courtesy and attention received from the staff at Manchester University Press.

1

The United States consular service in Ireland: appointments and conditions, 1790–1906

It was ironic that in the century after Ireland lost its legislative independence that the newly created United States of America demonstrated its autonomy and power by establishing and expanding its foreign service. Britain and its remaining colonies now provided the new government with an opportunity to illustrate its independence and legitimacy. Appointing consular officers to Ireland may be seen against the background of state-formation, specifically the expansion of foreign representation and consolidation of sovereign status. The aims of this chapter are to examine the rationale behind the decision to appoint a representative in Ireland, to document the men who were selected for the posts, their reasons for applying and ultimately leaving, to identify whether the pattern of appointments to Ireland betrayed the main weakness of the nineteenth-century consular system, namely that it was flawed by being non-professional and exposed to patronage and corruption. Finally, it examines how reforms after 1856 affected the consular service in Ireland.[1]

Establishing the United States foreign service in Ireland: recruitment and terms of employment, 1790–1856

Appointing a US consular officer to Ireland took place in the context of American-British relations. In 1785, two years after the Treaty of Paris was concluded, the British government accepted John Adams as the American minister although they did not reciprocate at the time by appointing a representative to Washington.[2] Once installed as minister in London, Adams hoped that an American consul general might be appointed to England with vice consuls in Scotland and Ireland because they would explore 'new markets for our produce'. US Secretary of Foreign Affairs, John Jay, a former minister to Spain, informed Congress

---

1 Charles Stuart Kennedy, *The American consul: a history of the United States consular service, 1776–1914* (Westport, 1990), 16.
2 Ibid., 11–12.

that it would be advisable to have consuls in Russia, Sweden, Denmark, Germany, the Netherlands, Britain, Ireland, France, Portugal, Spain, the Canaries, Madeira and certain ports in the Mediterranean. In addition he wanted five consuls general to be appointed, including one for Britain and Ireland resident in London. He believed that it would be sufficient to have consuls in London, Bristol, Dublin and Cork. Congress did not agree and between 1783 and 1789, one consul was appointed to Europe, a consul and vice consul to Canton in China and some commercial agents. Despite this slow development, there was much discussion about the structure of the consular service and its role. It was the establishment of the executive branch of government in 1789, particularly the appointment of Thomas Jefferson as the first Secretary of State (1790–3), combined with the lack of cost involved, that signalled the expansion of the consular service. As a former minister to France, Jefferson had practical experience of the importance of the consular officer.[3]

In 1789, in order to encourage direct trade between Ireland and the new republic, Benjamin Franklin suggested that the Irish parliament sign a 'speedy commercial treaty with the States', appoint a consul and monopolise some branches of trade. The idea was welcomed by Sir Edward Newenham who had mooted the idea a few years before. But the proposal was not feasible as the Irish parliament did not possess such powers.[4] Instead, the American consular presence in Ireland was initiated after President Washington informed Congress on 8 December 1790 that 'the patronage of our commerce, of our merchants and seamen, has called for the appointment of consuls in foreign countries'.[5]

Already Ireland and America were connected by transactions in people and commerce. Indeed Jay's motivation for suggesting consular representation in Ireland rested on the importance of its ports to America's Atlantic trade, transatlantic communication and travel routes. Additionally, there were no reasons presented why Ireland, like Scotland and Wales, should not have US consular representatives. Finally, the presidency of Andrew Jackson (1829–37) is noted for establishing a spoils system, where a new administration rewarded its party supporters with appointments at home and abroad. Carroll suggests, however, that Thomas Jefferson initiated this

---

3 *Ibid.*, 5, 20; *Papers relating to foreign affairs accompanying the annual message of the president, 1783–89, vol. 2* (hereafter *PRFADC*), Report of Secretary Jay respecting the number of consuls to be appointed, 19 September, 13 October 1785 (Washington, 1837), 809–12.
4 Pádraig Ó Snodaigh, 'Benjamin Franklin in Ireland', *Ulster Local Studies*, 7:1 (1981), 9.
5 *American state papers, foreign relations, documents legislative and the executive of the congress of the United States* (hereafter *ASPFR*) *from the first session to the session of the 23rd congress inclusive, 3 March 1789 to 3 March 1823, class 1, vol. 1*, Washington, 8 December 1790 (Washington, 1833).

practice in 1801 when he replaced Federalists with his own Democratic–Republican supporters within his administration.[6] Prior to that, however, favouritism also accounted for some of the early consular appointments to Ireland under Presidents Washington, Adams and Jefferson.

Washington decided that applicants should directly canvas the president which led to such a flood of communications in his first weeks of office that he did not reply to many. By April 1789 he believed that merit was a key consideration for any appointment in addition to 'service during the Revolution, firm support of the new Constitution and equity among the states'. Obviously, geographical distribution mattered more when it came to apportioning important posts in the judicial, cabinet and civil service. However, at all levels Washington wanted men of integrity and standing in their communities exemplified by the revolutionary officer corps.[7] Even though consular duties and responsibilities were not defined by legislation until 1792, there were no additional criteria for entry to the consular service. He was fortunate to be able to draw from an extensive pool of candidates for all federal posts. Neither age nor more significantly for the Irish immigrant, citizenship were issues until late into the nineteenth century. Until 1792 most consuls were merchants and after receiving a commission from the president, the consul had to be in a position to submit a renewable bond of $2,000 as surety vouched for by two respectable merchants, to the State Department.[8] Consular posts were much sought after and appointees reflected the strengths and weaknesses of the evolving system.

An early applicant for the honour of becoming the first US consul to Ireland was John Talbot Ashenhurst from Dublin who wrote directly to George Washington on 29 March 1790. He explained how Denmark, Spain and Portugal had consular representatives in Ireland who were 'natives of this country and still are merchants resident in this city'. Ashenhurst described his suitability for the post 'I am ... a native of this country, a resident of this City ... of independent fortune and ... unsullied reputation'. Also he was a supporter of Irish legislative and financial independence and secretary to the Irish Insurance Company for Ships,

---

6 Carroll, *The American presence*, 33 fn.
7 Dorothy Twohig, 'George Washington' in Melvin I. Urofsky (ed.), *The American presidents* (New York and London, 2000), 8–9; Michael J. Gerhardt, *The Federal Appointments Process: a constitutional and historical analysis* (Durham and London, 2000), 50–1.
8 D. B. Warden, *On the origin, nature, progress and influence of consular establishments* (Paris, 1813), 13; National Archives and Records Administration, Maryland, US (hereafter NARA), State Department (hereafter D/S), Despatches from US consuls in Dublin (hereafter USD), 1790–1906, 1, 1, T199, Wilson to Secretary of State, 12 March 1834.

Merchandise and Lives.⁹ Ashenhurst was not appointed. Instead in June 1790, William Knox was appointed in circumstances that illustrate the spoils system while also offering an example of how foreign appointments could be used to deal with personal problems within America's élite families.

By September 1789, Washington had appointed Alexander Hamilton as Secretary of the Treasury and Henry Knox, Secretary of War. Both men had served under him in the war, were trusted servants and from the 1770s a lifelong and affectionate friendship bound Knox and Washington.¹⁰ Knox was not descended from John, the Scottish reformer, as is often thought but from his elder brother William. During the reign of James I (1603–25), many Scotch Presbyterians settled in northern Ireland and it was from Londonderry that William Knox and other Scottish–Irish sailed to Boston in 1729. Henry was the seventh of ten sons born in 1750 at 247 Federal Street in Boston to William and Mary Knox. William, born in 1756, was the youngest of the family. Following their father's death in 1762, Henry became the sole support of his mother and younger brother who eventually became his ward, a financial and emotional dependence that lasted through William's life. Between 1771 and 1790 when he was appointed to Ireland, he had worked in his brother's bookshop, twice joined his brother's side during the revolutionary war, incurred debts as a merchant, failed to profit from privateering and worked as a clerk for Henry at the War Office.¹¹ He divided his time between Boston and Henry's home in New York and throughout suffered from head pains and nervous problems. In June 1790 Washington appointed him as consul for Dublin but not for Cork and Limerick as William had requested.¹² An

---

9 W. W. Abbot (ed.), Dorothy Twohig (associate ed.), *The papers of George Washington*, 5 series, 52 vols, *Presidential series*, 3 June–September 1789 (hereafter *PGWPS*), (Charlottesville, 1989), Ashensurst to Washington, 29 March 1790.
10 Noah Brooks, *Henry Knox: a soldier of the revolution* (New York, 1900), 36.
11 *Ibid.*, 3–158 throughout; North Callahan, *Henry Knox: General Washington's general* (New York, 1958), 16, 17; Gilder Lehrman Institute for American History (hereafter GLI), Henry Knox Papers (hereafter HKP), Lucy to Henry, 18 March 1777; *ibid.*, William to Henry, 30 August 1781; *ibid.*, Henry to William, 19 November 1780; *ibid.*, Messrs De Kneufville and sons, Amsterdam to William Knox, 1 March 1781; *ibid.*, Kneufville to William, 25 July 1781; *ibid.*, Major Grauchau to William, 6, 19 August; *ibid.*, William to Henry, 25 July 1781; *ibid.*, William to Henry, 27 June 1781; *ibid.*, Henry to William, 14 December 1784; *ibid.*, Killingby, Green and Son, Nottingham, England to William, 20 July 1785; William to Henry, 14 June 1787; *ibid.*, William to Henry, 14 June 1787; *ibid.*, William to Henry, 14 September 1788; *ibid.*, William to Henry, 21 October 1788; *ibid.*, Account from the War Office, 1 July 1790.
12 *PGWPS*, 9, Knox to Washington, 13 November 1791, fn., p. 188; LC, Thomas Jefferson Papers (hereafter TJP), 17, 1 December 1790; GLI, HKP, William to Henry, 30 September 1790.

improvement in his health and disposition appears to have contributed to his wish for the post. In addition, Henry's confidence in him was evident from his giving power of attorney to William to offer his St Lawrence lands to potential European buyers.[13] As indicated above, Knox was not the only candidate for the Dublin post. Along with Ashenhurst, newly installed Secretary of State Thomas Jefferson requested it for Paul R. Randall from New York.[14] But it was William Knox who was offered and accepted the Dublin consulate.[15] The question why did Knox choose the Irish post may be raised. One clue may be that although William had some private income, he still hankered to make his fortune facilitated by his business and family connections in Ireland, England and continental Europe.

The choice of Knox as first consul to Dublin epitomised the strengths and weaknesses of the appointment system at this early stage. On the one hand, he had the perfect credentials to secure the post; he had helped in the fight for the republic, had excellent family and political ties, was familiar with the region and his political allegiance would make him another valuable source of information. Also, he appeared committed, informing Jefferson that he would lose no time in starting his duties.[16] On the other hand, his career up to June 1790 revealed that he had been unable to take full advantage of the variety of employment opportunities that came his way to establish a career as a merchant. Second, he owed his work in the bookshop, the clerkship and the consular appointment to his brother's, rather than his own, endeavours. The reason for the frequent change of career – his mental illness – was already known to his family. But this did not prevent Henry Knox from sponsoring his brother, Secretary Jefferson from recommending him and President Washington from appointing him to Dublin. Henry may have hoped that his brother's problems would settle once he arrived in Ireland.[17] Knox left New York for London on the *Rachel* in September, survived its shipwreck and arrived in London on 23 October 1790. One month later, *The Times* carried the announcement of George III's approval of his appointment and he assumed his duties in Dublin in late November.[18] Knox's appointment typified Washington's stated selection criteria and

13 GLI, HKP, William to Henry, 9 August 1790; *ibid.*, Henry to William, memorandum of power of attorney, 3 September 1790; *ibid.*, Henry to William, 4 September 1790.
14 LC, TJP, 17, 1 December 1790, 28 February 1793, 1 May 1793.
15 *PGWPS*, 9, Knox to Washington, 13 November 1791, fn., 188.
16 NARA, D/S, USD, 1, 1, T199, Knox to Jefferson, 26 November 1790.
17 *PGWPS*, 9, Knox to Washington, 13 November 1791, fn., 188; GLI, HKP Catalogue, James Webber to Henry, 2 December 1790.
18 *PGWPS*, 9, Knox to Washington, 13 November 1791, fn., p. 188; *The Times*, 22 November 1790.

the additional one of relieving the personal difficulty of a political ally and friend. As we will see, Knox's personal and professional failings soon outweighed his qualifications for the posting.

Personal aggrandisement was a priority for Knox. He desired control of not just the Dublin consulate but of Cork and Limerick in order to make a trading profit while expanding official transatlantic trade. But it was the appointment of the first US consular officer to Belfast which reveals the reality of economic ties between the two countries and, second, represents the traditional selection criteria. James Holmes was born in Belfast in 1747 and his firm of Holmes and Davis traded in tallow, rum and barilla and was involved in finance and milling partnerships. By the mid-1790s he and his brother had established the Belfast Chamber of Commerce and he had entered the American market buying potash and flaxseed for sale in Belfast. He was in the US from spring 1795 to summer 1796 where he probably visited Philadelphia, cradle of Scottish–Irish culture in America, and met with members of Washington's administration. His commercial and political contacts would have assisted his acquisition of the post though Carroll states that the deterioration of US relations with France at a time when many radical, pro-French United Irishmen were arriving in the US added a political imperative for the US to have a presence in Belfast. As a successful businessman, with contacts among the United Irishmen, Holmes met many needs. Whatever the exact motivation, Secretary of State Timothy Pickering recommended to Washington on 12 May 1796 that the Belfast and other appointments were 'necessary to be immediately decided upon'. Washington signed the papers for Holmes' appointment on 27 May.[19] Holmes was fortunate that his selection was not made a few months later as James Monroe, US minister to France, had waged a campaign to have American citizens appointed as consuls. Eventually Washington agreed that if possible an American citizen was to replace the consul at Hamburg.[20] The Holmes appointment was not affected. Holmes survived three changes of administration until 1815 at which time his friend, William Phelps, who had assisted him during past absences, styled himself as 'vice consul' in Belfast.[21] Phelps did not

---

19 Joseph J. Kelly, 'Philadelphia' in Michael Glazier (ed.), *The encyclopedia of the Irish in America* (Indiana, 1999), 769; Carroll, *The American presence*, 23–5; George Chambers, 'The early years of American consular representation in Belfast', *Familia: Ulster Genealogical Review*, 12 (1966), 4–9.

20 Stanislaus Murray Hamilton (ed.), *The writings of James Monroe including a collection of his public and private papers and correspondence now for the first time printed*, 7 vols (New York, 1899–1903), ii, Monroe to Secretary of State, 16 October 1794; *ibid.*, Secretary of State to Monroe, 13 June 1796.

21 NARA, D/S, Despatches from US consuls in Belfast (hereafter USB), 1798–1906, 1, 1, T368, Phelps to Monroe, 10 October 1815.

become consul. Instead the Belfast merchant brothers, Joseph and Samuel Luke, held the post between 1815 and some time after August 1821. Chambers suggests that they obtained the post through the political influence of their brothers, Campbell in Philadelphia and William in New York. By 1824, Samuel had established the consulate at 6 York Street where he was a partner in the mercantile firm of Luke and Thompson of the same address.[22]

Similar economic circumstances accounted for the appointment of John Church as the first US consul to Cork in 1798 by President Adams. Church operated one of the oldest mercantile companies in the city, Church, Sons and Busteed which had vessels travelling the Atlantic route.[23] He was well placed to have benefited from the growth in the city's trade during the eighteenth century, based largely on the export of salted beef, pork and butter to the West Indies, and supplying the British Navy. This commerce had expanded further during the American War of Independence when large British fleets sheltered in the harbour. Textile industries were part of its economy too and during the 1790s, its tanning, brewing and distilling industries expanded. It was ironic that Church was appointed in 1798, the year of the rising which shattered the political stability upon which Cork's growth had been based and just before the Napoleonic wars heralded economic stagnation.[24] His appointment also represents a further trend within the consular system: institutional nepotism. In December 1805, Church requested permission from Secretary Madison to appoint his son, James B., as vice consul. His qualification was his mercantile experience working in his father's company. John explained that he needed a replacement if he wanted to visit 'English watering places' or conduct US official business outside of Cork. Secretary Madison's approval arrived in mid-April 1806 and from then until 1813 when John Church died, his son ran the office and effectively operated as consul. After his father's death, James now head of the family firm, applied to President Madison on 26 December 1813, for promotion to the consular position citing three reasons; his experience, his conduct and the presence of many American vessels in the port during times of peace. His letter did not receive a reply and he had to write on five further occasions. During this period, he assumed

---

22 NARA, D/S, USB, 1, 1, T368, Holmes to Pickering, 6 October 1796; *ibid.*, Holmes to Madison, 15 June 1804; *Ibid.*, Phelps to Monroe, 10 October 1815; *ibid.*, Lake to Adams, 13 August 1821. Chambers, 'Early years', 9–11; *Pigot and Co.'s city of Dublin and Hibernian provincial directory* (London, 1824), 350.
23 NARA, D/S, Despatches US consuls in Cork, 1800–1906 (hereafter USC), 1, 1, T196, Church to Rufus King, 18 April 1800; *ibid.*, Church to Madison, 24 December 1805.
24 Cormac Ó Gráda, *Ireland: a new economic history 1780–1939* (Oxford, 1994), 293.

all consular functions, though he could have had little official business because no American vessel visited the harbour during the War of 1812. But at the end in 1815, James hoped to see the harbour 'crowded' and he expected his services to be in demand. In other words, he assumed he had been elevated to the consulship and wanted confirmation of it. For over three years, he received no communication from the State Department.[25] Two reasons may account for this. First, Michael Hogan, a naturalised US citizen from New York, was appointed by President Madison as consul for Cork in late 1815. Though Hogan never travelled to Cork, he held the post until June 1817.[26] Second, when Madison became president in 1809, he removed only twenty-seven federal officials and in an effort to appease regional and party interests, his first cabinet largely consisted of men who were 'undistinguished, disloyal or both'. The weakness of American-born, Irish Presbyterian, Robert Smith who became Secretary of State forced Madison to take on the post himself for two years which led to inefficient decision making.[27] Instead of Hogan, Jacob Mark of Maryland became consul at Cork from 1817 to 1826, with an office at Charlotte's Quay, where he also established himself as an agent for the Liverpool Underwriters' Association.[28]

Madison's difficulties may explain why John English assumed his consular duties in Dublin without being officially appointed. His brother Thomas, a Philadelphia merchant, and a friend of Smith's, was appointed in 1809 but was unable to take up the post immediately because he had to close his affairs. Instead Thomas appointed his brother John, from New York as vice consul to execute his duties in Ireland. Thomas reassured Smith that the public interest would not suffer from the arrangement because his brother was well qualified. John English was still in place in July 1811. Irrespective of the nepotism, his presence at least ensured a continuity of representation in Dublin that contrasted with other posts left unfilled for many years. Indeed, consular officials

25 NARA, D/S, USC,1, 1, T196, Church to Madison, 24 December 1805, *ibid.*, 15 August 1806; *ibid.*, James B Church to Madison, 26 December 1816; *ibid.*, Church to Madison, 2 January, 12 October 1815; *ibid.*, Church to Madison, 12 February, 18 May 1816; *ibid.*, Church to Secretary of State, 3 February 1817.
26 NARA, D/S, USC, 1, 1, T196, Hogan to Monroe, 7 November 1815; *ibid.*, 10 June 1817.
27 Gerhardt, *The federal appointments process*, 53, 94; David Noel Doyle, 'The Irish in North America, 1775–1845' in J. J. Lee and Marion Casey (eds), *Making the Irish American: history and heritage of the Irish in North America* (New York, 2006), 183.
28 Philadelphia merchant Joseph Wilson, also a friend of Washington's, replaced Knox in 1794 and served for fifteen years. NARA, D/S, USD, 1, 1, T199, Wilson to Secretary of State, 23 September 1833; *ibid.*, Wilson to Pinckney, 5 August 1796; *Pigot's directory* (1824), 246.

in Washington found his report in July 1810 sufficiently informative to have it forwarded to Albert Gallatin, Secretary of the Treasury. Thomas only arrived in Dublin in July 1812 some three years after his original appointment.[29]

Soon it became clear that Thomas English did not immediately operate as consul either. In August 1814, Thomas Wilson, a merchant, shipowner and son of a former consul from North Wall in Dublin, who harboured ambitions for the post, asked Secretary of State Monroe if he could replace Thomas English who was absent from his post and considering resignation. Unfortunately for Wilson, English returned to Ireland and because he had been unfortunate in business decided to remain as consul. Wilson apologised to Monroe but left him in no doubt that English was unreliable and was planning to move to England or America.[30] But again Wilson did not get his chance as English remained *in situ* until his death on 11 January 1825. Immediately the English family moved to keep the post in the family. On 13 January, Isaac, another English brother with a merchant business at 20 Bachelor's Walk, Dublin, requested Secretary of State John Quincy Adams, to appoint him in his brother's place because he had been doing the job for the past fifteen years particularly in the previous five years when his brother was absent, and Dublin merchants connected with the American trade supported his candidacy.[31] Obviously the English brothers had shared the duties, responsibilities, status and benefits of the Dublin consulship. By the end of March 1825, Adams had not replied and Isaac forwarded his biannual report as usual to the new Secretary of State, Henry Clay, asking him to take up the matter with President Adams.[32] Throughout the year, Isaac described himself as 'late consul *pro tem*' and Thomas Wilson as acting in that capacity. Wilson's application had not been ignored and along with his father's previous tenure between 1794 and 1809, he possessed other credentials for the post because he had lived in New York, still had business contacts and friends there and his sister, Mrs Timothy Williams, lived in Boston. Thomas Wilson replaced Isaac English in 1826.[33]

Even before President Jackson institutionalised a spoils system in 1832, each president used patronage, to some degree or other, to reward personal and party loyalty. In 1816, President Monroe recorded that

---

29 NARA, D/S, USD, 1, 1, T199, English to Smith, 15 July 1809; *ibid.*, English to Smith, 10 July 1810; Thomas English to James Monroe, 25 July 1812.
30 NARA, D/S, USD, 1, 1, T199, Wilson to Monroe, 14 February 1815.
31 *Ibid.*, English to Adams, 13 January 1825; *Pigot's directory* (1824), 57.
32 NARA, D/S, USD, 1, 1, T199, English to Secretary of State, 31 March 1825.
33 *Ibid.*, English to Secretary of State, 3 April 1827; *ibid.*, Munson and Barnard to Clay, 12 August 1826; *ibid.*, English to Clay, 3 April 1827.

he had been forced either to distribute offices among his supporters' friends or to appoint those whom he knew personally. Democrat Jackson, however, rewarded party supporters with appointments both at home and abroad.[34] The consular service did not experience the full impact of the spoils system until after the American Civil War. Consequently, Thomas Aspinwell of Massachusetts was consul in London from 1815 to 1853, Alexander Hammit of Maryland held the Naples post from 1809 to 1861 and members of the Sprague family were consuls in Gibraltar from 1815 to the end of the nineteenth century.[35] The Wilson and English families held the Dublin post for thirty-six and seventeen years respectively, and James Holmes was in Belfast for nineteen years. Reuben Harvey represented Cork from 1827, being appointed by the John Adams administration, to 1836 by which time Andrew Jackson was president.[36] Harvey, however, possessed credentials sufficiently imposing to impress from one administration to the next.

The Harveys were a county Cork merchant family trading from Youghal to England, Newfoundland and the West Indies. Members of the Religious Society of Friends (Quakers), Reuben's father and namesake, was a strong advocate for America. During the American War of Independence, he corresponded with General Washington, passed on news of events to sympathetic politicians in London and provided succour to American seamen imprisoned in French Prison in Kinsale, county Cork. The Continental Congress commended him and entitled him 'to the esteem of every American.' In the following years, Harvey's premises became a haven for Americans who found themselves in distress in the region. He died in 1808 but his third son, Reuben was able to utilise these endorsements and the presence of his kinsmen Edward Harvey in Philadelphia and Jacob Harvey in New York, to support his application for the consular position in his home city.[37] Jacob was a guarantor for Reuben's application and his ships were used by the State Department to forward correspondence direct to Reuben in Cork.[38] Although he was a

---

34 Gerhardt, *The federal appointments process*, 52; Murray Hamilton (ed.), *The writings of James Monroe*, vii, Monroe to Jefferson, 22 March 1824.
35 Kennedy, *The American consul*, 72.
36 NARA, D/S, USC, 1, 1, T196, Harvey to Clay, 6 June 1827; *ibid.*, Harvey to Van Buren, 5 April 1831.
37 C. J. F. MacCarthy, 'The American prisoners at Kinsale', *Journal of the Cork Historical and Archaeological Society*, 94 (January–December 1989), 46–51; Dublin Friends Historical Library (hereafter DFHL), '1809–1912: Journal of Margaret Boyle Harvey, 1786–1832', part iii; Sheldon Samuel Cohen, *British supporters of the American revolution, 1775–1783: the role of the 'middling-level' activists* (Suffolk, 2004), 83–107.
38 DFHL, 'Journal of Margaret Boyle Harvey'; NARA, D/S, USC, 1, 1, T196, Harvey to McLane, 23 May 1834.

wealthy man with a fine residence in Blackrock, near Cork, Reuben was disappointed to be replaced by John Murphy in 1836.[39] He handed over the consular effects to Murphy, but Secretary Forsythe's letter dismissing him was published in several newspapers including the *Cork Constitution*, and clarified that the change did not result from Harvey's actions but the US government's preference for its own citizens.[40]

In this early period, 1790 to 1829, candidates who wanted to be appointed to Ireland sought such an appointment. While it is not possible to identify the specific ethnic, political or indeed religious allegiance of each man or to establish whether acquiring the post represented further evidence of the Irish advance in American politics, each was recommended and sponsored by individuals close to the government parties. Moreover, each had to be appointed by the president and confirmed by the Senate.[41] Appointees were already engaged in commerce to some degree and all believed that personal and national commercial advantage could be gained from an Irish post, so much so that the Wilson, English and Harvey merchant families attempted to keep control of their respective consulships for family members. A further trend evident in the 1820s was the prominence of Quakers as consuls. Three of the six men in place in 1824 were Quakers: Robert Jacob, Reuben Harvey and Jacob Mark, perhaps confirming their commercial as well as political prowess, despite their usually non-partisan politics. Other qualifications evident during this first period were private income and US citizenship.

From the beginning of the consular service, salaries to American representatives abroad were a matter of contention between Congress and the State Department. In 1785 Jay wanted consuls to be unsalaried and be awarded consular service fees and be permitted to trade. Consuls general and ministers would have a salary. Jefferson tried to have these increased, arguing that they were much less than those usually paid by their European counterparts. He believed the absence of salaries for consuls was detrimental to the public good by discouraging competent men from applying for the consular service. In the end Jefferson settled for increased allowances payable to ministers in London, The Hague and Madrid.[42]

---

39 NARA, D/S, USC, 1, 1, T196, Harvey to Forsythe 2 May 1836; *ibid.*, Murphy to Forsythe 10 May 1836; *ibid.*, 2, 2, T196, Seymour to Pierce, 7 December 1854.
40 *Ibid.*, 1, 1, T196, Murphy to Forsythe, 25 June 1836; *ibid.*, Murphy to Forsythe, 24 December 1837; *ibid.*, Murphy to Forsythe, 27 September 1836; DFHL, 'Journal of Margaret Boyle Harvey', part ii; *Cork Constitution*, 17 May 1836. A relative, Reuben Harvey, was also a consular agent in Limerick in 1824. *Pigot's directory* (1824), 285.
41 Ruth Kark, *American consuls in the Holy Land 1832–1914* (Detroit, 1994), 161.
42 Report of Secretary Jay, 19 September 1785, PRFADC, 2, 809–10; Stuart, *The Department of State*, 21; Raymona E. Hull, *Nathaniel Hawthorne: the English experience, 1853–64* (Pittsburgh, 1980), 20; Kennedy, *The American consul*, 20.

Section five of the 1792 Consular Act, indicated that annual salaries, not exceeding $2,000, were provided for consuls appointed to the Barbary coast states, Morocco, Tunis, Tripoli and Algiers. All other consular officers would live on consular fees for taking statements and holding and inventorying estates, and from earnings arising out of private trading. Consuls, therefore, were empowered to handle appeals, documents and bequests of American seamen, travellers and merchants whether resident or visiting their jurisdictions. Congress accepted that the consuls in the Barbary coast states would be too busy to trade.[43] Fees ranging from fifty cents for verification of a solicitor's letter to two dollars for any act requiring the consulate seal could be charged.[44] Thus the quality of a consular living depended on the geographical location, the extent of American trade and personal income. Consuls could collect further fees after 1823 when they were required to verify in triplicate every invoice of goods sent to the US which was then presented to customs officials in US ports who calculated the *ad valorem* duty. Not only was the consul obliged to take the oath or statement of a manufacturer or exporter as to the actual value of the goods for export but he was expected to be familiar enough with local trade to know that the statement was accurate and in turn, be able to detect any undervaluation, fraud or collusion. By the 1830s, however, the State Department was receiving complaints from merchants about improper consular practices. Unlike British and French practices, the US government did not have a sufficient number of experienced US citizens from whom to choose and, therefore, appointed not just foreigners but some without experience. Moreover, a combination of the spoils system, a lack of consular training and an increase in the number of consuls from six in 1790 to 129 in 1830, and of consular agents also, exacerbated this situation. Not all followed William Knox's practice of working with respectable merchants.[45] The lack of scrutiny from the State Department and the absence of salaries led some officials to advance their own personal business and commercial interests.[46] The US consular service, therefore, became tainted by allegations of bribery and corruption which in turn brought criticism from officials and politicians in Washington.[47]

Although there is no evidence that William Knox had resorted to

---

43 Quoted in Kennedy, *The American consul*, 22.
44 Warden, *On the origin*, 150.
45 NARA, D/S, USD, 1, 1, T199, Knox to Jefferson, 15 May 1792.
46 Report of Secretary Jay, 19 September 1785, *PRFADC*, 2, 809–10; Stuart, *The Department of State*, 21; Kark, *American consuls*, 51; Eugene Schuyler, *American diplomacy and the furtherance of commerce* (London, 1886), 49; Kennedy, *The American consul*, 20.
47 Kennedy, *The American consul*, 76.

illegal practices, he was unable to survive on the fees available in the Dublin district.[48] Knox had expected his income to comprise consular fees, revenue from his land agent work in England on Henry's behalf and private mercantile work. But the trading contacts were not lucrative and by January 1791 his debts to James Webber, a friend of Henry's in London, had increased and he did not expect to clear them for two years.[49] He appealed to Henry to have Jefferson provide him with a salaried post and apologised to him because one of his debtors demanded Henry pay his brother's debts.[50] Part of his problem was funding his social life in the 'partly civilised ... country of strangers.' In these pre-Act of Union days, he had become a part of the political and social circles surrounding the Irish parliament and administration.[51] He had nothing to complain of 'on the score of invitations' but he never drank so much wine.[52] Nevertheless, between 1792 and 1796 the cost of living rose by one-third. Kennedy suggests that the increases were offset by rising incomes and wages but Knox would not have benefited. Instead he experienced the full brunt of rising costs of foodstuffs, clothing and rent and his meagre income could not sustain him.[53]

His straitened financial circumstances forced him to go to London in order to negotiate funds to keep him 'from sinking' although he still hoped to become a successful merchant and repay Henry.[54] While there he met with US Consuls Johnson and James Maury based in England. Both were successful merchants who found their duties considerable whereas William's situation was the reverse on both counts. However, he came up with another plan to prevent him 'from starving'. On two occasions, he asked Henry to secure the post of US minister to London.[55]

On his return to Ireland his pleadings became more feverish and critical of his brother's apparent inaction.[56] He asked Washington for an annual salary of £300–400 but in early May 1792 he asked for permission to return to the US. In the interim Henry wrote to say that he had

48 NARA, D/S, USD, 1, 1, T199, Wilson to Secretary of State, 23 September 1833.
49 GLI, HKP, William to Henry, 15 January 1791.
50 Ibid., 13 February 1791; ibid., 18 February 1791; ibid., William to Henry, 27 June 1791.
51 Ibid., 26 April 1791; ibid., catalogue, William to Henry, 11 May 1791; ibid., HKP, 15 January 1791.
52 Ibid., HKP, William to Henry, 26 April 1791.
53 Liam Kennedy, 'The cost of living in Ireland, 1698–1998' in David Dickson and Cormac Ó Gráda (eds), Refiguring Ireland: essays in honour of Louis Cullen (Dublin, 2003), 257.
54 GLI, HKP, William to Henry, 27 June 1791.
55 Ibid.; ibid., William to Henry, 18 July 1791.
56 Ibid., William to Henry, 30 September 1791.

spoken to Jefferson about a posting to London but there was no firm news.⁵⁷ A few weeks later Knox received a copy of the 1792 Consular Act from Jefferson. The Secretary of State justified the exclusion of salaries for consuls, except in the Barbary states, because the posts were given to gentlemen who accepted the attendant financial responsibilities and if that changed, they could resign.⁵⁸ Knox, a gentleman with some, but limited financial means, had been appointed to Dublin but he found that a living could not be made purely on the basis of fees collected.

Knox left Ireland on 22 July 1792, and arrived in Philadelphia on 15 September with debts owing to Webber and James D'Olier in Dublin.⁵⁹ By May he admitted that he was in a distressed state and in the following year, he was incarcerated in the Pennsylvania Hospital for the Insane in Philadelphia where he died in 1797.⁶⁰ Despite his persistent money difficulties, Knox had never resorted to corruption to augment his income but his case highlighted that from the earliest stage, the consular service was open to abuse by men less honourable than him. In 1829 the President of Western Union Company complained to Secretary McLane, that US Consul R. R. Hunter based in Cowes, England, was guilty of a long series of abuses. He charged that Hunter had pocketed money intended for repairs to a damaged boat, mutilated the log book of a ship and made false entries in his fee book to cover himself.⁶¹ Secretary Van Buren in 1830 attempted the first reform by eliminating practices that were harming America's reputation internationally and bringing the consular service into disrepute. Van Buren received a report from US Consul Daniel Strobel in Bordeaux, France, who highlighted that the British, French, Spanish, Portuguese and Russian governments had each improved their consular systems by reducing the fees collected and prohibiting consuls from trading and paying fixed salaries. It fell to his successor Edward Livingston to pursue the matter. On 2 March 1833, he proposed to Congress that in order to end suspicion of consular enhancement and complaints, some thirty consuls should each receive salaries of $2,000 and 126 consuls and commercial agents would receive salaries

57 PGWPS, 9, Knox to Washington, 13 November 1791, fn., 188; NARA, D/S, USD, 1, 1, T199, Knox to Washington, 13 November 1791; GLI, HKP, Henry to William, 15 May 1792.
58 Quoted in Kennedy, *The American consul*, 24.
59 PGWPS, 9, Knox to Washington, 13 November 1791, fn., 188; NARA, D/S, USD, 1, 1, T199, Knox to Jefferson, 28 May 1792; *ibid.*, Knox to Jefferson, 18 September 1792; *ibid.*, William to Henry, 6 March 1793; *ibid.*, 1 May 1793.
60 *Ibid.*; Callahan, *Henry Knox*, 358.
61 NARA, RG 59, Diplomatic instructions of the Department of State, 1801 to 1906 (hereafter DIDS), 73, M77, Van Buren to Louis McLane, 27 December 1830; *ibid.*, DIDS, 73, M77, President of Western Union to McLane, 20 July 1829.

averaging $1,000. Additionally, Livingston wanted to restrict commercial work and limit the collectible fees. He also issued a set of instructions to guide consuls in the performance of their duties.[62]

Livingston's report on the consular establishment was forwarded to the overseas officers for comment. Consul Thomas Wilson in Dublin believed that it would be possible for the State Department to recruit American 'men and respectable men too' for the proposed salaries and that such men would agree not to carry on any mercantile business.[63] But, echoing William Knox's view, he warned Livingston that such men would not be of the 'same class or rank in society' as those who had filled the positions to date. He argued that even if consular officials could retain some fees arising out of notarial services, a salary of $1,000 per year would be too small to induce a respectable man to take up the post.[64] Wilson had earned consular fees worth $182 in 1834, $223 in 1835 and $121 in 1836.[65] Nevertheless, he said he would abide by the new restrictions if they were adopted 'so far as it was practicable' but he would not be giving up all his business activities.[66] Even though the cost of living in Ireland declined between 1820 and 1835 and the costs of provisions were low by the mid-1830s, Wilson could not have survived on his fee income alone. An annual average fee income of $200 was dismally low when compared to the $500 earned by Jasper Chasseaud, US consul in Beirut in 1835, which prompted American missionaries to appeal to Secretary of State Forsyth for a reasonable salary for him.[67]

No action was taken by Congress on Livingston's proposals. Because of his personal wealth, Wilson was able to carry the small expenses incurred and he prided himself that his 'demand upon the government is but small'.[68] He was so mindful of the need for financial prudence that in 1837 he advised Levi Woodbury, Secretary of the Treasury, that savings could be made on the cost of sending books to consulates in Ireland by directing them to the consul in Liverpool who could then forward

---

62 Wilbur J. Carr, 'The American Consular Service', *The American Journal of International Law* (January and April 1907), 898–9.
63 NARA, D/S, USD, 1, 1, T199, Wilson to Secretary of State, 23 September 1833.
64 *Ibid.*, Wilson to Secretary of State, 23 September 1833.
65 *Ibid.*, Wilson to Secretary of State, 9 July 1834; *ibid.*, Wilson to Secretary of State, 2 January 1834, Consular statement of fees (hereafter Fees); *ibid.*, Wilson to Secretary of State, 30 June 1835, Fees; *ibid.*, Wilson to Secretary of State, 1 January 1836, Fees; *ibid.*, Wilson to Secretary of State, 1 January 1837, Fees.
66 *Ibid.*, Wilson to McLane, 23 September 1833.
67 Kennedy, 'The cost of living', 258; Cited in Kark, *American consuls*, 163.
68 NARA, D/S, USD, 1, 1, T199, Wilson to Secretary of State, 5 May 1834; Wilson to Secretary of State, 11 January 1838.

them.⁶⁹ Thomas Moore Persse, the first US consul in Galway, offered to send in his reports only every six months to save on postage.⁷⁰ By way of contrast, US Consul Thomas Gilpin simply replied that the administrative requirements had been adopted in the Belfast and Londonderry offices.⁷¹ Gilpin collected $270 in fees for July to December 1833, $718 in 1834, $718 in 1835, $908 in 1836 and $677 in 1837 due largely to the growth in the linen trade in the northern port. However, his consular agent and later consul, James Corscaden collected just $124 in 1834, $92 in 1835, $178 in 1836 and $124 in 1837. In the latter three years his fees increased from notarial work for his own business. In partnership with Daniel Baird and William McCorkell and Company, Corscaden operated ships from Londonderry to New York, Philadelphia and St John, New Brunswick.⁷² Despite the absence of salaries and indeed emergency and rent allowances, for the Irish posts in the Livingston reforms, and though the Dublin post was less lucrative than Belfast and more equal to Londonderry, none of these men engaged in nefarious activities.

Despite the Livingston reforms and other efforts to pay all consuls and end the existence of the merchant consul, change was not forthcoming until 1856. Instead the Livingston tenure gave a further fillip to the spoils system and also saw an increase in the number of consular or commercial agents. On 25 January 1832, Secretary Livingston indicated to Minister Van Buren in London, that more consular agents would strengthen American commercial links with Britain and Ireland.⁷³ Appointment as a consular agent was straightforward enough and resulted mainly from an individual applying either to the consul, consul general, minister or the secretary of state. Most of the appointments in Ireland were made by consuls and were generally Irish citizens already involved in commercial activities with an American aspect. Even though they had no status as 'consular officers' until 1856, and the State Department had no official list of their names, the position held an element of prestige and was eagerly sought.⁷⁴ Thomas Moore Persse in Galway complained to Louis McLane in April 1834 that Limerick and Sligo should have a vice consul or consular agent.⁷⁵ Three years later, Thomas Evans was appointed consular agent in Waterford by Cork Consul John Murphy. Evans succeeded vice consul Robert

---

69 Ibid., USD, 1, 1, T199, Wilson to Woodbury, 1 April 1837.
70 Ibid., USG, 1, 1, T570, Persse to Secretary of State, 10 May 1837.
71 Ibid., USB, 1, 1, T368, Gilpin to McLane, 20 August 1833.
72 Sholto Cooke, *The maiden city and the western ocean: a history of the shipping trade between North America in the nineteenth century* (Dublin, 1950), 81.
73 NARA, D/S, RG 59, 73, M.77, Livingston to Van Buren, 25 January 1832.
74 Jones, *The consular service*, 23.
75 NARA, D/S, USG, 1, 1, T570, Persse to McLane, 26 April 1834.

Jacob of Bridge Street, Waterford. The latter was a general merchant and an agent for the Liverpool Underwriters' Association.[76] Londonderry consul James McHenry's need for additional income led him to request Secretary Abel Upshur in February 1844 to permit him establish a consular agent in Sligo which he said was within his Londonderry consular district. It was his successor, Robert Loughead, who eventually appointed James Harper as vice consul in Sligo in January 1847 to cope with the increased emigration traffic from that port during the famine. Harper still acted in that position in 1857 and Fleming Harper, his son, replaced him in 1871.[77]

Another of the Livingston reforms tackled eligibility but solely relating to citizenship. Jefferson had indicated that only American citizens should represent the US as consuls. If there was no American citizen available at a port, then a 'reputable foreign' subject should be chosen and made vice consul. But this principle was not widely applied.[78] Naturalisation had been a grievance for Irish immigrants since the 1790s when John Jay and Rufus King attempted to limit the naturalisation of foreigners by raising the residency requirement of two years set in 1798 by James Madison to fourteen years. As Doyle indicates, Catholic Irish joined Presbyterian Irish in carrying on this campaign, securing repeal of the Naturalisation Act in 1802 although the Irish remained frustrated about local restrictions until the 1850s. In the 1830s Jackson's decision to appoint US citizens only to foreign consular posts was a natural one for him and his 'populist' faction, soon to be known as the Democratic party. In turn it offered him more posts for his political supporters including the Irish. However, there were insufficient American merchants living abroad to fill all the available posts and so the practice of appointing foreigners continued although some preferred a system staffed by wealthy, native-born Americans, more akin to the diplomatic section.[79] In reality, these two issues – abuses due to the absence of salaries and citizenship – like the rest of the Livingston reforms, were not pursued by Congress.

Having been born in the US, John Murphy was the first naturalised American citizen appointed to the consular position in Cove in 1836. But he soon discovered that it was not a 'place of emolument or profit' and

---

76 Ibid., USC, 1, 1, T196, Murphy to Forsythe, 18 May 1837; *Pigot's directory* (1824), 319.
77 NARA, D/S, Despatches from US consuls in Londonderry, 1780–1906 (hereafter USL), USL, 1, 1, T216, McHenry to Upshur, 28 January 1844; *ibid.*, Loughead to Buchanan, 29 January 1847; *ibid.*, 2, 2, T216, Smith to Marcy, 1 January 1857; *ibid.*, 3, 3, T216, Livermore to Secretary of State, 25 March 1871.
78 Carr, 'The American consular service', 896.
79 Doyle, 'The Irish in North America', 182; Schuyler, *American diplomacy*, 80–1.

he was forced to ask Secretary Forsythe for financial aid in May 1837.[80] Although it is unclear if he received it, Murphy was able to pay his predecessor Reuben Harvey £7 for the recovery of the consular seal. Murphy set up office at Lynch's Quay, the same address as shipowners and agents, C. and W. D. Seymour and company. Later, Murphy's daughter married Nicholas Seymour and the connecting of the two families raised suspicions about the nature of the consul's true loyalty. In early 1843 because of ill health he went to Baltimore on leave and in November, he requested Secretary Upshur in John Tyler's administration, if he could take charge of 'any other consulate you may have in Europe'. But he had not received permission to abandon his post in the first place and he was back in Cove by January 1844 complaining that the consulate did not have a US flag because he would have had to purchase one with his own money.[81]

The first US citizen appointed in Belfast was Thomas Gilpin born in Delaware and living in Philadelphia by the time of his appointment in 1830. Gilpin's father, Henry, may have secured the appointment for his son through political connections with Jackson's Democrats as he corresponded directly with Secretary Louis McLane during his son's tenure in Ireland and successfully obtained a six-month leave of absence for him to spend time with his parents. Nonetheless, Henry was unable to obtain a transfer for Thomas to the Martinique consulate.[82] At any rate by 1833 Gilpin was in residence at 35 Castle Street and secured official premises in Commercial Court in Donegall Street, Belfast.

Applying the citizenship regulation in the appointment of consular agents was problematic at this early stage. Just like elsewhere in the service, most of the agencies were established by consuls and were under their control. One of Alfred Mitchell's first actions as the new consul in Queenstown in August 1849 countered his instructions as he appointed Michael Robert Ryan as consular agent for Limerick and Christopher Bolton Cole in Waterford.[83] By 1853, Ryan was still in place and another non-American, Josiah Williams, was now consular agent in Waterford. But the State Department was reassured that Williams was a respectable, honourable, wealthy man and a member of the Society of Friends.[84] Later

---

80 NARA, D/S, USC, 1, 1, T196, Murphy to Forsythe, 19 May 1837; *ibid.*, Murphy to Forsythe, 19 May 1837.
81 *Ibid.*, Murphy to Forsythe, 24 December 1837; *ibid.* Murphy to Forsythe, 24 March 1837; *ibid.*, Murphy to Forsythe, 24 December 1838; *ibid.*, Murphy to Forsythe, 15 June 1840; *ibid.*, Murphy to Webster, 20 November 1843; *ibid.*, Murphy to Upshur, 15 January 1844; *ibid.*, Murphy to Buchanan, 1 January 1846.
82 *Ibid.*, USB, 1, 1, T368, Mr Gilpin to McLane, 13 March 1833. *United States, Official Register*, 1833, Department of State.
83 NARA, D/S, USC, 1, 1, T196, Mitchell to Clayton, 5 September 1849.
84 *Ibid.*, 2, 2, T196, Higgins to Marcy, 26 November 1853. Ryan died in office in 1874.

in 1853, Marcy queried the appointment of foreigners to these positions. Naturalised US citizen and consul in Cork, John Higgins, explained that there were no US residents in either district and the demands on the agents were few and, consequently, their duties limited.[85] Three years later he was reprimanded again for the same offence. By now consul in Belfast, Higgins was forced to appoint a local merchant and shipowner, James Corscaden as agent in Londonderry because there was no US citizen available or interested. Corscaden also had the support of the mayor, Alexander Curry, and other merchants.[86] Despite the wish to have US citizens as representatives at the lowest level of the service, it was often not possible. Consuls appointed non-Americans who were either known or recommended to them because they believed that experience, reliability and promptness mattered most. James Carraher became vice consul for Drogheda, Dundalk and Newry. Belfast Consul John Young appointed Danzig-born, merchant, shipbroker, insurance agent and Prussian consul, Gustavus Heyn as agent to assist vessels in distress on the coast between Belfast and Londonderry. Francis Harper, an agent for Lloyds Shipping Company, gave money to two destitute sailors from the *Niagara* and became agent in Wexford in September 1859. The only American citizen who applied for the Wexford agency in 1861, Thomas W. Rowntree, was appointed but after his resignation in August 1862, Irishman Jasper W. Walsh took over. Michael Murphy, agent in Kingstown, was employed by the American shipping line, Palgrave, Murphy and Company operating out of the North Wall in Dublin. By 1858, Samuel Talbot believed that the absence of direct trade between Sligo and Westport and the US, justified the lack of consular agents there.[87]

The Livingston reforms had attempted to deal with the citizenship issue as well as the poor consular remuneration. However, the new measures were honoured more in the breach than in the observance. Following Congress' failure to reform the service in the early 1830s, consuls remained unpaid, untrained and liable to dismissal every four years. During the period 1829 to 1831, roughly one-quarter of all consuls

85 *Ibid.*, Higgins to Marcy, 9 January 1854.
86 *Ibid.*, USB, 2, 2, T368, Higgins to Marcy, 16 March 1855; *ibid.*, Higgins to Marcy, 27 July 1855; *ibid.*, Higgins to Marcy, 17 April 1856; *ibid.*, Higgins to Cass, 10 June 1857; *ibid.*, 2, 3, T368, Appleton to Higgins, 19 June 1857; *ibid.*, 2, 3, T368, Higgins to Cass, 29 July 1857. Higgins resigned because he could not survive on the income.
87 NARA, D/S, USD, 1, 2, T199, Foy to Carraher, 9 June 1853; *ibid.*, USB, 2, 3, T368, Young to Seward, 28 October 1861; *ibid.*, Young to Seward, 18 December 1861; 'Belfast/Ulster Street Directory' online at www.lennonwylie.co.uk (accessed 20 July 2008); NARA, D/S, USD, 3, 3, T199, Talbot to Black, 23 January 1861; *ibid.*, Hammond to Seward, 12 February 1862; *ibid.*, Hammond to Seward, 14 August 1862; *ibid.*, Talbot to Cass, 10 January 1861; *ibid.*, USG, 1, 1, T570, Talbot to Cass, 30 September 1858.

were replaced by new appointees. Other reform efforts fell in Congress in 1838 and 1844. Two years later the House Committee of Commerce reported that the service was inadequate.[88] It was not until August 1856 that 'An act to regulate diplomatic and consular systems' became law.[89] By this time the irregularities in the consular system, including Ireland, necessitated urgent Congressional action.

Bribery, corruption and consular reform

While State Department officials at home and in the field, were lobbying Congress to improve conditions of employment for its officers, improper consular conduct continued. Thomas Gilpin in Belfast was a casualty of the Whig victory under William Henry Harrison in 1841 and was replaced by James Shaw, a US citizen. From the beginning he adopted a businesslike approach and soon uncovered 'laxity' in his predecessor's practices. In winter 1842 he toured his district and learned that while Newry manufacturers and exporters of goods to the US might have the value of goods authenticated by the Belfast consul, the final manifest was signed by the US consul in Liverpool. Consequently, it was the latter official who received the fee while the former lost out.[90] The nature and structure of US–Irish transatlantic trade will be examined later but suffice to say here that the value of linen exports from Ireland in 1835 was £3,731,000. Most of it originated in Ulster, and was then shipped from Belfast or Newry to Liverpool where it was forwarded to the US.[91] As a consequence, by mid-century, Liverpool had become a prominent port for the Irish linen trade. Shaw's complaint was to be the first of many. There was little understanding of the situation in Washington where Secretary of the Treasury John C. Spencer approved the practice [92]

Shaw did not let the matter go and his investigation revealed that the activity went beyond his jurisdiction and the financial losses were greater than he first realised. In 1843, he accused James McHenry, the

---

88 William Barnes and John Heath Morgan, *The foreign service of the United States: origins, development and functions* (Washington, 1961), 90, 85–6.
89 Carr, 'The American consular service', 900–01.
90 NARA, D/S, USB, 1, 1, T368, Shaw to Webster, 2 December 1842; Barnes and Morgan, *The foreign service*, 97.
91 Cormac Ó Gráda, 'Poverty, population and agriculture, 1801–45' in W. E. Vaughan (ed.), *A new history of Ireland, v, Ireland under the Union, 1, 1801–70* (Oxford, 1989), 136. In the colonial period 'Whigs' opposed British rule and in 1834 the term applied to the party comprising the remnants of the old National Republicans who opposed excessive presidential power. See comments on imprecise nature of figures for this period; Carroll, *The American presence*, 39.
92 NARA, D/S, USB, 1, 1, T368, Spencer to Ran, 24 August 1843.

Larne-born consul in Londonderry, of irregularities, namely interference in his jurisdiction.⁹³ McHenry had employed Francis Skelly in Ballymena, thirty-three miles from Londonderry, to fill up, seal and issue certificates of invoice for local merchants and agents of textile companies. Not only was he not delegating his duty but Ballymena merchants should have gone to the Belfast consulate just eighteen miles away for the service while McHenry was also accused of interfering with the fee record. McHenry had ignored Shaw's instruction to stop and the latter appealed to Secretary Upshur and Minister Edward Everett in London to end the practice.⁹⁴ Everett, with Upshur's approval, warned McHenry that he had no authority to grant consular certificates 'out of limits' of his own district.⁹⁵ McHenry's convenient deal with Skelly was sufficiently valuable for him to write directly to Washington. He claimed that Ballymena was the largest market for unbleached linen in Ireland and he was often asked by linen manufacturers, agents and shipowners to issue the certificates out of convenience. Second, he argued that if this source of income was permanently taken from him, he would have to be transferred to another post and he thought that President Tyler had 'intended to do me a kindness rather than an injury' by appointing him to Londonderry.⁹⁶ Skelly continued issuing certificates in Ballymena.⁹⁷ McHenry was intent on using any means to make money. Before he took up the post, he learned that it would earn him annual fees worth only $200 and that mercantile interests were inconsiderable in Londonderry. He agreed to be a 'temporary loser' but once installed, he twice requested Webster to find him another consulate and to appoint his son James as his consular agent. These requests were all refused.⁹⁸ When called upon again to explain his behaviour in January 1844, he informed Upshur that Ballymena shipowners preferred to get the certificates from him in Londonderry via Skelly, because it was closer than Belfast or Liverpool.⁹⁹ A few months later, Shaw again reported the same irregularities in Ballymena and despite further reprimands, the practice continued even though in January 1845, Skelly's certificates recorded incorrect values. It is possible that McHenry and Skelly had been bribed to undervalue the cargoes which would result in

93 *Ibid.*, Shaw to McHenry, 12 July 1843.
94 *Ibid.*; *ibid.*, Upshur, 22 September 1843.
95 NARA, D/S, RG 59, 74, Upshur to Everett, 8 September 1843.
96 NARA, D/S, USL, 1, 1, T216, McHenry to Webster, 7 October 1843.
97 *Ibid.*, USB, 1, 1, T368, Shaw to Upshur, 11 January 1844.
98 *Ibid.*, USL, 1, 1, T216, McHenry to Webster, 25 January 1843; *ibid.*, 27 October 1842; *Ibid.*, 7 January 1843; *ibid.*, note on 7 January 1843 dated 10 January 1843; *ibid.*, 14 February 1843; *ibid.*, 1 May 1843.
99 *Ibid.*, McHenry to Upshur, 28 January 1844.

lower duties at the port of entry.[100] Even after the post became a salaried one, Belfast consuls still complained about the violation and loss of customs revenue to the US government. By this stage there was another consideration for them because a consulate's rating and salary level was calculated according to the amount of fees collected.[101] Consul Ruby in 1889 calculated that 1,000 invoices were signed elsewhere for goods that originated in Ulster and the government was being defrauded of $2,500 annually. Moreover, the possibility of goods being valued incorrectly by consuls outside the consular district was voiced again, thereby raising the issue of fraudulent conduct by consuls. All attempts to stop it failed. Ruby's successor, James Taney, determined that more than 10 per cent of merchandise manufactured in the Belfast district, worth more than $1.6 million, and exported to the US was declared outside the consular district. He was relieved to receive a ruling from the Treasury Department in 1895 supporting his position. But there was a loophole which allowed the practice to continue. It was not until 1925, after the new Northern Ireland state was created with Belfast as its capital, that the State Department instructed that goods manufactured there had to be certified there prior to export to the US.[102] The practice had continued for over eighty years thus revealing the extent to which the consular system was unregulated and without oversight for most of the period. It was this type of local practice in Belfast that the 1856 act was directed at.

There were other forms of improper consular conduct also. When Secretary of State James Buchanan informed Thomas Wilson, who had served as consul in Dublin from 1826 to 1847, that there was no complaint against him in the discharge of his duty and he was being replaced because he was not an American citizens, it was not the full truth.[103] Hugh Keenan had solicited the appointment. He was born around 1798 in Castleblaney, county Monaghan, to Thomas Keenan and Betty Smith and aged 18, he and his brother emigrated to the US. He became a US citizen in 1828 and two years later was admitted to the Pittsburgh Bar. His law firm operated in the US, England, Scotland and Ireland. Among his circle of friends was Jimmy May, a wealthy businessman from Pennsylvania, who recommended him to President's

100 *Ibid.*, USB, 1, 1, T368, Shaw to Calhoun, 11 October 1844, 15 January 1845; *ibid.*, Gilpin to Buchanan, 1 October 1845.
101 Carroll, *The American presence*, 40.
102 NARA, D/S, USB, 10, 10, T368, Ruby to Wharton, 30 September 1889; *ibid.*, Wharton, 12 October 1889; *ibid.*, Taney to Quincy, 6 March 1894; *ibid.*, Taney to Uhl, 12 December 1895; Carroll, *The American presence*, 40.
103 NARA, D/S, USD, 1, 1, T199, Wilson to Secretary of State, 25 February 1848.

Polk's Secretary of State, James Buchanan, as a 'faithful and competent agent'.[104] Polk was besieged by Democrats including May, looking for posts and he was guided by the need to implement his policy objectives, to reward the party faithful and to unite the Democrats. He made as many enemies as friends.[105] Hugh Keenan had successfully used his legal and political connections to secure the Dublin post.

By 13 December 1847 Keenan had left the US side of his business in the hands of his nephew, Thomas, and arrived in Dublin having received his commission and *exequatur* from George Bancroft, US minister in London. Keenan owned property in Dublin and was worth 'fifty or sixty thousand dollars' and from the time of his return to Ireland, he was determined to extract as much as he could from the consulship and other business transactions.[106] He may not have anticipated the surge in cost of living and doubling of prices during these famine years.[107] Although he made no reference to this in his correspondence, he established his professional business as a solicitor, bill discounter and money broker. The Irish banking system was still evolving and lawyers often acted as bankers for clients. Keenan appeared to prosper but he ended up in the court of Chancery charged with deducting too much commission from bills paid on behalf of Patrick James Richardson, a bills agent. Keenan attended the proceedings dressed in his consular uniform of blue coat with buttons bearing the US emblem. Richardson claimed that Keenan owed him £4,868 but a State Department investigation later noted that this claim was unsupported by affidavit or proof. However, in 1851 the court found him 'not to have come into court with clean hands, nor has he sworn truly' and he unlawfully withheld documents.[108] His need for a larger income led him to apply for a transfer to the more lucrative Queenstown post after John Murphy's death there in May 1849.[109] Keenan explained to the new Whig Secretary of State, John Clayton,

---

104 *Ibid.*, Keenan to Buchanan, 22, 6, 22 October 1847; 'The Keenan families of county Monaghan, Ireland' online at http://members.aol.com (accessed 24 July 2008).
105 Gerhardt, The *federal appointments process*, 54; Holman Hamilton, *Zachary Taylor: soldier in the White House* (Connecticut, 1966), 53.
106 NARA, D/S, USD, 1, 1, T199, Keenan to Buchanan, 17 December 1847, online at http://members.aol.com (accessed 24 July 2008). *Thom's Directory, 1848*; NARA, D/S, USD, 1, 1, T199, Keenan to Buchanan, 14 July 1848.
107 Kennedy, 'The cost of living in Ireland, 1698–1998', 258.
108 The latter occupations involved buying and selling bills of exchange for a commission or a fee and were respected activities. NARA, D/S, USC, 2, 2, T196, Petition to President Pierce; Department of State, Summary of certain complaints filed against Hugh Keenan, United States, consul at Cork; Ó Gráda, 'Industry and communications, 1801–1845' in Vaughan (ed.), *A new history of Ireland*, v, 150–5.
109 NARA, D/S, USD, 1, 1, T199, Keenan to Clayton, 20 July 1849; *ibid.*, USC, 1, 1, T196, Keenan to Secretary of State, undated, late May 1850.

that a number of individuals had left for Washington immediately after Murphy's death to press their case for appointment but they were not American citizens and would use the post for personal gain. He advised Clayton that an intelligent individual was needed in Queenstown to deal with the emergencies that frequently arose due to shipwrecks and the arrival of US vessels in distress or in need of repair. Not only did he see himself as the ideal replacement in Queenstown but he recommended his nephew, a native of Pennsylvania, to replace him in Dublin.[110] But Whig President Zachary Taylor had his own promises to fulfil. Taylor replaced almost two-thirds of his predecessor' appointees during his first year in office and while his party had brought some Irish-Americans in New York to its side on the issue of denominational education, the Democrats remained their preferred political alignment.[111] However, Alfred Mitchell from New York with links to the Whigs became US consul in Cork.[112] Keenan lost out once more when Whig Vice President Millard Fillmore replaced Taylor following the latter's sudden death in July 1850. Daniel Webster became Secretary of State and he nominated James Foy of Pennsylvania to the Dublin post in September following representations by former Attorney-General of Pennsylvania and Whig senator, James Cooper.[113] Foy was established at number 2 Lower Buckingham Street in Dublin by late November 1850.[114] Keenan was furious because he felt he had carried out his duties without giving rise to any complaint despite the upcoming court case and because Foy, a Briton, was not an American. Furthermore, he had learned that Foy and members of his family held positions under the British government and, therefore, could not be totally loyal to the US.[115] Some of Keenan's arguments might have been turned against himself. They revealed a man tired of crossing the Atlantic and desperate to hold onto a consular post in Ireland.

Keenan's appointment to the Cork office resulted from the return of the Democrats to power under President Franklin Pierce in 1853 and he may have indirectly benefited from the military service of another nephew James during the Mexican war (1846–8). Hugh had survived the negative publicity arising from the court case in 1851, a critical State Department investigation into his conduct and an ambivalent endorsement of

110 *Ibid.*, Keenan to Secretary of State, undated, late May 1850.
111 Doyle, 'The Irish in North America', 199–200; David Noel Doyle, 'The Remaking of Irish America, 1845–1880' in Lee and Casey (eds), *Making the Irish American*, 215.
112 NARA, D/S, USC, 1, 1, T196, Mitchell to Clayton, 3 July 1849.
113 *Ibid.*, USD, 1, 1, T199, James Cooper to Webster, 31 December 1850.
114 NARA, D/S, USD, 1, 1, T199, Foy to Webster, 18 November 1850.
115 *Ibid.*, 1, 2, T199, Keenan to Webster, 1 January 1850.

his culpability at the end of it.¹¹⁶ Keenan's avariciousness brought him trouble.

Two versions of the events emerge; one from Keenan and the other from local shipowner and shipping agent, Nicholas George Seymour of C. and William Deane Seymour and Company, Lynch's Quay, Queenstown. The latter was also agent for Norway, Prussia, Belgium, Netherlands, Hanover, Mecklenberg, the Ottoman Empire and the East India Company. According to Nicholas Seymour, soon after he arrived in the port Keenan offered to sell him the consular position for an annual sum of $6,000 in order that he could continue to reside in Dublin. Seymour who had acted previously as vice consul to his father-in-law Consul John Murphy and held consular property after John Higgins' departure, informed President Pierce that Keenan had threatened he would enter into 'relations with other parties ... [for] great pecuniary advantages' if Seymour refused. Seymour understood he would be 'indirectly purchasing the office' and indignantly refused to comply with Keenan's terms. Two days later, Keenan offered Seymour modified terms set out in a contract. On a third visit, Keenan demanded that Seymour hand over the seal, flag and statutes which he then deposited with the French consular agent in Queenstown.¹¹⁷ Keenan defended himself against the allegations stating that when he told Seymour he would not appoint him as vice consul or agent, he was subjected to threats and unwarrantable language. Neither would Seymour hand over the coat of arms and consular records. Keenan's two-page letter devoted just one of four paragraphs to the meetings, unlike Seymour's detailed letter and supporting documents. This suggests that Keenan was deliberately downplaying the many encounters.¹¹⁸ Seymour kept an eye on Keenan's movements and reported to Secretary William Marcy on 29 December that he had not appeared in Queenstown since the beginning of the month and that the French consular agent remained in possession of US consular property, displaying the US flag underneath the French standard outside that office in Queenstown. In addition Seymour seemed genuinely concerned at not being able to assist a distressed US citizen, Henry Williams, who had attempted suicide by throwing himself into the River Lee but was saved by a policeman who wished to hand him over to the US consul.¹¹⁹

---

116 James Keenan obtained a consular post in Hong Kong on 24 May 1853. Laura A. White, 'The United States in the 1850s as seen by British consuls', *Mississippi Valley Historical Review*, 19:4 (March 1933), 531; http://members.aol.com (accessed 25 July 2008); Kennedy, *The American consul*, 210.
117 NARA, D/S, USC, 2, 2, T196, Seymour to Pierce, 7 December 1854; *ibid.*, 9, 9, T196, Piatt to Porter, 4 November 1885.
118 *Ibid.*, 2, 2, T196, Keenan to Marcy, 8 December 1854.
119 *Ibid.*, Seymour to Marcy, 29 December 1854.

Keenan was back in Queenstown by early February 1855 hoping 'to avoid all altercations and take no notice' of Seymour. He maintained his innocence and denied dereliction of duty because he was simply moving his family from Dublin to a new house in Queenstown. It was Seymour who offered him a partnership agreement, whereby they share the consular fees and Keenan could continue to live in Dublin. Keenan also intimated that Seymour had maintained a similar type of relationship in 1853 and 1854 with former Consul Higgins. Keenan also denied knowing the French consular agent and said he left the consular property with an unnamed local merchant.[120] Later in April, he forwarded affidavits detailing Seymour's threatening behaviour against local merchants and captains. He outlined a campaign of harassment that Seymour and his agents waged against him and his family. Keenan believed that Seymour wanted to render the consulate profitless thereby, forcing him to leave the post. He asked Marcy for some sign of official disapproval to finally discredit Seymour and re-establish the prestige of the US consulate in Queenstown.[121] This did not happen but Keenan's other business interests would bring him further official attention.

Keenan earned a fee income in Queenstown of $310 between August 1853 and November 1854 and $225 between January and June 1855, thus averaging approximately $200 per annum.[122] It was a pathetic amount when compared to the $6,000 he had expected and was forced to engage in other money-making ventures. In September 1855, he advertised in the *Cork Examiner* that he would be embarking on a visit to the US 'for the collection of legacies and debts, executors' documents, making searches and transactions of all American business as heretofore'.[123] The conflict of interest was obvious. During his absence, the State Department compiled a summary of complaints against him including negligence, failure to return papers and inconveniencing the master of *Wandering Jew* in September 1855, and the appointment of an inefficient, British citizen, George Scott, as his agent.[124] In October, Keenan complained that Seymour was behind the campaign to have him

---

120 *Ibid.*, Keenan to Marcy, 6 February 1855; *ibid.*, Mitchell to Marcy, 13 September 1853; *ibid.*, Mitchell to Marcy, 24 November 1853; *ibid.*, Keenan to Marcy, 5 March 1855.
121 *Ibid.*, Keenan to Marcy, 13 April 1855; *ibid.*, Keenan to Marcy, 6 October 1855.
122 *Ibid.*, Fees, 26 August 1853–27 November 1854; *ibid.*, January–June 1855.
123 *Ibid.*, Enclosure in Patrick J Hayes to Marcy, 6 September 1855.
124 *Ibid.*, Keenan to Marcy, 28 February 1855. Keenan returned to the US in September 1855, *ibid.*, Department of State, 'Summary of certain complaints filed against Hugh Keenan, United States consul at Cork'; *ibid.*, J. DeWitt [a US citizen living in Middleton] to Marcy, 28 September 1855; *Cork Examiner*, 17 September 1855. NARA, D/S, USC, 2, 2, T196, Keenan to Marcy, 6 October 1855.

US consular service: appointments and conditions, 1790–1906

removed from or resign from the consulate. In September 1857, Captain Sorle of the *Roebuck* of Boston, refused to hand over his papers to Keenan, on Seymour's advice.[125] Keenan was replaced in 1859 believing it was due to Seymour's corruption charges.[126]

The Keenan–Seymour dispute suggested that US consuls in Queenstown at least, had benefited financially from an association with local merchants, ship agents, brokers and owners of shipyards whereby they could receive payment to certify lower values of export goods on invoices, and to direct masters of American vessels to certain local shipyards for supplies or repairs. In turn, Keenan outlined that locals businesses profited:

> by charging double concessions – first, a large fee percentage deducted from bills furnished for work materials and for supplies for American ships, and then charging the bill in full to the shipowners, and also charging them an additional commission or brokerage for these important services, and finally, to reconcile conscientious squeamish captains to this system, dividing the spoils with them in several cases.[127]

Keenan exposed other examples of irregular consular behaviour. John Murphy maintained his consular office in his son-in-law's Seymour's building. John Higgins had a close relationship with Seymour also. Keenan believed that Alfred Mitchell (1849–53), had been compelled to connect himself to a shipbroker or agent who acted as his consular agent while he usually attended to other business and even lived elsewhere. Consequently, Keenan admitted that the consul could realise considerable money in a dubious manner and bring disrespect on the office.[128] Later in Dublin Consul Henry Hammond was convinced that Keenan, Michael Lynch (Dublin 1853–4), James Arrott (Dublin 1855–8, Belfast 1858) and Samuel Talbot (Galway 1856–8, Dublin 1859–61) had all engaged in bribery during their tenures. He had gathered information from 'influential' men in Dublin that indicated each consul 'had relied … upon the money bag of the ship broker'. As soon as Hammond arrived in Dublin in 1861, he was approached by a broker who was desirous of having the consular office located over his own premises and would give Hammond £100 in return. Hammond described by Benjamin Moran, secretary in the London legation, as an 'educated gentleman' with a 'most agreeable manner', declined but later told Secretary William Seward that if he had involved himself in this system of bribery, he could have

---

125 *Ibid.*, Keenan to Marcy, 6 October 1855; *ibid.*, Keenan to Marcy, 2 September 1857.
126 NARA, D/S, USC, 4, 4, T196, Keenan to Cass, 5 September 1860.
127 *Ibid.*, Keenan to Marcy, 13 April 1855.
128 *Ibid.*, Keenan to Marcy, 28 February 1856.

gained much. Hammond's statement was credible.[129] Other accusations were made by James R. Smith, consul in Londonderry, who believed that former consul James Corscaden (1834–42) often used his position 'to accomplish his own and his friends' purposes'. Between 1856 and 1858, Smith experienced a 'great many annoyances and troubles' from Corscaden. The latter was not removed, serving again as agent in 1854–6, 1857–8, 1861–2, 1863–71 and was replaced only because a younger man was needed. Smith also believed Belfast Consul John Higgins (1854–8), formerly of Queenstown, to be untrustworthy, with a poor reputation among the Belfast business community.[130] Such activities, real or alleged, in Queenstown, Dublin, allegedly Galway, Londonderry and Belfast which spurred on the introduction of the 1855 and 1856 reform legislation. The accused miscalculated the extent of the consular fees and when they discovered their mistake, unlike other impecunious consuls who returned home, resorted to unlawful ways of surviving.[131]

The reimbursement of monies given to destitute American sailors was another source of abuse. John Church's expenditure in this regard in 1840 was queried by the State Department. Other consuls submitted bogus claims for clothes, accommodation and hospital charges. The 1846 House Committee recorded many other cases particularly in consulates located in the southern hemisphere where there were few trading opportunities. In one year, four consuls based in seaports in the South Pacific, claimed for $114,000, $8,000 'more than the disbursements of all ... other consulates' and way above what might have been expended to the few penniless Americans discharged from whaling schooners.[132]

The 1856 act represented the first serious effort by Congress to deal with the problems of corruption, bribery, inefficiency and indiscipline within the consular system. First, fees were to be regulated; consuls were permitted to charge $2 for authenticating documents of most types, 0.5c. for registering each ton of vessel whose paperwork was processed

129 *Ibid.*, USD, 3, 3, T199, Hammond to Seward, 3 December 1861. Wallace and Gillespie (eds), *The journal of Benjamin Moran, 1857–65*, ii, 3 July 1862. William West also believed Talbot to have engaged in corrupt activities. NARA, D/S, USD, 4, 4, T199, West to Seward, 23 April 1864. Wallace and Gillespie (eds), *The journal of Benjamin Moran, 1857–65*, ii, 4 April 1863.
130 NARA, D/S, USL, 2, 2, T216, Smith to Cass, 9 April 1857; *ibid.*, 3 June 1857; *ibid.*, 3, 3, T216, Livermore to Secretary of State, 18 March 1871; *ibid.* C. Henry, note 29 August 1872; *ibid.*, Livermore to State Department, 12 October 1872. According to George Dallas, Smith's money-making efforts to recruit 33,000 labourers 'riled ... Downing Street' and he ordered Smith to be 'more measured and guarded.' George Mifflin Dallas, *A series of letters from London written during the years 1856, '57, '58, '59 and '60* (Philadelphia, 1869), Dallas to Marcy, 3, 10, 14 October 1856.
131 Barnes and Morgan, *The foreign service*, 98.
132 Lloyd Jones, *The consular service*, 41.

through the consul's office, $1 for every seaman discharged or shipped, 5 per cent of the gross amount for administering the estates of deceased US citizens, 0.25c. for administering an oath, $1–$2 for noting a protest, 0.50c. for recording any document, $5 for preparing a power of attorney and $3–$5 for valuing goods. Additional fees could result from other services performed usually as a result of violence aboard ships, deaths and disaster at sea.[133] The list of fees was to be posted in the consular office, receipts given for fees received and reports on all monies collected would be forwarded annually by the Treasury Department to Congress. No other fees were charged, more offices would be salaried and freed from the need to scrabble for fees or engage in dubious money-making ventures. Officers could devote all their time to consular matters, particularly the promotion of trade.[134]

The act created two schedules of posts and salaries: diplomatic posts (schedule A), consular posts and agencies with higher responsibilities (B) and with lower responsibilities (C). Ninety-two consuls general, consuls and consular agents in the B schedule received salaries ranging from $1,000 to $7,500 but could not trade, do business or retain consular fees. The forty consular and consular agent posts in schedule C received salaries from $500 to $1,000, could be merchants but could not retain fees. In addition there were thirty consuls not included in either schedule who could trade, do business and keep fees. The salary levels were still lower than those offered by other countries and were allocated according to post and not an individual's rank in the service. The reasons for allotting salaries to posts was not revealed but more likely reflected the former fee capacity of various posts.[135]

The salary rates signalled the order of importance of posts. Table 1.1 notes that Belfast and Cork were in schedule B, therefore consuls would receive a salary of $2,000, could retain fees but were forbidden from trading. Dublin, Londonderry and Galway were not listed as they were among thirty unsalaried posts where the consul could trade and keep fees.[136] While the act improved the situation, it did not eliminate the trading consul. The inadequate salary level in the salaried posts and absence of salaries for others drew an immediate response from consuls.

133 James O'Donald Mays, *Mr Hawthorne goes to England: the adventures of a reluctant consul* (New Forest Leaves, 1983), 74.
134 Kennedy, *The American consul*, 84.
135 Barnes and Morgan, *The foreign service*, 109; Kark, *American consuls*, 165; 'An act to regulate the diplomatic and consular systems of the United States' in *The American almanac and repository of useful knowledge for the year 1857* (Boston, 1856), 147–9.
136 Barnes and Morgan, *The foreign service*, 109. Kennedy, *The American consul*, 83–4; 'An act to regulate the diplomatic and consular systems', 147–9.

Table 1.1 Salary scales for some consular posts under the 1856 legislation

City	Salary $
Liverpool	7,500
London	7,500
Le Havre	5,000
Paris	5,000
Virgin Islands	4,000
Sandwich Islands	4,000
Bremen	2,000
Hamburg	2,000
San Juan del Norte (Nicaragua)	2,000
Beirut	2,000
Belfast	2,000
Cork	2,000
Jerusalem	1,000–500

Source: Barnes and Morgan, *The foreign service*, 109; Kark, *American consuls*, 165; 'An act to regulate the diplomatic and consular systems of the United States' in *The American almanac*, 147–9.

In the lucrative Liverpool posting (also in schedule B), where the novelist Nathaniel Hawthorne was consul from 1853 to 1857, the salary was $7,500. This was at the highest level but less than half that actually earned by him.[137] When Hawthorne had accepted the post, he had hoped to put by $5,000 to $7,000 per year but soon revised that downwards when he included wages for his staff, office expenses and maintaining his family.[138] Hawthorne resigned a few months before the act became effective but the new salary would have disappointed him and not compensated for the drudgery.[139] James R. Smith in Londonderry pointed out to Secretary Marcy that as there was no salary attached to his post, it meant that no respectable American could live there. Within a few months, he complained that it was impossible to live on the fees that averaged $50 a quarter in 1856 and he requested authority over the vacant Galway consulship. By January 1857, Smith had decided to resign due to financial difficulties (he could not even afford to pay the passage home) and

137 NARA, D/S, USB, 2, 3, T368, Statement concerning the United States Consulate at Liverpool.
138 O'Donald Mays, *Mr Hawthorne*, 73.
139 Kennedy, *The American consul*, 83–4; Hull, *Nathaniel Hawthorne*, 35, 57; Barnes and Morgan, *The foreign service*, 106.

he faced charges from the local prison governor for illegally carrying a flask of brandy into the prison during a visit to a US Captain Bouttel.[140] Smith's replacement, Irish-born naturalised US citizen Alexander Henderson, made no comment about the 1856 legislation and the absence of a salary. He collected fees worth $152 in 1858. But he had a private income having accumulated property in Pittsburgh and his company carried government mail between Philadelphia and Pittsburgh.[141]

In the other northern office in Belfast, it was John Higgins (former Cork consul) who received the new $2,000 salary which was less than the $2,071.75c. in fees collected in 1854.[142] Higgins did not comment on the new legislation and its consequences for him.[143] But he continued to engage in business in the busy city leading Acting Secretary of State John Appleton in June 1857 to ask for an explanation.[144] The matter was clarified sufficiently that Higgins was granted two months' leave of absence in January 1858 to attend to business in the US.[145] However, on reaching New York he resigned from the Belfast post for personal reasons and left James Joseph Higgins in charge.[146]

In Dublin, Consul James Arrott learned about the new legislation from an American newspaper. Under the new arrangements, his post was not salaried but he was permitted to retain fees and trade. He reported to Secretary Marcy that the fees amounted to $228.97c. in 1855 and he earned only $100 in the year to October 1856. He needed a salary of at least $1,000 not least because of the particular financially-demanding local conditions.[147] In the decades after the Act of Union, Dublin experienced the gradual retreat of many of its wealthy nobility while the middle classes increasingly made their impact on the economic, social and architectural, and ultimately the political life of the city.[148] Yet, Dublin still remained the centre of administration, the judiciary, police, revenue,

---

140 NARA, D/S, USL, 2, 2, T216, Smith to Marcy, 1September 1856; *ibid.*, Smith to Marcy, 16 October 1856; *ibid.*, Smith to Marcy, 26 October 1856; *ibid.*, Smith to Marcy, Fees, March, June, September Quarters 1856; *ibid.*, Smith to Marcy, 1 January 1857; *ibid.*, Smith to Cass, 26 March 1857.
141 *Ibid.*, Henderson to Cass, 13 May 1858, 7 July 1858; *ibid.*, Fees, 1858; *ibid.*, Hugh Campbell to Buchanan, 30 October 1858.
142 *Ibid.*, USB, 2, 2, T368, O'Neill to Marcy 11 May 1854; *ibid.*, O'Neill to Marcy, 19 June 1854; *ibid.*, Higgins to Marcy, 20 November 1854; *ibid.*, Higgins to Marcy, 12 December 1855.
143 *Ibid.*, Higgins to Marcy, 8 December 1856.
144 *Ibid.*, 2, 3, T368, Appleton to Higgins, 19 June 1857.
145 *Ibid.*, Higgins to Cass, 26 January 1858; *ibid.*, Higgins to Cass, 21 March 1858.
146 *Ibid.*, Higgins to Cass, 31 March 1858; *ibid.*, Higgins to Cass, 18 May 1858.
147 *Ibid.*, USD, 1, 2, T199, Arrott to Marcy, 2 October 1856.
148 Oliver MacDonagh, 'Ideas and institutions, 1830–45' in Vaughan (ed.), *A new history of Ireland*, 193–4.

education and postal service and was the residence of the lord lieutenant, the official representative of the sovereign in Ireland.[149] By the mid-nineteenth century, it was the chief secretary who had day-to-day control of government but during the 'Castle season' from January to March, the lord lieutenant and his retinue resided in the viceregal apartments in Dublin Castle. The 'season' dominated the élites' social life, even though for many the London 'season' took precedence. Arrott along with other foreign consuls in Dublin, went annually to the levées, balls, banquets and dinners associated with the season, all of which would have incurred expense.[150] The second problem Arrott identified – helping American citizens – also required the consul to have personal funds readily available. Arrott requested a transfer to a salaried consulate in either Scotland or England, or in France as he had fluent French. He repeated to Marcy that he could not establish himself in business because Dublin was not a commercial city and as an elderly man, he did not have the energy to establish himself.[151] Unfortunately, he and his family faced a rise in living costs which continued into the mid-1870s.[152] Twice in February and again in June 1857, Arrott reminded President Buchanan that he had loaned the Madison government $80,000 during the War of 1812 and he requested a transfer to a salaried post.[153] His request was refused and Arrott remained in Dublin consul and contracted debts. In July 1858, however, he was relieved to be temporarily transferred to the salaried Belfast post after John Higgins' resignation, even though James and his daughter, Elizabeth, disliked the damp climate.[154] Despite the salary and greater commercial opportunities in Belfast, by the end of 1858 Arrott had not paid off his debts. Elizabeth implored President Buchanan in November not to replace her father until the following spring so that he could save some money to pay for their fare back to the US, rather than in the winter which would harm his health. Before she completed the letter she learned that Theodore Frean had been appointed to Belfast and she reminded Buchanan of her father's old age, ill health, past military record and asked that he be given a salaried post in England or France. She claimed that her father was the oldest person to have represented the

---

149 W. E. Vaughan, 'Ireland c. 1870', in Vaughan (ed.), *A new history of Ireland*, 788–9.
150 Barnes and Morgan, *The foreign service*, 92, n. 48.
151 NARA, D/S, USD, 1, 2, T199, Arrott to Marcy, 2 October 1856; *ibid.*, Arrott to Marcy, 6 November 1856.
152 Kennedy, 'The cost of living in Ireland', 260.
153 NARA, D/S, USD, 1, 2, T199, Arrott to Marcy, 20 February 1857; *ibid.*, Arrott to Buchanan, 4 June 1857.
154 *Ibid.*, Arrott to Cass 7 May 1857; *ibid.*, USB, 2, 3, T368, Arrott to Cass, 24 July 1858; *ibid.*, Arrott to Cass, 26 August 1858.

US abroad with the exception of Franklin.[155] Buchanan received petitions from Arrott's friends and he asked Secretary Cass if anything could be done in this 'extreme case'?'.[156] A four-month delay ensued before Frean received his consular passport and it was not until 1 April 1859 that Frean gained control of the Belfast office.[157] Arrott's impecunious state combined with the social demands and absence of a salary in Dublin revealed that the capital's place, albeit now less significant, in the British empire had not been considered during the formulation of the 1856 legislation.

Irish-born New York resident Samuel Talbot who had previously served as US consul in Mazallan in Mexico, arrived in Galway in September 1856 and one month later, learned that the post there was not salaried. He requested Marcy to transfer him to a salaried post. But he was still in Galway in December 1857 even though he had collected only $14 in fees and had not claimed compensation for the small sums given to destitute seamen. His isolation could not have been helped by the non-arrival of a seal, press and stationery from the State Department.[158] In 1857, he collected $364 in fees but he had other means of support. Repeatedly he asked for a transfer to the Dublin consulate which had become vacant upon Arrott's departure. Although it was unsalaried and the fee potential was not much higher than Galway, Talbot felt that he could make a living there because of his business connections there.[159] In early 1859, President Buchanan appointed him to Dublin where his tenure was problematic. Captain Simpson of the *Caroline A. Simpson*, of Rochester, New York, protested that Talbot had unduly delayed the vessel's departure by not issuing documents on time. Benjamin Moran, secretary in the London legation, thought the complaint well founded and US Minister Dallas rebuked Talbot for the 'unwarrantable detention.' One possible reason for Talbot's conduct was that he acted on instruction from a Dublin firm owed money by Simpson. During the American Civil War he charged emigrants for visas, contrary to orders. By this time Moran regarded correspondence from Talbot to be among the 'most stupid' he received.[160]

155 *Ibid.*, Elizabeth Arrott to Cass, 18, 22 November 1858.
156 *Ibid.*, Buchanan, 22 December 1858.
157 *Ibid.*, Arrott to Cass, 1 April 1859.
158 NARA, D/S, USG, 1,1, T570, Talbot to Marcy, 29 July 1856; *ibid.*, Talbot to Marcy, 24 September 1856. The wealthy, merchant Anglo-Irish Persse family held the Galway consulship for fifteen of the first eighteen years. Monaghan-born John Duffy lasted a few months in Galway because it was financially worthless to him. See NARA, D/S, USG, 1, 1, T570.
159 *Ibid.*, Talbot to Cass, 15 July 1858; *ibid.*, 19 August 1858.
160 *Ibid.*, Talbot to Cass, 3 May 1859; Wallace and Gillespie (eds), *The journal of Benjamin Moran, 1857–65*, i, 27 December 1859; *ibid.*, i, 3 January 1860; *ibid.*, ii, 4 January 1862; ii, 7 October 1861.

Talbot, Arrott and Smith were each disappointed at the absence of a salary for their post.

The legislation had stipulated $1,000 per year for the Queenstown post. Once Hugh Keenan heard about the reform process, he lobbied for Queenstown to be salaried for three reasons: interference by Nicholas Seymour in consular affairs, the port's importance to American vessels and the consul was responsible for consular agencies in Limerick and Waterford.[161] After he received a copy of the act, Keenan repeated the arguments for a higher salary and added that the consul incurred expense visiting the docks and courts in Cork city and the dry docks in Passage West. Following the change in administration in March 1857 and the installation of Democrat James Buchanan, Keenan requested a transfer to either of the higher-salaried posts in Glasgow, Antwerp or Marseilles or appointment as consul general based in Ireland. The latter, he argued, would enhance the prestige of the US government and provide an additional source of income as the post holder was entitled under British shipping law to claim wrecked property from shipwrecks if the shipowner or agent were absent. His requests were refused and, unfortunately for him, when the Queenstown fees peaked at $500 for the last quarter of 1858, the highest since 1854, he had been replaced by Robert Dowling, a naturalised American citizen born in Dublin and resident of Iowa.[162] Keenan returned to Dublin where he engaged in currency exchange.[163]

The 1856 act underpinned the consular service for the following fifty years. While it represented a major attempt to regulate fees, control the consular representatives and reduce corruption, it had weaknesses. It did not provide for a professional, trained service, appointments were a consequence of political influence and salaries were too low or non-existent, thereby tempting corrupt practices and ineptitude. For example, the salary levels for Ireland did not take into account that consuls whether salaried or not, were liable for payment of taxes on income earned and for poor rates, just like any other resident.[164] The allowance paid to the salaried consuls was for office rent but it was so low that many consuls were located in second-rate rooms and garrets which occasionally contributed to consular ill health. Stationery, seals, presses, ledgers, flags and coats of arms were provided by the State Department

161 NARA, D/S, USC, 2, 2, T196, Keenan to Marcy, 28 February 1856; *ibid*., Keenan to Marcy, 18 April 1856.
162 *Ibid*., 3, 3, T196, Keenan to Marcy, 12 March 1857; *ibid*., Keenan to Secretary of State, 19 March 1857; *ibid*., Keenan to Cass, 1 September 1857; *ibid*., 12 November 1857; *ibid*., 18 November 1857; *ibid*., 4, 4, T196, Dowling to Appleton, 25 January 1859; *ibid*., Keenan to Cass, 31 March 1859.
163 *Ibid*., Keenan to Cass, 13 August 1859.
164 *Ibid*., 6, 6, T196, Eastman to Seward, 7 November 1863.

along with postage costs. An allowance to hire a clerk from 1874 and an increase in rent allowance relieved the financial pressure on consuls.[165]

Soon after the passing of the act, the Treasury Department appointed agents to inspect consular offices and accounts. The agents discovered abuses such as indebtedness, 'plunder and profligacy' and poor performance.[166] Liverpool consul Beverly Tucker from Virginia, was identified as one culprit; another was Tipperary-born, naturalised American, Patrick J. Devine, who returned as consul to Cork in 1861. Immediately he associated himself with Nicholas Seymour by establishing the consulate in his building. Several ships' masters protested to Secretary Seward that confidential conversation with Devine was almost impossible because he was based at a desk in Seymour's private office. Seymour could hear all their business and frequently interfered in conversations in a 'very insulting manner', especially if a ship's business was not in his hands. Seymour's business cards also contained Consul Devine's details and were distributed to all ships' masters upon arrival in Queenstown. Ultimately, the captains felt that Devine was unduly influenced by Seymour and consular business was conducted by Seymour's clerks.[167] Not only were they intimidated by the arrangement but felt obliged to give their business to Seymour. Evidence of continuing bribery in the Queenstown post was verified by Consul Henry Hammond in Dublin. He had heard these complaints from other foreign consuls and that Seymour had 'secured' the consul.[168] Seymour was also accused of giving Devine £1,000 and the use of a residence.[169]

Against the background of the American Civil War (chapter 3), Devine denied 'the tissue of false and malicious fabrications' in March and again in April 1862. But he admitted renting an office and residence from Seymour and that he was naïve in his actions.[170] Yet, he had connected himself to US Consular Agent Isaac Arthur based in Crookhaven along the Cork coast. Arthur kept two pilot boats off Cape Clear, the southernmost point of Ireland and landmark for most transatlantic traffic. His ships intercepted any vessels in difficulty and directed them into Crookhaven despite the absence of a dockyard there. He would then sell the repair contract to other ship agents for an 'underground commission' which would be concealed in the repair bills. Eventually the shipowner

165 Barnes and Morgan, *The foreign service*, 122–3.
166 *Ibid.*, 124.
167 NARA, D/S, USC, 5, 5, T196, Petition to Seward, early 1862.
168 *Ibid.*, USD, 3, 3, T199, Hammond to Seward, 31 July 1862.
169 *Ibid.*, USC, 5, 5, T196, Devine to Seward, 23 April 1862; *ibid.*, Turner to Seward, 30 June 1862.
170 *Ibid.*, Devine to Seward, 15 March 1862; *ibid.*, Seward to Devine, 23 April 1862.

would have to pay this additional expense and any others arising from the hire of a steamer to tow the ship from Crookhaven to the dockyard at Passage West further along the Cork coast. Arthur's lucrative scheme in relation to American vessels, was dependent on his consular status which Devine continued.[171] The relationship emerged after Devine's dismissal when Arthur asked his successor Edwin George Eastman to reappoint him. Arthur offered Eastman, a former shipmaster and friend of US minister to Belgium Henry Shelton Sanford, a share in the profits which amounted to roughly £100 per year. Eastman refused the offer because he did not want to 'forward the … nefarious business'.[172] Seward backed his consul's judgement. Eastman appeared to be a man of honesty as was Hammond in Dublin who would not accept 'bribes' and insisted that the only way to end consular corruption in his district was for the post to become salaried. He offered Seward other reasons also; Dublin was a 'beautiful and fine city … the largest city of Ireland and the third city in the United Kingdom … to which so much importance is attached by Great Britain'. He believed he was sent 'to protect American interests not to destroy them'.[173] In March 1862, however, Hammond requested a transfer to a paid post because he could no longer bear the expense. He repeated the request in May and July and solicited the help of Benjamin Moran in London and his own father who wrote to Seward also.[174] Seeing no hope of a transfer to another post, Hammond resigned on 9 July 1863.[175] Eastman remained in Queenstown until 1869 but both men's financial difficulties and honesty highlighted the unprofessional and dishonest behaviour of other consuls.

The continuing absence of selection procedures, appropriate salary scales, relevant training and promotion opportunities ensured that men without qualification or experience became consuls. Benjamin Moran's views on the quality of consuls in 1859 resonated down the subsequent years:

> [as a] class a most pretentious and ignorant set … at this time there are not more than three in the entire Dominions fit for their places. Three-fourths of them are dishonest, always side with the master against the seamen as a matter of policy, regardless of justice, and there are but three who know

---

171 *Ibid.*, Eastman to Seward, 26 March 1863.
172 *Ibid.*, Devine to Seward, 2 August 1862.
173 *Ibid.*, 6, 6, T196, Eastman to Seward, 27 July 1869; *ibid.*, USD, 3, 3, T199, Hammond to Seward, 3 December 1861.
174 *Ibid.*, Hammond to Seward, 13 March 1862; *ibid.*, Hammond to Seward, 22 May 1862; *ibid.*, P Hammond to Seward, 22 July 1862; *ibid.*, Hammond to Seward, 24 July 1862; Wallace and Gillespie, *The journal of Benjamin Moran*, ii, 3 July 1862.
175 NARA, D/S, USD, 4, 4, T199, Hammond to Seward, 9 July 1863.

their duty ... while they get salaries this legation in fact performs their duties.[176]

Moran was a Buchanan Democrat and by 1861 was even less enamoured by President Lincoln's consular appointments: 'our consuls are enough to provoke a saint ... the most pretentious and stupid I have yet seen'. Those in Ireland featured prominently in his judgement. He liked Frean in Belfast because his wife was 'a very pleasant lady, and he is far above the ordinary run of the stuff of which Am[erican] consuls are made'. Unfortunately, Dr John Young who replaced Frean, was a 'mere pompous windbag.' Young was born in Balloughan, county Antrim, emigrated to the US where he became a preacher, a lawyer and an active Republican party member. His appointment was a reward for party loyalty which would not have endeared him to Moran in the first place. Talbot, consul in Dublin since 1859, was unacceptable because he asked questions 'which were properly answered, and ... he turns round to argue with the Minister out of his convictions!'. Thomas McGunn in Londonderry was an 'illiterate fellow' but for Moran, James Cantwell personified the worst aspects of the spoils system.[177]

Cantwell was appointed consul to Dublin on the nomination of General Thomas Francis Meagher, a former leader of the 'Young Ireland' nationalist movement, who eventually made his way to the US and formed the pro-Union Irish brigade during the Civil War. After Cantwell received notification of his appointment, he contacted the Wexford-born, Vice Consul in Dublin, William West, who refused to hand over the seal, press, flag and archives of the consulate.[178] Initially, West had arrived as consul in Galway, obtained the Dublin vice consulship also and aspired to the full post in the capital. He established an office at 17 Eden Quay in Dublin and lived at 15 Lower Gardiner Street. Seward would not promote him to consul and instead appointed Cantwell. West then began a campaign to discredit him. He refused to give Cantwell consular property not out of 'ill-feeling' for him but in accordance with

---

176 Wallace and Gillespie, *The journal of Benjamin Moran*, i, 17 August 1859.
177 *Ibid.*, ii, 11 October 1861; *ibid.*, 1 November 1861; Carroll, *American presence*, 63; Wallace and Gillespie, *The journal of Benjamin Moran*, ii, 18 July 1861; *ibid.*, ii, 11 October 1861; *ibid.*, ii, 1 January 1862.
178 NARA, D/S, USD, 4, 4, T199, Cantwell to Seward, 10 October 1863. In 1866 Meagher was appointed governor of Montana territory. Young Ireland was led by Thomas Davis, Charles Gavan Duffy and John Blake Dillon who worked to achieve a 'spontaneous peasant-led social revolution.' Peter Gray, 'Meagher, Thomas Francis' in Connolly (ed.), *The Oxford companion*, 353; Timothy Walch, 'Meagher, Thomas Francis' in Glazier (ed.), *The encyclopedia*, 601–2; Peter Gray, 'Young Ireland' in Connolly (ed.), *The Oxford companion*, 602–3; Peter Gray, 'Rebellion of 1848' in *ibid.*, 473–4; *Thom's directory*, 1869.

regulations because Cantwell had not received his *exequatur*.[179] Second, Cantwell 'kept a petty grogery' and West believed that consuls should be 'gentlemen ... who reflect honour and credit on the countries they represent', men of 'superior not common education, with the tact and knowledge of an experienced lawyer'. Moreover, West highlighted that Cantwell would represent his government at vice regal occasions where he would be accompanied by his daughter who worked in his tavern, again implying his unsuitability for the position. Finally, Cantwell was charged with being a nationalist sympathiser. West's 'dissent' was endorsed by the US consuls in Liverpool, Bristol, Cardiff and Cork, former Consul Hammond, foreign consuls in Dublin, leading merchants and manufacturers. One unnamed merchant asked if the US government could not find a better consul for Dublin than a publican and a 'Young Ireland rebel?'. West felt that Cantwell's appointment would not please the London government either.[180]

By the 1860s, the appointments process no longer involved the newly appointed consul presenting himself in London to receive a royal *exequatur*. Instead, the US legation in London applied to the Foreign Office which in turn requested the Home Office to inquire of the Irish chief secretary whether there was any objection to the candidate. Consequently, the local mayor and police inspector were asked for an opinion and with this approval, the *exequatur* was issued allowing the consul to begin his official business. During the investigation into Cantwell's suitability, the appointment stalled in the chief secretary's office.[181] In November 1863 Thomas Larcom, the Irish Under-Secretary, received the standard Home Office letter inquiring about any possible objections to Cantwell's appointment. But before a reply was drawn up, Foreign Secretary Earl Russell received an anonymous letter, probably from West, outlining reasons why Cantwell would not be a proper person and recommending further inquiries.[182] In late February 1864, Detective Superintendent Daniel Ryan of the Dublin Metropolitan Police confirmed that Cantwell was a tavern-keeper and that he was a 'very unfit person' to be the American consul. In addition to his economic, social and personal unsuitability, there was his politics; 'his antecedents in 1848 are not such

179 NARA, D/S, USD, 4, 4, T199, West to Seward, 12 October 1863.
180 *Ibid.*, West to Seward, 28 November 1863; *ibid.*, West to Seward, 18 February 1864; *ibid.*, West to Seward, 18 February 1864.
181 For examples see National Archives of Ireland (hereafter NAI), Chief Secretary's Office Registered Papers (hereafter CSORPP), 1861, 2128, 26 March 1861, 2255, 2 April 1861 about the appointment of Josiah William in Waterford and Michael Robert Ryan in Limerick.
182 NAI, CSORP, 1863, H. Waddington to Larcom, 10 November 1863; *ibid.*, 1864, 12617, H. Waddington, Whitehall to Chief Secretary, 16 February 1864.

as to recommend him ... and the class of meetings held at his tavern [were] of a kind abhorrent to the authorities'. Cantwell had been charged with 'treasonable practices' in 1848 and along with others had fled to the US. He returned to Dublin in 1858 or 1859, married the daughter of a tea importer and eventually became proprietor of the Star and Garter Hotel at 16 D'Olier Street. Contrary to West's assertion, the police officer reported that the hotel could not be designated a 'low tavern' though it was confirmed as a centre of nationalist political activity because the organising committee of the Irish National League Association held their meetings there.[183] Founded by Young Ireland leader, John Martin, in Dublin in January 1864, the Association sought to restore a separate and independent Irish legislature.[184] Cantwell and his hostelry were at the heart of this latest attempt to mobilise nationalist public opinion. Unsurprisingly, neither the civil or police authorities could recommend him for the consular post. It was ironic, however, that there were no objections to West's appointments to either Galway or Dublin, even though he espoused separatist beliefs through his association with James Roche, a founding member of the National Brotherhood in New York.

Against the background of the American Civil War, tense Anglo-American relations and continuing Fenian planning for a rising, the British government signalled in spring 1864, its refusal to grant an *exequatur* to Cantwell and asked the US government to cancel the appointment. After a meeting with Russell, Benjamin Moran recorded: 'it appears he is a Fenian and very obnoxious to the British government [it was] perfectly disgraceful that such an appointment should have been made. The man is a low Irishman and keeps a rum shop in Dublin.' Russell did not want to announce publicly the decision but asked that someone else be appointed. Facing the opposition of the host government, his minister and long-serving legation secretary in addition to that of the authorities and private groups in Dublin, Seward decided that 'West now in charge ... will continue until further notice'.[185] West felt vindicated and informed Seward that Cantwell had intended to 'farm' out the post

---

183 NAI, CSORP, 1864, 12920, Ryan to Chief Secretary's Office, 22 February 1864; *ibid.*, Chief Secretary of Ireland, 26 February 1864.
184 R. V. Comerford, 'Churchmen, tenants and independent opposition, 1850–56' in Vaughan (ed.), *A new history of Ireland*, v, 412, 425; Comerford, 'Gladstone's first Irish enterprise, 1864–70' in *ibid.*, 431.
185 NARA, D/S, Diplomatic Instructions of the Department of State, 1801–1906, Great Britain (hereafter DIGB), RG 59, M77, 78, Seward to Adams, 21 March 1864; Wallace and Gillespie (eds), *The journal of Benjamin Moran, 1857–65*, ii, 5 April 1864; NARA, D/S, DIGB, RG 59, M77, 78, Seward to Adams, 4 May 1864; *ibid.*, Seward to Adams, 19 May 1864; NARA, D/S, USD, 4, 4, T199, West to Seward, 9 April 1864.

to former disgraced Consul, Samuel Talbot. Cantwell unsuccessfully appealed the decision to the Irish chief secretary.[186] Unfortunately for West, despite his commitment and constant petitioning, he was never upgraded to full consul and in 1869 Edward D. Neill replaced him in Dublin. Undoubtedly West had pursued Cantwell because of the absence of a salary for the Galway post and the inadequacy of the Dublin wage along with his personal ambition for the post. Nonetheless, the details about Cantwell's occupation and his political leanings helped to define for Seward the desirable features of a consular officer in Ireland at this time. He should be educated, socially acceptable, politically neutral or at least not anti-British and, if in business, keeping a public house and hotel ranked low. Indeed as noted earlier, a view existed within the State Department that 'uneducated, unpolished, and utterly inexperienced men' should not be appointed.[187]

Ireland was not the only country still causing problems for the State Department. Beginning in July 1870, DeBenneville Randolph Keim, a Treasury official, inspected consular offices during a worldwide tour. Accepting that he was an accountant and his visits were short, he discovered that almost every consulate had some defects owing to the 'incompetency, low habits and vulgarity of some if its officers'. Among the abuses were the illegal collection of fees, improper exercise of power, fraudulent accounting procedures, faulty administration of deceased Americans' estates, the sale of illegal passports and the American flag, collusion with shipmasters and imposition of unauthorised taxes on intending emigrants to the US. He commented on the ingenuity displayed by consular officers since 1856 particularly in 'defrauding the government and grasping gains from various outside sources'. There were, he admitted, honest officers but they were few in number. The main cause of these 'evils' was political patronage. Among his recommendations were increased levels of remuneration and selection on merit.[188]

Ironically, the Keim review took place under the auspices of the Republican administration of Ulysses Grant (1869–77) which in itself represented the nadir of the spoils system. Grant involved himself in all manner of lowly appointments; few competent men were chosen and others who were, such as Eastman and West, were removed. Consular ranks swelled with former generals, colonels, lower-ranked officers, politicians and family friends. Secretary of State Hamilton Fish, a capable lawyer from New York who had never been abroad, ignored Grant's

---

186 *Ibid.*, 4, 4, T199, West to Seward, 23 April 1864; *ibid.*, T199, West to Seward, 18 June 1864.
187 Barnes and Morgan, *The foreign service*, 142; Schuyler, *American diplomacy*, 98.
188 *Ibid.*, 124–6; Kennedy, *The American consul*, 172.

consular appointments preferring instead to use his influence to prevent some of the more ludicrous appointments to diplomatic positions, and to temper Grant's foreign policy ideas.[189] Eastman was not surprised by Grant's decision to replace him because he had no political influence in his native state of Maine to lobby on his behalf in Washington. Moreover, Henry Shelton Sanford, his regular correspondent and benefactor, had retired from the service. So, Eastman had to make a case to hold on to his job based on his leadership during the 'most eventful period in the history of our country'. He asked for reassurance that he was not being moved by 'fault of his own'.[190] On 16 August 1869, Eastman handed over the post to former Belfast Consul, US-born Thomas R. King, a 'person who has stronger political friends than I have' but reiterated that his family and friends were astonished at his removal. Fortunately, Eastman was transferred as acting consul to Glasgow, Scotland, but stricken with tuberculosis, lasted just six months there. He returned to the US to live in Florida and then Chicago where suffering from depression, he committed suicide in December 1872.[191] Keim would have classified Eastman as one of the few officers of integrity even though his appointment resulted from the spoils system.

Keim also uncovered evidence of inadequate vice consuls and clerks in the system. Just as there was an inadequate allowance for accommodation, there was no appropriation for clerk hire until 1874. In offices where help was needed, consuls offered low salaries which led to abuses. In 1869, 22-year-old Hugh McCormick in Belfast passed on confidential information obtained from one linen manufacturer to a rival company. Fortunately, the case was settled out of court.[192] Dublin Vice Consul John Shaw duplicated invoices and did not record others in order to pocket the fee. Consul Barrows never checked his work and blamed Shaw's behaviour on a marriage on 'slender means' and excessive drinking.[193] A State Department investigation found Barrows innocent and Shaw's original guarantors were contacted presumably to retrieve some of the

---

189 Kennedy, *The American consul*, 168–9.
190 NARA, D/S, USC, 6, 6, T196, Eastman to Fish, 16 August 1869; Sanford Historical Society Florida (hereafter SHSF), 'Henry Shelton Sanford Papers Catalogue', 6–9, 51.
191 NARA, D/S, USC, 6, 6, T196, Eastman to Fish, 27 July 1869; *ibid*., King to Fish, 24 August 1869; *ibid*., 16 August 1869. King was appointed to Belfast by the Johnson administration where he replaced Gwyn Heap who moved to the US consulate in Tunis in April 1867. King left Belfast for Cork in August 1869. Carroll, *The American presence*, 85–6.
192 NARA, D/S, USB, 5, 5, T368, King to Seward, 4 February 1869; *ibid*., Rea to Fish, 14 April 1870.
193 *Ibid*., USD, 9, 9, T199, Barrows to Davis, 1 April 1884; *ibid*., Chilton, 30 April 1884; *ibid*., Barrows to Davis, 1 April 1884.

embezzled funds.¹⁹⁴ Barrows' faulty record-keeping specifically the failure to record separately his notarial and private fees, was later uncovered.¹⁹⁵ Keim had also proposed the establishment of an inspectorate system to investigate procedures as well as consuls' behaviour. A full inspectorate system was created in 1906.

Excessive patronage continued into Grant's second term in 1873. The frustration experienced by consuls who aspired to promotion clearly emerges from Arthur Livermore's letter to Secretary Fish on 17 April 1876: this 'deserving' consul saw vacancies elsewhere filled by 'strangers to the service'. Prior to his appointment in Londonderry in 1871, Livermore, a lawyer, from a wealthy New Hampshire family, was consul in Stuttgart, but during the Grant administration he saw himself as a 'forgotten' servant and perhaps a victim of a corrupt government. He viewed the Irish post as a short-term one prior to a salaried position. His letter was acknowledged by the State Department but no action followed. In 1877 when Republican President Rutherford Hayes was installed, Livermore wrote again emphasising the financial burden, that his duties were not numerous but diversified and he complained of the appointment of 'strangers', by which he meant political appointments to the service. He hoped that 'justice [and] enlightened government' would bring him promotion.¹⁹⁶ Hayes prioritised civil service reform and his successors, Republicans James Garfield (4–19 March 1881) and Chester Arthur (1881–5), upheld it, but the consular and diplomatic services remained vulnerable to patronage.¹⁹⁷

Livermore remained in Londonderry for sixteen years, surviving on the small salary and income from his legal business and American property, as he saw more 'strangers' appointed ahead of him to salaried and lucrative posts. By 1880 he was disappointed and disgusted with the spoils system but he knew that not having any influence in Washington hindered him.¹⁹⁸ In July 1886, aged 76, he offered his resignation to Democrat President Grover Cleveland (1885–9). He recognised that Cleveland might not want to maintain 'incumbents trained to political notions repugnant to his own views'. But Livermore still harboured hopes of being kept on, adding that if the post was of 'greater value and importance', it should probably go to a better man. However, the

194 Ibid., Barrows to Davis, 1 April 1884.
195 Ibid., McCaskill to Porter, 3 April 1886.
196 Ibid., USL, 3, 3, T216, Livermore to Secretary of State, 17 April 1876; ibid., USB, 9, 9, T368, Livermore to Secretary of State, 29 March 1877; ibid., Livermore to Secretary of State, 30 December 1880. Carroll, The American presence in Ulster, 104.
197 Urofsky (ed.), The American presidents, 222, 228.
198 NARA, D/S, USL, 9, 9, T216, Livermore to Secretary of State, 30 December 1880.

work could be easily performed by an 'old man' whose hours were not otherwise filled. His hopes of being retained were not helped by Consul General Thomas Waller in London who reminded Assistant Secretary Porter of the complaints by US pensioners against Livermore. Either way, Cleveland had many favours to repay and used the consular and diplomatic service to do so. Livermore was dismissed in September, and vented his anger to Porter at the lack of 'courtesy' and 'justice' shown to him by his government. The Londonderry consulate was downgraded to a consular agency in November 1886.[199]

In the absence of real reform in the 1880s, unsuitable consuls continued to be appointed. Edward Brooks from King George's County, Virginia, was appointed to Cork in January 1880, having worked as a clerk of the circuit court for two judges whose patronage appears to have secured him the post from President Hayes. However, he left a trail of unpaid bills behind him in Washington and when he resigned from Cork in March 1882, his deputy, George Dawson, discovered that he was heavily in debt and owned large sums to various people including Dawson, the Bank of Ireland and Queenstown General Hospital for medical aid to seaman Edward Staines. The US Treasury was defrauded also and Brooks' guarantors were pursued.[200]

Just as a monarch patronised the arts, in the American democracy there was a view that the government should support writers, poets and artists by awarding them foreign service positions. Writer Washington Irving worked in the Madrid legation and became secretary in the London legation in the 1820s. Novelist James Fennimore Cooper was awarded the consulship in Lyons, France, in 1826 for his literary achievements.[201] Nathaniel Hawthorne secured the consulship in Liverpool in 1853 from President Pierce.[202] Poet William Dean Howells wrote a biography of Lincoln's campaign and was rewarded with the consulate in Venice, Italy, in 1861. In 1877, 'foremost American man of letters of his time', John

---

199 *Ibid.*, USB, 9, 9, T368, Livermore to Porter, 28 July 1886; *ibid.*, Porter to Livermore, 9 August 1886; *ibid.*, Livermore to Porter, 10 September 1886; *ibid.*, Livermore to Porter, 4 November 1886; *ibid.*, Stewart to Porter, 20 November 1886.
200 *Ibid.*, USC, 8, 8, T196, Brooks to Robert R. Hitt, Assistant Secretary of State, 25 July 1881; *ibid.*, Dawson to Bancroft Davis, Assistant Secretary of State, 3 May 1882; *ibid.*, Ralph Hodges to Dawson, 1 May 1882; *ibid.*, note, 9 June 1882; *ibid.*, Davis to Dawson, 9 June 1882.
201 Clare Dowler, 'John James Piatt: representative figure of a momentous period', *Ohio Archaeological and Historical Quarterly*, 45 (January 1936), 17, fn. 33; Alan Taylor, 'Fenimore Cooper's America', *History Today* 46:2 (February 1996), 21; Kennedy, *The American consul*, 72–3.
202 Kennedy, *The American consul*, 82–3; Hull, *Nathaniel Hawthorne*, 3; O'Donald Mays, *Mr Hawthorne goes to England*, 56–191.

Russell Lowell, became US minister to Spain and three years later moved to the London post. Francis Bret Harte became a commercial agent in Crefeld, Germany, and later transferred to Glasgow in 1880.[203]

Ireland received its share of literary and artistic men. James McHenry, born in Larne, county Antrim, on 20 December 1785, became a doctor, emigrated to the US in 1817 and settled in Philadelphia. As a student he wrote poetry, including 'Patrick' (1810) concerning the 1798 rebellion, to help pay his way. His earliest poem published in the US was 'The pleasures of friendship' (1822). Described as a 'successful writer on romantic Irish topics', one of his central themes was to offer an Irish Presbyterian perspective on Ireland's revolutionary past. Among these were 'The insurgent chief: or the pikemen of '98: a romance of the Irish rebellion' (1820) and 'O'Halloran: or the insurgent chief: a tale of the United Irishmen' (1844). His work was praised by Edgar Allan Poe and his play *The usurper: an historical tragedy* was performed to acclaim at the Old Chestnut Street theatre in Philadelphia. McHenry was a Jacksonian Democrat and wrote the poem 'Jackson's wreath' as a tribute. He may have become one of the discontented Jacksonians who left for the Whig party and helped bring President Harrison to prominence and following his death, Vice President John Tyler to power in 1841. Whatever his political connections, McHenry obtained the consular position in Londonderry in 1842. Like many others he hoped it would be financially lucrative, but he too would be disappointed.[204] He remained in office for just three years until his death on 21 July 1845.

Following this pattern, Republican Presidents Garfield and Harrison respectively, appointed poet and writer John James Piatt as Consul to Cork in April 1882 and to Dublin from February to June 1893. Piatt was born on 1 March 1835 in Dearborn County in Indiana and grew up in Milton, Indiana. Piatt's poems, 'The lost farm', 'The pioneer's chimney' and 'Riding to vote' glorified the movement westwards of people and modern machines and pioneer life in the newly settled states. Although Dowler maintains that the poetry was mediocre, his poetry captured a 'stirring picture' of contemporary events. After working as a

---

203 Dowler, 'John James Piatt', 17, fn. 33; See also Dowler, 'John James Piatt', online at http://publications.ohiohistory.org (accessed 20 August 2008); Barnes and Morgan, *The foreign service*, 139; Kennedy, *The American consul*, 128, 149, 209, 211–12; NARA, D/S, USB, 9, 9, T368, White to Livermore, 8 December 1885; *ibid*. Wood to Porter, 16 June 1885.
204 Carroll, *The American presence*, 42; Nathaniel Vance, *Irish literature since 1800* (London, 2002), 61–3; *The Oxford companion to United States history* (Oxford, 2001), 789; NARA, D/S, USL, 1, 1, T216, Fees, 1837; McHenry to Webster, 7 January 1843.

clerk in the Treasury Department in Washington, editing a newspaper, serving as a clerk and librarian in the House of Representatives and finally as clerk in the Cincinnati Post Office, he petitioned Garfield for a consular post. His request was endorsed by Henry Longfellow, Oliver Wendell Holmes, Thomas Bailey Aldrich and John Hay among others and it resulted in his appointment to Cork. Although he had a number of volumes published in Cork, Dublin and London including *At the holy well* in 1887, these were mainly reprinting of old material. However, his wife, Kentucky-born Sarah Morgan Piatt, was also a prolific poet, publishing 120 poems in US magazines and the *Irish Monthly* during her stay. Katharine Tynan may have captured the intellectual isolation felt by the two Piatts in the title of her review, 'Poets in exile: Mr and Mrs Piatt at Queenstown'.[205] Piatt moved to Dublin but did not survive the return of the Democrats under Grover Cleveland in March 1893.[206] But Piatt wanted to remain in Dublin and had gathered supporters. The *Irish Times* published two petitions signed by every Irish member of parliament, every professor in Trinity College, Dublin, Protestant and Catholic bishops, the mayor of Cork, chairman of the Harbour Board and the Queenstown Town Commission and president of the Cork Literary and Scientific Society. The Piatts had made an impact on the cultural as well as economic and political circles in both cities. But all had to accept that Piatt would have to live with the consequences of a spoils system.[207]

Irrespective of their quality, rewarding men on the basis of literary achievement or their feats as explorers and adventurers, emphasised the continuing weaknesses in the system. Up to the early 1880s few politicians were willing to initiate reform.[208] The desire for change within the State Department was evident from the work of the former Consul Bureau head, Arthur B. Wood, who was appointed to Belfast in 1881. He arrived with all of the experience of the headquarters desk man who transferred his diligence and rigour to the field. He also submitted a plan for the future of the service in Ireland. He recommended that the Dublin and Cork salaries be increased to $2,500 per year as the current level provided a 'living only' and that Londonderry be downgraded to a consular agency. From his own experience in Belfast, Wood suggested

---

205 Dowler, 'John James Piatt', 1–17.; NARA, D/S, USC, 8, 8, T196, Piatt to Frelinghuysen, Secretary of State, 24 April 1882; John James Piatt, *At the holy well with a handful of new verses* (Dublin, 1890).
206 NARA, D/S, USD, 10, 10, T199, Ashby to Gresham, 16 June 1893.
207 *Irish Times*, 19 June 1893; *ibid.*, 25 April 1894; Robert L. Gale, 'Piatt, John, James' in *American national biography*, 24 vols, 17 (Oxford, 1999), 464.
208 Carr, 'The American consular service', 902–3.

that the vice consul and deputy consul should be US citizens, appointed by the State Department as part of a career path rather than unpaid and appointed by the consul.[209]

Wood also surveyed the five consular agencies; Ballymena ($300 annual fee income), Lurgan ($1,300), Waterford ($75), Limerick ($110) and Sligo ($50).[210] He believed the agents served a useful purpose by cultivating trade links between the US and Ireland without expense to government. His successor, Savage, agreed with the downgrading of Londonderry because it had no trade or commerce of interest to the US.[211] Despite much competition for the post, Pat Rodger became the first consular agent in April 1888. Educated in Glasgow, a justice of the peace, magistrate for county Donegal, nursery owner and seed merchant, his application was strengthened by the absence of any previous involvement in the emigration trade and the *Derry Standard* commented 'he has never taken part in politics'. At a politically sensitive time when views on Irish home rule were hardening, Rodger had 'friends in all parties and of both religions'. Assistant Secretary of State Rives waived the citizenship condition.[212] Rodger successfully resisted a transfer of the agency to Moville, county Donegal, sixteen miles away, in order to facilitate the Allan Line Steam Ship Company and he threatened to resign twice in the 1890s over inadequate compensation for his demanding emigration duties. He lasted until 1905 at least and Philip O'Hagan, the last consular agent, was *in situ* when the Londonderry agency closed in 1920.[213]

There was a break in the continuity of US consular representation at Sligo between 1871 and 1882 and Galway between 1869 and 1901. William Eccles had been appointed to Sligo and would prove his usefulness when asked to investigate state-aided emigration from the Carrick-on-Shannon poor law union. Wood felt the Sligo agency was important to promote US trade with the west coast and as Sligo was located in excess of 100 miles from Dublin, abolishing it would cost the master of a vessel a lot of time and money to receive a consular service. Yet, by 1890 there was little business being done there and it was closed, much to the disgust of many locals and of John Tighe, Eccles' successor.[214] When

209 NARA, D/S, USB, 8, 8, T368, Wood to Asst. Secretary of State, 11 September 1883.
210 *Ibid.*
211 *Ibid.*, Wood to Asst. Secretary of State, 11 September 1883; *ibid.*, 9, 9, T368, Savage to Porter, 19 June 1885; *ibid.*, Savage to Porter, 13 September 1886.
212 *Ibid.*, 10, 10, T368, Savage to Rives, 6 January 1888; *ibid.*, Savage to Rives, 29 March 1888; *ibid.*, Waller, 3 April 1888; *ibid.* Rives, 11 April 1888; *ibid.*, Rodger to Rives, 25 August 1888; *Derry Standard*, 24 August 1888.
213 NARA, D/S, USB, 10, 10, T368, Ruby to Taney, 6 March 1894.
214 *Ibid.*, USD, 9, 9, T199, Reid to Wharton, 15 July 1890; *ibid.*, 10, 10, Reid to Wharton, 28 July 1891; *ibid.*, Ashby to Rockhill, 10 August 1896.

US consular service: appointments and conditions, 1790–1906 47

the matter was revisited in April 1901 Thomas Cridler, third assistant secretary, saw no reason to reopen it.[215] Shipbroker and shipowner, William Farrell of Matthew Farrell Ship and Steamship Agents of 13 The Quay, was consular agent in Waterford from 1880 and held the office for twenty-five years to 1906 at least.[216] A request to re-establish a US official presence in Galway came in January 1894 from the Allan Line Steamship Company which had recently established a transatlantic passenger service from Galway to the US. The company wanted to avoid paying the expenses of Consular Agent John Burgess who travelled to Galway from Athlone. Following extensive lobbying by among others Senator Henry Cabot Lodge from Boston and Connecticut trial lawyer, Charles S. Hamilton, Scottish born, 34-year-old Robert Allen Tennant, a ship agent for J. P. Hutchinson of Glasgow, was appointed in 1901 to the post. He believed he was qualified for the work because 'being in business ... in a fairly prosperous town ... seldom being absent and being of average intelligence'.[217] Burgess in Athlone was relieved because he was located in the 'seat of the woollen industry in the west of Ireland' and was too busy with that work to attend to Galway also.[218] From 1882, a court clerk and commissioner of oaths, Frederick Maghan, was the agent at Lurgan, the 'most important agency in Ireland' because of the many large linen factories. He satisfied the demands made by the 'large circle of merchants and shippers.'[219] Requests for an agency in Larne by the G. N. Nichols Company in 1885 and ten years later, by the Bessbrook Spinning Company and the Bedford Street Weaving Company in Newry, were opposed by the State Department.[220] Attempts to establish an agency in Ballina, county Mayo, were resisted because it was just eighty-eight miles from Athlone and connected to it by railway. Officials in the Consular Bureau commented in 1900 'we can't open consular agencies all over the

215 *Ibid.*, 11, 11, T199, Wilbour to Hill, 13 April 1901; *ibid.*, Cridler, undated.
216 *Ibid.*, USC, 12, 12, T196, Gunsaulus to Secretary of State, 18 July 1906.
217 *Ibid.*, USD, 10, 10, T199, note on cover note, undated; *ibid.*, 11, 11, T199, Wilbour to Hill, 16 October 1900; *ibid.*, Wilbour to Hill, 19 March 1901; *ibid.*, 'approved Cridler', undated; *ibid.*, 'Application for office', 4 March 1901.
218 *Ibid.*, 9, 9, T199, McCaskill to Porter, 14 February 1887; *ibid.*, 26 April 1888; *ibid.*, USD, 10, 10, T199, Ashby to Uhl, 26 February 1894; *ibid.*, J. Wilson Lynch *et al.* to Ashby, 31 August 1893; *ibid.*, James and Alexander Allen to Ashby, 25 January 1894.
219 NARA, D/S, USB, 9, 9, T368, Savage to Porter, 19 June 1885; *ibid.*, Savage to Porter, 13 September 1886; *ibid.*, Savage to Porter, 3 December 1886; *ibid.*, 8, 8, T368, Wood to Asst. Secretary of State, 11 September 1883; *ibid.*, 10, 10, T368, Ruby to Wharton, 13 November 1890.
220 *Ibid.*, 9, 9, T368, Savage to Porter, 19 June 1885; *ibid.*, Savage to Porter, 13 September 1886; *ibid.*, 10, 10, T368, Taney to Uhl, 31 January 1895; *ibid.*, Stokes to Taney, 26 January 1895; *ibid.*, 11, 11, T368, Touvelle to Hill, 10 November 1902; *ibid.*, Carr, undated.

world to suit the convenience of people who have unofficial papers to execute or others who want to be appointed agents'.[221]

Despite increasing demands to do so, there was no expansion in the consular agency service in Ireland in the last decades of the nineteenth century. Elsewhere, the increase in the number of consular agencies was accounted for by the growth in America's international trade from $308 million in 1850 to $1,697 million in 1893. A report compiled by Senator John T. Morgan of the Committee on Foreign Relations criticised Congress for neglecting the consular service and the negative impact of the spoils system on it. He believed that the guiding principles behind appointments should be the 'fitness of candidates, permanency of tenure during good behaviour and impartial methods of selection and promotion'.[222] The varying quality of the work of the mainly foreign-born, part-time, consular agents confirmed Morgan's conclusions. In time many of Wood's recommendations were implemented and his report became part of the reform process, underpinning the increasing professionalisation of the service.[223] Indeed Wood himself experienced the vulnerability of consular life in 1885. Acknowledging the 'coming change in administration [and] its possible result to me as a consul', Democrat Cleveland replaced him with West Point-born George W. Savage.[224]

Reform regains momentum

Reform came slowly. In the 1890s, America's foreign affairs had become more complex and required greater professionalism. Moreover, the onset of economic depression in 1893 made US business leaders and some congressmen even more vociferous in their criticism because US manufacturers relied on exports more than ever before and needed the services of efficient consuls. Also the tightening of immigration regulations increased the consul's role in the transfer process.[225] In his second term of office, Democrat President Grover Cleveland finally got to grips with reforming the consular service. In 1895 an anti-patronage act aimed to ensure that posts in the consular service, with salaries between $1,000 and $2,500, would be filled by a person 'designated' by the president and having passed examinations. This momentous move, however, came

221 *Ibid.*, USD, 11, 11, T199, Wilbour to Hill, 26 June 1900; *ibid.*, Chelton to Cridler, 6 July 1900.
222 Quoted in Barnes and Morgan, *The foreign service*, 150.
223 Carroll, *The American presence*, 99–100.
224 NARA, D/S, USB, 8, 8, T368, Wood to Davis, 27 January 1885; *ibid.*, Savage to Porter, 19 June 1885.
225 Library of Congress (hereafter LC), Wilbur Carr Papers, Box 16, 'Uncle Sam's diplomatic agents', 3.

only after Cleveland had fired many serving consuls and replaced them with 'deserving' Democrats. These new appointees who had helped the Democrats win back the White House weakened the impact of the 1895 order. Cleveland had undermined his own reforming zeal and, therefore, gave his successor the Republican William McKinley a reason to follow suit in 1897. McKinley did not revoke the 1895 act but recalled 259 of 320 consuls and appointed 'deserving' Republicans in their place. The examination procedure also became a farce with one candidate rejected out of 112 tested.[226]

In 1905 President Theodore Roosevelt (1900–9) ordered the extension of the appointment on merit to all consular posts carrying annual compensation of more than $1,000. Examinations would be required for entrance to the service. Promotion would be on the basis of merit, a salary scale introduced and the fee system abolished. Consulships would be classified and consuls transferred from post to post, within their respective grades. Each consular office was to have full clerical staff composed entirely of Americans.[227] In June 1906, therefore, the central elements of a modern consular service were in place. Congress had classified the service into nine classes, arranged it on a salaried basis between $2,000–$8,000, allowed for greater Americanisation of the personnel and created a corps of inspectors at consul general at large level.[228]

The new system had immediate impact. Consul General At Large Horace Lee Washington made the first inspection tour of the consulates and agencies in Ireland in May and June 1908. Washington was obliged to complete a standard twenty-nine page form on each office. In addition to providing biographical information, outlining the activities of the consulate particularly trade extension, he had to rate the individual officers. New Jersey man, Alfred K. Moe, had been transferred to Dublin from his consular position in Tegucigalpa, Honduras, where he had built up extensive experience dealing with conflicts between American syndicates and companies and Honduran landowners.[229] He found Dublin dull and had asked for promotion on the basis of his record to the post of consul general in Mexico.[230] Washington admitted that Dublin was

226 Kennedy, *The American consul*, p. 178; Carr, 'The American consular service', 904–5.
227 Barnes and Morgan, *The foreign service*, 155–65, appendix 2, 337; Carr, 'The American consular service', 908–13.
228 Richard H. Werking, *The Master Architects: building the United States foreign service 1890–1930* (Lexington, 1977), 103.
229 NARA, D/S, USD, 11, 11, T199, enclosure in Moe to Loomis, 23 November 1904; *Bulletin of the American Geographical Society*, 36:12 (1904), 777–8; Lester D. Langley, Thomas David Schoonover, *The banana men: American mercenaries and entrepreneurs in Central America, 1880–1930* (Lexington, 1995), 55.
230 NARA, D/S, USD, 11, 11, T199, Moe to ass. secretary of state, 2 January 1906.

the second city in population and commercial importance to Belfast but Moe had not taken advantages of the opportunities available to promote American commerce or to develop a social profile. He was suited to a 'quiet post'. Significantly, Washington thought Dublin was rated too highly at class five instead of four.[231] Another officer in the Dublin consulate at 9, Leinster Street, whose personal expectations were not met after the passage of the 1906 act was deputy and Vice Consul Arthur Donn Piatt. In Dublin for fifteen years, Piatt was highly rated on the basis of his efficient record, his qualifications and his 'morals' but he had applied twice for promotion and a transfer to the Lisbon consulate.[232] Washington commented that Piatt was 'intelligent, and has a quick, active mind … a valuable subordinate and employee … is undoubtedly capable of performing more responsible consular work'.[233] Piatt died in Dublin on 12 April 1914 still at the level of vice and deputy consul.[234]

Washington discovered deficiencies in Henry S. Culver's performance in Queenstown. A lawyer and former mayor of Delaware, Ohio, he had been consul in London, Ontario, and was then moved to Queenstown in 1906 when along with his wife, Mary, they practised the Bahá'ís religion.[235] Culver was interested in his work and did not neglect any branches of it and enjoyed substantial social standing in the community But Washington felt that he would be better suited to a post where there was more commercial and less shipping work. The principal work in the port was connected to emigration which Washington felt Culver was physically unable to handle. Not only did Washington intimate that Culver be moved but also that a new clerk and vice consul be appointed for the busy port and that it be upgraded to the same class as Dublin. Culver remained in Queenstown until 1910 when he was appointed as consul to St John, New Brunswick. He failed to secure a transfer back to Europe.[236]

Washington's findings at the Dublin and Queenstown consulates contrasted with those from Belfast. In the latter office at 2 Wellington Place,

231 *Ibid.*, Department of State, RG59, Inspector's Report Foreign Service Personnel, Dublin (hereafter IRFSPD), 25 May 1908.
232 Ibid., D/S, USD, 11, 11, T199, Moe to Ass. Secretary of State, 9 January 1906.
233 *Ibid.*, IRFSPD, 25 May 1908.
234 *New York Times*, 13 April 1914.
235 Armstrong-Ingram, R. Jackson, 'Early Irish Bahá'ís: issues of religious, cultural and national identity', *Research notes in Shakai, Babi and Bahái studies*, 2:4 (July 1998), online at www.h-net.org/~bahai/notes/(accessed 2 September 2008). The Culvers' four years in Ireland represents the earliest documented presence of the Bahá'í sect in the country. *Ibid.*
236 Armstrong-Ingram, 'Early Irish Bahá'ís'; NARA, IRFSP, Cork (hereafter IRFSPC), 5 June 1908.

he encountered Samuel Knabenshue and his son Paul, both of whom personified the new professional, career diplomat. In 1905 Belfast was Samuel's first foreign service appointment. After examining the workings of the Belfast office, Washington concluded that as Belfast was commercially and industrially the 'principal city of Ireland' with declared exports, mostly paying *ad valorem* duty, amounting to $14,700,000 in 1907, there was considerable office activity without a great deal of work outside the office. Knabenshue's temperament, he felt, was suited to the work; 'he seems to have a high sense of official obligations, and to be in every sense a most trustworthy officer'. Knabenshue remained in Belfast until 1909 when he was promoted to consul general in Tientsin, China. His son, Paul, was a messenger in the Belfast office before becoming vice and deputy consul.[237] He was interested in his work and was an 'intelligent young man, of good habits and a fondness for outdoor exercise'. In 1911, he left to continue a successful foreign service career and, after transferring to the diplomatic side, became minister to Iraq in 1932 where he died in February 1942. Under his direction, the American legation in Baghdad became known as the 'White House on the Tigris' and a refuge for British subjects during the failed rebellion by Rashid Ali in 1941.[238]

Unlike Culver and Moe, the personality and efficiency records of the Knabenshues met the new criteria for promotion and their careers progressed. There were mixed results from the inspection of consular agents also. The prosperous merchant John Burgess (Athlone) was not 'entirely a suitable person' to be an agent and the Scottish steam ship agent Robert A. Tennant (Galway) made a 'suitable' officer. Solicitor, notary public and commissioner of oaths Wilson McKeown (Ballymena) could 'not be said to be attentive as an agent' and his 'manner' would not be 'pleasing to Americans'. The court clerk Frederick W. Maghan (Lurgan) was an elderly man 'of a kindly disposition' and of 'excellent social standing' but brought 'no advantage to the work'. Shipbroker and owner William Farrell (Waterford) was a 'suitable' person for the post while solicitor, notary public and commissioner of oaths while Philip O'Hagan (Londonderry) would make a 'good officer'. Similarly, the Edmund Ludlow (Limerick) would make an 'excellent officer'.[239]

237 *Ibid.*, D/S, USB, 11, 11, T368, Knabenshue to Loomis, 28 January 1905; *ibid.*, 1 March 1905; *ibid.*, Knabenshue to Bacon, 15 January 1906; *ibid.*, 24 May 1906; *ibid.*, 27 July 1906.
238 *Ibid.*, IRFSP, Belfast (hereafter IRFSPB), 10 June 1908; Carroll, *The American presence*, 110; Robert Lyman, Howard Gerrard, *Iraq 1941: The battles for Basra, Habbaniya, Fallujah and Baghdad* (Botley, 2006), 50.
239 NARA, IRFSP, Athlone, 28 May 1908; *ibid.*, Galway, 30 May 1908; *ibid.*, Ballymena, 17 June 1908; *ibid.*, Lurgan, 13 June 1908; *ibid.*, Waterford, 8 June 1908; *ibid.*,

Following the inspection visits, for the first time the State Department had detailed reports on every US consular office. The information could now assist with determining the quality of personnel, the exact nature of business transacted and the physical condition of consulate buildings. An officer with aspirations to progress in the service was obliged to produce positive results and not just remain untainted by complaints or criticism. As Wilbur Carr, chief of the Consular Bureau, noted in 1907, 'the only friend of real service to him now is a record of efficient and faithful performance of duty'.[240]

The nineteenth-century US consular service did not develop along professional lines with salaries, rotation in posts and promotion, but had an *ad hoc* evolution. Instead patronage and profit dictated its growth until the beginning of the twentieth century.[241] In Ireland between 1790 and 1906, the background and personalities of the appointees betrayed the consequences of this haphazard growth. Men were appointed because of their political loyalty and influence within political circles whether Federal, Democratic-Republican, Whig, Democrat, Reform or Republican. No consular post was left unfilled for any significant length of time. In most cases the candidates themselves solicited the appointment armed with recommendations from patrons and sponsors in the party that were victorious at the presidential election. Thus in the early period, Americans and some British citizens with American connections filled the posts. Many of them were naturalised Americans of varying ages, conjugal status and religious and ethnic affiliations.

Though their biographical details differ, their reasons for seeking posts were similar; concern for their own or family members' health, desire to study, research and write, pursuit of religious aspirations, earn money and a return to their place of birth.[242] Until 1906, the last two were particularly applicable to Ireland. Few of the consuls had any relevant experience or training. Their previous occupations ranged from businessmen, soldiers, sea captains, journalists, lawyers and doctors to writers and poets. Some had skills to compensate for the absence of official training and, therefore, were equipped for their posts. Others were not and in the hope of making as much money as possible, used their talents in unsavoury ways. Some demanded excessive fees for services, overcharged the

---

Londonderry, 15 June 1908; *ibid.*, Limerick, 1 June 1908.
240 Carr, 'The American consular service', 912, 913.
241 Kennedy, *The American consul*, 7.
242 *Ibid.*, 224–5; Henry E. Mattox, *The twilight of amateur diplomacy: the American foreign service and its senior officers in the 1890s* (Kent, 1989), 29; Kark, *American consuls*, 155–6.

US consular service: appointments and conditions, 1790–1906

US Treasury, engaged in corruption, particularly in the Queenstown port where it was more than likely that the consular post was owned by a local merchant or shipping agent or owner for most of the century and finally, employed relatives in subordinate positions. Undoubtedly, some engaged in these practices because of the absence of or inadequate salary which was a constant theme in consular correspondence from William Knox onwards.

Until 1906 few men served longer than the term of the president who appointed them. Unfortunately, the reform thrust was set back in 1913 by the patronage practices of Woodrow Wilson's Secretary of State, William Jennings Bryan, but it recommenced with the Rogers legislation in 1924 which unified the consular and diplomatic services.[243] Throughout the period 1790 to 1906, these consuls' duties and functions highlighted the increasing transatlantic contact between the US, Ireland and Britain. Chapter 2 begins the examination of their consular work.

---

243 Mattox, *The twilight*, 170, n. 3.

2

'Oh Lord, not in my district, Amen':*
consular work in Ireland, 1790–1907

The triumph of the American cause in 1783 did not signal internal political unity or stability in foreign policy. It took until 1789 for the authority of the Federalist Convention to be accepted by each state and between 1789 and 1815 the leaders struggled to keep the union intact, expand America's boundaries and survive in the world being redefined by the French Revolution and the Napoleonic wars. There was little agreement between, and within, the respective federalist and anti-federalist camps as to whether America's predominant foreign relationship should be with Britain which still controlled northern parts of its territory and which sold the US twice as many goods as it bought or, with France which acquired the Louisiana Territory from the Spanish in 1801 and purchased seven times more commodities than it traded to the US.[1] It was in this unstable economic and political climate that US foreign representatives began to appear in European ports and that its formal involvement in Ireland was initiated. This chapter examines the administrative side to consular work, the circumstances in which US citizens came to the consul's attention, how consuls engaged with the mid-century famine crisis and their efforts to expand trade between the two countries.

Protecting American citizens

In 1790 Jefferson instructed consuls and vice consuls to report every six months on the number of American vessels entering their respective ports, to provide a description of the ships and their cargoes, to describe any military preparations or indications of war in their respective districts and finally, to warn American ships of dangerous situations so that they would be on their guard.[2] These duties revolved around the protec-

---

* Kennedy, *The American* consul, 81.
1 Walter LaFeber, *The American age: United States foreign policy at home and abroad since 1750*, i, (London, 1989), 46.
2 Carr, 'The American consular service', 895–6.

tion of individual American citizens, particularly seamen. At this early stage, the protection and promotion of American commercial interests including certification of goods, was not proscribed as a statutory duty although both would later become a key consular activity.[3] The judicial and administrative duties of the consul were, and they remain, to act as a notary public, particularly to authenticate foreign documents for use in US courts. Verifying birth, marriage, death and property documents belonging to intending emigrants became increasingly demanding.[4]

On 18 April 1800, John Church, US Consul in Cork, acknowledged receipt of a State Department note directing him to protect US property and persons present in his district.[5] Fulfilling this duty was not always straightforward because as the experienced London legation secretary Benjamin Moran put it, 'Americans are always getting into trouble in Europe'.[6] Safeguarding the interests of US citizens varied greatly from post to post. For example, consuls in the Holy Land provided services to American missionaries and Christian settlers along with American-Jewish settlers, pilgrims and tourists.[7] In Ireland, the central responsibility for consuls lay in relation to US seamen and shipping.

The long series of wars between Britain and France during the revolutionary period and the War of 1812 between the US and Britain directly challenged the abilities of the consular officials to carry out their responsibilities towards sailors and vessels. Two issues predominated; impressment of sailors and seizure of ships and cargoes. During the former conflict, neither the British nor French governments respected the neutrality of US naval and merchant shipping. Successive US governments considered the Royal Navy's practice of impressment particularly repugnant because it ignored US nationals' rights and ultimately their country's sovereignty, and deprived the US Navy of seamen while augmenting the British Navy. In 1790, Congress offered naturalisation to all foreigners who had been resident for two years. It was expanded to fourteen years in 1798 but reduced to five in 1802. Thus, British seamen who became naturalised US citizens had equivalent status to native-born American seamen. However, British naval authorities clung tightly to the right of their captains to board and search vessels without warning, sometimes seize vessels and impress sailors into its service and also to launch press gangs into ports to coerce men into its service. Impressment was motivated by the principle of inviolable allegiance, in other words, sailors

---

3 Barnes and Morgan, *The foreign service*, 58.
4 Kennedy, *The American consul*, 144.
5 NARA, USC, 1, 1, T196, Church to King, 18 April 1800.
6 Wallace and Gillespie (eds), *The journal of Benjamin Moran*, i, 7 February 1857.
7 Kark, *American consuls*, 197–243.

born in British territory were, and always would be, British citizens. A further reason for impressment was the high level of desertion from the British Navy due to atrocious living conditions on board ship. American shipowners also offered wages double those available on British ships.[8] When Gouverneur Morris, unofficial US agent in France, visited London in 1790–1 to negotiate a solution to the remaining problems arising out of the Treaty of Paris (1783), he sent a short memorial on impressment of American seamen to the Lords of the Admiralty.[9] On 20 May 1790, he told Foreign Secretary, the Duke of Leeds, 'I believe, my Lord, this is the only instance in which we are not treated as aliens'. Leeds acknowledged the 'wrong' in the practice and Prime Minister William Pitt concurred. Morris came up with the idea that American sailors should be required to carry certificates of citizenship which could be issued by consuls throughout Britain and Ireland.[10] This followed from US Secretary of War Henry Knox's idea that upon arrival in a British port, US sea captains should bring their crew before a local magistrate to have them certified as US citizens while US Consul James Maury in Liverpool wanted sailors to obtain certificates of citizenship before they left US territory.[11] Despite securing Leeds' sympathy which accorded some legitimacy to American claims, the practice continued. American anger intensified and the issue placed US consuls in Ireland at the heart of US–British relations.

The presence of press gangs in Irish ports was not unknown.[12] The *Dublin Chronicle* reported that between 24 July and 7 August 1790, Royal Navy ships arrived in Dublin bay 'for the purpose of conveying impressed seamen, mariners and those who have voluntarily entered into His Majesty's Service'.[13] Consul William Knox was not long in Dublin before he became exercised by the issue because 'the Americans feel more of this from operating the same language than any other nation' and he expected that more American citizens would be soon impressed from Irish ports. He was at a loss to think of any method to determine what circumstances (exclusive of birth) 'constitute an American on this side of the water'.[14] A few days later, he complained to Robert Hobart,

8 James Fulton Zimmerman, *Impressment of American seamen* (New York, 1925), 22–7.
9 John E. Findling, *Dictionary of American diplomatic history* (Westport, 1980), 335.
10 Anne Cary Morris (ed.), *The diary and letters of Gouverneur Morris: minister of the United States to France; member of the constitutional convention*, 2 vols, i (New York, 1888), 326–8.
11 Zimmerman, *Impressment*, 52–3.
12 See 'An Act for the impressing of soldiers for the service of the Commonwealth in Ireland (1851).'
13 K. D., 'The press gang in Dublin, 1790', *The Irish Sword*, 2 (1954–6), 363–6.
14 GLI, KNP, William Knox to Henry Knox, 7 April 1791.

Chief Secretary of Ireland, and to Philip Stephens, secretary to the British Admiralty, that American vessels in Belfast were 'stripped of all their sailors' and he demanded an end to the practice and the release of the sailors as the ships were still in the port. Stephens replied that if Knox's information was correct, then Captain Drury of HMS *The Squire* would ensure that the sailors were freed. Next Knox notified his contacts in Limerick, Londonderry, Cork and Newry to 'warn [US] sailors to be on their guard'. He advised Jefferson to ensure that each sailor's name, place of birth, size and age should be detailed in the ship's manifest along with other proofs that they were US citizens. He concluded in May 1791 that the British government was determined not to relinquish the idea 'that no seaman born in His Brittanick Majesty's Dominions can transfer his allegiance'. Knox reported further evidence of the practice to Secretary Jefferson in early 1792 and again asked him to introduce legislation which required ship captains to have evidence of his crew's citizenship.[15]

Jefferson had in 1792 urged US Minister Pinckney in London, to produce a permanent agreement with Britain to protect US citizens. Pinckney did not regard Morris' idea of certificates of citizenship as workable because it would permit the British government legal authority to seize all seamen without papers and, thereby exacerbate the problem. Jefferson wanted an agreement based upon the presence of sufficient crew for the vessel's size. Press gangs would not be allowed to board vessels unless the crew was above a certain ratio and searches of vessels in port had to be conducted in the presence of an American consul.[16] Soon after Pinckney's arrival he received letters of complaints about impressment and other British Navy interference with US vessels, cargoes and citizens. John Pridy of the *Santa Margarita* ship in Cove described himself as a 'pressed man' and US citizen. On 9 August 1795, he pleaded to be set free so that he could return to the US where his wife and five children lived.[17] Pinckney made no headway on the matter and returned to the US in 1796.

By this time, the terms of the Jay Treaty which resolved outstanding issues after the American Revolution, were announced. Although war with Britain was avoided and limitations placed on US–West Indian trade, nothing was gained on neutral rights or impressments.[18] This

15 Howard Temperley, *Britain and America since independence* (New York, 2002), 27; NARA, D/S, USD, 1, 1, T199, Knox to Stephens, 12 April 1791; *ibid.*, Stephens to Knox, 21 April 1791; *ibid.*, Stephens to Jefferson, 19 April 1791; *ibid.*, Stephens to Jefferson, 7 May 1791; *ibid.*, Knox to Jefferson, 17 January 1792.
16 Jack L. Cross (ed.), *London mission: the first critical years* (East Lansing, 1968), 24.
17 Charles Colesworth Pinckney, *Life of General Thomas Pinckney* (Boston and New York, 1895), 110–1.
18 Samuel Flagg Bemis (ed.), *The American secretaries of state and their diplomacy* (New York, 1963), 141.

incensed the Irish-American community in Philadelphia because sailors or travellers born in Ireland were more vulnerable to impressment than native-born Americans. Many protested in the streets and a copy of Jay's Treaty was burned outside the office of the British minister. The British government retained the right to search US vessels for French goods, remove contraband from US vessels in British ports and seize British-born deserters even if protected by US citizenship.[19] Although the Jay Treaty was passed by the Senate in June 1795 and the House of Representatives voted for monies for its implementation, it did not guarantee US neutral rights and the agitation continued as did the problem itself. In 1796 an 'Act for the Relief and Protection of American Seamen' instructed two officials to examine impressment which underlined that it was a problem throughout the British empire.[20]

Secretary of State Pickering had a 'deep admiration of England' but recognised that British aggression on the high seas and impressment might lead to another war between the two countries.[21] His minister in London, Rufus King, admitted in 1796 that 'the subject ... I confess, is much greater than I had supposed it'. But the British government adhered to its right to impress. As Beamis points out, it did not claim the right to impress American citizens but only British subjects including naturalised Americans. In reality British captains rarely discriminated between the two groups and took as many men as needed. During 1796 and again in 1797, the British government attempted to restrict the consul's right to issue certificates of American citizenships to seamen. Moreover, such documents were regarded with suspicion because there was a thriving market in forged citizenship papers. Nonetheless, Minister King maintained US consuls' right to verify US citizenship and Consul James Holmes in Belfast did also on behalf of his relative, Thomas Sinclair Pollock, who was impressed from the *Thomas Jefferson*.[22] Rufus King met with some success. Between July 1796 and April 1797, he applied for the discharge of 271 seamen who claimed US citizenship from British men-of-war ships and at least 86 were released. These successes were

---

19 Peter Thompson, *Cassell's dictionary of modern American history* (London, 2000), 207; David A. Wilson, *United Irishmen, United States: immigrant radicals in the early Republic* (Dublin, 1998), 79; Brian Jenkins, *Fenians and Anglo-American relations during reconstruction* (Ithaca, 1969), 9; LaFeber, *The American age*, 47.
20 Kennedy, *The American consul*, 42–3.
21 Gerard H. Clarfield, *Timothy Pickering and American diplomacy, 1795–1800* (Columbia, 1969), 70, 74.
22 *ASPFR*, iii, extract from a letter from King to Secretary of State, 13 April 1797, 18 November 1796; *ibid.*, King to Lord Grenville, 28 January 1797; *ibid.*, Grenville to King, 27 March 1797. Bemis, *The American secretaries*, 211; Kennedy, *The American consul*, 44; NARA, D/S, USB, 1, 1, T368, Holmes to Madison, 25 August 1804.

insufficient to appease John Adams' administration. In September 1800, Secretary of State John Marshall declared that Britain had no right to impress the 'native of America' especially those who had evidence of citizenship.[23] The practice intensified: between 1793 and 1802, US consuls and agents reported that 2,410 fellow citizens were impressed with few released. But the most active period was from 1803 to 1813.[24]

Following Horatio Nelson's defeat of the French fleet at Trafalgar in 1805, the US government found its naval and mercantile fleets caught up in the opposing British and French economic blockades and embargoes. US Minister James Monroe declared that the British Navy 'boarded our vessels, annoyed our commerce, and violated our rights, not for goods only, but likewise for seamen'.[25] The overall number of impressed US citizens of Irish birth is not available, in 1803 Consul John Church knew of no cases in Cork though some Irishmen turned up in Secretary James Madison's regular bulletins on impressment delivered to Congress during these years. William Wall, Henry Clark and James Clark were impressed at London from an American ship. They did not have certificates of protection but claimed American citizenship as did four men taken from the *Loire* off the port of Cove. Madison informed the House of Representatives that between 1 May 1804 and 5 March 1806, the aggregate number of impressments of US citizens into the British Navy was 2,273.[26] American–British relations worsened as Britain tightened control of the Atlantic and asserted its rights.

Crisis point was reached in June 1807 when HMS *Leopard* attacked the USS *Chesapeake* off the coast of Virginia leaving three US citizens dead, eighteen wounded and four alleged British deserters were impressed. The event united Irish immigrants and most Americans in protest. Among the chorus of outrage were the United Irishmen whose Irish republicanism now converged with their American patriotism. Jefferson favoured an economic tactic to force Britain and France to respect its neutral rights. He persuaded Congress to pass the Embargo Act in December 1807 and Macon's Bill Number Two in May 1810 to force recognition of US neutrality. The President believed that British and French dependence on US trade would compel them to negotiate.[27] Consul Joseph

23 Bemis, *The American secretaries*, 211, 273.
24 Zimmerman, *Impressment*, 106, 255, 256.
25 Stuart Gerry Brown (ed.), *The autobiography of James Monroe* (Syracuse, 1959), 186.
26 NARA, D/S, USC, 1, 1, T196, Church to Madison, 5 July 1803; *ASPFR*, II, Abstract of impressment of seamen belonging to American agents by agents of foreign nations, 593; *ibid.*, II, Madison to House of Representatives, American Seamen Impressed, 5 March 1806.
27 Wilson, *United Irishmen*, 78–9; Miller et al. (eds), *Irish immigrants*, 616.

Wilson reported in July 1809 that the *Mary* carrying flaxseed, tar and cotton had recently arrived in Dublin port from New York and broken the embargo.[28] Jefferson's action proved to be short-sighted as it would virtually halt all US overseas commerce. It was clear, however, that the US authorities were exasperated at British high-handedness which brought war between the two countries closer.[29]

Between 1 April 1809 and 30 September 1810, 1,042 American seamen and citizens were impressed including 229 who were 'natives' of England, Scotland, Ireland or Wales.[30] Although there was no evidence of impressment of American sailors in Dublin port during the period 1810 to mid-1811, James Widdington was removed in July 1811 by the British Navy from the *General Armstrong*. Also Consul Thomas English applied to the Lords of the Admiralty for the release from impressment of William Swain and John Brown but was informed that 'it could not be guaranteed'. All three were eventually released and no further impressments in the Dublin and Belfast consular districts were reported during the period May 1811 to September 1812.[31] Nevertheless, British seizure of vessels and cargo along with impressments, continued. The situation worsened when the Royal Navy intercepted passenger ships, including those carrying Irish immigrants to the US.

In the period 1808–11, the British Navy impressed more than 6,000 Americans, although newspapers and campaigners made claims of between 10,000 and 50,000.[32] Among the many incidents reported was that in summer 1811 concerning the immigrant ship, *Belisarius*, bound for New York from Dublin. It was boarded by the crew of HMS *Atalanta* and sixty-two passengers were removed on the grounds that they had not cleared the Custom House in Dublin. However, a more accurate explanation was offered by one officer who commented, 'You shan't go into that damn'd Republican country ... we are going to have a slap at them one of these days, and you shan't be there to fight against us'. Most of the passengers were taken to St John's Island (present day Prince Edward Island) and forced into becoming tenants on Lord Townshend's estate, while seventeen were impressed into the British Navy. Wilson describes the event as 'Irish-America's *Chesapeake*'. Criticism flowed from American politicians and public alike, and the demand for revenge against British oppression was intense, particularly among the

28 NARA, D/S, USC, 1, 1, T199, Wilson to Monroe, July 1809.
29 Temperley, *Britain and America since independence*, 28–9.
30 Zimmerman, *Impressment*, 264.
31 NARA, D/S, USD, 1, 1, T199, English to Smith, 15 July 1811; *ibid.*, 25 July 1812; English to Monroe, 2 September 1812.
32 Zimmerman, *Impressment*, 256.

radical Irish. Edward Gillespy of the New York newspaper *Shamrock*, argued that British impressment was 'a prosecution of war waged against Ireland for nearly seven centuries, and which will never be terminated by concession, submission or liberty'. The United Irishmen advocated war with Britain. Within Congress, politicians from the southern and western states regarded British actions as an intolerable attack on national interests.[33] In June 1812, Madison asked Congress for a declaration of war against Britain. Once declared, the ensuing land engagements, primarily along the US–Canadian border, were accompanied by a complete British blockade of US ports and seizure of Irish-American sailors from US vessels, who were subsequently charged with treason. As these men were naturalised American citizens, Irish-American leaders were furious and James Madison's government retaliated by suspending the exchange of prisoners for a period.[34] When news of the war became known, some American consuls who were US citizens and located in the British empire left their posts, as did British consuls in the US.[35] In Ireland, the first US consuls appointed to Cork and Belfast, John Church and James Holmes respectively, were British subjects and remained *in situ*. Thomas English in Dublin was a naturalised American but with an established mercantile business and stayed.

The war continued until 24 December 1814 when the Treaty of Ghent was signed by American and British negotiators even though it failed to address the original grievance; impressment. Consuls reported that during the period 1803 to 1815, at least 1,500 US ships were seized, two-thirds by the British and one-third by the French.[36] Consuls soon encountered the problem of discharged sailors. Church in Cove had to deal with them during winter 1815–16.[37] Thomas English in Dublin encountered numerous American sailors discharged from British ships of war. Most applied to him for financial assistance which he granted along with arranging passage back to America. He found masters of US ships to be most accommodating.[38] But after a winter of experience, Church was critical that seamen would 'wander about … idle' and indulge in 'unfavourable conduct'. Many soon turned to him for help but some tried to deceive him and he had to distinguish between 'the worthy' and the 'unworthy'. He believed that fear of impressment made other seamen less

---

33 Wilson, *United Irishmen*, 80, 82, 83; Thompson, *Cassell's dictionary*, 436.
34 *Ibid.*, 436–7; Jenkins, *Fenian*, 11–2.
35 Kennedy, *The American consul*, 45–6.
36 *Ibid.*, 42; NARA, D/S, USD, 1, 1, T199, Wilson to Monroe, July 1809; *ibid.*, English to Rush, 30 January 1826; *ibid.*, English to Goulbourne, Dublin Castle, 21 July 1825.
37 *Ibid.*, D/S, USC, 1, 1, T196, Church to Madison, 12 February 1816.
38 *Ibid.*, USD, 1, 1, T199, English to Monroe, 1 November 1815.

willing to leave their ships and 'indulge in vicious practices on shore'.[39]

The number of impressments declined in 1815, though British authorities continued to claim the right to board American vessels. It was a cause of concern for Richard Rush, US minister in London between 1817 and 1825, but there was some support for him. Against a social reforming background, Royal Navy Lieutenant Standish Haly published *Reasons for abolishing impressment* in 1822 and his arguments for an end to the 'diabolical practice' merited attention in *The Times*.[40] Meanwhile impressment continued. In October 1848, Consul Hugh Keenan in Dublin complained to James Buchanan, that impressment deserved the 'interference of our government'. Although the practice waned, both the right of search and the issue of US citizenship became frequent themes in US–British diplomatic relations and placed some US consuls in the centre of the ongoing disagreement between the two countries.[41]

Irrespective of the direction of US foreign policy, consular work changed little in relation to assisting needy seamen who arrived into their districts due to impressment, their vessels being sunk or condemned as unseaworthy, the sale by the captain of his cargo and vessel, the replacement of seamen with less expensive labour and desertion. Even if a captain had paid wages to the seamen or the consul could extract the three months' wages that seamen were due, they often disappeared in the taverns and brothels of a port. Both the US Congress and Executive considered the protection of seamen seriously and by 1815 a welfare system was in place. But there was no set sum which the consul could use to relieve such men. Fulfilling his duties in relation to seamen often depended on the type of relationship the consul had with individual ship's captains and local authorities. The former relationship was always problematic. Under the 1792 act, consuls had judicial duties prescribed by law and they held the equivalent to police functions over American captains and shipowners. Yet, captains exercised full authority over crews, cargo and property on the high seas while ownership of vessels provided owners with certain rights. As early as 1802 James Holmes in Belfast favoured a strengthening of the consul's authority.[42] On the other side, the captain had a difficult task. They had to guide ships across the Atlantic with crews often comprising 'misfits, alcoholics, criminals, returning emigrants and

---

39 *Ibid.*, USC, 1, 1, T196, Church to Madison, 18 May 1816.
40 Lt. R. S. Haly, *Reasons for abolishing impressment* (London, 1822); J. H. Powell (ed.), *Richard Rush: republican diplomat, 1780–1859* (Pennsylvania, 1942), 110; Philip Ziegler, 'Introduction' in Richard Rush, *Century lives and letters: a residence at the court of London* (London and Melbourne, 1987), x.
41 NARA, D/S, USD, 1, 1, T199, Keenan to Buchanan, 1 October 1848.
42 *Ibid.*, USB, 1, 1, T368, Holmes to Madison, October 1802.

illiterate foreigners with little or no skills'.[43] Also the widespread recruitment practice of getting sailors drunk and carrying them on board ship in an unconscious state often added to tensions during voyages, particularly if the sailor's wages had been paid in advance to the shipping master who had arranged the abduction.[44]

Conditions on board ship allowed for mistreatment of and cruelty towards sailors, violence between crews and attacks on captains. Most disagreements between crew and captain on US-owned vessels would have been settled between themselves and those that came to consular attention usually involved death or serious injury. Over time some consuls were described as a 'captain's consul' because they automatically sided with the captain in a dispute with seamen.[45] Indeed Robert Loughead in Londonderry believed that a captain's authority had to be upheld on principle because vessels required a full complement of crew to navigate journeys, otherwise it would disrupt the trading life of the port and American trade would be 'completely in the power of wandering crews'. Consequently, he preferred criminal cases to be handled by local courts and few seamen were returned to the US for trial.[46] Similarly, the experienced Consul Thomas Dudley in Liverpool confirmed that sailors' protests were common but he attached little importance to them.[47] On the other side, in September 1830, Consul John Murphy had no difficulty helping mutinous American seamen on board the *Oxnard* from Liverpool en route to Boston. Once they landed in Cove, they were jailed but were not further punished and when freed, Murphy provided assistance.[48] When James Smith in Londonderry encountered Captain Boutell of the *Ella* who mistreated his crew, refused to pay consular fees, used insulting language towards Smith and even struck him, he complained about him to Secretary Cass.[49] The drunken behaviour of Captain Hodge of the US vessel *EJ*, resulted in damage to the ship and violent treatment of the crew who were left without food and wages. In December 1861, Consul Devine in Queenstown provided aid to the crew.[50] Moran in the London legation, believed the 'charges of murder and cruelty against American merchant captains' to be almost always true. Such bad behaviour had been common for years and he had no sympathy for captains

---

43 O'Donald Mays, *Mr Hawthorne*, 118.
44 NARA, D/S, USD, 7, 7, T199, West to Fish, 10 April 1869.
45 The phrase appears in Wallace and Gillespie (eds), *The journal of Benjamin Moran, 1857–65*, i, 17 August 1859.
46 NARA, D/S, USL, 1, 1, T216, Loughead to Buchanan, 19 October 1848.
47 *Ibid.*, USD, 4, 4, T199, West to Seward, 7 March 1865.
48 *Ibid.*, USC, 1, 1, T196, Returns 13 July to 20 January 1845.
49 *Ibid.*, USL, 2, 2, T216, Smith to Cass, 9 April 1857.
50 *Ibid.*, USC, 4, 4, T196, Devine to Seward, 21 December 1861.

or for consuls who instinctively defended them over seamen.[51]

Issues over desertion also exercised consuls. By mid-century James McDowell in Belfast queried the 'evil' whereby consuls were obliged to help these undeserving sailors.[52] In 1848, Vice Consul Harper in Londonderry devoted no time to investigating the reasons for the desertion of a number of American seamen in his port. Instead he was annoyed when Mayor Robert MacBride fined one ship's captain on 'the crew's most frivolous charges … without legal or just cause'. He wanted MacBride to arrest the sailors. Fortunately, for the men, MacBride consulted the legal authorities in Dublin Castle who advised against the action because he did not have the power.[53] There was no change in the US government's position on deserters and in 1862, William West in Galway complained to Secretary Seward about having to pay the passage of six 'coloured' men who had received and spent their three months' wages but technically were deserters from the *Jenny Pitts*. In the following year, having dispatched fifteen sailors to the US and another to hospital, he asked for a change in the system that allowed captains to set the amount of wages they could claim for deserted seamen.[54] Nevertheless, the traditional consular function of assisting seamen continued to be a duty, irrespective of the consul's assessment of how deserving they were.

Dealing with captain–crew disputes, local police and judicial authorities was demanding. Consul Hawthorne who left Liverpool in 1857, recalled that a 'great part of the wear and tear of [my] mind and temper resulted from the bad relations between the seamen and officers of American ships'. Nonetheless, he could see the validity of both crew and captain's respective arguments: 'Looked at judicially, there appeared to be no right side to the matter nor any right side possible in so thoroughly vicious a system as that of the American mercantile marine'. He proposed a US government investigation into conditions on board mercantile ships and stressed the importance of having professional training for US captains and seamen.[55] Reform of the maritime legislation that might have improved conditions was resisted due to the shortage of US seamen. The onus remained on consuls to deal with the consequences arising from the illegal recruiting and wretched circumstances on board US vessels. By the 1880s, Consul Brooks in Queenstown, where almost 1,000 vessels

51 Wallace and Gillespie (eds), *The journal of Benjamin Moran, 1857–65*, i, 17 August 1859.
52 NARA, D/S, USB, 1, 1, T368, McDowell to Buchanan, 14 December 1848.
53 *Ibid.*, USL, 1, 1, T216, Loughead to Buchanan, 19 October 1848; *ibid.*, MacBride to Lord Lieutenant, 7 September 1848; *ibid.*, Redington to MacBride, 18 September 1848.
54 *Ibid.*, USG, 1, 1, T570, Fees, 1862.
55 O'Donald Mays, *Mr Hawthorne*, 118.

docked in one year, was proud that US shipping laws guaranteed to the sailor of whatever nationality under the American flag, 'better provisions for his personal comfort, better defence against mistreatment and generally better opportunity of extra wages in the event of inter-voyage discharge than those of any other native in the world'.[56] It was not until 1892 when the National Union of Seamen of America (later the International Seamen's Union) was formed that circumstances improved specifically in relation to reducing penalties for desertion and disobedience, ensuring maximum levels of hours, food, pay and safety standards and curtailing owners' rights.[57] Few incidents of consular involvement with on-board disputes were reported in subsequent decades. However, a continuous theme in consular correspondence related to shipwrecks.

By 1790 sea travel around Ireland was safer than it had ever been with the increasing publication of atlases, maps and globes, construction of lighthouses and establishment of lifeboat services. The Customs Board was responsible for eight coastal lights at Howth Baily, Copeland Island, the Old Head of Kinsale, Loop Head, Hook Head, Wicklow Head, Arranmore and South Rock. This network of lighthouses continued to expand under the direction of the Custom Board and the Dublin Port Authority as did the number of lifeboat stations.[58] Unfortunately, these measures did not mean the end of shipping tragedies. The Irish coastline was perilous due to changing wind strengths, dangerous waves, fogs and tides. Yet, Irish waters also attracted more traffic as sea-borne trade expanded.[59] Along with documenting the arrival and departure of US-owned vessels from their ports, consular responsibility included reporting the loss of vessels, cargoes and life, assisting the survivors to return to the US and helping to take possession of the cargo for the owner. The consul was reliant on the co-operation at local level of the coastguard, the local constabulary, the judiciary, fishermen, resident foreign consuls and Lloyd's Shipping Company to inform him of the incident, the conditions of the vessel, cargo, captain and crew and in his absence, to provide assistance. Obviously not all shipwrecks involving American vessels and crew came to the consul's attention but when he

56 NARA, D/S, USC, 7, 7, T196, Brooks to Hay, 6 October 1880.
57 'International Seaman's Union', online at http:seafarers.org/ (accessed 21 October 2008).
58 John de Courcy Ireland, *Ireland and the Irish in maritime history* (Dun Laoghaire, 1986), 130–1, 170–2, 256–7.
59 John de Courcy Ireland, *Wreck and rescue on the east coast of Ireland* (Dun Laoghaire, 1983), 12, 30; W. Forsythe, C. Breen, C. Gallagher, R. McConkey, 'Historic storms and shipwrecks in Ireland: a preliminary survey of severe synoptic conditions as a causal factor in underwater archaeology', *International Journal of Nautical Archaeology*, 29:2 (2000), 247–59.

was informed about an incident he was obliged to assist in every way possible although some consuls avoided visiting the location.

The survival of captain, crew, passengers and cargo depended on the vessel's location, weather conditions and the extent of the damage sustained. If a ship was in danger at sea, usually it was the crew of other vessels who were expected to assist in the first instance. The *Mobile* was en route from Liverpool to New Orleans under Captain J. H. Tarbox with a crew of twenty-three and sixty passengers when on 29 September 1852 it struck the Arklow Bank on the east coast in heavy seas and violent gales. It soon began to break up and despite the efforts of the crew to launch lifeboats, it was 'fruitless'. By the time two schooners, one of which was the *Mary Elizabeth* from Nevin, Wales, came across the wreckage, only eight sailors and one passenger were alive. Four were landed at Wexford and the rest at Dundalk. The Swedish vice consul in Dundalk and the Harbour Master arranged a collection 'to provide little comforts for the poor fellows saved'. US Consul James Foy who travelled to Dundalk, provided the US citizens among them with clothes and money and made arrangements for them to travel on the Steam Packet Company's *Pride of Erin* to Liverpool where US Consul Critenden took responsibility for their welfare and passage home. Foy was then obliged to travel to Arklow to look after the others and the wreck. The Swedish vice consul also offered an additional reason for the incident; 'the second mate having been tipsy ... steered the vessel contrary to the captain's orders'.[60]

When a ship was damaged closer to land, the work of all foreign consuls located in Ireland was greatly helped by the creation of a rescue service around the coast. The Dublin Ballast Company had located a lifeboat in Sandycove, county Dublin, in 1803 and two others in Old Dunleary and Howth respectively in 1817. But it was the establishment of the National Institution for the Preservation of Life from Shipwreck in 1824 that initiated a national lifeboat service staffed by trained crew, most on a voluntary basis. By the end of the 1860s, fifteen rescue stations had been set up around the Irish coast, which had increased to eighteen by 1900.[61] If a coastguard or rescue service was not present, more often than not local people, particularly fishermen, came to the assistance of crews. The US consuls do not appear to have risked their own lives to rescue crews. Nonetheless, they did recognise the bravery of rescuers. Consul O'Neill in Belfast recorded in late January 1854, the extraordinary actions of a few fishermen in the northern channel who saved the

60 *New York Times*, 19 October 1852.
61 'Royal National Lifeboat Institution', online at www.rnli.org (accessed 21 October 2008).

lives of the crew of the *Mermaid* en route from Liverpool to Maine.[62] James Arrott asked Secretary Marcy in November 1855, if he would pay the claim for services submitted by two fishermen from Arklow who rescued two sailors after the *John Bright* ran into trouble off the coast. Also Arrott wanted compensation for the officers of the Arklow Marine Society who had advanced money to the sailors for clothing and travel expenses.[63] The practice was in accord with well-established custom 'to promote humanity at sea', as one consul put it.[64] In each case the consul had to assess the extent of the risk involved and whether a rescuer could be nominated for a reward and if so, of what type. Captains and officers involved in rescues received a gold medal, gold watch, gold chain and sums of money. Individual sailors, local men usually fishermen and coastguards, were rewarded with sums of money.[65] Rewards did not come automatically. The crew of the Swedish brigantine *Tertius* saved the twenty-one man crew of the US-owned *Moravia* of Maine. But in February 1875 when Captain Franz A. Helberg presented an invoice for £20 for expenses incurred in the diversion and subsistence of the ship-wrecked crew, Arthur B. Wood in the Consular Bureau declared that 'nothing appears to show that there was any risk run in the rescue'. However, Consul Townsend was instructed to pay it because the crew had been treated with kindness.[66]

If the rescuers perished during the rescue, their dependants could receive US government assistance. In 1868, four coastguards lost their lives trying to rescue the crew of the American vessel, *R. H. Tucker*, on the Blackwater Bank off the Wexford coast, leaving four widows and twenty children in a state of utter destitution. Secretary Seward awarded each widow $100. But Consul William West in Dublin who learned that the widows would receive pensions from the British Admiralty, decided not to pass on the money and returned the vouchers for $400 to the State Department.[67] A delay in paying such rewards could lead to disappointment. Two years after rescuing the crew, including an American seaman, of the Norwegian brig *Hilding* off the northern coast in January 1878, Samuel and James McCandless and six other fishermen complained to Consul Livermore in Londonderry about not being awarded either medals or money. Livermore was particularly embarrassed because he

62 NARA, D/S, USB, 2, 2, T368, O'Neill to Marcy, 20 January 1854.
63 *Ibid.*, USD, 1, 2, T199, Arnott to Marcy, 15 November 1855.
64 NARA, D/S, USC, 7, 7, T196, Richmond to Seward, 25 January 1878.
65 NARA, D/S, USD, 7, 7, T199; *ibid.*, 9, 9, T199, Barrows to State Department, 24 February 1883.
66 *Ibid.*, A. B. Wood, 15 April 1875.
67 *Ibid.*, USD, 5, 5, T199, West to Seward, 25 September 1868; *ibid.*, Seward, 2 October 1868; *ibid.*, West to Seward, 1868.

had already publicised the gesture.⁶⁸

The role of those on shore was also acknowledged. In January 1870, local people from the southern Cork coast had to deal with four 'bruised and mutilated' bodies from the American-owned *Sautee* from Portsmouth, New Hampshire, which foundered off Cape Clear the previous August. The American ship *Alfred D. Snow* of Thomaston, Maine, en route from San Francisco to Liverpool went down in the entrance to Waterford harbour with a cargo of wheat on the morning of 4 January 1888. The captain and crew of twenty-eight escaped but their lifeboats then capsized and all were drowned. Seven bodies including that of Captain Willey, were washed into Captain's Bay at Arthurstown, county Wexford, and were found by Nicholas Roe and Matthew Walsh. Consul Piatt in Queenstown, recommended the award of some remuneration to Roe and Walsh for their 'honesty and to encourage these men and others in a similar occasions in future'. The two locals had notified John Hill the coastguard at Arthurstown station and delivered the valuable ship's papers found in Willey's pocket. Both received a sum of money. In April, the board of the New Ross Poor Law Union contacted Piatt to request payment for the funeral expenses including whiskey for those involved in washing and 'coffining' thirteen corpses that washed up along the coast. The State Department approved the reimbursement of £20 6s. 10d.⁶⁹

Once a consul received news of the shipwreck, he was obliged to ensure that the survivors received food, shelter, clothes and to assist their return journey to the US. More often than not the consul relied on the coastguard or police superintendent to look after them once they came on shore, then consular funds would be used to transport all onto his district where he would secure them passage to the US. In addition to providing money, a consul could rely on the expanding system of relief for destitute seamen run by philanthropists, religious and charitable organisations and in time the British government.⁷⁰

After dealing with survivors, the next major responsibility for the consul was to look after the owners' interests. Ownership of the wrecked cargo was determined by law and practice. Over time, legislation gave rights to the survivor, the owner of the wreck or cargo and the receiver was warranted to administer the wreck. But salvage and wreckage disputes

68 *Ibid.*, USB, 9, 9, T368, Livermore to Hitt, 18 January 1882.
69 *Ibid.*, USC, 7, 7, T196, King to Fish, 8 March 1870; *ibid.*, 10, 10, T196, Piatt to Rives, 11 February 1888; *ibid.*, Hill to R. Boyd, Receiver of Wrecks, Waterford; *ibid.*, Rives to Piatt, 2 March 1888; *ibid.*, Piatt to Rives, 17, 23 May 1888; *ibid.*, Pat Pope, clerk of the union to Piatt, 28 April 1888; *ibid.*, Piatt to Rives, 29 June 1888.
70 Chapters of the Seaman's Missionary for Ireland were in place by 1822, the Sailors' Home in Belfast was established in 1842, the Dublin Home in 1848, the Sailors' Institution in Belfast in 1874 and the Lansdowne Sailors' Home in Limerick in 1907.

continued as did plundering and the murdering of survivors who would have permitted the legitimate owner claim the salvage.[71] It was against this background that a US consul was legally obliged to take responsibility of the cargo in the absence of the captain or other representative of the owner. During the winter of 1790, five American vessels, crews and cargo were lost due to bad weather. After *The Clara* went down two miles off Dublin in February 1791, Consul Knox applied to the Lord Mayor of Dublin to call out the police to recover the cargo. Sufficient cargo was recovered from this large ship to sell and pay expenses and the sailors' wages.[72] It is not known whether any prosecutions arose from this case but fifty years later matters were different. On 6 March 1854, the emigrant ship, *Robert Kelly* from Liverpool bound for New York went ashore at Jack's Hole on the Arklow Bank. Local fishermen saved all and brought the crew and 690 passengers to safety in Wicklow from where they re-embarked on the *Iron Duke*. However, some of the fishermen stayed on board the wreck, plundered the passengers' property and cargo. They refused to allow anyone on board including the ship's captain, Captain Laurence, and the harbour master, and threatened to sink any approaching ship. On 10 March, the Custom's tide surveyor boarded the ship and saw the extent of the damage. In the interim Captain Laurence travelled to Dublin seeking help from Consul Keenan who appealed to Colonel Brown at Dublin Castle. The police evicted the fishermen from the vessel and 150 of them were later arrested drunk in the town. Forty-five of the 'marauders' as Keenan called them, were tried and fined while twenty-one were imprisoned in Kilmainhaim gaol in Dublin. The ship was re-floated and towed by two steamers into Kingstown harbour.[73]

The increase in the number of shipwrecks led to the introduction in 1854 of the British Merchant Shipping Act which established the modern principles of salvage. The act categorised wreck as jetsam, flotsam and lagan and stipulated that the receiver could summon men and sailors to requisition carts or equipment. Penalties were specified for plundering wreckage and failing to report salvaged goods to the receiver.[74] But locals still regarded salvaged goods and wreckage as their own and consuls continued to call on the local authorities to assist them in recovering the cargo in order to retrieve some profit for the shipowners. Generally, it

---

71 Edward J. Bourke, *Shipwrecks of the Irish coast, volume 2, 932–1997*, 3 vols, 2 (Dublin, 1998), 183.
72 NARA, D/S, USD, 1, 1, T199, Stephens to Jefferson, 19 April 1791.
73 *Ibid.*, 1, 2, T199, Keenan to Marcy, 13 March 1854; de Courcy Ireland, *Wreck*, 59; Bourke, *Shipwrecks*, 3, 134–5; *ibid.*, 2, 76.
74 Bourke, *Shipwrecks*, 2, 183.

was the captain of the vessel, as representative of the owner, who either arranged for the re-transportation of surviving cargo or could pass it into the hands of the local consul, the representative of the insurance company such as Lloyd's, or engage a local salvage operator or merchant to recover the cargo after which the captain received a percentage of the profits. The case of the 549-ton *George A. Hopley* en route from Liverpool to its home port of Charleston with a general cargo which sustained damage in bad weather and came into Portrush on the northern coast in April 1856 is illustrative of the process. Despite the presence of Consul James Smith in nearby Londonderry, the captain sold it to the local Lloyd's agent and made a profit of almost $10,000. Smith was furious at the loss of income and because the captain had ignored him.[75] Occasionally shipwrecks also offered opportunities for consuls to submit bogus claims.[76]

In the second half of the nineteenth century, Ireland's importance in the global maritime network increased largely because of the growth of transatlantic emigrant traffic from and through Irish ports. But ships still sunk in bad weather and natural hazards around the southern coast also caused damage. Not surprisingly, consuls greatly welcomed news of the proposal to build a new lighthouse at Blackwater Bank on the south-east coast. Consul Keenan regarded the bank as a 'most dangerous one' that had caused the loss of many vessels. He asked that the information be circulated to the US marine community.[77] The consuls did not comment on other safety improvements introduced into vessels at this time or that in 1853 the telegraphic cable between Ireland and Britain was reconnected and came into permanent service which meant that weather predictions, sailing instructions and other information could be passed quickly from shore to shore and assist in the campaign to reduce the loss of life at sea. Despite these measures, throughout the rest of the century the continued flow of sea-borne commerce and emigrant trade from Europe combined with inadequate coastal lighting and regulations, the unreliability of vessels and the pressure on owners to compete for cargoes, resulted in US consuls continuing to devote their time to protecting survivors and cargoes.[78]

The greatest challenges faced by consuls in Ireland concerned emigration. In the first half of the nineteenth century, beyond forwarding copies of recently enacted legislation to Washington, consuls were not requested to report on the causes and course of emigration, unlike later. Nonetheless, the arrival and settlement of over one million Irish emigrants in the US

75 NARA, D/S, USL, 2, 2, T216, Smith to Marcy, 16 October 1856.
76 O'Donald Mays, *Mr Hawthorne*, 86.
77 NARA, D/S, USC, 3, 3, T196, Keenan to Cass, 22 August 1857.
78 de Courcy Ireland, *Wreck*, 53, 75, 81.

by 1845, increased consular correspondence (see chapter 5). Not only did consuls have to respond to instructions from the State Department and other government agencies but US politicians regarded it as their prerogative to demand consular action usually on behalf of constituents. Other consular duties relating to emigration arose from protecting US citizens imprisoned in Ireland for political offences (see chapter 4). Also the consul would administer pensions to former soldiers retired to Ireland or to their dependants on their death. This work remained a routine duty into the twentieth century.

Clearly consular responsibilities and duties were diverse. However, they centred on protecting the interests of US citizens, trade and transportation, all of which came together during the Irish famine of 1845 to 1851. Caused by long-term and short-term factors including an increase in population from four million in 1800 to eight million in 1841, uneconomic subdivision of land and an over-reliance by one-third of the population on the staple food, the potato, which was hit by the fungal disease *phytophthora infestans*, the famine affected different parts of Ireland at varying times and rates but few whether rich or poor remained unaffected by it.

Reporting the famine, 1845–51

On 1 October 1845, and again on 1 April and 1 October 1846, Consul Thomas Wilson in Dublin reported 'nothing remarkable or worthy of notice has occurred within this consular service [since] the date of my last communication'.[79] His conclusion was incorrect. In 1845, the potato crop was one-third less than usual and in 1846, three-quarters of it was lost by a recurrence of the fungal blight. On 9 September 1845, the *Dublin Evening Post* had reported that an unknown blight from North America was ravaging the European potato crop. Two days later the disease had appeared in Waterford and Wexford and by 20 September, it had affected the potato crop in seventeen counties.[80] Wilson first referred to the 'failure' of crop on 1 January 1847. He explained that in the previous October 'very great and serous apprehensions were entertained' which had been 'too well-founded' and the British Parliament would meet shortly to devise means to provide food and employment for the 'distressed population'. But as a consular officer and shipowner,

79 NARA, D/S, USD, 1, 1, T199, Wilson to Secretary of State, 1 October 1845; *ibid.*, 1 April 1846; *ibid.*, 1 October 1846.
80 E Margaret Crawford, 'Great famine' in Connolly (ed.), *The Oxford companion*, 228; Helen E. Hatton, *The largest amount of good: Quaker relief in Ireland 1654–1921* (Montreal, 1993), 79.

he identified that the crisis might be attended by commercial possibilities. He continued, 'it is ... highly probable that Indian corn from the United States and other countries will have to be imported in very large quantities'.[81] Thomas Gilpin arrived in Belfast in September 1845 and wrote five letters to the State Department before noting on 10 February 1847 'the failure of the staple food of the country'. He agreed with Wilson and expected an 'increase and raising' of US trade with Belfast. He anticipated a doubling of US imports into Ireland in the following two years which would result in the potato being replaced by American corn as the 'common' diet.[82] Gilpin was incorrect about the long-term prospects for Indian corn but he was correct about its increased value during the crisis.[83] John Murphy in Cork, in a postscript to a letter of 15 December 1846 stated that 'Indian corn is now selling in this market at £17 to £18 per ton' but offered no further explanation. Nine months later he informed Secretary Buchanan, the demand for bread stuffs still continued and prices were coming down.[84] Robert Loughead arrived in Londonderry in December 1845 and provided an inventory of consular property and two fee returns before he noted in a general report, on 1 January 1847 that distress was widespread, food shortages and high prices prevailed and emigration was greater than it had been for a few years. Also he had learned that some 'poor houses' were expected to charter vessels to convey 'inmates' to America.[85] Not only did he anticipate an increase in emigration to the US from ports in the north-west – in 1847, fifty ships with 12,385 passengers left Londonderry for America – but also an increase in US trade. Later in the month, he appointed James Harper, a Scottish merchant, as vice consul in Sligo because of the arrival of a number of US vessels and others carrying relief supplies were expected in the following months.[86]

Each of the US officers was located in regions variously affected by the potato failure in 1845–6. In early 1846 the blight was most prevalent in counties Armagh, Clare, Kilkenny, Louth, Monaghan and Waterford where over 40 per cent of the crop was lost. Each of the consular districts included these counties but none of the consuls seemed overly concerned about the local situation. Neither did they refer to the increasing numbers of paupers seeking relief from the poor houses

81 NARA, D/S, USD, 1, 1, T199, Wilson to Secretary of State, 1 January 1847; *ibid.*, Keenan to Secretary of State, 7 April 1848.
82 *Ibid.*, USB, 1, 1, T368, Gilpin to Buchanan, 10 February 1847.
83 Carroll, *The American presence*, 47.
84 NARA, D/S, USC, 1, 1, T196, Murphy to Buchanan, 15 December 1846; *ibid.*, Murphy to Buchanan, 1 September 1847.
85 *Ibid.*, USL, 1, 1, T216, Loughead to Buchanan, 1 January 1847.
86 *Ibid.*, Loughead to Clayton, 1 May 1850; Carroll, *The American presence*, 48.

even in relatively prosperous poor law unions, although Loughead may have been referring to the scheme adopted by the poor law guardians of the Sligo union who selected fifty-six paupers for emigration in August 1846.[87] Furthermore, there were no reports of the food riots when the government's corn depots failed to open on 15 March 1846 or of the estimated 400,000 excess deaths during the winter of 1846. Moreover, by December 1846, over half of workhouses were full and some were forced to turn people away.[88] Instead the consuls focused on the opportunities available for US food suppliers as did George Bancroft, US minister in London. On 3 November 1846, he alerted Buchanan to an increased British demand specifically from members of parliament, for the names of American suppliers of Indian corn. He felt that the increasing dependence on American corn would extend to 'meat, wheat and pork' and was due to first, the recent repeal of the Corn laws, second, 'the scarcity in Ireland and England' and third, 'the appalling distress occasioned by the famine in Ireland'. Despite his concern about the situation, he focused on 'the benefits that will come to our country which is becoming the most opulent in the world'.[89]

Bancroft and Wilson's analysis of the British government's response to the conditions in the first year of the famine was accurate as was their prediction concerning potential profits. Sir Robert Peel's Tory government purchased Indian meal from US suppliers, established a programme of public works and repealed the Corn laws which removed duty on imported grain and permitted US ships to land in Irish ports with supplies of maize. Peel's government spent £185,000 on food supplies including £105,256 for American corn, until it was replaced in June 1846.[90] The new Whig government, led by the *laissez-faire* exponent, Lord John Russell, increasingly allowed the British Treasury to dictate policy on Ireland specifically Charles Trevelyan, Treasury assistant secretary, who administered the government's relief plan. The public works schemes which operated until September 1847 provided three million meals daily at one stage. But at a time of economic recession in Britain, financial restraint dictated that the schemes should end and that further relief provided by the workhouse system should be funded by local taxpayers in the future. Many landlords baulked against these measures

---

87 Christine Kinealy, *A death dealing famine: the great hunger in Ireland* (London, 1997), 60–1, 79, 95.
88 Gerard Moran, *Sending out Ireland's poor: assisted emigration to North America in the nineteenth century* (Dublin, 2004), 128–9.
89 Quoted in Timothy J. Sarbaugh, '"Charity begins at home": the United States government and Irish famine relief, 1845–9', *History Ireland*, 4:2 (summer 1996), 31–2.
90 Crawford, 'Great Famine', 228–9; Hatton, *The largest amount*, 82.

at a time of reduced rent receipts. Evictions increased, some entered the workhouse while others fled to North America, Britain and Australia.[91] The US consuls in Ireland offered Secretary Buchanan a clear-eyed, if predatory, account of the situation but none suggested US government involvement to relieve the deteriorating conditions.

Until 1847, US politicians may have been distracted by the ongoing war with Mexico over control of California but they also seemed to have paid more attention to English newspaper reports which characterised the famine conditions as exaggerated and pleas for help as politically motivated.[92] But with the complete decimation of the potato crop in 1846, increasing numbers of famine emigrants arrived on US shores, including those carried on two ships owned by Consul Wilson of Dublin. Gilpin in Belfast informed Buchanan on 25 June 1847 that 'emigration is very extensive and applications to me for information on the subject have been very numerous and interested'.[93] Private letters began to arrive in the US from relatives in Ireland detailing the situation and the Irish Society of Friends' detailed reports and circulars sent in late 1846, were widely distributed and used by them and others to raise funds. In early 1847, there was extensive coverage of the famine in the US press and fundraising meetings were held throughout the country. Democrat Vice President George M. Dallas, attended a meeting in Washington on 9 February, at which thirty-one senators and representatives along with other influential citizens, recommended to the American people a 'general contribution in money or provisions' and representatives were appointed for each state and territory to assist with raising funds.[94] Congress' response went further and forced a reaction from the Polk administration.

On 8 February 1847, Whig Congressman Washington Hunt of New York, introduced legislation in the House of Representatives requesting a government contribution of $500,000 in money or provisions for Ireland. But the bill languished in a special committee. A similar bill, sponsored by Whig Senator John J. Crittenden of Kentucky, was proposed in the Senate on 26 February, subsequently passed and then sent to the House where opposing positions centred on the Democrats' appeal to the Irish-American voter versus the Republicans' hostility to foreigners and Roman Catholics. The bill was defeated in the House on 3 March.[95] But even if it had passed, Polk had told his cabinet the previous day that

---

91 Crawford, 'Great Famine', 228–9.
92 Hatton, *The largest amount*, 112.
93 NARA, D/S, USB, 1, 1, T368, Gilpin to Buchanan, 25 June 1847.
94 Kinealy, *A death-dealing famine*, 113–5; Hatton, *The largest amount*, 113; see also Carroll, *The American presence*, 48–9.
95 Hatton, *The largest amount*, 113, 117; Sarbaugh, '"Charity begins at home"', 33.

because of 'its unconstitutionality … I could not sign it'. Even though he was of Scottish-Irish origins and president of the Democratic party that had relied heavily on Irish votes in New York to defeat Whig Henry Clay in the 1844 presidential election, he could not overcome 'the want of constitutional power' to appropriate public money to charities either at home or abroad. After the cabinet meeting, he noted in his diary 'I have all the sympathy for the oppressed Irish and Scotch which any citizen can have' and a few days previously he contributed his 'mite' of fifty dollars for Irish relief.[96]

Despite the failure of the relief bills, in March 1847 Congress passed a proposal from the Irish Relief Committee of Boston to permit the use of two warships, the USS *Jamestown* and the USS *Macedonian*, to transport relief supplies to Ireland organised mainly by a private Boston relief committee and by Captain Robert Forbes of the *Jamestown*.[97] By 22 April, Forbes had arrived in Cork and having been fêted by city dignitaries, and his cargo of corn, breadstuffs, hams, port, oatmeal, potatoes, flour, rye, beans, rice, dried fish and clothing unloaded, the *Jamestown* departed. Consul John Murphy in Cove offered no comment on the events even though two public receptions were held for Forbes and local newspapers praised the swift US response compared to British hesitancy.[98] By late August, the *Macedonian* under Captain George deKay, had unloaded its cargo of 15,160 bushels of Indian corn in Cove and departed.[99] The gesture provoked the British government to instruct Foreign Secretary Lord Palmerston, to thank the American people 'for this kind and honourable manifestation of sympathy … for the sufferings of the Irish people'. Palmerston minimised British government responsibility for the famine, preferring instead to note that it was 'an awful visitation of Providence'.[100] During the famine, particularly up to summer 1847, private aid consisting of food, clothes and money, was received from the US. It came from many sources and through different channels. For example, the contributions organised by the Quakers in the US and Canada amounted to £149,824 5s. 9d. ($749,120) and came from individuals of Irish and non-Irish descent, young and old, wealthy and poor in rural and urban areas.[101]

---

96 Milo Milton Quaife (ed.), *The diary of James K Polk during his presidency, 1845 to 1849*, ii (Chicago, 1910), 2, 3 March 1847, 396–8; LC, Manuscripts Division (hereafter MD), James K Polk Presidential Papers, reel 59, 3 March 1847.
97 Hatton, *The largest amount*, 113, 117; Sarbaugh, '"Charity begins at home"', 35.
98 Kinealy, *A death dealing famine*, 115–6.
99 NARA, D/S, USC, 1, 1, T196, Report of American vessels which entered the port (hereafter Returns), 1 July 1847 to 1 January 1848.
100 Hatton, *The largest amount*, 125.
101 *Ibid.*, 124.

These private relief efforts combined with the British government's purchase of American food contributed to a significant increase in direct US traffic into Irish ports. Consul Murphy detailed that a total of sixty-seven vessels arrived into Cove in 1847, nineteen discharged their cargoes of Indian corn, meal and flour valued at $441,679 and four of them brought supplies for the Quakers' Central Relief Committee. Once unloaded, the vessels prepared to depart with cargoes of either passengers or ballast. Also in 1847, thirty-five vessels arrived for mercantile orders and then proceeded to unload cargo at other ports around the Irish coast, while others sailed to London, Liverpool, Gloucester and Glasgow. Murphy's office collected $733 in consular fees for 1847, a sixty-six per cent increase over 1846.[102] Not only did American producers profit but consuls earned more fees.

In Londonderry, Loughead's usual duty to report the loss of a US ship at sea was more poignant than usual. On 7 April 1847 the *Juliette* was bound for Rathmelton in county Donegal, with a cargo of grain. It sank about forty miles out from Londonderry, though the cargo was saved most of it was carried away by desperate local people despite the presence of the police who rescued just a small portion of it. According to Loughead, the people also turned on the officers and seamen who were robbed of their clothes and he was forced to replace the crew's clothes before they travelled onwards.[103] This incident emphasised the worsening conditions in the north-west of the country as does the significant increase in direct US trade into Londonderry and Sligo. Six vessels arrived into Londonderry in 1846 and forty-five in 1847. The circumstances of these arrivals emphasises the complexity of famine conditions. Some of the ships in 1847 carried cargoes of corn, oats, flour, potatoes and salt and one came from Liverpool with passengers. It was not scheduled to call but it had been forced into Belfast and then Londonderry due to the poor condition of the ship and sickness among the passengers. Of those vessels that departed from Londonderry for US ports in the same year, thirty-one left with passengers only and thirteen left predominantly with ballast and some iron ore, valued at £9,028. Ironically, the increased business brought Consul Loughead, just like Murphy, fees of $437 58c. for the first six months in 1847, compared to $38 5c. for the same period in 1846.[104]

---

102 NARA, D/S, USC, 1, 1, T196, Returns 1 January to 1 July 1847; *ibid.*,1 July 1847 to 1 January 1848; *ibid.*, I January to 1 July 1846; *ibid.*, 1 July 1846 to 1 July 1847.
103 *Ibid.*, USL, 1, 1, T216, Loughead to Buchanan, 30 April 1847.
104 NARA, D/S, USL, 1, 1, T216, Loughead to Buchanan, Fees, January to June 1847; *ibid.*, July to December 1847. In Sligo, in 1847, fifty-nine vessels arrived in the port, thirty-four were from UK ports but forty-three originated in US ports. They carried

Consul Wilson reported from Dublin in July 1847 that nineteen American vessels had arrived via Cork and departed from the port during the previous three months. This 'unusually large' number of vessels was due to the 'failure of the potato crop'. The ships brought 'provisions' and returned either with 'passengers or in ballast'.[105] But Wilson's replacement, Hugh Keenan, appeared less interested in reporting on the countrywide calamity and devoted the first weeks after his arrival in early December 1847 to establishing his office. He warned Buchanan that he would 'probably have nothing to report until … say June'.[106] Similarly, Gilpin did not report from Belfast between February and December 1847 when he died.[107] In January 1848, Loughead in Londonderry temporarily took over the Belfast office and up to July, sent five communications to Secretary Buchanan providing a general report and details of his appointment of a consular agent in Sligo, the loss of a US vessel and cargo, an 'unpleasant occurrence' involving discharged seamen in Sligo port in July 1847 and he forwarded his returns of fees.[108] Despite the absence of any analysis of the situation, the regularity of his reporting to the State Department merited notice by one official in Washington.[109]

Potato yields were average in 1847 but fewer potatoes had been sown and the amount harvested was just 10 per cent of the 1844 crop. The loss of a staple part of the Irish diet for one-third of the population led to the institution of relief measures by both private organisations and the British government. High levels of mortality and disease, rising crime rates, increasing evictions and emigration became widespread in the southern and western counties. In Ulster, the failure of the potato, oat and flax harvest struck small tenants, weavers and their families, while the economic depression in England reduced the demand for textiles and led to unemployment and shortened hours for linen workers. Emigration and eviction became widespread. Despite the worsening conditions, the first priority for Tyrone-born James McDowell, a former governor of Virginia and congressional politician, was to inform the Belfast commercial community of his availability and services. His first reference to the famine came on 30 November 1848, when he indicated that seventy-six

---

meal, corn, flour, wheat and meal and presumably emigrants departed. *Ibid.*, Loughead to Buchanan, Fees, January to June 1847; *ibid.*, July to December 1847; Liam Kennedy, Paul S. Ell, E. M. Crawford, L. A. Clarkson, *Mapping the great famine* (Dublin, 1999), 36, 108, 113.
105 NARA, D/S, USD, 1, 1, T199, Wilson to Secretary of State, 1 July 1847.
106 *Ibid.*, Keenan to Buchanan, 17 December 1847.
107 *Ibid.*, USB, 1, 1, T368, Loughead to Buchanan, 14 January 1848.
108 *Ibid.*, USL, 1, 1, T216, Loughead to Buchanan, I, 29 January 1847; *ibid.*, 30 April 1847; *ibid.*, 16 July 1847; *ibid.*, Fees, January to July 1847.
109 *Ibid.*, USD, 1, 2, T199, undated, probably after 26 September 1850.

US vessels arrived in the ports of his district in 1847 carrying Indian corn and flour and some left with passengers. This almost fivefold increase in traffic compared to 1846 was due to continuing 'famine'. Indeed his office benefited from this business as $1,310 in consular fees was collected for 1847. Although the spread of the blight had slowed, and more potatoes planted in 1847, by the summer of 1848, the disease returned and for the next six years it afflicted the potato harvest, which was only 50 per cent of 1844 yields.[110]

None of the officers in Dublin, Cork, Galway, Belfast or Londonderry dedicated a report to the worsening situation and apparently none was requested. Keenan wrote in July 1848, that the British government was 'pouring into this country immense bodies of troops and carrying [out] their coercive measures by military force. The inhabitants are in the most wretched conditions'.[111] Neither he nor his colleagues commented further on the ultimately unsuccessful Young Ireland rebellion on 29 July 1848 even though it had been brewing from February in the aftermath of the Paris revolution, and returned Irish-Americans were entangled in it.[112] Once the British government learned from its foreign service and spy networks in the US and Canada that Irish-Americans were considering launching diversionary tactics by raiding Canada and sending arms, ammunition and men to Ireland to support a rebellion there, on 21 July it suspended the writ of *habeas corpus* in Ireland.[113] Americans arriving into Ireland or resident became in the words of Thomas Redington, Under-Secretary for Ireland, 'agents of the sympathisers with the revolutionary party' and a 'strict watch' was kept on them. Innocent Americans were arrested and appealed to the US minister in London, George Bancroft, for protection and aid. He secured the release of W. A. Newbold, Franklin Taylor, Thomas N. Taylor, George S. Pepper and Frederick Pepper. Afterwards, the men complained bitterly about their treatment but Redington admitted that an American passport was not accepted by the authorities as 'conclusive evidence either of the[ir] identity or ... previous movements'.[114] In other words, the naturalised status of

---

110 Kinealy, *A death-dealing famine*, 92, 96–7; Crawford, 'Great Famine', 228; Miller, *Emigrants and exiles*, 282; Carroll, *The American presence*, 53; NARA, D/S, USB, 1, 1, T368, McDowell to Buchanan, 30 November 1848; *ibid.*, Fees, January to June 1847; *ibid.*, July to December 1847. Between January and December 1849 seventeen American vessels arrived into Belfast port with Indian corn, flour, maize, bacon and provisions. *Ibid.*, January to June 1849; *ibid.*, July to December 1849.
111 *Ibid.*, USD, 1, 1, T199, Keenan to Buchanan, 14 July 1848.
112 Peter Gray, 'Young Ireland' in Connolly (ed.), *The Oxford companion*, 602–3; Peter Gray, 'Rebellion of 1848' in *ibid.*, 473–4.
113 Jenkins, *Fenians*, 14–16.
114 K. Bourne and D. C. Watt (general eds), *British documents on foreign affairs* hereafter

Irish-born Americans was not automatically accepted by the authorities who still regarded them as British citizens vulnerable to any emergency coercive measures. Consequently, even if they had proof of citizenship, they should not be surprised at official attention. Foreign Secretary Palmerston refused to release others such as James Bergen in Dublin's Newgate prison.[115] Bancroft sought copies of the arrest orders but Palmerston refused, annoyed at the US government's tolerance of the activities of anti-British Irish groups in the US. Eventually Bergen was released and while Bancroft wanted to abandon the matter, President Polk and his Democrat cabinet were not. Under pressure from a Congress concerned about the fate of American citizens in Ireland, Polk instructed Bancroft to protest formally against the British authorities making a distinction between native and naturalised Americans. Bancroft eventually complied in early 1849.[116] The Young Ireland rebellion in 1848 was a failure not least because the government was forewarned, the leaders' lacked a co-ordinated plan, clerical opposition and the rapid dispersal of public support when confiscated land and food were not distributed.[117] Yet, the potential for, rather than actual, American involvement had threatened the US–British diplomatic relationship and would do so again in 1865 following the end of the American Civil War. The contrasting responses from within the Democratic party to the Irish situation when the legitimacy of the American state was threatened and to the unfolding human calamity, was noticeable.

Meanwhile, Keenan maintained his sporadic reporting. Between July and October 1848 he asked Buchanan for more blank forms to complete his quarterly reports and for a response to a proposal to cultivate tea in the US. His seeming disinterest continued; in April 1849 when the blight struck again and evictions were ruthless in places, he asked Buchanan's successor, John Clayton, to write a complimentary letter to the British government praising the assistance given by Captain William Holt of HMS *Dragoon* to the US vessel *Washington* which had been in trouble at sea.[118] In the same month, Robert Loughead detailed his success in securing the release of Captain William Garrick from Lifford prison. Garrick had arrived from Liverpool into Londonderry on 10 February

---

BDFA), 25 vols, part 1, series C, North America, vol. 3, The Irish problem of immigration, 1848–1870 (Bethesda, 1986–7), Brodhead to Redington, 30 August 1848; *ibid.*, memorandum drawn up by the under secretary for Ireland, 15 August 1848.
115 BDFA, 1, C, North America, 3, 'The Irish problem of immigration, 1848–1870', Brodhead to Redington, 30 August 1848.
116 Jenkins, *Fenians*, 17–19.
117 Gray, 'Rebellion of 1848' in Connolly (ed.), *The Oxford companion*, 473–4.
118 NARA, D/S, USD, 1, 1, T199, Keenan to Buchanan, 14 July 1848; *ibid.*, 19 July; *ibid.*, 1 October 1848; *ibid.*, 1 April 1849. Kinealy, *A death-dealing famine*, 140.

1849, in charge of the US-owned *Brutus*. It had 217 passengers on board, was bound for Boston but cholera had appeared among the emigrants, seven of whom died at sea and the vessel put into the port. Garrick, under the influence of morphine for his cholera, shot a young boy rowing around the boat, was tried at the Lifford assizes and acquitted by the jury on the grounds of temporary insanity. Garrick successfully appealed to the Lord Lieutenant for his release and returned to Liverpool to board another vessel for the US.[119] Loughead did not elaborate any further on his reference to cholera. Yet, by 1849 cholera which had first appeared in Ireland in 1832, was the second major cause of deaths after fever. The disease had reappeared in Ireland in November 1848 and its arrival prompted government legislation to prevent its advance. But this failed and soon it had spread throughout the country particularly in places with major ports, although northern counties were less affected. Even though the famine survivors were severely struck by the disease, particularly in spring 1849 when it was at its peak with 11,129 reported cases, Loughead appeared unconcerned about the consequences of the Garrick case for either himself or the local population.[120]

In 1848 and up to his death in May 1849, Consul Murphy in Cork provided the State Department with an accurate balance of the monies owed him by the US Treasury and a defence of his non-reporting of the arrest of US citizen James McNamara by the local police on board a US vessel *Lehuse*, in Cove. With the defeat of the Democrats in November 1848, Murphy's replacement, Alfred Mitchell, had arrived in Cove by 9 August 1849 and after he had settled, forwarded his first report on 9 September from the town from then known as Queenstown. It outlined only his appointment of consular agents for Limerick and Waterford.[121] Galway was without a consul from 1844 to 1848 when local man, Thomas Moore Persse was reappointed to the position, having served previously for ten years from 1834 to 1844. His first consular report dated 7 November 1848, made no reference to the famine but noted that emigration from Galway to the US was greater than preceding years.[122]

Persse also reported on the potential development of Galway as a packet station and in a later bulletin in May 1850 commented on the

---

119 NARA, D/S, USL, 1, 1, T216, Loughead to Clayton, 5 April 1849.
120 Kennedy et al., *Mapping the great famine*, 123–4; Joseph Robins, *The Miasma: epidemic and panic in nineteenth-century Ireland* (Dublin, 1995), 62, 137–49.
121 NARA, D/S, USC, 1, 1, T196, Murphy to Buchanan, 20 January 1848; *ibid*., 4 August; *ibid*., 20 November; *ibid*., Buchanan to Murphy, 26 January 1849; *ibid*., Murphy to Buchanan, 7 March; *ibid*., 2 May; Mitchell to Clayton, 5 September 1849.
122 *Ibid*., USG, 1, 1, T570, Persse to Secretary of State, 7 November 1848.

new railway line, the recently completed university, the building of a canal to allow ships navigate into lakes Corrib, Mask and Carra and the consequent commercial potential.[123] Meanwhile in Belfast, James McDowell (who died in April 1849), had been more exercised by the increased number of destitute American seamen discharged into his care, than the ongoing disaster. However, McDowell's Vice Consul and local man Thomas McLure offered a dramatic insight into the daily situation in the Belfast district. On 18 September 1849 he wrote 'the rot has spread within the last ten days in the potatoes and threatens the distribution of the great bulk of the crop'. Clearly he was well informed, perhaps because he was Irish but unlike Persse, not of the wealthier class. Yet, McLure was mindful of his official responsibilities also and commented that 'there is no doubt a large quantity of Indian corn will be required to make up the deficiency. I do not think, however, that it is likely at any time to attain to a high price.' This warning to American exporters not to become reliant on Irish markets was echoed again by McLure in April 1850; 'potatoes are again set very extensively and if these thrive the consumption of Indian corn will be really interfered with'.[124]

One other official report during these latter stages of the famine came from an unexpected source, and tried to offer some explanation for the calamity. American Minister Abbot Lawrence in London, was not a professional diplomat, but he was an active one who corresponded regularly with Washington. Unlike his predecessors, he toured Ireland and wrote a lengthy dispatch on the conditions he encountered in autumn 1851. His initial aim was 'to investigate the social and political condition of Ireland' and somewhat incredulously, to find out the causes of the drop in population from 8.1 million in 1841 to 6.5 million in 1850.[125] Accompanied by his wife and daughter, his route took him from the east to west coasts, south to Kerry and Cork and back to Dublin. He praised the condition of harbours and the national school system but the country had not progressed because it was a 'conquered country, and governed by the conquerors'.[126] His report was forwarded to Washington, but failed to elicit a response from Lawrence's superiors. On his return to London, he met with Foreign Secretary Palmerston but it was to discuss the fate of another island, Cuba, whose security and strategic

123 *Ibid.*, Persse to Secretary of State, 9 May 1850.
124 *Ibid.*, USB, 1, 1, T368, McDowell, circular, 20 July 1848; *ibid.*, McDowell to Buchanan, 30 November 1848; *ibid.*, 14 December 1848; *ibid.*, McLure to Clayton, 18 September 1849; *ibid.*, McLure to Clayton, 17 April 1850.
125 Hamilton Andrews Hill, *Memoir of Abbott Lawrence*, 'Condition of Ireland' (Boston, 1884), appendix, 224.
126 *Ibid.*, 222–6.

significance to US domestic and foreign policy was immense. Lawrence resigned in summer 1852. His last dispatch to Washington, stated that he had aimed to cultivate friendly relations with Britain which had 'never in my judgement been so cordial or on so firm a basis of good understanding ... I have found every administration of this government animated with a desire to preserve this happy state of things and every class vieing with every other manifestation of respect and good will'.[127] Despite his obvious sympathy for the Irish situation, it was the healthiness of US–British relations that mattered most to him and by which he judged the success of his tenure.

But while US consular officials failed to report fully on the desperate situation in Ireland, 1.5 million people left for the US between 1845 and 1855. Fifty-five per cent of Irish emigrants to the US arrived into New York port. Between 1846 and 1851, 76 per cent of Irish emigrants arriving into New York left from Liverpool, 3 per cent from Belfast, 2.3 per cent from Glasgow, 2.2 per cent from Dublin, 2.1 per cent from Cork and Limerick respectively and 2 per cent from London. Thus, the indirect routes predominated during the famine period as a whole but closer examination indicates that while 93.5 per cent of all Irish arrivals into New York came from Liverpool in 1846, by 1849 the figure had declined to 69 per cent. Indeed by 1850–1, the southern ports of Queenstown and Limerick featured in the emigrant trade alongside Londonderry, Belfast and Dublin.[128] By 1851–2, consuls reported that emigrants comprised the bulk of the cargo carried by US vessels out of Queenstown and by 1854 the same situation pertained in Dublin.[129]

Beyond, vague, albeit increasing, references to the mass departures, and Minister Laurence's report, no US consul in Ireland attempted to explain events. Instead they provided statistical information on vessels and cargoes. They also reacted to restrictions imposed on shipowners by changes to the British and American passenger legislation. In early 1847 Loughead in Londonderry was overwhelmed with inquiries from local merchants and shipmasters who had just received news of recent US legislation requiring passenger vessels to provide appropriate ventilation, living quarters, food and cooking facilities for passengers.[130] In theory, the new measures would limit the numbers of passengers that could be

127 Willson, *American ambassadors*, 266–70.
128 Mageean, 'Emigration from Irish ports', 1, 2, 10.
129 NARA, D/S, USC, 2, 2, T196, Fees, 1 January to 1 July 1851; *ibid.*, 1 July to 31 December 1851; *ibid.*, 1 January to 1 July 1852; *ibid.*, USD, 1, 2, T199, Fees, 30 June to 31 December 1854.
130 *Ibid.*, USL, 1, 1, T216, Loughead to Buchanan, 30 April 1847; Carroll, *The American presence*, 53.

carried on each vessel. Failure to comply could result in a heavy fine, imprisonment or loss of the shipowner's right to transport passengers within certain limits.[131] The aim of the US legislation and the equivalent amendments in 1848, 1849, 1852 to the British passenger acts, was to reduce the number of overcrowded and poorly fitted ships and destitute emigrants arriving from Ireland. The consequences were immediately recognised by shipowners at least those known to Loughead who were 'very much alarmed, for fear of difficulties on their arrival' in the US. At the end of April 1847, adopting a slightly rebuking tone, Loughead indicated that he had not yet received formal notification of the act. Instead he gave the owners documents that certified 'his ignorance of the requirements of the law' and exempted them from the legislation, temporarily at least.[132] It is not known whether this assisted in their flouting the new measures but conditions for emigrants did not improve until steamships came to dominate the passenger trade.[133]

Other evidence of consular collusion with shipowners came from Dublin. In early April 1848, Hugh Keenan commented on the 'very large' emigration from the region but he had not given bills of health to all the ships leaving the port, except those belonging to former Consul Thomas Wilson. Nonetheless, Keenan warned that 'fever and sickness still prevail to a considerable extent among passengers'.[134] In other words, the horrific conditions still existed but surprisingly not on any ships belonging to Wilson. Certifying the health of emigrants became a vital task. Between July and December 1851, Consul James Foy filled out 'certificates to emigrate' for nine people described as 'cripples' each of whom had 'ample means 'to survive in the US. Others were issued to Jane Keefe and Catherine Howard who as 'single women' had sufficient 'means and protection' and also to Mary Keogh, Mary Price, John Fisher and John Brerton and their respective children.[135] At this stage, consuls did not have an official role in the emigration system and would not acquire that until 1875 when Congress began to legislate on the matter (see chapter 5). Consequently, it is more likely that Keenan and Foy were assisting specific shipowners and captains to meet the legislation introduced by the New York legislature in May 1847. The commissioners of immigration were legally required to control and protect new immigrants and could impose the payment of a bond of $300 on ship captains for every passenger liable to become dependent on city charity.

131 Moran, *Sending out Ireland's poor*, 104.
132 NARA, D/S, USL, 1, 1, T216, Loughead to Buchanan, 30 April 1847.
133 Carroll, *The American presence*, 53.
134 NARA, D/S, USD, 1, 1, T199, Keenan to Buchanan, 7 April 1848.
135 *Ibid.*, 1, 2, T199, Fees, 1 July to 31 December 1851.

This legislation and similar Massachusetts laws were struck down by the US Supreme Court in 1849 but in the interim shipowners scrambled to comply.[136]

During the famine years, US consuls in Ireland continued to protect US interests reporting on US vessels, crews and cargoes. Rarely did they go beyond this brief. Most of them were naturalised Americans with Irish ancestry, but any sympathy they may have had for the distressed local population, was not reflected in their reports. On the rare occasion some information was given on local circumstances, no analysis was provided and neither did any consul request US government intervention. Such an appeal would have gone beyond the strict interpretation of the boundaries of consular responsibility. A call for official involvement came within the ambit of the US minister in London. Though consuls struggled to do their duty in trying times and endured periods without communication from the State Department, under-reporting continued. During the end of the 1850s and the early 1860s when poor weather escalated the already severe poverty and widespread destitution: Keenan at Queenstown tersely recorded in September 1858 'bad harvest weather'. One year later, his successor, Dowling reported that the 'crops were below a fair average, the potato crop particularly being 'seriously blighted' and in October 1860 the potato crop was 'almost a total failure' in the southern district. Dowling's comment in summer 1859 that the number of US vessels arriving and departing Queenstown was 'unprecedentedly limited' and that most merely stopped for orders. The situation changed in 1861. Between 1 October 1861 and 20 May 1862, thirty-five US vessels discharged wheat, Indian corn and flour.[137] Alexander Henderson in Londonderry recorded the arrival of eleven US vessels between April and September 1861 carrying Indian corn and flour.[138] He did not comment that it was a tenfold increase in traffic compared to the same period in 1860 nor the reasons why corn was needed again. His counterpart in Dublin, Samuel Talbot, recorded the arrival of twenty-five vessels with cargoes of wheat, corn and flour, compared to six the previous year, an increase he explained by the 'deficient harvest.'[139] This was an accurate reason even if he did not go into the background.

William West, the Irish-born Consul in Galway and Dublin from 1861 to 1869, offered a fuller picture and constantly commented on

---

136 Robbins, *The Miasma*, 181.
137 NARA, D/S, USC, 4, 4, T196, Keenan to Cass, 30 September 1858; *ibid.*, Dowling to Cass, 30 September 1859; *ibid.*, Dowling to Cass, 5 October 1860; *ibid.*, 5, 5, T196, Returns of Imports, 30 September 1862.
138 *Ibid.*, USL, 2, 2, T216, Fees April to June 1861; *ibid.*, July to September 1861.
139 *Ibid.*, USD, 3, 3, T199, Talbot to Seward, 22 October 1861.

the 'misery and death' that he encountered.¹⁴⁰ West, a writer by profession and sympathiser to the Irish nationalist cause, returned to Ireland with few resources himself, was sensitive to the prevailing conditions and critical of the Lincoln administration's bad management of pensions for Irish families of dead or missing soldiers from the recent Civil War (chapter 3). Few consuls empathised with or articulated the complexity of the Irish emigrant's situation as well as West.

Developing trade and commerce

The promotion of trade, specifically the search for new export opportunities, became an official consular duty and a major function in the 1880s. Prior to that, however, US governments used consuls to collect commercial information of value to the administration and manufacturers and to describe local conditions.¹⁴¹ In November 1790, William Knox arrived into a thriving city. Dublin's commerce had increased so much during the last half of the century that the construction of the Customs House began in 1781 and signalled the city's expansion towards the bay. In later years new docks and warehouses were built on both sides of the river Liffey.¹⁴² Immediately Knox met with the Earl of Westmoreland, Lord Lieutenant of Ireland, to discuss trade.¹⁴³ In 1791 he found that commerce between America and Ireland was 'increasing materially', with between eighty to one hundred vessels annually travelling between the US and Dublin, Cork, Belfast, Newry, Londonderry and Limerick. Between six to ten US vessels visited Sligo, Killybegs, Donegal, Ballyshannon and Waterford. Transatlantic vessels carried American 'flax seed, pott pearl ashes, lumber' into Ireland and returned with 'great quantities of linens' which, according to Knox, were bought in Ireland for twelve to fifteen per cent cheaper than in London. Indeed, the linen industry was 'increasing' and had led James Holmes the first US Consul in Belfast, to purchase American supplies of flax seed and potash for sale as a chemical fertiliser to modernising farmers.¹⁴⁴ More generally, Knox identified a number of characteristics of the trade. First, that it had expanded beyond the Ulster counties, second, the doubling of linen exports between the late

140 Ibid., USG, 1, 1, T570, West to Seward, 23 January1863.
141 Barnes and Morgan, *The foreign service*, 79–80; Davies, 'Roofing Belfast and Dublin 1896–8', 32.
142 Joseph Robins, *Custom House people* (Dublin, 1993), 20–3.
143 GLI, HKP, William to Henry Knox, 15 January 1791.
144 NARA, D/S, USD, 1, 1, T199, Knox to Jefferson, 7 September 1791; *ibid.*, Knox to Washington, 13 January 1791; *ibid.*, 17 January 1792; *ibid.*, 8, 8, T199, Barrows to Asst. Secretary of State, 3 July 1878; Chambers, 'The early years', 4–9.

1750s and the mid-1780s and its continual growth into the early 1790s, and third, he noted one of the weaknesses of the industry, namely that traditional techniques were still employed in spinning and weaving. To this extent he endorsed and recommended the advertisement by Messrs McCabe and Pearse of a new loom which would 'double the quantity' and produce 'superior' linen.[145]

At this stage, the balance of trade between the two countries was in America's favour as vessels usually returned to the US with 'incomplete cargoes' and the Irish market was 'over-stocked with American produce'. The over supply of Irish markets with American goods, exacerbated the grievance felt by the Irish mercantile community already antagonised by re-exporting. Knox informed Secretary of State Jefferson that because prices of US goods were 'so low in Ireland', he had been approached by 'respectable mercantile characters' to ensure that any future trade negotiations between the US and Britain should discuss a measure whereby US produce could be 're-shipped' from Ireland to London, Liverpool and Bristol for sale.[146] While Knox's request does not appear to have brought immediate action on the American side, the British parliament introduced a navigation act in 1793 that permitted Ireland to re-export colonial products to Britain.[147]

Knox also noted that there was a 'great' demand for American tobacco but sales were low because excessive duties pushed up the price. So, it was not surprising that Knox also commented on the 'immense' smuggling trade particularly along the west and north-west coasts, and the efforts by Irish revenue officials to end it.[148] In early 1792, Knox warned Jefferson that American ships carrying tobacco were liable to seizure if they attempted to enter any Irish port or if they even appeared off the coastline. But he did forward a proposal to Jefferson from the Irish Customs authorities offering a reduction in duties if the US government instructed the master of each vessel carrying tobacco to lodge a certificate at the Dublin Customs House declaring the quantity of tobacco in the cargo and to be subject to penalties if the full quantity was not present. The aim was to reduce the smuggling trade while increasing legal sales, thereby, benefiting both governments.[149] The illegal trade continued into

---

145 Ó Gráda, *Ireland*, 283; NARA, D/S, USD, 1, 1, T199, enclosure in Knox to Jefferson, 19 April 1791, McCabe and Pearse, Dublin 24 January 1791; Report on the petition of Thomas McCabe and William Pearce.
146 *Ibid.*, Knox to Jefferson, 7 September 1791.
147 S. J. Connolly, 'Navigation acts' in Connolly (ed.), *The Oxford companion*, 385.
148 NARA, D/S, USD, 1, 1, T199, Knox to Washington, 13 November 1791; *ibid.*, Knox to Jefferson, 7 September 1791; *ibid.*, Knox to Jefferson, 17 January 1792.
149 NARA, D/S, USD, 1, 1, T199, Knox to Jefferson, 28 May 1792; *ibid.*, Knox to Jefferson, 15 February 1792.

the nineteenth century to meet the strong Irish demand for tobacco.[150]

Knox encouraged the expansion of US–Irish trade not only for professional but also personal reasons. Following his discussion with Westmoreland in early 1791, he spent September and November travelling throughout the country making contact with merchants interested either in developing or expanding trade links through him. He reported to George Washington that 'no country in Europe contains more real friends to America ... who rejoice more in her rising prospects'. But in order to promote US commercial interests, he thought it proper to cultivate connections with the class that governed the country and formed public opinion. Consequently, he met again with Westmoreland who was 'courteously accessible' to him, Robert Hobart, his Chief Secretary and John Foster, speaker of the Irish House of Commons among others who had 'extensive commercial knowledge'.[151] Knox believed that the newly independent Irish Parliament was important to the development of trade between the two countries but worried about the increasing radicalisation of Irish politics evident in the establishment of the Society of United Irishmen in Belfast and Dublin in late 1791, along with the possibility of Britain 'plunging the greater part of Europe into a war by sea and land'. Knox hoped the Irish matter would be resolved and he cautioned his political masters in Washington to not 'be ambitious of participating in the politics ... of European courts' and instead 'supply naval stores'.[152] But he was convinced that Irish Catholics would not accept 'anything less than a participation in the elective franchise'. Throughout the first half of 1792, he assiduously reported the United Irishmen's demands for full political independence.[153]

His contacts with merchants such as Edward Forbes in Dublin and Messrs Harvey and Deaves in Cork, indicate the fine line negotiated by consuls who engaged in trade on their own behalf while simultaneously representing official American interests.[154] Unfortunately, Knox was unable to take advantage of the good-will, credit terms and existing demand for popular American products that were 'liked and sell well' such as American timber, wax, oil and potash, to benefit financially

150 Ó Gráda, *Ireland*, 83.
151 GLI, HKP, William to Henry Knox, 30 September 1791; NARA, D/S, USD, 1, 1, T199, Knox to Washington, 13 November 1791.
152 *Ibid.*, Knox to Washington, 17 January 1792; S. J. Connolly, 'United Irishmen, Society of', in Connolly (ed.), *The Oxford companion*, 567; NARA, D/S, USD, 1, 1, T199, Knox to Jefferson, 15 February 1792; GLI, HKP, William to Henry Knox, 7 April 1791.
153 NARA, D/S, USD, 1, 1, T199, Knox to Jefferson, 28 May 1792; *ibid.*, Knox to Jefferson, 17 January 1792; *ibid.*, 28 May 1792.
154 GLI, HKP, Edward Forbes to William Knox, 19 July 1792; *ibid.*, Harvey and Deaves, Cork to William Knox, 19 July 1792.

while expanding American–Irish trade. A heavily indebted and demoralised Knox departed for Philadelphia in July 1792 and did not return to Ireland again. Yet, even in February 1793, he still saw the same potential and indeed imbalance in the US–Irish trading relationship not least because of the 'value of the numerous cargoes sent to Ireland' and the 'small proportion of the amount ... returned to this country in goods'.[155]

Knox's departure meant he avoided dealing with the economic consequences of the turbulent 1790s. While the British and French navies battled for supremacy over the world's shipping lanes, neutral America found its transatlantic trade disrupted. Merchants on both sides of the Atlantic struggled to maintain their commercial links. The absence of a US consul in Dublin was noted in early 1793 by James D'Olier and John Lindsey, friends and creditors of William Knox. The former believed that Knox's 'residence here was highly ... beneficial to the trade of the American states' while Lindsey believed 'that the want of an American consul has been experienced'. But Lindsey expected 'prosperity' in US–Irish trade particularly because the duty on tobacco was to be reduced in March 1793 and he hoped 'it may become again an article worth millions'. Holmes in Belfast did inform Secretary Pickering in October 1796 that owing to the war, the Navigation acts had been largely dispensed with which meant that American and other ships were allowed to enter Irish ports without having to pay the usual duties. As evidence of this opportunity for US vessels and captains, he noted the arrival into Belfast from St Petersburg of the *Eliza* of Salem, Massachusetts, laden with tallow.[156] Yet, the wars provided a stimulus to Irish production as did Britain's growing population and Ireland's expanding domestic demand.

The economic impact of the Act of Union in 1800 remains controversial. Some claim that the reduction and eventual elimination of protective tariffs on Irish industries after 1800 permanently damaged the economy. On the other hand, Ó Gráda suggests that the impact was short term and that other factors such as the 'Industrial Revolution, war [and] political change' must have contributed to the subsequent decline of Irish industry.[157] None of the consuls reported on the immediate effects of the legislative union implemented in January 1801 not least of which was the loss of Dublin's status as the parliamentary capital of Ireland and the economic consequences arising from the departure of 271 peers and 300

---

155 *Ibid.*, William Knox, New York to Henry Knox, 10 February 1793.
156 *Ibid.*, James D'Olier Dublin to William Knox, 14 February 1793; *ibid.*, John Lindsey to William Knox, 16 February 1793; NARA, D/S, USB, 1, 1, T368, Holmes to Pickering, 6 October 1796; Carroll, *The American presence*, 26.
157 Ó Gráda, *Ireland*, 45–6; L. M. Cullen, *An economic history of Ireland since 1660* (London, 1972), 104.

members of the Irish House of Commons and their respective families and households to London.[158] However, this might be explained by irregular contact and by the narrow terms of reference employed in consular reporting. Knox's successor, Joseph Wilson did not report and neither did he comment on the Robert Emmet-led insurrection in July 1803.[159] However, Holmes reported in September on the great concern in Belfast about the 'late rising in Dublin' and its possible effects on the domestic economy.[160] Neither did it feature in Church's report from Cove later in December. Instead he recorded an increase in American imports into the port and he expected it to continue as the authorities had decided to permit all imports of provisions duty free for the following year. In 1804, he noted the arrival of twenty-seven US vessels carrying cotton, flax seeds, skins, hides, timber, ash, turpentine and tar. Moreover, he felt that there would soon be further new opportunities for US growers and merchants in the aftermath of the poor harvest and famine in 1800–1.[161] Holmes in Belfast seemed to be less interested in the fate of US trade with Ireland and more concerned in securing permission for his journey to Leghorn, Italy, to protect his business interests there.[162] However, US Minister James Monroe in London paid close attention to any British interference with American trade and instructed all consuls to report any such cases. In 1805, Joseph Wilson was asked by Monroe to identify any exports from Ireland to the US in the period 1802 to 1804 on which a higher duty had been imposed than on similar goods exported to continental Europe.[163] A year later, Church informed Monroe that one American vessel, *Mary* from Charleston, South Carolina, carrying wine from the Canary Islands to Drontheim, Germany, was detained by HMS *Argus*, brought to Cork on 28 July 1805 and was not 'liberated' until 9 September 1805.[164]

Despite these difficulties, neutral America profitably shipped goods to France and Britain at least until early 1807 and equally the war years were generally a period of rapid expansion for the Irish economy.[165] However,

---

158 Fergus D'Arcy, 'An age of distress and reform: 1800 to 1860' in Art Cosgrove (ed.), *Dublin through the ages* (Dublin, 1988), 96–7.
159 See NARA, D/S, USD, 1, 1, T199.
160 *Ibid.*, USB, 1, 1, T368, Holmes to Monroe, 8 September 1803.
161 *Ibid.*, USC, 1, 1, T196, Church to Madison, 31 December 1803; *ibid.*, 31 December 1804; *ibid.*, Returns 1804. Returns for 1805 are missing from the microfilm; Ó Gráda, *Ireland*, 4, 5, 12.
162 NARA, D/S, USB, 1, 1, T368, Holmes to Monroe, 15 June 1804.
163 *Ibid.*, USD, 1, 1, T199, Wilson to Monroe, 10 July 1805.
164 *Ibid.*, USC, 1, 1, T196, Church to Monroe, 7 May 1806.
165 Quoted in Andrew Burstein, 'Thomas Jefferson', in Melvin I. Urofsky (ed.), *The American presidents* (New York, 2000), 41; Cullen, *An economic history*, 100.

in February 1807, Wilson reported from Dublin that the Irish revenue commissioners had introduced a new regulation under the Navigation acts that prohibited the importation into Ireland of mahogany from British Honduras and the West Indies on US vessels. Cork merchants were particularly incensed. Timber merchants, Harvey, Deaves and Harvey of Charlotte's Quay and Joshua and Thomas Carroll of Patrick's Street along with iron merchants Messrs Houghton, tobacco merchant William Clark and general merchants Lecky and Mark, wrote to the Duke of Bedford, lord lieutenant, Sir John Newport, chancellor of the still distinct Irish Exchequer and Minister Monroe in London to explain the impact on their business. Acting on behalf of the Dublin and Cork merchants and perhaps protecting his own interests, Wilson also appealed to the Irish authorities. However, he learned that the British Privy Council was 'averse to any relaxation' of the Navigation acts even though Newport admitted that he was 'anxiously disposed to promote the trade of Ireland with the United States by every means within my power'.[166] In early March 1807, Wilson again appealed to Monroe to act.[167]

More provocative towards the US were the introduction in November 1807 by the Duke of Portland's Tory government of the Orders in Council which banned French trade with Britain, its allies or neutral countries and threatened seizure of neutral shipping and the British attack on the USS *Chesapeake*. Congress' response was the passage of the Embargo Act in December. Jefferson believed that British dependence on US trade would force it to negotiate. But the action proved to be short-sighted as it virtually ended all US overseas commerce and also restricted British imports. Not only did US trade collapse but British mercantile activity flourished as did smuggling. Church in Cork reported the arrival of just three American vessels in 1808 and the 'reduction of our trade with the United States'. In December 1808, he appealed to James Madison that 'the circumstances which have caused the cessation of intercourse may be speedily removed', particularly as trade was expanding.[168] Within two years, Madison introduced the Non-Intercourse Act in March 1809 and US commerce resumed, though not with British and French ports.[169] Thomas English in Dublin reported in July 1810 that many US ships had landed in Dublin in contravention of the new act. The masters of these

166 NARA, D/S, USD, 1, 1, T199, Wilson to John Newport Hart, 31 January 1807; *Ibid.*, Wilson to Monroe, 19 February 1807; *ibid.*, USC, vol. 1, roll 1, T196, Harvey to Monroe, 3 March 1807, Memorial to Sir John Newport, 25 February 1807.
167 *Ibid.*, USD, 1, 1, T199, Wilson to Monroe, 6 March 1807.
168 *Ibid.*, USC, 1, 1, T196, Returns 1808; *ibid.*, Church to Madison, 2 January 1808; *ibid.*, Church to Madison, 31 December 1808.
169 Paul Johnson, *A history of the American people* (New York, 1997), 213–14; Temperley, *Britain and America since independence*, 28–9.

vessels did not possess papers and, therefore, concealed the identity of owners, sailors and origin of cargoes. One year later, more US vessels arrived and the duties on US goods (cotton, timber, tobacco) arriving into Irish ports on American ships had increased. Consul John English believed the additional duties were adopted with the view to 'giving an advantage to Britain over foreign shipping'. Their imposition did not prevent the arrival of more US vessels in Dublin during 1812. But only one ship left for New York between January and June 1812 with a 'valuable' cargo of linen, glass and saltpetre under the protection of the British Navy.[170]

The outbreak of war between the US and Britain on 19 June 1812 may have been inevitable. As indicated previously, Madison had listed America's grievances to Congress on 1 June; the impressment of US sailors, violation of the country's neutral rights, the blockading of its ports and the continuing ban on trade into British ports. The war was conducted on land along the Canadian border, in Florida and on sea. Ireland's foreign trade in 1807 was described by Cork merchants as in 'its infancy', and by June 1812 when war broke out exports to the US such as they were had collapsed. By December 1813, Church reported that commerce between the two countries had 'ceased'.[171] Eventually the might of the British Navy prevailed, the Treaty of Ghent was signed on 24 December 1814 and Britain emerged from the war politically and economically stronger. The combination of its great power status, peaceful conditions and technological developments combined to produce unprecedented economic growth in America.[172]

After 1815, Irish exporters benefited from the American and British post-war conciliatory mood although, as Cullen notes, the value of exports declined. Thomas English, absent from Dublin between 1812 and 1815, informed Monroe in September 1815 that the same duties applied to American and British goods shipped in and out of Ireland.[173] Coincidentally James Holmes was absent also from Belfast from 1810 onwards and Vice Consul William Phelps indicated that US–Belfast trade for the six-month period to October 1815 was of 'much greater moment' than previously. But linen exports, in a pattern of stagnation since the 1790s, continued to decline until the 1820s. Church in Cove commented

170 NARA, D/S, USD, 1, 1, T199, English to Smith, 10 July 1810; *ibid.*, 15 July 1811; *ibid.*, English to Monroe, 25 July 1812; *ibid.*, English to Monroe, 2 September 1812.
171 *Ibid.*, USC, 1, 1, T196, Church to Madison, 26 December 1813; *ibid.*, Church to Madison, 2 January 1815.
172 Ó Gráda, *Ireland*, 307; Temperley, *Britain and America since independence*, 29–37. NARA, D/S, USC, 1, 1, T196, Memorial to Sir John Newport, 25 February 1807.
173 *Ibid.*, USD, 1, 1, T199, English to Monroe, 1 November 1815; Cullen, *An economic history*, 101.

in February 1816 that a considerable number of American vessels had unloaded here within the past few months and he welcomed the 'renewal of intercourse and commerce', not least because it increased his fees.[174] But while the volume of vessels entering Irish ports recovered after 1815, it would have been difficult for Church and the other consuls to identify structural weaknesses then occurring in the Irish economy.

The second quarter of the nineteenth century saw the continued decline in agricultural output, greater competition for Irish manufactures particularly from Britain, and more generally contracting markets. Short-term crises occurred also such as the potato failure in 1817 and 1819, an agricultural crisis in 1820, the onset of further famine conditions in the southern counties in 1822 and severe economic depression in 1825–6. The contraction in woollen and cotton industries even in Belfast continued although the stagnation in linen in the first two decades of the century was reversed in 1817 and from the mid-1820s it grew rapidly and was increasingly centred in and around Belfast. Outside of the textile industry, however, there was no general crisis.[175] Nonetheless, the balance between Irish and British industry generally shifted in the latter's favour although American markets remained vital for the continued growth of Irish linen, shipbuilding and brewing. But the difficulties in agriculture were more serious with a widespread fall in prices after 1815. Exports of beef and pork declined not only to Britain but to other markets. This trend may have disproportionately affected the Cork district more than others because it was at the centre of the transatlantic provisions trade. Yet, despite the decline in beef and pork, the volume of agricultural exports rose during the 1820s and 1830s.[176] Increasingly, however, Britain came to dominate the market for Irish agricultural produce, a pattern that persisted into the twentieth century.[177]

A new era in Anglo-American trading relations was signalled in 1830. Louis McLane's tenure as US minister in London was dedicated to negotiating an understanding on reciprocal trade. Three years earlier, President Adams prohibited British vessels from trading with American ports until US ships could return to the British West Indies. Consul Wilson in Dublin and the other US consuls and agents, were instructed by Andrew Jackson to prevent the 'introduction of foreign goods' into the US. Shipowner and merchant Wilson abided by the direction and he did not expect other

---

174 NARA, D/S, USB, 1, 1, T368, Phelps to Madison, 10 October 1815; Ó Gráda, *Ireland*, 283; NARA, D/S, USC, 1, 1, T196, Church to Madison, 12 February 1816.
175 Cullen, *An economic history*, 100–8, 124.
176 *Ibid.*, 103; Andy Bielenberg, *Cork's industrial revolution: development or decline?* (Cork, 1991), 3. These authors differ on this point.
177 Cullen, *An economic history*, 186.

Dublin merchants to break the ban but he warned Secretary Van Buren on 26 August 1829 that trade between the port and the US 'which was considerable some years since ... has lately become very insignificant'.[178] Van Buren and McLane's conciliatory approach was welcomed by the Duke of Wellington's government and led to the signing of the British Reciprocity Agreement in 1830 in Washington. The British government agreed that American ships could trade with the West Indies in return for the opening of American ports to British vessels.[179]

The agreement had little impact on the decline of direct US–Irish trade. Yet, in mid-1829, Wilson believed that despite the drop in the number of American ships docking in Dublin, the 'consumption of American produce' had not reduced. Instead, the establishment of various packet ship companies travelling the Dublin–Liverpool route and resultant 'daily or almost hourly' communication between the two cities meant that Irish demand for American goods could be supplied from Liverpool. Wholesale merchants in Dublin had ceased importing directly from the US and instead imported American goods from Liverpool. Wilson admitted that direct US trade with Ireland was 'small' and Irish exports to the US 'are still more so'.[180] His report detailing the eleven US vessels that entered Dublin between 16 January 1827 and 1 July 1829 and the four ships between July 1829 and June 1833 supported his opinion. Wilson concluded 'the direct intercourse between this port and the United States has almost ceased to exist, in consequence of the great facility by communication by steam navigation between United States and Liverpool'. Between January and June 1833, four ships brought cotton, flax seed and tobacco – the staples of the US–Irish trade. In the following six months no US vessel entered Dublin, two arrived there between January and June 1834 with flax seed, naval stores and dry goods and none between July 1834 and January 1847.[181] Wilson repeated the obvious twenty times in his annual report on American traffic between 31 March 1835 and 1 October 1846; 'nothing has occurred within the consulate worth communicating during the last three months'.[182]

178 NARA, D/S, USD, 1, 1, T199, Wilson to Van Buren, 26 August 1829.
179 Deane and David Heller, *Paths of diplomacy: America's secretaries of state* (Philadelphia, 1967), 56–8.
180 NARA, D/S, USD, 1, 1, T199, Wilson to Van Buren, 26 August 1829.
181 *Ibid.*, Wilson to Van Buren, Returns enclosure to 26 August 1829; *ibid.*, 30 June 1833; *ibid.*, 31 December 1833; *ibid.*, Wilson to Van Buren, 30 June 1834; *ibid.*, 31 December 1834; *ibid.*, Harvey to McLane, 23 May 1834; *ibid.*, Wilson to Forsythe, 30 June 1835; *ibid.*, Wilson to Forsythe, from 31 September 1835 to 1 January 1846; *ibid.*, Wilson to Buchanan, 1 July 1846, 1 January 1847.
182 NARA, D/S, USD, 1, 1, T199, Wilson to Forsythe, 31 March 1835; *ibid.*, USC, 1, 1, T196, Returns 31 December 1832 to 30 June 1833; *ibid.*, 1 July to 30 December

Obstacles to trade between the US, Britain and its colonies continued to be removed. In the period 1838 to the end of 1840, US imports into Dublin faced no discriminatory regulations, laws, tariffs, decrees or royal orders. Unfortunately the relaxation of barriers did not assist the growth of direct US trade with the Dublin district. Wilson wrote that while the trade 'at one time was considerable, [it] has for some year back almost altogether ceased'. He explained in 1841 that 'the introduction and the very great facility of the steam communication between the ports of this consulate and Liverpool … enables consumers of American produce to supply themselves on cheaper terms than by direct importations' and guaranteed them the quality and quantity of the article and delivery at the precise time. The reasons echoed those offered in 1829. Wilson also confirmed that in 1841 only a 'small demand' existed for American flaxseed because Dutch and Russian equivalents suited the 'soil better'. In November 1842, only a 'few parcels of linens' were exported from Dublin to the US via Liverpool.[183] Approaching mid-century Ireland had become a market for American products but direct trade with Dublin had collapsed and most goods were imported from English ports particularly Liverpool. Other consuls in Ireland reported a similar pattern.

Nine US vessels entered Cork in 1833 four of them 'in distress' not landing any cargo. In the following year, there was 'no trade' between New York and Cork except via Liverpool: two US vessels, the *Harvest* from Rhode Island and *Neva* from Boston, entering the port were 'in distress'. Indeed in May 1834, one of Consul Reuben Harvey's relatives in New York, the merchant Jacob Harvey, doubted whether any US vessel would sail from New York to Cork in 1835 because there was no ongoing direct trade between the two ports. In December 1835, Harvey confirmed the absence of direct trade with the US during the year.[184] Between January and October 1837 and in 1838, seventeen US ships docked because of emergencies. Their cargoes of cotton, wine, wheat, coal, glass and passengers were intended for the US. Thirteen were repaired and proceeded on their journey while the others were condemned and sold and the cargo sent to Liverpool.[185] The pattern continued into 1841 when only one of the eleven US vessels that entered Cove collected orders for goods and

1833; *ibid.*, Harvey to McLane, 23 May 1834; *ibid.*, USD, 1, 1, T199, Wilson to Forsythe, from 31 September 1835 to 1 October 1845; *ibid.*, Wilson to Buchanan, 1 April 1846, 1 October 1846.
183 *Ibid.*, Wilson to Forsythe, 31 December 1841; *ibid.*, 1 November 1842.
184 *Ibid.*, USC, 1, 1, T196, Returns from 31 December 1832 to 30 June 1834; *ibid.*, Harvey to Forsythe, Returns from 30 to 31 December 1835.
185 *Ibid.*, Returns 1 December 1836 to 5 May 1837; *ibid.*, 3 May to 6 October 1837; *ibid.*, 16 February to 24 December 1838.

the others required repairs and proceeded on their respective journeys. No US vessels were reported as entering Cove between April and the end of May 1841. There was no evidence of direct exports from Cork between 1837 and March 1843.[186] Consular agent George Scott vividly described the situation in September 1843: 'there is no commercial intercourse between this district of Cork and the United States.'[187] Direct trade between the US and Cork and vice versa had collapsed. In Galway, one US vessel had visited the port in 1833–4. In April 1834, Thomas Persse expected another to leave 'in a short time'. During the following three years, Persee had 'nothing of any importance' to report; 'few vessels sail from here direct to the United States'.[188]

Trade between the US and Belfast formed a different pattern. Belfast was thriving; 772 vessels arrived in 1786 and 3,655 in 1845. This 'vast increase' in the number of vessels was reflected in the same period in the growth in tonnage from 34,287 to 445,537 and revenue from £1,553 to £25,001.[189] By the 1830s, American products carried into Belfast consisted of flaxseed, cotton, tea, tar, potash, salt and turpentine, while exports consisted of linen, whiskey, pig iron, oats and potatoes.[190] The most important imports were flaxseed for the linen industry and raw cotton for spinning. Although the Irish cotton industry declined during the nineteenth century due to English competition, trade liberalisation and transport improvements, its development in Belfast was less straightforward. Ó Gráda suggests that Belfast producers continued to export for longer and might have survived except for the lure of greater profit from linen.[191] Consul Gilpin acknowledged in August 1833 that linen output was expanding. It was Belfast's most important export to the US and it had changed from being a cottage industry to an increasingly mechanised process which continually adapted throughout the century. A further identifiable trend was the concentration of production in the 'linen triangle' of Belfast, Newry and Dungannon. However, Gilpin identified serious problems with the linen trade. First, inferior fabrics called 'unions' made of a mixture of linen and cotton fibres were manufactured and sold in America as genuine linen. He requested Secretary McLane to introduce a regulation forcing Irish manufacturers to label their goods correctly with their value and composition and have the cargo certified

---

186 NARA, D/S, USC, 1, 1, T196, Returns from 28 October 1838 to 1 April 1841; *ibid.*, Murphy to Webster, 29 May 1841.
187 *Ibid.*, Scott to Secretary of State, 2 September 1843.
188 *Ibid.*, USG, 1, 1, T570, Persse to McLane, 26 April 1834; *ibid.*, Persse to Forsythe, 10 May 1837.
189 *Thom's Directory*, 1849, 563.
190 See NARA, D/S, USB, 1, 1, T368 and *ibid.*, USL, 1, 1, T216.
191 Ó Gráda, *Ireland*, 278.

by the consular officer. This action would have addressed his second concern also, namely that the bulk of linen exports from Ulster were still not being certified by the consul. While most of the linen cargo left from Belfast and Newry, it went to Liverpool for reshipment to the US and elsewhere. Liverpool dealers and bankers provided better credit terms and the city offered greater possibilities of further cargo to fill a vessel on the return journey.[192] Consequently, even if the US consul in Belfast authenticated the value of goods, it was his counterpart in Liverpool who signed the ships' manifests and obtained the fees which were a bone of contention for all Belfast-based consuls throughout the nineteenth century. For example, no US vessel entered or left Belfast port in the six month period to December 1833, but two British vessels with cargoes of linen originating in Belfast valued at £1,023 35s., left for Liverpool where the US consul certified the cargo, en route to the US.[193] Two years later, three US vessels arrived in Londonderry from New York with flax-seed, hides and naval stores worth £17,000 and departed with whiskey, potatoes, linen worth £1,900 and passengers. In the same year, thirty-one British vessels carrying linen and hosiery departed from Londonderry for Philadelphia and New York via Liverpool including eight owned by the US consul, local merchant and shipping agent, James Corscaden. Two years later, three US vessels arrived with coal and iron and left with linen and passengers for Providence and New York but seventeen British vessels left for New York and Philadelphia again via Liverpool with a cargo of linens, potatoes and salt.[194]

Gilpin's successor, James Shaw confirmed in 1843 that the trade between Belfast and the US consisted primarily of linen goods but was 'more limited than formerly' and most of the cargoes were carried on British vessels.[195] Like Gilpin, Shaw identified the 'irregularities' in certification, complained to Secretary Webster and as chapter two indicated, uncovered James McHenry and Francis Skelly's involvement. Treasury Secretary Spencer did not have any 'authority' to interfere in the situation and believed that compelling 'shipment from Belfast ... would seriously obstruct trade'.[196] In other words, Spencer's main priority was to facilitate US trade. Future consuls pursued the matter but to no avail. During the famine years of the 1840s, Consul McDowell clarified for

192 NARA, D/S, USB, 1, 1, T368, Gilpin to McLane, 27 August 1833; Carroll, *The American presence*, 39.
193 NARA, USB, 1, 1, T368, Returns, 1833.
194 *Ibid.*, USL, 1, 1, T216, Returns from 1 January 1835 to 31 December 1837.
195 *Ibid.*, USB, 1, 1, T368, Shaw to Webster, 11 January 1843; *ibid.*, Shaw to Upshur, 17 November 1843; Ó Gráda, *Ireland*, 289.
196 NARA, D/S, USB, 1, 1, T368, Shaw to Webster, 2 December 1842; *ibid.*, Shaw to Upshur, 22 September 1843; *ibid.*, Spencer to Ran, 24 August 1843.

Secretary Buchanan that the huge increase in US vessels arriving in the Belfast district in 1847 was related to famine relief and was not due to 'any increase of the regular trade, either to or from this district' and, of course, would not lead to a permanent increase in consular fees.[197] As predicted, US mercantile traffic into Irish consular districts soon returned to normal levels and its indirect pattern. However, opportunities to develop direct trade and communications emerged.

In late 1850, Belfast Vice Consul Thomas McLure became aware of British government investigations into the possibility of establishing a port on the west coast of Ireland as a point of arrival and departure for their mail packets with connecting railways to Dublin, thereby avoiding the 'risk and delay' of travelling through the English channel. He suggested to Secretary Webster in October, that it would be very desirable that such a port be made into a packet station for the US.[198] US Minister Abbot Lawrence in London supported the idea as it would expedite the mail service and facilitate emigration.[199] Both men may have heard about the efforts of local people including that of Consul Persee in Galway, to develop it as the hub of the steam service to America. In November 1848, Persee informed Secretary Buchanan that Galway would become 'one of the most flourishing cities in Ireland', it would be within one day's communication with London and as it had a 'magnificent bay' and a 'splendid dock ... no other port in Ireland' could compete with it 'as to its eligibility for a packet station'.[200] As owner of the barque, *Bonita* which traded on the Atlantic routes and part-owner of other Galway-based sailing vessels which operated on many other routes, Persee had many reasons to support the campaign led by Peter Daly, a Roman Catholic priest in the parish of Saint Nicholas North in Galway city.[201] His successor, John Duffy, was equally enthusiastic not least because in March 1854 he could not afford to take up the offer of the Galway post because the 'stars and stripes' had not floated over an American vessel in Galway port since 1850, hence he would not gather fees. But he emphasised that if Galway became a packet station, it would possess all the 'elements of greatness both in a commercial and manufacturing point of view'.[202] Two years later, Samuel Talbot adopted a

197 NARA, USB, 1, 1, T368, McDowell to Buchanan, 30 November 1848; *ibid.*, Returns January to December 1847.
198 *Ibid.*, McLure to Webster, 30 October 1850, 12 December 1850.
199 Hill, *Memoir of Abbott Lawrence*, 93.
200 NARA, D/S, USG, 1, 1, T570, Persse to Secretary of State, 7 November 1848.
201 Walter S. Sanderlin, 'Galway as a transatlantic port in the nineteenth century', *Éire–Ireland*, 5:3 (1970) 25; Collins, *Transatlantic*, 17, 21, 116.
202 NARA, D/S, USG, 1, 1, T570, Persse to Secretary of State, 23 March 1854. In 1852, Senators Stockton and Shields respectively presented petitions, on behalf of Andrew

similar course.²⁰³ A breakthrough for the Galway entrepreneurs came in 1858. The *Indian Empire* was bought by the Atlantic Royal Mail Steam Navigation Company (the Galway Line) with Persee among its shareholders. The vessel safely left Southampton and eventually arrived in Galway after running aground west of Mutton Island. At the inauguration of the line in Galway on 19 June, Consul Talbot was given a prominent place and toasts were made to the health of President Buchanan. The *Indian Empire* departed on its first formal voyage carrying mail to and from the US and Canada.²⁰⁴ Between 1858 and 1861 and 1863 and 1864, fifty-three westbound voyages and fifty-one eastbound voyages were made by the sixteen Galway Line steamers. Talbot was optimistic for the expansion of the service and when the vessels on the US routes displayed the US flag, he decided to return the 'compliment' by having a flag pole erected at the harbour for the US flag.²⁰⁵ Despite the best efforts of all involved, the line did not survive because of the withdrawal of the government mail contracts due to bad administration of the company, increased competition from the British government-backed Cunard and Inman lines based in Liverpool, the beginning of cablegram communication and the outbreak of the American Civil War. In 1864, it ceased to exist and ended hopes that it would make 'the Citie of the Tribes the Liverpool of Ireland'. Although trading activities continued in Galway and the possibility of developing it into an embarkation port for the US remained an aspiration, direct transportation and trading ties with the US continued to decline.²⁰⁶

In mid-century, Irish manufacturing had fallen behind British, although output in linens, ship building, brewing and distilling increased. Belfast's central position in the linen trade was confirmed by Consul Holmes in January 1852, when he described it as the 'seat of the linen manufacture of Ireland.' Linens 'designed for the United States' were forwarded

---

Thompson, to the Senate asking the postmaster general to authorise the transportation of US mail in steamers from New York to Galway. It was referred to the Committee on Naval Affairs. *Journal of the Senate*, 1st session, 32nd congress, Wednesday, February 4, 1852, 175 and Thursday, March 4, 1852, 246.
203 NARA, D/S, USG, 1, 1, T570, Talbot to Marcy, 31 December 1856.
204 *Ibid.*, Talbot to Cass, 23 June 1858; *ibid.*, 19 August 1858.
205 Collins, *Transatlantic triumph*, 9–11, 53–4; NARA, D/S, USG, 1, 1, T570, Talbot to Cass, 30 September 1858; *ibid.*, 1 October 1858. The company's offer to the British Admiralty to supply its ships at St John's, Newfoundland with coal, was refused. National Maritime Museum, Caird Library Manuscripts Department, Milne, Sir Alexander, 1st Bt., Admiral of the Fleet, 1806–96 Collection, No. 2 NA and WI stations, General letters, commencing 16 July 1861 ending 27 October 1862, Secretary Fred James Fegen to N. Shea, St Johns, Newfoundland, 24 October 1862, 196.
206 Collins, *Transatlantic*, 9–11.

from Belfast port to Liverpool for re-shipment to the US.[207] Nevertheless, the general picture of post-famine industrial stagnation (except for Belfast), did not apply to agriculture. After the 1870s this sector was characterised by innovation, rising potato yields and 'buoyant' livestock and butter exports.[208] Other trends were evident also. In 1852 in Belfast there were 'daily lines of steamers' sailing in and out but Consul Holmes reported that imports and exports were 'almost entirely secured through and trans-shipped from British ports'. Four years later, Consul Higgins confirmed that there was 'no direct trade' between Belfast and the US, while his successor James Arrott repeated the comment in 1858. In April 1859, the Liverpool and New York Steamship Company commenced a direct service between Belfast and New York with two steamships, *City of Manchester* and *Vigo*, carrying linens. But after making five voyages the service was discontinued in September.[209] In Queenstown, however, between November 1853 and August 1854, forty-five US vessels arrived with cargoes of wheat, maize, molasses and cotton, while just two discharged cargoes. The others collected orders and proceeded to Limerick, Liverpool, Glasgow, Bristol and London. By the end of the 1860s, Consul Eastman believed that the port was no longer an important one for direct US trade.[210]

Dublin was no different. In October 1859 Consul Talbot wrote that the port 'has lost all the direct trade with the United States … it is dependent in a great measure upon Liverpool and Glasgow for all the staple articles of consumption and export'. Just four US vessels arrived in Dublin direct from the US in 1859 but as with Belfast, an extensive trade was carried on with British and continental ports. Talbot calculated that 565 non-American vessels entered Dublin port in 1858, 405 arrived in Cork and 307 in Belfast. Between 1858 and 1861, the main staples imported indirectly into Dublin from the US were tea, sugar, wine, spirits, tobacco, cotton, tobacco, flour and corn and wheat due to the 'deficient harvest'.[211] In the same year, Thomas Larcom, Under-Secretary for Ireland, commented 'as American corn has been followed by American bacon, so American

207 NARA, D/S, USB, 2, 2, T368, Holmes to Webster, 5 January 1852; *ibid.*, 28 July 1852.
208 Ó Gráda, *Ireland*, 309, 257.
209 NARA, D/S, USB, 2, 2, T368, Holmes to Webster, 28 July 1852; *ibid.*, Higgins to Marcy, 21 July 1856; *ibid.*, 2, 3, T368, Arnott to Cass, 22 December 1858; *ibid.*, Frean to Cass, 16 November 1859.
210 *Ibid.*, USC, 2, 2, T196, Fees, 26 August 1853 and 27 November 1854; *ibid.*, 6, 6, T196, Eastman to Seward, 12 October 1863; *ibid.*, Eastman to Seward, 9 July 1868.
211 *Ibid.*, USD, 3, 3, T199, Talbot to Cass, 8 October 1859; Talbot to Cass, 8 October 1859; *ibid.*, Talbot to Cass, 22 October 1860; *ibid.*, Talbot to Seward, 22 October 1861.

bacon is followed by American butter'.[212] Although the American Civil War would reduce all commerce into Irish ports, an Irish taste for American goods had developed. Indeed Consul Livermore in Londonderry commented in 1880 'the Irish peasant now sells his hog and with the proceeds buys American bacon'.[213] But most American products arrived from British ports because the prices were keener and the quantities and delivery times better suited Irish merchants than if directly imported.[214]

US consuls did not hold out much hope of a revival in direct exports to the US either. Irish exports to the US were underpinned by linen, leather, skins, wood, potatoes, porter, ale, whiskey and of course, emigrants. For example, exports out of Dublin in 1859 and 1860 consisted mainly of porter, ale, whiskey, leather, glue, oil, skins and most of it went direct to Liverpool and Glasgow for re-export. Nonetheless, Consul Talbot felt that Ireland's expanding countrywide railway network and its prosperous banking system, growing mining industry and declining levels of 'pauperism' would benefit the 'nation at large after centuries of oppression and neglect.' But significantly he concluded in late 1860 that outside of the distilling and brewing industries, the manufacturing sector 'had not been prosecuted with the same vigour and skill as in the north'. Outside of Belfast, he felt that there were few new opportunities for skilled, manual labour.[215] Consul Lewis Richmond in 1877 confirmed the predominance of agriculture in the south of Ireland and the practical absence of direct trade between Queenstown and the US because 'the wants of this country being entirely supplied from England' and 'the spirit of the people leans toward contentment with things as they are than toward the adoption of anything new'.[216]

Ireland's subsequent economic development bore out the consuls' mid-century predictions about its structural problems and the nature of the American-Irish trading relationship. By the beginning of the twentieth century excluding food and drink, the three southern provinces were 'virtually without industries' or to use Belfast Consul Samuel Knabenshue's words in 1908 'the manufactures of Ireland are unimportant'.[217] Whereas industrial success in the north-east based on textiles, engineering and ship building was well established by now.

212 *Ibid.*, 6, 6, T196, Eastman to Seward, 21 September 1864; Quoted in H. D. Gribbon, 'Economic and social history, 1850–1921' in Vaughan (ed.), *A New history of Ireland vi*, 267.
213 NARA, USB, 9, 9, T368, Livermore to Secretary of State, 23 October 1880.
214 *Ibid.*, USD, 3, 3, T199, Talbot to Cass, 22 October 1860.
215 *Ibid.*, Talbot to Cass, 8 October 1859; *ibid.*, Talbot to Cass, 22 October 1860; *ibid.*, Talbot to Seward, 22 October 1861.
216 *Ibid.*, USC, 7, 7, T199, Richmond to Seward, 15 December 1877.
217 Ó Gráda, *Ireland*, 313; NARA, RG 59, IRFSPB, June 1908, 19.

Consul Savage commented that Belfast was the 'commercial capital of Ireland'.[218] According to US Consul General at Large Horace Lee Washington who visited the Athlone, Ballymena, Belfast, Dublin, Galway, Limerick Londonderry, Lurgan, Queenstown and Waterford offices in 1908, 'commercially and industrially' Belfast was the 'principal city of Ireland'. The value of declared exports from Belfast to the US in 1906–7 was $14,703,678 14c., of which linens comprised $10,328,061 and cottons, $1,077,339 7c.[219]

The principal export from Dublin to the US was porter and no single item reached one million dollars in value while total exports were only worth $1,339,984 12c. By 1907, although Dublin was the capital, it was the second city in commercial importance.[220] The returns for Queenstown, the main port for Cork, the third largest city in Ireland in terms of commerce and population, declared exports to the US for 1907 to be worth $97,374 16c. of which mackerel comprised the largest export commodity.[221] Yet, the value of exports from Queenstown to the US in 1907 was less than Lurgan or Londonderry. In the former, which had a population of just 12,000 and was without a shipping port, $1,068,679 57c. worth of exports was certified by the consular agent of which linen accounted for $757,725 54c.[222] In the other northern port, Londonderry, exports in 1907 were valued at $125,809 47c. and consisted largely of pickled herring.[223] At the other end of the scale, Limerick exported $38,204 5c. worth of goods to the US and two-thirds were mackerel. Galway's exports valued just $9,716 in the same year, most were salted fish, marble and whiskey. While in Waterford, declared exports to the US of grass seed and furze sticks were valued at $2,282 68c.[224] Washington's reports had clearly identified a vital feature of the Irish economy in 1900: most of its export trade was carried on British vessels through British ports.[225] According to the consuls, no American-owned vessel cleared

218 NARA, D/S, USB, 9, 9, T368, Savage to Porter, 5 March 1886.
219 NARA, RG 59, IRFSPB, June 1908, 27, 11.
220 *Ibid.*, IRFSPD, June 1908, 10.
221 *Ibid.*, IRFSPC, June 1908, 11. In May and June 1904, a number of local authorities in counties Cork, Kerry, Tipperary and Galway protested to Swiney about the duty charged on pickled and salted fish and the decline in the trade and later thanked him when it was repealed. See NARA, D/S, USC, 12, 12, T196, Swiney to Loomis, 20 June 1904.
222 NARA, RG 59, IRFSP, Lurgan, June 1908, 27.
223 *Ibid.*, IRFSP, Londonderry, June 1908, 10, 11.
224 *Ibid.*, IRFSP, Limerick, June 1908, 11; *ibid.*, Galway, May 1908, 12, 27; *ibid.*, Waterford, June 1908, 28.
225 There were brief periods when the US factor stood out in the trading relationship. In 1885 imported American meat depressed prices. *Ibid.*, D/S, USD, 9, 9, T199, Barrows to Porter, 4 November 1885.

from Belfast, Dublin, Queenstown, Londonderry, Limerick, Galway or Waterford in 1906-7.[226]

The American goods that arrived in Irish ports were mainly carried in cross-channel steamers from Liverpool, London, Glasgow and Manchester and then distributed by railway and coastal steamer. The absence of a direct line of steamers between the US and Belfast, Dublin, Queenstown and Londonderry districts respectively, was identified as a major obstacle in the expansion of US–Irish commercial relations as were excessive freight rates and complex bills of lading. Additionally, Consul Moe believed that 'a systematic hostility' existed in some circles in Dublin towards foreign-produced articles particularly among supporters of Sinn Féin who adhered to the slogan 'Ireland for the Irish.' Consular Agent Ludlow also identified 'the Home Industries agitation' as an obstacle to the expansion of openings for American trade and industries in his Limerick district. Moreover, there was no American–owned export or import firm located in Belfast, Dublin, Queenstown or Londonderry in 1907 although there were a number of agencies established for the sale of various US manufactures, with head offices in London. For example, there were eight Irish-owned firms in Londonderry which imported American goods including four that traded in maize, timber, cotton cake and oils. However, the existence of a largely indirect trade did not mean that a further characteristic of the mid-century economy was not present. A demand, although small, for American products particularly oil, timber, tobacco and wheat still existed.[227] These products accurately represented the predominance of raw and agricultural commodities in the profile of US foreign trade by the turn of the century.

Table 2.1 reveals the indifference of US manufacturing and commercial interests to foreign trade until the 1880s when the US consular service was harnessed by government and manufacturing interests in the effort to expand exports generally and manufactured products specifically. Cotton manufacturers were the first group in 1880 to directly request the government to obtain through consuls, information on the market for their products abroad. From then, greater obligation was placed on consuls to find openings for American trade. Daily, monthly and annual commercial reports detailed foreign customs regulations, food and

---

226 *Ibid.*, RG 59, IRFSPB, June 1908, 15, 16, 19; *ibid.*, Ballymena, June 1908, 14; *ibid.*, Athlone, May 1908, 14; *ibid.*, Dublin, May 1908, 15, 16; *ibid.*, Cork, June 1908, 15, 27; *ibid.*, Limerick, June 1908, 15; *ibid.*, Londonderry, June 1908, 15, 16, 28; *ibid.*, Waterford, June 1908, 15, 16.

227 NARA, RG 59, IRFSPB, June 1908, 15, 16, 19; *ibid.*, Ballymena, June 1908, 14; *ibid.*, Athlone, May 1908, 14; *ibid.*, Dublin, May 1908, 15, 16; NARA, *ibid.*, Cork, 1908, 15, 27; *ibid.*, Londonderry, June 1908, 15, 16, 28.

Table 2.1 Exports of domestic merchandise, 1860–1903

	Raw and agricultural Products (%)	Manufactured products (%)
1860	87.24	12.76
1880	87.52	12.48
1900	68.35	31.65
1903	70.72	29.28

Source: Lloyd Jones, *The consular service*, 60

patent laws, local demand and prejudices, business methods, packaging, means of sale and advantages which America's competitors might enjoy due to direct shipment. Consuls' commitment to trade extension was also intensely scrutinised during the regular inspection visits from 1906 of the consul general at large.[228] Despite transportation, administration and political obstacles, consuls in Belfast, Dublin, Londonderry and Queenstown saw opportunities for American manufacturers. One such opening came in the mid-1890s during an expansion in housebuilding in Ireland when a shortage of Welsh roof slates coincided with a surplus of slate in the US. Consuls Ashby in Dublin and Taney in Belfast identified the opportunity and put American manufacturers in contact with Irish buyers. As a result, more than £125,000 worth of American slate was imported into Ireland between 1897 and 1900.[229] More often than not, given the impermanence of the consular service and constant loss of consular experience and contacts with the local economy, it was the consular agents located in the smaller towns who were more realistic in their commercial judgement. Most were merchants or traders or solicitors working in the locality and were familiar with the needs and demands of local markets and recognised the dominance which British manufacturers, suppliers, shippers and distributors had over Irish trade.[230]

Protecting US interests could be routine in nature but also at times exciting. The work ranged from certifying the composition and value of exports to providing food, clothes, shelter and sometimes protection to American seamen. Undoubtedly the imposition of wartime conditions particularly

228 Lloyd Jones, *The consular service*, 65–9; NARA, RG 59, IRFSP, Form.
229 NARA, RG59, IRFSPD, May 1908, 14; Davies, 'Roofing Belfast and Dublin', 26–35.
230 Another mid-century trend had been sustained namely, the flight from the land, despite agricultural innovation and an expansion in farm productivity. NARA, RG 59, IRFSP, Athlone, May 1908, 12; *ibid.*, Galway, May 1908, 28; *ibid.*, Limerick, June 1908, 19; Ó Gráda, *Ireland*, 259.

involving the US and Britain, made life more difficult for consuls located in Ireland. But the extent to which consuls and consular agents engaged with this work depended on the individual and the local circumstances pertaining in his consular district and less on whether he was a US or Irish citizen at least during the first half of the century. Thus, the onset of extensive famine conditions from 1845 to 1851 provoked little comprehensive comment, except from William West in Galway. Yet, none of the consuls called on either the Polk or Taylor or Fillmore governments to intervene either politically with the Peel or Russell governments in London or to provide food or financial aid. Instead, they adhered strictly to their consular role and commented on the economic opportunities for US companies. This may seem harsh and unsympathetic. However, each man was dependent to some extent on fees received for certifying and verifying export and import cargoes going to and from the US for his livelihood. Consequently, the undoubted growth in imports during the famine years and growing departures of people resulted in increased consular incomes. Second, the mercantile and maritime emphasis of the consular post meant that many incumbents were also engaged in shipping as owners or suppliers and again benefited financially from any increase in traffic between the two countries. Finally, the formal nature of the contact between consul and Secretary of State may belie the extent to which the famine affected them personally although it did not inhibit William West or US Minister Lawrence from providing more extensive reports. Nonetheless, this variation in US consular reporting was not specific to Ireland.[231] In the absence of official instructions, US consuls refrained from formal intervention in the mid-century famine crisis in Ireland. However, the onset of the American Civil War crisis in the United States in 1861 would provide an altered context for the consular service.

---

231 See *Business History*, 23:3 (November 1981).

3

Protecting the Union: the American Civil War, 1861–5

In March 1861 among the immediate tasks facing Republican President Abraham Lincoln was to keep the United States together. This he failed to do and on 12 April when the southern states attacked Fort Sumter in South Carolina and then seceded from the Union, civil war became inevitable. There were many reasons for the conflict but the most significant was the future status of the institution of slavery. The four-year war caused political, economic, social and military upheaval, the effects of which would be long felt. The conflict had immediate consequences for all parts of the Union administration including the foreign service where diplomats and consuls became crucial figures. In Ireland, consuls and their offices became important listening posts for local opinions on the conflict. Temporarily, they also encouraged British neutrality. Ultimately, they acquired new duties providing intelligence and information on any unusual movements on land or at sea, recruited for the Union army under the guise of promoting emigration ensuring that the Confederate government did not gain any advantage. This chapter will examine the role of Union consuls based in Ireland during the Civil War and the extent of their involvement in the subsequent victory.

Lincoln had many political debts to repay. His first days were spent making appointments not least to the consular service. Heavily populated by southern Democrats 'of more or less doubtful loyalty', many were in strategic locations which concerned Lincoln and his Secretary of State, William Seward. The key diplomatic post was London to which Charles Francis Adams, the Massachusetts Republican leader and son of John Quincy Adams, was appointed while other important Lincoln appointees were William L. Dayton as minister to France and Henry Shelton Sanford as minister to Belgium. At the consular level, Freeman H. Morse who replaced the former South Carolina congressman, Robert Campbell, as Consul in London and John Bigelow appointed as Consul General to Paris, became crucial figures during the hostilities.[1] Liverpool

---

1 Barnes and Morgan, *The foreign service*, 112–16; Harriet Chappell Owsley, 'Henry

was an important port where the efficient and loyal Thomas Dudley replaced the Virginian Beverly Tucker.² In Queenstown, Patrick J. Devine replaced Robert Dowling, 'a most violent partisan, and advocate of the southern rebellion and equally violent in his abuse of the administration'.³ Alexander Henderson replaced Thomas McGunn in Londonderry, John Young, Lincoln's political supporter, exchanged with Theodore Frean in Belfast and Henry B. Hammond switched with Samuel Talbot in Dublin. William West was appointed to Galway due to Seward's 'influence ... friendship [and] sympathy for all foreigners and Irishmen' and amid complaints of disloyalty against the incumbent Thomas Moore Persse who was also a justice of the peace and 'can't serve two masters'.⁴ These appointments and others were based on party loyalty and patronage rather than on competency. In contrast, the Confederate government had no consular service but had agents abroad, while some of the recently released consuls formally transferred allegiance to the southern cause. Beverly Tucker became a Confederate agent in Britain, as did A. Dudley Mann, formerly in the Bremen legation. Robert Dowling was appointed 'commercial agent of the Confederate States of America at Cork'.⁵

Among Lincoln's earliest concerns was to establish and preserve a naval blockade of the southern coastline from New Jersey to Florida and the Gulf of Mexico. His government had a capable navy, money to expand it, shipbuilding yards, skilled craftsmen, trained crews and unblockaded ports. On the other side, the Jefferson Davis-led Confederate government worked to circumvent the blockade in order to pursue its 'King Cotton' strategy in the belief that Britain's need for southern cotton would bring it to the Confederacy's side. But the south had few of the north's resources and had to quickly move to create a modern navy .⁶

Shelton Sanford and Federal surveillance abroad, 1861–1865', *The Mississippi Valley Historical Review*, 48:2 (September 1961), 212
2 Kennedy, *The American consul*, 127.
3 NARA, D/S, USC, 4, 4, T196, Devine to Seward, 30 June 1861.
4 *Ibid.*, USL, 2, 2, T216, McGunn to Seward, 28 September 1861; *Ibid.*, USG, 1, 1, T570, West to Seward, 10 July 1861.
5 Kennedy, *The American consul*, 129; See NARA, D/S, USC, 4, 4, T196; *ibid.*, 5, 5, T196, Eastman to Seward, 8 July 1863.
6 The historiography on the American Civil War is extensive. The following have been consulted Clement Eaton, *A history of the southern Confederacy* (New York, 1954); D. P. Crook, *The North, the south and the powers, 1861–65* (New York, 1974); Frank J. Merli, *The Alabama, British neutrality and the American Civil War* (Bloomington and Indianapolis, 2004); R. J. M. Blackett, *Divided hearts: Britain and the American Civil War* (Baton Rouge, 2001); Kennedy, *The American consul*, 129; *Official records of the Union and Confederate navies in the War of the Rebellion* (hereafter ORUCN), series ii–volume 3 of 30 (Washington, 1922, reprinted 1987), J. P. Benjamin, Secretary of State, 7 March 1863, 143; Kevin J. Foster, 'The diplomats who

Combating Confederate navy-building and blockade-running

For economic and political reasons, the British government led by Lord Palmerston with Lord Russell as Foreign Secretary, was unwilling to intervene on either side even though it was increasingly dependent on northern states for grain and for its markets. On 9 March 1861, Secretary of State William Seward sent a circular to his foreign service which stated that 'recognition of the revolutionary government of the so-called Confederate states would be an unfriendly act on the part of any European government'. Adams was to explain the 'evils of dismemberment and prevent recognition'. In the case of Britain, Seward further clarified the Union position on 27 April: 'Great Britain cannot recognise the Confederate states and retain the friendship of the United States'.[7] Britain did not recognise the Confederacy during the war but its declaration of neutrality in May 1861 with its implied recognition of the south's belligerent status, angered Seward and Lincoln. Seward responded with a threatening note which Adams in London toned down before delivering it to the Foreign Office. The British government in turn believed that Seward 'never chooses to understand' its position, namely that if it refused facilities to Confederate vessels 'it would be at once declaring herself a party to the war'.[8] Adams and his consuls had a difficult task ensuring that British neutrality was upheld.

British policy also complicated the work of Commander James Dunwoody Bulloch, the naval officer of Ulster origin, in charge of acquiring and arming vessels and buying war supplies for the Confederates.[9] Bulloch arrived in Liverpool on 4 June 1861 with a budget of one million Confederate dollars. Initially he planned to buy and forward naval supplies and ammunitions. Following the Confederate government's decision to build gunboats at its home ports and inland waterways, he was ordered to supply every 'wants of the service' from submarine batteries and wire to blankets and to recruit skilled mechanics. Later on, he supervised the building of new ships and the buying of old ones.[10] He

---

sank a fleet: the Confederacy's undelivered European fleet and the Union consular service', *Prologue: Quarterly of the National Archives and Records Administration*, 30:3 (autumn 2001), 182.
7 NARA, D/S, Diplomatic Instructions of the Department of State, 1801–1906 (hereafter DIDS), M77, 76, RG59, Seward to Dallas, 9 March 1861; *ibid.*, Seward to Dallas, 27 April 1861.
8 Bourne and Watt (general eds), *BDFA*, 1, C, North America, 1837–1914, 5, The Civil War Years, 1859–5 (Bethesda,1986–7), Russell to Lyons, 22 November 1861.
9 Owsley, 'Henry Shelton Sanford', 213.
10 James D. Bulloch, *The Secret Service of the Confederate states in Europe or, How the Confederate cruisers were equipped*, first published 1959 (New York, 2001 edition), 459–77.

worked swiftly and succeeded in circumventing the Foreign Enlistment Act (1819) that forbade British subjects from 'equipping, furnishing, fitting out or arming, of any ship or vessel, with intent or in order that such ship or vessel shall be employed in the service' of a state 'with intent to ... commit hostilities' against a country with 'whom His Majesty shall not be at war.' This he did by contracting with British businesses to build unarmed vessels. Once built, the ships left the yards without weaponry that were later fitted at sea outside British jurisdiction. The onus was on the Union government to provide evidence of a violation of British law. In early July, Consul Dudley in Liverpool and Adams made great efforts to investigate the building of two vessels at Liverpool. From reports received from 'tradesmen, workmen and spies', there was 'no doubt' that these were gunboats. However, the evidence was insufficient to force the British government seize the ships.[11] Both were eventually released to the Confederate side.

As 'Hull no. 290' later named the CSS *Alabama*, prepared to depart from the Laird yard in Liverpool, Bulloch learned of the departure of the USS *Tuscarora* from Southampton for Queenstown, where he believed it would await news of the *Alabama*'s progress and then move either to intercept or follow it out to sea.[12] 'Hull no. 290' left Liverpool on 28 July 1862 the day before the British government agreed that 'the vessel, cargo and stores may be properly condemned'.[13] Immediately Dudley warned all consuls to be vigilant and prevent 'Hull no. 290' from being 'armed or fitted out in your jurisdiction'.[14] The vessel headed towards the northern coast of Ireland and helped by bad weather, avoided light houses, coastguard and customs stations from which its movements could be observed. On the evening of 31 July, it halted off the Giant's Causeway where Bulloch and the pilot, George Bond, went ashore and returned to Liverpool.[15] On 5 August, Devine in Queenstown, learned that 'a confederate privateer built and fitted up by Mr Laird of Birkenhead, sailed from Liverpool on, or about, the 29th ultimo, laden as it is believed with war material for the southern rebels'.[16] Once news of 'Hull no. 290's' departure from Liverpool reached Dublin, the

11 Wallace and Gillespie (eds), *The journal of Benjamin Moran, 1857–65*, ii, 7 July 1862.
12 Bulloch, *The secret service*, 171. On 2 July, Adams accepted the loss of 'No. 290' and ordered the *Tuscarora* to pick up the crew at the next convenient port, Queenstown. James Tertius deKay, *The rebel raiders: the astonishing history of the Confederacy's secret navy* (New York, 2002), 75.
13 Foster, 'The diplomats', 182.
14 NARA, D/S, USC, 5, 5, T196, Circular, 30 July 1862.
15 Bulloch, *The secret service*, 171, 178.
16 NARA, D/S, USC, 5, 5, T196, Devine to Seward, 5 August 1862.

USS *Tuscarora*, now in Kingstown, outside Dublin, immediately left to pursue it.[17] On 15 August, Young in Belfast, received a note from George Hill, one of his agents, resident at Ballycastle on the north-east Antrim coast, that 'no. 290 passed this place on 31 July' but took no notice of the coastguard's order to stop.[18] West, based on the west coast seemed to have knowledge of the 'Hull no. 290' building project and reported on 16 August that it had delayed the completion of two Galway Line steamers, *Hibernia* and *Columbia*. He continued 'I have had confidential agents on the western coast watching for her, and got information, I fear too late, of her being in Killary Harbour last Saturday night, and left in the morning westward, having, it now appears, taken in her guns ... by previous arrangement off that coast, the following day.' He believed the British authorities had turned a blind eye 'to the whole proceedings of this Rebel gun-boat!'.[19] The Union consuls' information was remarkably accurate but was of little use to Dudley and Adams. Bulloch's decision that once out of Liverpool, the vessel should head north and not south combined with the worsening weather provided the opportunity for it to escape without interference. The ship quickly cleared the Irish coast. Bulloch's contact in Queenstown, perhaps Dowling, informed him that the *Tuscarora* remained on the lookout but on 11 August, 'Hull no. 290' arrived at the island of Terceira in the Azores where it was armed from two supply boats and commissioned as the CSS *Alabama*.[20] In London, Moran commented 'she is now at her hellish work' and it went on to sink many Union merchant vessels including the American built and owned USS *Lafayette* on 29 October.[21] Destined for Irish ports, its cargo of grain was the property of Messrs Shaw and Finlay and Messrs Hamilton, Megault and Thompson in Belfast. According to Captain Raphael Semmes of the *Alabama*, the cargo belonged to the 'Yankee shippers', Craig and Nicoll and the Montgomery Brothers in New York and, therefore, liable to forfeit. By the end of October 1862 the *Alabama* had captured twenty-one vessels worth in all more than one million dollars.[22]

Bulloch had circumvented British legislation by engaging a private shipbuilder, recruiting crews from its own employees and sailing the completed vessel outside British waters where it was outfitted by a Confederate captain and crew. Seward and Adams had learned a costly

17 *Ibid.*, USD, 3, 3, T199, Hammond to Seward, 14 August 1862.
18 *Ibid.*, USC, 5, 5, T196, Hill to Devine, 15 August 1862; *Ibid.*, Young to Seward, 16 August 1862.
19 *Ibid.*, USG, 1, 1, T570, West to Seward, 16 August 1862.
20 Bulloch, *The secret service*, 171, 178.
21 Wallace and Gillespie (eds), *The journal of Benjamin Moran*, ii, 1 September 1862.
22 Foster, 'The diplomats', 185; deKay, *The rebel raiders*, 108–10.

lesson. Although Dudley had employed spies to watch the building of the *Alabama* and Union Minister Henry Shelton Sanford, working through Consul Freeman H. Morse, had employed a police detective, Ignatius Pollaky, and his private detectives, to report on Bulloch's movements, it was only after *Alabama* had escaped that Union consuls asked Seward to establish an intelligence system to help them supply the State, War and Navy departments with information on Confederate shipbuilding activity in Britain and Ireland.[23] Already many consuls received information from contacts in textile mills, factories, shipbuilding yards, post offices, telegraph offices and other government agencies but upon the outbreak of the war, more regular and reliable information was required. However, they had no additional funds to cover this activity and often had to pay from their own pockets with no hope of reimbursement.[24]

Investigations by Union consuls in Ireland was hampered by an additional factor. At the beginning of the war, nationalists in Ireland regretted the possibility of the break-up of the Union though there was much sympathy for the south and opposition to the coercion policy of the north. In addition, Joyce suggests that the Catholic hierarchy was concerned about the secular and liberal direction of the United States while there remained resentment against the anti-Catholicism and anti-Irishness of the Know-Nothing party of the previous decade.[25] Irish unionists, supporters of the Confederates, were impressed by the 'gallant and chivalrous southern gentlemen' while denying this meant support for slavery.[26] In Belfast, Young felt 'deep disappointment and regret at the state of public feeling with regard to our affairs in America'. He expected the Irish people to dislike slavery and, therefore, to naturally sympathise with the 'needful struggles of a paternal government for self existence'. Most of the newspapers in his town showed 'strong partiality for the south [and] magnify insignificant advantages into victories'. He identified the 'mercantile class' and the 'Catholic clergy' to be the main supporters of the Confederate cause while the middling and working classes championed the Union cause.[27] Young's suggested remedies provoked Moran in London to note:

---

23 Bulloch, *The Secret Service*, 177; Foster, 'The diplomats', 185; Owsley, 'Henry Shelton Sanford', 213. In comparison, Union Minister Sanford had funds to pay for his intelligence network from June 1861 onwards. *Ibid.*, 214.
24 Owsley, 'Henry Shelton Sanford', 212.
25 Toby Joyce, 'The American Civil War and Irish nationalism', *History Ireland*, 4:2 (summer 1996), 38–9.
26 Joseph M. Hernon, 'Irish sympathy for the southern confederacy', *Éire–Ireland*, 2:3 (1967), 74.
27 NARA, D/S, USB, 2, 3, T368, Young to Seward, 30 October 1861.

When he first arrived, he was anxious to make speeches on the subject of our troubles to the Irish public, and being snubbed at that, he now wants to enlighten the denizens and citizens of Paddy's Land by furnishing articles to certain newspapers and taking it upon himself to contradict all the slanders on America that appear in the Irish journals.[28]

The *Trent* affair in November 1861 provoked an even stronger reaction and an Anglo-American war seemed possible. Captain Wilkes of the USS *San Jacinto* seized two Confederate commissioners, James M. Mason and John Slidell, from the Royal Mail Packet, *Trent*, in the Bahamas channel on 8 November. They were imprisoned in Boston. When reports of their seizure reached Britain and Ireland, there was an immediate reaction. On the one hand, it was believed that Wilkes was following a long-established Royal Navy practice that had already led to the War of 1812, while on the other, his activities were seen as provocative and nothing less than piracy. The *Trent* affair encouraged the drift of nationalist support toward the Confederate side and the possibility of a war involving Britain. Irish unionists were furious about the insult to the British flag and many desired war too. But there were some who hoped for a peaceful conclusion.[29] West viewed the commissioning of articles by the recently established conservative and unionist *Irish Times*' from the South Carolina-born Edwin De Leon, former US Consul in Alexandria and confidential agent abroad for the Confederate department of State, as evidence of an anti-Union stance. De Leon was a personal friend of President Davis, and Secretary Benjamin gave him $25,000 to pay the press in England and France to report favourably on the Confederacy. De Leon did not admit to conducting propaganda work in Ireland but West suspected that he was subsidising the Dublin press with southern money. Later, West wrote that the *Irish Times* was 'more bitter towards us than nearly the entire press of the United Kingdom'.[30] Devine in Queenstown described the *Cork Examiner*'s editorial position as 'one of the bitterest revilers of the government and persevering advocates of the southern rebellion'.[31] In December, Hammond reported from Dublin that 'there are many influential persons … who sympathise with the secessionists'. He

28 Wallace and Gillespie (eds), *The journal of Benjamin Moran, 1857–65*, ii, 1 November 1861.
29 Kennedy, *The American consul*, 131; LaFeber, *The American age*, 1, 143; Carroll, *The American presence*, 67; Hernon, 'Irish sympathy', 74.
30 NARA, D/S, USD, 4, 4, T199, West to Seward, 21 August 1863; *ORUCN*, ii, 3, Benjamin to Mason, 12 April 1862, 385; NARA, D/S, USD, 4, 4, T199, West to Seward, 12 October 1864. Kennedy, *The American consul*, 127, 129, 136; William C. Davis (ed.), Edwin De Leon, *Secret history of Confederate diplomacy abroad* (Lawrence, 2003), 135–50. De Leon wrote under the pseudonym 'Virginian.'
31 NARA, D/S, USC, 5, 5, T196, Devine to Seward, 15 November 1862.

even doubted his predecessor, Samuel Talbot's support for the northern cause and was critical of his silence. Hammond tried to counter this apparent pro-Confederate propaganda campaign by supplying information about the 'state of American affairs' to 'leading men' who agreed to place favourable articles in the press. He encouraged Seward to launch a propaganda campaign to gather support for the Union cause even though he knew that it might embarrass the Secretary because of his personal compassion for Irish nationalist aspirations. In 1853, Seward as a New York senator, had supported a resolution of sympathy for the imprisoned Young Irelanders, William Smith O'Brien and Thomas Francis Meagher. In the following year, he visited Ireland, described the Irish Act of Union as 'disgraceful' and wished for its 'repeal' and expressed 'a deep interest in the welfare of Ireland'.[32] In Belfast, although Young's first attempt at countering the public pro-Confederacy position was thwarted by Moran, he gave legal texts to newspaper editors which supported the Union's right to search and seize.[33]

War was avoided over the *Trent* affair and Mason and Slidell were released through the diplomacy of Lord Lyons, British minister to the US, and Adams. Nonetheless, both nationalist and unionist attitudes against the Union cause had hardened.[34] Many of the merchant and administration classes became more sympathetic towards the south and increasingly anti-northern. Events in the battlefield had an impact also; even when there were Union victories in 1862, Young found that the 'people here will hardly allow themselves to believe it'.[35] Confederate victories particularly by Robert E. Lee at Bull Run on 29 and 30 August 1862, confirmed for many Irish people that the south was a nation while Lincoln's Emancipation Proclamation in September and the presence of many Irishman among casualties at the battle of Friedricksburg in December, further encouraged nationalist support for the Confederates.[36] Union consuls in Ireland believed that this opposition hampered their intelligence work and furthermore, slowed emigration of potential recruits and workers from Ireland to the Union states. During 1862, Hammond in Dublin found it increasingly difficult to gather intelligence concerning 'suspicious vessels' from customs officials and instead obtained it from 'the lower classes of the people, those who usually emigrate to the United

---

32 *Ibid.*, USD, 3, 3, T199, Hammond to Seward, 3 December 1861; *ibid.*, Hammond to Seward, 29 January 1862; *ibid.*, Hammond to Seward, 22 January 1862. George E. Baker (ed.), *The life of William H. Seward with selections of his works* (New York, 1855), 137; Hernon, *Celts*, 90.
33 NARA, D/S, USB, 2, 3, T368, Young to Seward, 29 November 1861.
34 Carroll, *The American presence*, 67; Hernon, 'Irish sympathy', 74.
35 NARA, D/S, USB, 2, 4, T368, Young to Seward, 14 May 1862.
36 Hernon, 'Irish sympathy', 77; Joyce, 'The American Civil War', 38–9.

States' and waited at the docks.[37] Among the agents Young had to use in Belfast in May 1862, were his clerk and a US citizen, Mr Hopkins, a tea trader.[38] Patrick Devine's informants in Queenstown were 'true and genuine friends of the government' and included people working for the shipping agents and 'rebel' sympathisers namely former Vice Consul Nicholas Seymour in Queenstown and former consular agent, Isaac Arthur based further along the coast in Crookhaven.[39] This Union intelligence network had failed to stop the building and departure of CSS *Alabama* and CSS *Oreto* (later renamed the *Florida*), on 10 March 1862. However, a legal precedent had been set. Consul Dudley and Minister Adams ensured that the British government prevented the delivery of further vessels to the Confederates by presenting proof of violations of British domestic law. The gunboat *Alexandra* built by William Miller of Liverpool and two turreted iron-clad rams built by Laird and sons in Birkenhead, never reached the Confederate navy.[40] The combination of systematic intelligence gathering and persistent diplomacy ensured that of the 214 ships commissioned by the Confederacy only five European-built, warships became active.[41] The last delivery, the CSS *Shenandoah*, built on the Clyde river in Glasgow, Scotland, was still attacking Union ships in the Pacific ocean in late June 1865 when its captain learned of the surrender of all other Confederate forces. No ships were recorded as having been built in Ireland but newly built ships came into Queenstown for supplies during trials though vessels were bought in Ireland for Confederate use as blockade-runners.

Immediately after the naval blockade was installed in April 1861, the Confederate government resorted to a variety of methods to avoid it and continue its export of cotton and tobacco and to import war supplies. The principle blockade-running routes were to and from Bermuda, Nassau and the southern ports of Wilmington, Charleston and Savannah. Initially, the Confederate government permitted privately owned vessels to run the blockade and make significant profits. In May 1861 the *Ivanhoe* and *Caphas Starrett* arrived in Belfast port from New Orleans under the flag of the 'insurrectionary rebellious and treasonable' Confederate government and in violation of the Union blockade.

37 NARA, D/S, USD, 3, 3, T199, Hammond to Seward, 5 June 1862. Hammond reported on a counterfeiting of treasury bills operation in August 1862. *Ibid.*, Hammond to Seward, 14 August 1862.
38 *Ibid.*, USB, 1, 4, T368, Young to Seward, 2 May 1862.
39 *Ibid.*, USC, 5, 5, T196, Devine to Seward, 17 July 1862; *ibid.*, Arthur to Seward, 3 February 1863; *ibid.*, 6, 6, T196, Eastman to Seward, 4 May 1864.
40 For further see Foster, 'The diplomats', 181–91.
41 John de Courcy Ireland, 'The Confederate States Navy, 1861–5: The Irish contribution', *Mariner's Mirror: Journal of the Society for Nautical Research*, 66 (1980), 259.

Adams instructed Theodore Frean to refuse to recognise the crew lists or authenticate the ships' cargo from the 'state of Louisiana ... now known to be in a state of open rebellion'. Frean was determined to 'uphold the Union and vindicate the constitution and laws of the United States'.[42] In the same month, Union consuls were instructed by Seward to gather intelligence and information about vessels sold as blockade-runners and the kind of assistance given to such vessels.[43]

Early in 1862 Hammond reported that the steamer *Herald* which travelled between Dublin and Liverpool had been sold to Cunard, Wilson and Company in Liverpool for the 'service of the rebels'. Subsequently, the steamer 'very suddenly' left Dublin port at night for an unknown destination. Hammond learned it had gone to Liverpool 'to fit out as a "privateer" or to take cargo and then try to run the blockade'. The steamer was well known in Europe because of its speed and Hammond felt that if 'the rebels have bought her they may do much mischief'. He could not establish its destination because there was 'silence' in Dublin among the mercantile classes. Adams and Dudley confirmed that the *Herald* was loading a cargo in Liverpool for Bermuda where it was expected to try and break the blockade. The *Herald* left Liverpool for Charleston on 15 February but had to stop into Falmouth four days later because of severe weather. Hammond hoped that this delay would give the Union's blockade squadron time to capture it when it eventually arrived off the Confederate coast. He reported on 1 March that it was heading for Savannah and under full steam would make one and half miles in one hour. It eventually got through a yet ineffective blockade and its captain, Lewis Mitchell Coxetter became one of the most successful blockade-runners.[44] A few months later on 7 May, Young in Belfast reported that the *Adela*, a small, swift steamer operating between Belfast and Scotland owned by a member of the Malcolmson family from Portlaw, county Waterford, had been bought by Mr McDowell residing in Dublin but formerly of New Orleans. The Malcolmson firm's steamship interests in Ireland, England and Scotland were built on the famous cotton mill founded by David Malcolmson at Portlaw in 1826. With the onset of

---

42 NARA, D/S, USB, 2, 3, T368, Frean to Seward, 30 May 1861; Ó Gráda, *Ireland*, 278–81; NARA, D/S, USB, 2, 3, T368, Adams to Frean, 4 June 1861. Moran was more succinct 'Mr. Frean can recognise no clearance but one from our US officer'. Wallace and Gillespie (eds), *The journal of Benjamin Moran, 1857–65*, ii, 4 June 1861; NARA, D/S, USB, 2, 3, T368, Frean to Seward, 5 June 1861.
43 Foster, 'The diplomats', 190.
44 NARA, D/S, USD, 3, 3, T199, Hammond to Seward, 12, 14, 21 February 1862; *ibid.*, Hammond to Seward, 1 March 1862; *ibid.*, Hammond to Seward, 11 December 1862; Glen N. Wiche (ed.), *Dispatches from Bermuda: the Civil War letters of Charles Maxwell Allen, United States Consul at Bermuda, 1861–1888* (Kent, 2008), 48.

the Civil War, the family supported the Confederacy because of their business interests and the firm attempted to break the Union blockade. Consequently, the sale of *Adela* into the service of the Confederacy can be seen as another sympathetic gesture towards the southern cause. Immediately after he received the news, Young sent word to Hammond in Dublin who confirmed that the *Adela* was ready to run the blockade with English goods and to return with cotton. Young's agents were busy with other business and he found it 'nearly impossible' to find out more information; 'my enquiries were met universally by negatives'. Consequently, he employed Hopkins, a tea trader, to board the *Adela* in Belfast on the pretext of securing a passage. Hopkins learnt that the vessel would be departing immediately but he could not discover the destination although Young believed it to be Bermuda. He indicated also that a company had been formed to buy similar vessels. Eventually the *Adela* was captured by the Union side, news which heartened Young.[45] Young and Hammond's reports along with all other rumours, affidavits and vessel descriptions were sent to Frederick Seward, Assistant Secretary of State.[46] He collated, printed and transmitted the information to the Navy Department and the North Atlantic Blockading Squadron. This meant that the captain of a blockader off the Carolina coast might know the name and description of a new blockade-runner before it had arrived in the area.

Union naval victories in April and May 1862 at New Orleans and Norfolk greatly increased the effectiveness of the Union blockade off the southern coastline and reduced revenue for the Confederate states by preventing cotton sales. But this did not deter blockade-runners and the detection efforts of the Union consuls. In June, Devine reported from Queenstown that nine vessels had departed from there laden with 'contraband of war' for the southern rebels and destined for Nassau. The local customs officials would not give him any additional information. But this excuse was unacceptable to Seward who expressed 'surprise to receive no information whatever in regard to several vessels lately in the harbour of Queenstown'. His officials had learnt from other US consuls, newspapers and a government official visiting that blockade-runners were 'loaded with arms and munitions of war purchased for the rebels'. Devine was charged with 'gross dereliction of duty' and warned to be 'more on the alert' to obtain and transmit important information to

---

45 NARA, D/S, USB, 2, 4, T368, Young to Seward, 7, 14 May 1862; *ibid.*, USD, 3, 3, T199, Hammond to Seward, 8 May 1862; *ibid.*, P. Hammond to Seward, 22 July 1862; *ibid.*, 22, 29 May 1862; *ibid.*, USC, 5, 5, T196, Young to Seward, 16 August 1862.
46 Findling, *Dictionary*, 439.

the government, otherwise he would be reported to President Lincoln 'for immediate removal'. Devine explained it was 'hard and difficult to obtain information' because of the many 'obstacles, impediments, difficulties and obstructions ... thrown in the way by government officials and others ... who sympathise with the rebels and their cause'. He also blamed Minister Adams to whom he had sent intelligence for not crediting him in his reports to Washington. But he promised to do better and embarked on a tour of US consular offices in London, Liverpool, Bristol and Cardiff. The rebuke produced more detailed and frequent reports from Devine including one on the *Alabama*, and another on the *Cornubia* which was taking on coal from Seymour's stores in Queenstown prior to running the blockade. Devine reported the arrival of the *Peterhoff* in Queenstown in October from Nassau. He had discovered that the vessel was bound for Liverpool with a cargo of cotton it had received from two other steamers that had successfully evaded the blockade. Owned by L. Pearson of Hull in England, Devine expected the *Peterhoff* to do the same in the future.[47] Towards the end of the year, the *Despatch*, a fast-sailing vessel based at Dundalk, sailed from Liverpool and the *Havelock*, a fast steamer, bought in October in Dublin left for its 'illegitimate business' in early November. It headed first to Glasgow and then to Nassau.[48] Devine in Cork confirmed the purchase of the *Havelock* owned by the Glasgow and Dublin Steam Company and the *Princess Royal* by the Glasgow and Liverpool Company, 'on Confederate account'.[49]

In November, former US Consul Hugh Keenan now living in Balieboro, county Cavan, informed Seward about the arrival of the *Eagle* in Belfast. It had carried passengers up and down the river Clyde in Scotland but was being refitted in Belfast to carry contraband cargo into the southern states. Subsequently, Young's agents learned from the crew that gunpowder was brought from London for the *Eagle*, it was to leave Belfast in early November for Madeira, then on to Nassau and then to a creek or river near Charlestown, South Carolina. Young spent two nights outdoors watching the vessel in case the gunpowder was taken on board. The *Eagle* finally left Belfast in early December but bad weather forced it into Dublin before heading to Queenstown for coal. A week later, Hammond in Dublin circulated details about its colour, insignia

---

47 NARA, USC, 5, 5, T196, Devine to Seward, 24 June 1862; *ibid.*, Devine to Seward, 17 July 1862; *ibid.*, Devine to Seward, 2 August 1862; *ibid.*, Devine to Seward, 14 August 1862; *ibid.*, Devine to Seward, 16 October 1862.
48 *Ibid.*, USD, 3, 3, T199, Hammond to Seward, 16 October 1862; *ibid.*, Hammond to Seward, 12 November 1862; *ibid.*, Hammond to Seward, 4 December 1862.
49 *Ibid.*, USC, 5, 5, T196, Devine to Seward, 15 November 1862; *ibid.*, *Cork Examiner*, 5 November 1862.

and design. He felt that the only reason the southerners had purchased it was because of its speed. He had also learnt that its captain had offered very high wages to obtain a pilot familiar with the Confederate coastline but had failed.[50] Hammond reported there were 'parties now in Dublin trying to buy other steamers and schooners ... to use in evading the blockade'.[51] Others ports also saw business, such as Waterford which was used as a coaling stop for the *Per* a blockade-runner.[52] By 1863 almost every major port in Ireland had dealt with traffic relating to the civil war. Furthermore, consular intelligence work highlighted first, the opportunism of Irish and British shipowners and merchants who quickly moved to profit from running the blockade and second, the authorities' tolerance of these activities which questioned British neutrality.

Despite a strengthened blockade, in 1863 there was evidence of continued Confederate success. In January and February, Seward received extensive reports from Devine and Eastman on the arrival into Queenstown of the blockade-runners, *Granite City*, *Emma*, *Gertrude*, *Banshee*. Eastman also provided hand drawings of the *Gertrude*, *Emma* and *Neptune* vessels.[53] In March, the *Fanny Lewis* arrived in the southern port from Wilmington, North Carolina, 'having run the blockade' with a cargo of cotton resin and pitch to be discharged at Liverpool. Hugh Keenan reported in June on the *Heroine* that had been purchased by rebel agents in Belfast and was being fitted out to run the blockade.[54] Two months later, the Confederate diplomatic representative, James Mason and his secretary, James McFarland, were in Dublin intent on commissioning two iron-clad Clyde built steamers then in Kingstown harbour as blockade-runners.[55]

Eastman also believed there was an increase in Confederate activity in Queenstown. On foot of receiving intelligence 'under oath', he informed British Rear Admiral Lewis Jones on 10 August 'that there is a strong suspicion that a vessel is about to receive her crew off this port and also that said vessel is intended to prey upon our commerce'. He asked Jones to detain the vessel 'until you are satisfied she and her crew are bound on

---

50 NARA, D/S, USD, 3, 3, T199, Keenan to Seward, 7 November 1862; *ibid.*, 4, T368, Young to Seward, 4 November 1862; *ibid.*, Hammond to Seward, 4 December 1862; *ibid.*, Hammond to Seward, 11 December 1862.
51 *Ibid.*, Hammond to Seward, 4 December 1862.
52 *Ibid.*, USC, 5, 5, T196, Eastman to Seward, 24, 29 January 1863.
53 *Ibid.*, Devine to Seward, 7, 15 January 1863, 5, 25 February 1863; *ibid.*, Eastman to Seward, 7, 15 January 1863, 3, 25 February 1863; *ibid.*, Eastman to Seward, 9, February 1863.
54 *Ibid.*, Eastman to Seward, 14 March 1863; *ibid.*, Keenan to Seward, 20 June 1863.
55 *Ibid.*, USD, 4, 4, T199, West to Seward, 21 August 1863.

legitimate business'.[56] Eastman believed there were several rebel officers in the port waiting for a steamer from Glasgow to put men on board. But he informed Adams that he could not 'get at the facts'.[57] Meanwhile Jones asked for 'some definite information on the description ... that may lead to the identity of the vessel'. Eastman regretted that outside of knowing that it was a screw steamer, had left the north of England and was en route to Queenstown to collect men already there, his information was 'not sufficient' to give an accurate description. He urged Jones to make his own inquiries, which would find his 'suspicions to be well-founded'.[58] It is unclear whether Jones followed this course but he reacted quickly. On 10 August he instructed Frederick Cassell, Customs Collector in Queenstown, to display a notice in the Customs House and the Shipping Office stating that 'any person or persons who shall be found aiding or abetting the shipments of any men for the purpose above mentioned [privateering against American commerce] will be prosecuted as an offender against Her Majesty's Proclamation of the 13th May 1861'. Second, he directed Captains Codd of HMS *Hawke* and Shadwell of HMS *Hastings* 'to have a gun boat ready to act if required to prevent a crew being shipped from this port' and third, on the following day HMS *Magpie* was sent to cruise off the harbour and if any vessel of a 'suspicious character' approached within the three mile limit and was found acting in contravention of British law, it was to be examined. If its register and other papers were unsatisfactory, or if its equipment 'lends to an inference that the object is to collect a crew for the purpose of privateering' it was to be detained and a report immediately sent to Jones. Additionally, if a boat or craft had evaded detection in the port and the *Magpie* found it to be 'conveying men to a suspected vessel in the offing', all parties would be arrested.[59] The gunboat was sent out but nothing happened. However, Eastman discovered that the CSS *Florida*, having just burned a vessel, arrived at a 'point near the port' early on 18 August and landed three officers. Eastman was convinced this accounted for the Confederate movements in Queenstown while Moran saw it as connected to the 'contemplated departure of rebel rams from Liverpool' perhaps as part of a convoy for them. Eastman's 'bomb' as Moran described this latest information, failed to stop the *Florida* from going

56 The National Archives (hereafter TNA), London, United Kingdom, Admiralty (hereafter ADM) 1/5814 1863, Eastman to Jones, 10 August 1863.
57 Wallace and Gillespie (eds), *The journal of Benjamin Moran*, 10 August 1863, 1196.
58 TNA, ADM1/5814 1863, Jones to Eastman, 10 August 1863; *ibid*., Eastman to Jones, 10 August 1863.
59 *Ibid*., Jones to Cassell, 10 August 1863; *ibid*., notice; *ibid*., J. Fanning for Cassell to Jones, 10 August 1863; *ibid*., Jones memo to Codd and Shadwell, 10 August 1863; *ibid*., Jones to Codd and Shadwell, 11 August 1863.

about its business of ensuring that the silver bars its crew had taken from the *Benjamin F. Hoxie*, an American ship, arrived safely in Liverpool, were forwarded to Southampton and on to Paris for smelting to the benefit of the Confederate government. Nonetheless, Adams telegraphed the Madrid embassy so that the USS *Kearsarge* could be sent after the *Florida*.[60] Eastman and Admiral Jones did not prevent the *Florida* from disembarking officers at Queenstown but the episode reveals the importance of securing reliable information and how the Queenstown posting was central to the Union's strategy.[61]

In 1863, Eastman's task had become more difficult because Robert Dowling had been appointed the Confederate commercial agent in Queenstown. Dowling, a former US Consul there from 1859 to 1861, possessed useful local knowledge and had vital contacts in the Cork district. From the beginning of the war, he had not concealed 'his sympathy for the southern cause.'[62] Once appointed, he set up office in Seymour's business premises where he flew the Confederate flag. Eastman believed that Dowling helped procure coal and supplies for blockade-runners from local merchants who were 'all in favour of the Southern cause' and had influenced the *Cork Examiner* to become 'completely pro-southern'.[63] Three prominent Queenstown merchants, Messrs Seymour, Scallen and Cummings passed on whatever information came their way to Dowling and he became a conduit between them and a network of pursers on the Inman-owned steamers trading between Richmond, New York and Queenstown, and Confederate ministers in London and Paris.[64] One of his informants was a Mr Fearnagh, the purser on the Inman line (for which Seymour was also a ticket agent). Eastman advised Seward to have a 'good detective' watch him when he arrived in New York by the *City of London* at the end of July 1863.[65] Within a few months, Eastman wrote that the 'merchants of Queenstown ... are all in favour of the southern cause as well as most of the wealthy inhabitants who believe nothing except what they read in the London *Times*'. The port had 'become a

---

60 Wallace and Gillespie (eds), *The journal of Benjamin Moran*, 18, 20, 23 August 1863, 1199.
61 TNA, ADM1/5814 1863, Jones to Secretary of Admiralty, 11 August 1863. In 1864, Eastman learned that the crew of the *Florida* off the Cork coast, was 'in a state of mutiny.' Wallace and Gillespie (eds), *The journal of Benjamin Moran*, 29 October 1864, 1343.
62 NARA, D/S, USC, 5, 5, TI96, Keenan to Seward, 7 August 1863.
63 Thomas J. Ryan, 'Out of Ireland into the Union army: the battle over Irish emigration', *The Irish Sword*, 23:91 (summer 2002), 13; NARA, D/S, USC, 6, 6, T196, Eastman to Seward, 4 May 1864.
64 NARA, D/S, USC, 6, 6, T196, Eastman to Seward, 4 May 1864.
65 *Ibid.*, 5, 5, T196, Eastman to Seward, 11 July 1863.

very unpleasant place for a consul to reside' and he requested permission to move the consulate to Cork city.[66] In the interim, he continued his work.

Much of the blockade-running was in the hands of private individuals and companies. However, in 1863 when Confederate leaders discovered that some ships were trapped in foreign ports and that some contained luxury rather than vital supplies, there was a change in policy. Beginning in 1864, more than one hundred vessels were bought either solely by the government or in partnership with private companies and the southern government instituted its own system of blockade-running. Confederate orders helped British shipbuilders keep full order books during the war.[67] West reported in November that thirty-six steamers had left within the previous nine months to run the blockade.[68] But many of the rebel ships turned out to be 'unfit, unlucky or untimely' and few were successful.[69] Nevertheless, this new Confederate policy led Seward to issue more detailed instructions to his consuls in early 1864. Now they should report any 'person who may have given aid to the rebellion by furnishing blockade-runners or munitions of war'. The directive had little relevance to the Union consuls in Ireland as most had continuously reported on blockade-running. By April 1864, Young was able to state that his port had not been 'heavily implicated'; four vessels had been sold out of Belfast from the beginning of the war to run the blockade and two of them were sold purely for profit, rather than for political motivation. But his intelligence work and that of other consuls, was still hampered by their having 'few friends'.[70]

West found himself in a similar situation. Adams telegraphed him in September 1864 'to look after a vessel at Limerick, said to be taking in arms and clothing for the rebels'.[71] On Thursday 27 October, the blockade-runner, *Evelyn*, arrived at nearby Foynes and proceeded to take on a cargo of ready-made army clothing from the Limerick Clothing Company owned by Peter Tait. The vessel took on coal and departed the following day. West believed that the arms must have been hidden inside the bales and cases but the Customs officials did not conduct an internal search of the cargo and the Limerick Consular Agent Michael

66 Ibid., 6, 6, T196, Eastman to Seward, 4 may 1864.
67 Peter Barton, 'The first blockade runner and "another *Alabama*"': some Tees and Hartlepool ships that worried the Union', *The Mariner's Mirror*, 81:1 (February 1995), 61.
68 NARA, D/S, USD, 4, 4, T199, West to Seward, 9 November 1864.
69 Foster, 'The diplomats', 190.
70 NARA, D/S, USB, 4, 4, T368, Young to Seward, 20 April 1864.
71 Wallace and Gillespie (eds), *The journal of Benjamin Moran*, ii, 21 September 1864.

Ryan failed to get any other information.⁷² Seward believed that blankets and army clothing, manufactured in Cork and Limerick factories, were delivered to the southern states along with arms. When the war ended again he demanded evidence of payment to Tait or others and when none was found, the Union government could not 'touch' either the contractor or manufacturers.⁷³ Moreover, the absence of a professional agent occasionally resulted in incorrect intelligence being gathered.⁷⁴ The *Lucian Victoria*, owned by Valentine O'Connor, a merchant of 3 Beresford Place in Dublin, took on a cargo of ale, porter and linens in Dublin. Hammond was suspicious because O'Connor had resided in Richmond and previously failed to evade the blockade. However, the vessel went straight to New York to deliver its shipment and collect a lucrative cargo of grain.⁷⁵ The *Pearl* arrived into Queenstown, heading for Cork city to take on 'powder'. Devine's conclusion – 'no doubt she intends to run the blockade' – which he applied also to the *Antonia* turned out to be untrue. He had obtained information on both these vessels from an employee of Confederate-sympathiser, Seymour.⁷⁶

Throughout the period, Union consuls lobbied for funds to establish a paid intelligence service modelled along the lines of Minister Sanford's intelligence and espionage system. Consul John M. Jackson in Halifax, Nova Scotia, supported the idea.⁷⁷ As early as August 1862, Young in Belfast wanted 'to employ a private observer at their discretion' because 'from the general public we can learn little'.⁷⁸ In the following year, William West who now operated between the Galway and Dublin consulates, suggested to Seward that one individual be paid to supervise and co-ordinate the intelligence activities of all consuls in Ireland.⁷⁹ The requests were unsuccessful, presumably because Sanford's work was already funded and his intelligence reports were circulated to the blockading squadrons.⁸⁰ But Young did not give up. In 1864, when Seward asked all consuls for information about persons selling vessels as blockade-

---

72 NARA, D/S, USD, 4, 4, T199, West to Seward, 29 October 1864; Wallace and Gillespie (eds), *The journal of Benjamin Moran*, ii, 29 October 1864.
73 NARA, D/S, USC, 6, 6, T196, Eastman to Seward, 7 December 1865.
74 Foster, 'The diplomats', 183–4.
75 NARA, D/S, USD, 3, 3, T199, Hammond to Seward, 14 February 1862; *ibid.*, Hammond to Seward, 1, 13 March 1862; *ibid.*, Hammond to Seward, 30 April 1862; *Thom's Directory*, 1862.
76 NARA, D/S, USC, 5, 5, T196, Devine to Seward, 29 October 1862; *ibid.*, Devine to Seward, 5 November 1862.
77 Foster, 'The diplomats', 187.
78 NARA, D/S, USB, 1, 4, T368, Young to Seward, 20 August 1862.
79 *Ibid.*, USD, 4, 4, T199, West to Seward, 21 August 1863.
80 Owsley, 'Henry Shelton Sanford', 226.

runners or selling munitions of war to the south, Young repeated that the only possible way of knowing 'what may be going on here' would be to pay a secret agent. But he told Seward 'you are aware that I have no such fund at my disposal. I think however that I ought to have such a fund and that it would pay itself fifty times over.'[81] Clearly, he felt that he did not have the time for the work, that his informants were unsatisfactory and that greater effort would bring better results. Seward finally established a 'secret service fund' to allow consuls pay for the activities of spies and informants which augmented Sanford's surveillance system.[82]

Consular reports rarely commented in detail on individual Irish people who assisted either side in the war. But some blockade-runners attracted attention. Eastman interceded with Seward in February 1864 on behalf of Samuel Johnson, a young man from Cork, who had joined the crew of the blockade-runner *Labunce*. The vessel was captured and Johnson was imprisoned in Fort Lafayette. His parents pleaded with Eastman to secure his release as he was their sole support. According to his father, Johnson had been 'induced to go by the promise of high wages', but if released he would look for work as a boiler maker in New York and promise never to run the blockade again. Eastman believed that such an 'act of charity' would create a 'favourable impression in the locality'.[83] Seward agreed as did the Secretary of the Navy Gideon Welles, and the young man was released much to the pleasure of his parents who confirmed that he would 'sin no more'.[84]

Perhaps a better known blockade-runner was the Right Honourable Thomas Conolly, one of the passengers on the CSS *Owl* captained by Captain John Maffitt 'the prince of the privateers', one of the last blockade-runners that reached the North Carolina coastline on 26 February 1865 just before the war ended.[85] Conolly was head of one of the leading protestant élite families, owner of a large estate at Castletown, county Kildare, and a member of the British House of Commons. He thus represented a class who mostly supported the Confederate cause and were critical of the British government's refusal to grant diplomatic recognition to the southern government. Although the Union side were beginning to win the war by autumn 1864, many Irish sympathisers

81 NARA, D/S, USB, 1, 4, T368, Young to Seward, 20 April 1864.
82 Foster, 'The diplomats', 187; Kennedy, *The American consul*, 135. Paid information was eventually obtained from dockhands, workers in shipyards, unemployed sailors, dock masters, Lloyd's register agents, customs inspectors, ships' captains, crews, couriers, purchasing agents, interpreters and private detectives.
83 NARA, D/S, USC, 6, 6, T196, Eastman to Seward, 10 February 1864.
84 *Ibid.*, Eastman to Seward, 22 April 1864.
85 The following is based on Nelson D. Lankford, *An Irishman in Dixie: Thomas Conolly's diary of the fall of the Confederacy* (Columbia, 1988).

including Conolly, still hoped for a Confederate victory. This expectation combined to his indebtedness led him to become involved with others in the purchase of a steamship to run the Union's naval blockade, bring back a cotton cargo and make a huge profit. Conolly joined the *Emily* in Cardiff and set sail on 7 December 1864. By January 1865 Secretary Seward was aware of the *Emily* although not of Conolly's presence on board. In March, Consul Dudley in Liverpool had established that Conolly had arrived safely in Richmond and not been captured by Union forces, as had been rumoured. This news along with a report from the US consul in Havana that Conolly was carrying dispatches, led Seward to instruct Dudley to investigate the matter. When Dudley reported in June, Conolly had returned to Ireland without a cargo and having lost money on the venture. His diaries suggest that he spent much of his time socialising while others such as President Davis and General Robert E. Lee, were unsure why he was there at all. Nonetheless, his position in Irish and British society and politics and the manner of his visit raised some concern in the State Department and among its consuls. At a time when the northern cause appeared to be on the brink of success, with Sherman moving through the Carolinas and Grant preparing for a final defence in Virginia, the possibility of any kind of fillip whether it be political or economic, for the southern side drew Seward's attention.[86]

This intelligence received from the consuls in Irish and British ports, expanded from one where a few individual consuls such as Hammond, West, Young, Devine and Eastman worked on their own and paid privately for information, into the wider Union intelligence and surveillance network functioning throughout Europe. Much to Eastman's satisfaction, more than half of the twenty-five steamers that called at Queenstown in 1863 and reported as possible blockade-runners would be captured by the Union navy.[87] The Queenstown consulate became the centre of a telegraph network whereby Eastman received and passed on intelligence telegrams on the movement of Union and Confederate vessels from captains of northern vessels and consuls in Madrid, Liverpool, Halifax and London, to Adams and Moran in the London legation, to Shelford in Brussels for a time, and to the State and War departments. Indeed Moran in London received so much political, military and financial information in one telegram from Eastman that he had to postpone a social visit and complained that he was 'obliged to do a good deal of work'.[88]

---

86 See Lankford, *An Irishman in Dixie*.
87 *Ibid.*, Eastman to Seward, 14 January 1864.
88 Wallace and Gillespie (eds), *The journal of Benjamin Moran*, 29 October 1864, 1343–4. By the start of 1862 Stanford's surveillance organisation was placed in

Recruiting Union soldiers and labour

Among the other challenges facing the Lincoln government when the war started, was a shortage of soldiers and also workers. Consuls in Europe were instructed to encourage emigration to the northern states from their respective districts. Those who left, it was hoped, would help the Union cause on the battlefield or in the factory. Encouraging Irish people to emigrate to the United States, irrespective of the reason should not have been difficult for Union consuls in 1861. Some 914,000 Irish had entered the US between 1851 and 1860, representing almost 35.2 per cent of total arrivals.[89] Prior to his appointment as consul in Galway in late 1861, William West was determined 'to send out thousands of hardy Irishmen to enrich themselves and this country' in this time of 'unparalleled crisis in our nation's history'.[90] Consequently, he welcomed Seward's instructions in 1861 to encourage emigration, although he hoped it would also bring financial gain if a fee for issuing a passport or visa was introduced.[91] However, he and other consuls faced a number of challenges.

The early 1850s had seen the emergence of the anti-Catholic, anti-immigrant Know-Nothing party but of greater importance was the commercial crisis of 1857 when Irish newspapers warned their readers of the 'utter madness' of emigrating to the US whose economy was in a 'paralysed condition'. Both developments (as is usual with migration movements), did not coincide with a decline in emigration but contributed to it after a delay of about one or two years.[92] Moreover, Lincoln's victory in 1860 posed a dilemma for some northern Democrats including Catholic Irish-Americans, by highlighting their loyalty to the Union but sympathy for the southern secessionists. Another strand of Irish-American opinion, expressed by Irish Protestant Samuel Nimiks, was the wish that war could be avoided but as anti-slavery campaigners they hoped for a northern victory. Moreover, upon the outbreak of the Civil War some Irish in the US and in Ireland warned the potential economic emigrant to stay at home.[93] Letters from Irish settlers were published in the newspapers and others circulated privately. In August, 1861, Ulsterman William McSparron recorded that the 'times is miserable in this countery [sic] … [since] this rebellion has stoped all publick works and men is going about in thousands [sic] that cant get any thing to Do'.

---

the hands of Consul Freeman H. Morse, at London, and Sanford co-ordinated the surveillance work on the Continent. Owsley, 'Henry Shelton Sanford', 219, 220.
89 Blessing, 'Irish', 528.
90 NARA, D/S, USG, 1, 1, T570, West to Seward, 17 August 1861; *ibid.*, 10 July 1861.
91 *Ibid.*, West to Seward, 8 January 1862; *ibid.*, 16 August 1862.
92 Arnold Schrier, *Ireland and the American emigration* (Chester Springs, 1997), 8.
93 Ural Bruce, *The Harp*, 50, 51, 53.

A few months later in November, Maurice Sexton, a Cork carpenter in Boston, warned his brother in Ireland, 'the business of the country is wholly prostrate, nothing ding [sic] in any le[level] of business or other industrial implowment [sic], and all the people who have lived by their labour and only from hand to mouth ... are gone to the war'. After the first battle of Bull Run in July 1861 when the Confederates were victorious, warnings about the lack of employment were tinged with an idea of the fate that awaited the Irish emigrant if he joined either Confederate or Federal army. Patrick Dunny in Philadelphia wrote to his family in county Carlow about two regiments that faced each other and whose casualties were 'grivious to every Irishman'. Some Irish newspapers reported that it would be foolish to emigrate to a country where war had broken out, emigrants could be 'preyed upon by ruthless recruiting agents' and as soldiers might end up fighting other Irishmen in a war of 'no concern to them'. In October 1862, the *Kilkenny Journal* printed a letter from an Irish farmer in Prairie Springs, Iowa, who expected one or both of his sons to be drafted soon.[94]

The impact of these dire predictions, particularly those published in the *Freeman's Journal*, the most popular newspaper in Ireland, was immediate. In early 1862, West reported from Galway that 'there are no emigrants leaving this port at present'. He believed this was due to the 'impression industriously made by those unfavourable to us, that no one could with prudence and safety emigrate to the US during the present disturbances which are generally supposed to extend all over the country, both north and south'. He felt that 'priests, press, and landlords' were generally opposed to emigration at the time even though the country was 'impoverished' and 'thousands ... only want the means to join their countrymen in the "far west" and if necessary, fight for the beneficent land of their adoption'. He asked for assistance for funds to purchase books on America which could be placed in public libraries for the education of potential emigrants. He also suggested that the equivalent of the *Galway American* newspaper be established in each province in Ireland to disseminate the Union message.[95] Former Consul Hugh Keenan reported in a similar vein on Dublin where he distinguished between the public's support for the Union cause and emigrating to the 'federal states' and the opposition of politicians to both.[96] West and Keenan had each identified similar reasons to account for assistance given to blockade-

---

94 Schrier, *Ireland and the American emigration*, 34–5, 178 n. 43; Miller, *Emigrants and exiles*, 359.
95 NARA, D/S, USG, 1, 1, T570, West to Seward, 8 January 1862; *ibid.*, 16 August 1862.
96 *Ibid.*, USD, 3, 3, T199, Keenan to Seward, 14 December 1861.

running; the Catholic hierarchy, the nationalist and unionist leadership and their respective newspapers. This climate of opinion also discouraged emigration to the northern states, at least for a period.[97] There were other factors.

Emigrants' motives for departure were a complex mix of the 'encouragement' offered by landlords, philanthropists, government agencies and shipping companies or third-party governments, who offered 'personal, on-the-spot recommendation and assistance' to the potential emigrants.[98] Eastman was in no doubt that the steamship agent was influential with intending emigrants.[99] Another competitor for the emigrant's attention was James Brown, a farmer and surveyor general of New Brunswick, who visited Scotland, Ireland and England in winter 1861–2 to entice emigrants to his province. New Brunswick authorities shared with other British North American colonies a need for settlers and Brown arrived in Dublin in November where he met with John Gray, owner of the *Freeman's Journal*, among others. He delivered eleven lectures in several towns, which were publicised in advance and covered in the newspapers. His standard lecture dealt with the province's location, its history, natural resources, economic progress and ready availability of land. Brown explained that between £200 and £500 would buy sufficient land that after clearance and improvement would make a good farm. Those who did not have capital were entitled to a grant of 100 acres of land at a cost of 2*s*. 5*d*. per acre which could be paid for in money or labour over a four-year period. Brown tailored his arguments to suit his audience but not all the lectures were fully attended, nor were all audiences receptive. In some places he competed with others such as T. L. Nichol whom he encountered in Kilkenny and whose lecture on American opportunities preceded his own. Also he met with 'rowdyism' forcing him to abandon his lecture in Waterford although the Athlone crowd 'were the most orderly' he had met in Ireland. Newspaper coverage was patchy and some times reported only the negative parts of his lectures. In Dublin, the *Evening News* of 11 November criticised Brown's reference that Ireland 'was most likely to rise and become prosperous' thereby raising doubts that such might not happen. The *Newry Telegraph* noted his concern that the 'American difficulty' should not spread to the northern territories because they would be in a 'pretty fix'.[100]

97 Joyce, 'The American Civil War', 38–9; Hernon, 'Irish sympathy', 72–5.
98 Miller, *Emigrants and exiles*, 134; quoted in Martin Hewitt, 'The itinerant emigration lecturer: James Brown's lecture tour of Britain and Ireland, 1861–2', *British Journal of Canadian Studies*, 10:1 (1995), 103.
99 NARA, D/S, USC, 6, 6, T196, Eastman to Seward, 6 September 1864.
100 Hewitt, 'The itinerant emigration lecturer', 103–19.

Protecting the Union: American Civil War, 1861–5 127

Brown enjoyed some success. The Glasgow shipping company informed him that his lectures had helped them to send a group of emigrants from Londonderry to St John and that a further sailing was planned. But ultimately Brown was disappointed. Up to 1860, two or three emigrant ships arrived in New Brunswick each year from Ireland. In 1860, 294 emigrants arrived, and rose to 545 in 1861, 548 in 1862 and 649 in 1863. Thereafter the flow declined to 396 in 1864, and 249 in 1865. For all his work, Brown acknowledged that he could not compete with the resources invested by governments of other British colonies particularly Canada, Nova Scotia, Western Australia, Queensland and Victoria. The southern hemisphere colonial governments provided assisted passages and free land grants. The Victoria government publicised its attractions by spending £5,000 on lectures. The Queensland Emigration Office based in London was also operating in Dublin at this time. Brown also felt that while the Civil War had diverted newspaper coverage of emigrant destinations away from America and towards the British colonies, New Brunswick featured little. His message could not match reports of discoveries of gold in Australia and Nova Scotia and positive news from emigrants already in the US.[101] But it was the attractions of Canada that provided his greatest competition and Union consuls encountered the same situation.

In 1862 Canadian government agents offered Irish emigrants free grants of land and peaceful conditions. In May, West sent Seward a circular announcing the establishment of an office by E. J. Charleton, emigration agent for the Canadian government at 25 Upper Sackville Street, Dublin. He sent Adams copies of handbills posted extensively in Galway by the Canadian Colonial Emigration Office which elevated Canada above the US as a superior place of settlement. In the following months West reported on the appointment of Thomas d'Arcy McGee, the former Young Irelander, as minister for emigration in Canada, Charlton's presence in Dublin and a sermon from a Catholic priest in county Kerry who advised parishioners to go to Canada 'where they had British law and British protection'. West was indignant that the Canadian scheme had British government support and hoped his own government would respond. Adams did not protest perhaps because of the more urgent need to build evidence of Confederate ship building in Liverpool.[102] In the following year, posters appeared across the Ulster counties urging people to emigrate to Canada rather than the US and giving details of emigrants

---

101 NARA, D/S, USD, 3, 3, T199, enclosure in West to Seward, 3 March 1864; Hewitt, 'The itinerant emigration lecturer', 103–19.
102 NARA, D/S, USG, 1, 1, T570, West to Seward, 3 May 1862; *ibid.*, West to Seward, 21 June 1862; *ibid.*, 16 August 1862; Wallace and Gillespie (eds), *The journal of Benjamin Moran*, ii, 14 May 1862.

who upon arrival in the US were disappointed and had to join the army. Consul Young complained that Canadian agents were 'not very delicate about publishing slanders about us'.[103] These consular concerns over the lure of Canada, were moderated somewhat by the introduction in the same month of the Homestead acts allowing any settler twenty-one years or more to claim 160 acres of public land provided that he or she had lived on and farmed it for five years. It affected immigration only in that 'aliens' who had declared their intention of becoming US citizens would benefit from its terms but soon enough there was a perception abroad that apart from registration fees, the land was 'free'.[104] Hammond who exercised 'considerable care' and 'judgement' in promoting emigration, felt that the legislation which the *Freeman's Journal* publicised, would greatly encourage departures for the US. But West criticised the measure because many emigrants now believed that they had to accept conscription prior to gaining possession of their land.[105] Nonetheless, in the absence of a formal protest from Adams to the British government about colonial agents' misrepresentation of conditions in the US, West acted. He used his close relationship with James Roche, editor of the *Galway American*, to pen an article quoting a State Department circular that gave 'glad tidings of the prosperous condition of the agricultural, manufacturing and mining interests' in the US and concluded with the claim that 'a true Irishman can never take root in Her Majesty's Siberian province'. Second, West had an article from the *Montreal Witness* newspaper reprinted which counselled prospective emigrants 'not to be led astray' by Canadian government advertisements. Throughout the period, he wrote a regular column in the *Galway American* comprising extracts from his book *The foreigner's book of American knowledge* and from the US Homestead legislation, all of which helped to combat a decline in emigrant numbers to the US and, West believed, 'Americanised its readers and removed a great deal of ignorance that previously existed in regard to our Country and its resources'.[106] Unsurprisingly, Schrier identified the years 1858–62 as a period of decline in Irish emigration to the US as did Miller who identified a decline of forty per cent in Irish departures to the US in 1861 and 1862.[107]

103 NARA, D/S, USB, 2, 4, T368, Young to Seward, 1 April 1863.
104 *Reports of the Immigration Commission, federal immigration legislation: digest of immigration decisions, steerage legislation, 1819–1908, state immigration and alien laws*, 39 (New York, 1970), 19; Thompson, *Cassell's dictionary*, 185.
105 NARA, D/S, USG, 1, 1, T570, West to Seward, 10 April 1863; *ibid.*, USD, 4, 4, T199, Hammond to Seward, 23 April 1863.
106 *Ibid.*, USG, 1, 1, T570, West to Seward, 30 August 1862; *ibid.*, 28 March 1863; *ibid.*, 10 April 1863.
107 Schrier, *Ireland and the American emigration*, 8; Miller, *Emigrants and exiles*, 359.

Table 3.1 Number of overseas emigrants from Ireland to the United States, 1851–65

Year	Number of emigrants
1851	219,232
1855	57,164
1858	31,498
1861	28,209
1862	33,521
1863	94,477
1864	94,368
1865	82,085

Source: *Commission on emigration and other population problems, 1948–1954 Reports* (Dublin, 1954), table 26, 314–16

The early 1860s were difficult years for Irish agriculture with poor weather, ruined crops and evictions particularly in the midland and western counties. The poverty and destitution, guaranteed a continuous interest in emigration and when passage was available, departures.[108] Henry Hammond in Dublin was astonished in spring 1862 by the outflow of people from Kingstown for New York via Liverpool, 'as has not been known for many years'.[109] In May, three passenger vessels left Galway and more emigrants departed daily by railroad, coaches and cars to Dublin and Cork for Liverpool. West concluded 'emigration to the US is not dormant here' so long as 'misery and starvation' was widespread.[110] By way of comparison emigration from parts of Ulster resulted from the 'distress' among linen workers where the disruption of markets unsettled an industry already in decline since the 1840s. Although the flow through Londonderry was interrupted in the summer and autumn of 1861, it soon recovered with mainly weavers, ruined by the cotton famine, emigrating.[111] So, despite all the warnings and forebodings, table 3.1 indicates that emigration to America continued and the volume tripled between 1861–2 and 1863–4.[112]

108 Miller, *Emigrants and exiles*, 359.
109 NARA, D/S, USD, 4, 4, T199, Hammond to Seward, 23 April 1862.
110 *Ibid.*, USG, 1, 1, T570, West to Seward, 8 May 1862; *ibid.*, 26 May 1862.
111 Carroll, *The American presence*, 76; Cooke, *The maiden city*, 140–1; David Fitzpatrick, 'Emigration, 1801–70' in Vaughan (ed.), *New History of Ireland*, v, 640.
112 Schrier, *Ireland and the American emigration*, 35; Miller, *Emigrants and exiles*, 359.

William West was the sole Union Consul in Ireland to express concern about the deplorable conditions on emigrant ships. He visited the *Hiawatha* due to leave Galway for New York with 132 passengers on board and 'could find no ventilation whatever'. He feared the conditions would produce ship fever and other sicknesses, either on board or after landing at Castle Garden and the emigrants would then be 'thrown on the care and expense of our government'. Adults who had paid £4 10s. for the passage were not fully supplied with food for the journey. Clearly West was a supporter of emigration as a remedy for Ireland's ills and a solution to Lincoln's shortage of recruits and workers. He expected three more emigrant ships to leave Galway and urged Seward to subsidise a transatlantic shipping company to meet the emigration and trading demand of the Galway district. Although some destitute immigrants would do little to benefit their new country, West believed most would become 'producers of wealth and population and payers of taxes'.[113] West, like other US consuls, remained critical of accommodation standards on board the vessels. Emigration became an increasingly lucrative business for shipowners and although reduced fares benefited the intending emigrant, they endured atrocious conditions particularly the steerage class passenger, despite the passage of the British Passenger acts. In the interim, West counselled intending emigrants in Galway and Dublin to leave New York as fast as possible and head inland, to settle in rural and not urban areas and appeased their fears about conscription.[114] Rumours circulated throughout Ireland that recently arrived emigrants were forced, and also duped, to join the Union army. West issued certificates of citizenship to reassure three intending emigrants that they would not be drafted into the army upon arrival in the US.[115] After March 1863 when conscription was introduced causing riots in New York, Eastman was 'often called upon' for the same service but he always refused, explaining that immigrants were not liable for the draft upon arrival in the US. He admitted 'still it is unsatisfactory to them'. He felt the only solution was for the State Department to issue a certificate to each intending emigrant outlining their status upon arrival in the US: 'it would be a great inducement to emigration and of course, would not prevent them from volunteering if they wished to'.[116] Young in Belfast refused requests made to him for 'passports' to avoid the draft.[117] Instead

---

113 NARA, D/S, USG, 1, 1, T570, West to Seward, 21 March 1863; *ibid.*, West to Seward, 28 March 1863.
114 *Ibid.*, West to Seward, 28 September 1863.
115 *Ibid.*, West to Seward, Treasury Returns, 1 July to 30 September 1862.
116 *Ibid.*, USC, 5, 5, T196, Eastman to Seward, 27 August 1863.
117 *Ibid.*, USB, 2, 4, T368, Young to Seward, 2 December 1863.

Seward circulated a despatch on 21 September 1863 to help consuls allay the widespread apprehension among intending emigrants.[118] However, in the autumn neither worries about the draft nor the 'largest and best produced' harvest and inducements to grow flax in parts of Cork, stopped the departures. Eastman recorded that 484 steamers called to Queenstown from Liverpool en route to New York and 24,800 passengers embarked from the port. He concluded 'emigration is now flowing as rapidly as ever'.[119] By early 1864 West now based in Dublin, referred to an 'emigration mania'.[120] He welcomed the amendment to the Homestead acts permitting Union veterans who desired to offset military service against the residency requirement to acquire land and the introduction of the Immigration Act on 4 July 1864 that for the first time saw the Lincoln government encourage immigration with direct legislation. The House of Representatives Select Committee that brought in the bill recorded that nearly 1.4 million men aged between 18 and 35 years, had joined the Union forces and created the unprecedented shortage of labour. The legislation authorised immigrant labour contracts whereby an intending immigrant received the costs of transportation and in return pledged his wages for a period not exceeding twelve months. The contract was to be legally binding and was not considered as creating 'the condition of slavery or servitude'. It also provided that no immigrant could be compulsorily enrolled in the military service unless 'he should voluntarily renounce allegiance to the country of his birth and declare his intention of becoming a citizen of the United States'.[121]

Following the law's enactment, it was expected that several companies would be established to deal in immigrant contract labour. However, the Bureau of Immigration in New York was soon criticised in Congress because it was working only with the American Emigrant Company. West complained in December 1864 that he was contacted daily by young men who would enter into 'any contract' to get to the US but the company was not operating in Ireland.[122] Miller indicates that 'relatively few' Irish emigrated as contract labourers because few investors were willing to risk paying for Irish emigrants whose combative reputation made them less reliable employees than other emigrants and at other times there was

---

118 *Ibid.*, USD, 4, 4, T199, West to Seward, 28 November 1863.
119 *Ibid.*, USC, 6, 6, T196, Eastman to Seward, 15, 28 October 1863.
120 Miller, *Emigrants and exiles*, 359. Fitzpatrick notes that the US became the majority destination for Irish emigrants only in the 1860s. David Fitzpatrick, 'Emigration: 1801-1921' in Glazier (ed.), *The encyclopedia*, 255. NARA, D/S, USD, 4, 4, T199, West to Seward, 30 April 1864.
121 *Reports of the Immigration Commission*, 20-3.
122 *Ibid.*

a sufficient pool of unskilled labour.[123] However, it is clear from West's reaction that both the immigration legislation and the promise of 'free land' had a psychological impact on the potential emigrant by adding to the attraction of life in the US, if any were required.

Joining the Union army demonstrated political allegiance but there were financial benefits for the soldier and his family: a bounty of between $50 and $1,000, a steady income and the possibility of a pension were all on offer.[124] But encouraging emigration for enlistment purposes was more problematic for Union consuls. As early as May 1861, Union Minister Sanford in Brussels had received many applications from men who wanted to join up and believed it to be the same in other legations.[125] In Dublin, in March, July and August 1862, 'every day numerous applications' were made to Hammond for a free passage to America to join 'our army'. They were made by 'stout, healthy, young men who would make fine soldiers'. Soon he became exasperated and almost convinced himself that the government was paying the passage. He asked Seaward if the government 'has any Agent for that purpose' and if so, he wanted to send him the 'large numbers'.[126] The Union government had not instituted a scheme and was acutely aware of the consequences should evidence of Union encouragement for enlistment purposes be proven. Consuls could not be involved in recruiting in foreign countries because first, foreign authorities might be outraged at a reduction of manpower for their own armies and the British Foreign Enlistment Act prohibited foreign recruitment of British subjects. Transgressions would damage diplomatic relations.[127]

Confederate officials such as A. Dudley Mann, Confederate commissioner to Belgium, had told Secretary Benjamin that Union recruiting agents were working in Ireland and central Europe. Moreover, De Leon, the Confederate propagandist, had noticed that the Union government was using its consuls and paying private individuals to encourage enlistment in Ireland. Indeed New York State Republican leader and editor, Thurlow Weed, conducted a joint mission with the Catholic Archbishop of New York, Tyrone-born John Hughes to 'speak authoritatively, though unofficially, on the views and wishes of the North' in England and France in 1861–2. A few weeks after Mann communicated with Benjamin, De

123 Miller, *Emigrants and exiles*, 356–7.
124 Phillip Thomas Tucker, *The Confederacy's fighting chaplain: Father John B. Bannon* (Tuscaloosa and London, 1992), 160; Ural, *The harp*, 146, 60.
125 Charles P. Cullop, 'An unequal duel: Union recruiting in Ireland, 1863–1864', *Journal of Civil War History*, 13:2 (1967), 103.
126 NARA, D/S, USD, 3, 3, T199, Hammond to Seward, 3 April 1862; *ibid.*, Hammond to Seward, 31 July 1862; *ibid.*, Hammond to Seward, 14 August 1862.
127 Kennedy, *The American consul*, 130.

Leon noted that Hughes was already in Ireland recruiting for the Union side.[128] Thus, Seward's response to his enthusiastic consuls' call to assist them with recruitment in summer 1862 had to be carefully worded. On 8 August all consuls were instructed to encourage emigration to the north, and to draw emigrants' attention to the work opportunities in the north. However, no passage money could be offered. Seward warned them to avoid any activity that might be seen as recruiting including 'making addresses to the public anywhere'.[129] Moran in London responded: 'this … it strikes me, must be inoperative'.[130] Indeed, Union Consul General John Bigelow in Paris persisted and asked for information about bounties paid to volunteers because it 'might induce a considerable emigration' especially from those ports 'whence the bounty money would defray the expenses of the voyage'.[131] It certainly would have been effective in Ireland as evidenced from his counterparts' responses to Seward's instruction. Hammond replied to Seward on 28 August that many of the applicants for a free passage were 'fine able-bodied looking young men' who would be of 'great service to our country at this time'. He was convinced that many more would emigrate if given the fare or the Union government chartered ships to come direct to Irish ports.[132]

West responded that soldiers of a militia regiment drilled in Galway during August 1862 and would 'most cheerfully emigrate to the US' and presumably enlist, if they had the passage. He proposed in October that the Union government order merchant vessels to carry one adult male free for every fifty tons, though the emigrant would be expected to provide his own food. He had already negotiated the passage on these terms for a young boy who wanted to join his three brothers in the US army.[133] While Consul Dudley in Liverpool forwarded a proposal from an emigration agent E. Bell, who could guarantee 50,000 Irish recruits for a 'consideration'. But Seward's emphatic reply to Bigelow on 19 September – 'nobody is authorized to do anything or pay anything for once entering into this kind of business there would be no end of trouble' – applied to all consuls. But Seward asked Edwin M. Stanton, Secretary of War, for a schedule of compensation to soldiers which he forwarded to

128 Cullop, 'An unequal duel', 103; De Leon, *Secret history*, 106.
129 Kennedy, *The American consul*, 130; NARA, D/S, USG, 1, 1, T570, West to Seward, 15 November 1862. Many visitors to the US consulate in London wanted a free passage in return for enlisting in the Union army. Manchester Consul Henry Lord also suggested Seward consider a scheme. Ural Bruce, *The Harp*, 203.
130 Wallace and Gillespie (eds), *The journal of Benjamin Moran*, ii, 1 September 1862.
131 Cullop, 'An unequal duel', 104.
132 NARA, D/S, USD, 3, 3, T199, Hammond to Seward, 28 August 1862.
133 *Ibid.*, USG, 1, 1, T570, West to Seward, 30 August 1862; *ibid.*, West to Seward, 4 October 1862.

Bigelow. The latter continued his undercover recruiting work but Union consuls in Ireland, part of neutral Britain, had to be even more careful.[134]

Consular adherence to Seward's instruction was uneven. In September 1862, Devine in Cork allowed Seward's circular on emigration to be published in *Saunders' Newsletter* with the additional comment 'No man is so great a dolt as to believe the object is merely [to] procure skilled labour in agriculture, manufactures and mining. It is human material for the war [that] is needed'.[135] West, inundated with 'many applications' from men wishing to enlist, cancelled a lecture entitled 'America as a field of emigration', that he was going to deliver to the Mechanic's Institute in Galway in November. He also refused to allow the Union flag be displayed at a fundraising meeting to erect a national monument to the deceased nationalist leader, Daniel O'Connell because the British 'Union Jack' was absent and he did not want to get 'mixed up in political questions'. He proclaimed to Seward that he behaved as an 'independent American consul'.[136] However, his political sympathies for and friendships within a group of revolutionary nationalists who unreservedly supported the Union cause represented an indirect contravention of Seward's instruction.

West was friendly with James Roche who had lived in New York for a few years and co-edited with Michael Doheny, the New York *Phoenix*. The paper was founded 'to advocate Irish freedom' by Roche and other members of the New York branch of the Ossianic Society a group dedicated to reviving the Irish language.[137] Roche was also an early member of the National Brotherhood of St Patrick, established in Dublin on 17 March 1861, to 'win for Ireland her freedom'. Among its activities was the organisation of the funeral of Terence Bellew McManus in late 1861. Roche returned to Ireland with the funeral cortège and remained on to edit the *Galway American* newspaper through which he may have met West.[138] Every week during 1862 West sent copies of the newspaper

---

134 Cullop, 'An unequal duel', 103–4.
135 NARA, D/S, USD, 3, 3, T199, Hammond to Seward, 11 September 1862 and enclosure.
136 Kennedy, *The American consul*, 130; NARA, D/S, USG, 1, 1, T570, West to Seward, 15 November 1862; *ibid.*, West to Seward, 6 December 1862; *ibid.*, West to Seward, 11 October 1862.
137 Kenneth E. Nielsen, 'The Irish language in New York, 1850–1900' in Ronald H. Bayor and Timothy J. Meagher (eds), *The New York Irish* (Baltimore, 1996), 264. The Ossianic Society declined during the early years of the Civil War and was soon supplanted by Fenian activity. Nielsen, 'The Irish language', 265.
138 Joyce, 'The American Civil War', 38–9; Hernon, *Celts*, 34; Louis R. Biscegelia, 'The Fenian funeral of Terence Bellew McManus', *Éire–Ireland*, 14:3 (1979), 58; Gerard Moran, 'The National Brotherhood of St Patrick in Britain in the 1860s', *Irish Studies Review*, 7:3 (1990), 325. After the 1848 rising, McManus was exiled to Tasmania,

to the State Department and asked the Secretary to provide a subsidy to alleviate its financial difficulties. West may even have been a regular contributor using the pseudonym 'James M. Burgess' and his own US address in Janesville, Wisconsin.[139] By early 1863, the *Galway American* was vigorously promoting the northern cause and enlistment on the grounds that Irish-American soldiers would fight in Ireland after the war. But in spring 1863 when West and Roche tried to use the *Galway American*'s pro-Union view to win an endorsement from the Lincoln administration for the National Brotherhood's agenda, it provoked strong reactions from the State Department.

One of the four meetings that took place in Ireland to support the abolitionists' cause was organised by the National Brotherhood. Police Superintendent Daniel Ryan reported that advertisements and placards announced the meeting in St Patrick's Hall at No. 3 Henrietta Street in Dublin on 25 May 'for the purpose of adopting an address to the American Republic'. One speaker warned the audience of approximately 200, that if the Irish 'did not exert ourselves and do something very soon, the slaves would beat us out, as they would be free and we would be slaves'. Charles D. Doran, Honorary Secretary, reminded the meeting that while 'sympathising with the Federals, you should regret that such a suicidal war is being carried out by the Confederates'. The address was proposed by Thomas O'Neill Russell and seconded by James Roche who then said the Irish 'had a great interest in the preservation of the American Union as it was a home for them when obliged to flee from the pauper's grave or the poor-house'. A young man named McDonnell proposed that the address should be forwarded to President Lincoln through the American consul at Galway. West knew that regulations prevented him from sending it directly to Lincoln and the proper channel was through Henry Hammond, US Consul in Dublin. But West dispensed with the protocol on the spurious grounds that the address reflected 'popular opinion' in Galway more than Dublin and second, that Galway was geographically closer to the US than Dublin. He failed to copy it to Union Minister Charles Adams in London also. In his cover letter addressed to Seward, he explained that the 'nationalist' organisation was a 'perfectly legal body' and he did not see any thing 'objectionable' in the address. He naïvely expected to get Seward and Lincoln's approval for the organisation.[140]

---

escaped to San Francisco in 1852 and died in November 1861. The Brotherhood was gradually infiltrated by the Fenians and was condemned by the Roman Catholic Archbishop Paul Cullen in December 1862.
139 NARA, D/S, USG, 1, 1, T570, West to Seward, 10 April 1863; *ibid.*, West to Seward, 11 January 1862.
140 NAI, Chief Secretary's Office Registered Papers (hereafter CSORP), 1863/4925,

When Hammond heard of the action, he informed Seward that he had not been asked to forward the address even though the society had its headquarters in Dublin. But he was not surprised because it was a 'political organisation of a very low order' and he had refused all invitations to attend their events. He preferred to associate with government officials rather than with people 'whose every object is to do something distasteful to the government of the kingdom'. He also felt that the address was not the 'unanimous voice of the aristocracy or of the middle class or the poor and labouring class but it is the sentiment of a very small uninfluential body' who wanted American help for an Irish rebellion.[141] Clearly, Hammond was intent on distancing himself from West and from the address and the nationalist movement behind it. Seward's reprimand of West may have surprised him because of his 'friendship' with Seward and the latter's sympathy for the Irish cause. But he failed to understand that the exigencies of the Anglo-American relationship determined that neither Lincoln nor Seward would overtly support Irish nationalists. Seward ordered West not to send any further despatches of a similar nature. On 10 July, West apologised to Seward for the 'oversight', pleading that the 'case was a novel one' and that he had acted in a hurry to help 'our numerous friends' in Ireland. He also apologised to Hammond in Dublin whose feelings, he had 'unconsciously wounded'.[142]

Seward's rebuff did not stop West from trying again. In summer 1863 both West and Roche moved to Dublin to commence publication of the *United Irishman and Galway American*, a successor to the *Galway American*. A few weeks later, West forwarded a second address from Roche on behalf of the National Brotherhood, 'our best and only friends in Ireland', to Lincoln but this time he followed protocol.[143] In the following months, the National Brotherhood, through its newspaper, encouraged emigration and enlistment thus siding with the American Fenian leader, John O'Mahony, and attacked nationalists who supported the opposite view held by James Stephens, the Fenian leader in Ireland. The Brotherhood was the only nationalist organisation to maintain this stance until its demise in mid-August 1864. West and Roche had failed to secure a 'propaganda coup' for the National Brotherhood but the

---

Dublin Metropolitan Police, 26 May 1863; NARA, D/S, USG, 1, 1, T570, West to Seward, 30 May 1863; *ibid.*, Charles D. Doran, Honorary Secretary, National Brotherhood to West, 27 May 1863; *ibid.*, West to Seward, 6 June 1863.
141 *Ibid.*, USD, 4, 4, T199, Hammond to Seward, 28 May 1863.
142 Hernon, *Celts*, 90; NARA, D/S, USG, 1, 1, T570, West to Seward, 10 July 1863; *ibid.*, 15 August 1863.
143 NARA, D/S, USG, 1, 1, T570, West to Seward, 15 September 1863; Joyce, 'The American Civil War', 39.

consul's enthusiasm for the cause was undimmed and he avoided being seen to promote enlistment.[144]

The challenge for West and the other Union consuls, therefore, was to not deter enthusiastic candidates while refusing to actually enlist them. Union consuls remained eager to fulfil their task. Early in 1863, West reported that 'thousands of fine, healthy young men and women in this locality would now gladly seize any opportunity to go to the United States'. A few weeks later, he pressed Seward to introduce the free passage for Irish emigrants, a gesture that would be a 'noble acknowledgement' of the recent casualties among the 'brave, patriotic Irish soldiers and sailors.' Every day in the office and on the streets of Galway, he encountered scenes of poverty and hardship and a desire to escape. Following the departure of the *Hiawatha*, two more emigrant ships were ready to leave at the end of March 'no doubt crowded with emigrants'. Thirteen men left for the US via Liverpool with the intention of joining the Union army upon arrival in New York and another 100,000 would leave if they had the price of the passage.[145] Similarly Hammond in Dublin reported on 29 April that the shipping lines had never carried so many emigrants from Dublin to the US and Australia. In the previous week, 260 had left Dublin for Chicago to work on the railways. Most were farmers but he said that if 'provided [with] the means' many more 'fine, able bodied industrious young men' were ready to leave and presumably enlist.[146] In the same month, Keenan reported from county Monaghan that several young men applied to him to join the Union army largely because of the widespread distress in the locality and absence there of government relief. Thousands were rushing from the countryside to escape the destitution and poverty.[147] Throughout 1863, rumours circulated in Galway and as far south as Cork, that the Union government was offering free passage to men who would enlist in its army.[148] In the northern counties, the merchant classes acknowledged that Union Consul Alexander Henderson did much 'to encourage the current of emigration'.[149] These

144 Joyce, 'The American Civil War', 39. The National Brotherhood did not last beyond mid-August 1864 when James Stephens exerted control over it. The only nationalist organisation that 'unequivocally supported the Union had become defunct.' *Ibid.*; Hernon, *Celts*, 34–5; Ural Bruce, *The Harp*, 200.
145 *Ibid.*, USG, 1, 1, T570, West to Seward, 23 January 1863; *ibid.*, West to Seward, 8 March; *ibid.*, West to Seward, 21 March 1863.
146 *Ibid.*, USD, 4, 4, T199, Hammond to Seward, 29 April 1863.
147 *Ibid.*, USC, 5, 5, T196, Keenan to Seward, 11 April 1863.
148 *Ibid.*, USG, 1, 1, T570, Cornelius Stokes, Youghal, county Cork, to West, 16 November 1862.
149 *Ibid.*, USL, 3, 3, T216, enclosure 'To the Honourable the Senate and House Representatives of the United States Washington' in Henderson to Seward, 3 March 1866.

reports emphasised that the desire to emigrate and to enlist was sufficiently intense among some groups to overcome the lack of sympathy for the Lincoln side felt by most nationalist and Catholic leaders. Others were inspired by the heavy losses endured by General Thomas Francis Meagher's Irish Brigade at Friedricksburg in December 1862 and by news of the New York city draft riots in mid-1863.[150]

While each of the consuls enthusiastically encouraged emigration for both economic and political purposes, the Lincoln administration had to avoid any accusations of enlistment and, therefore, violation of British legislation and the possibility of a further diplomatic crisis. In turn, the British government remained particularly sensitive to accusations of bias towards the Union side not least because of Britain's attempts to recruit soldiers in the US during the Crimean War (1854–6).[151] On 20 November 1862, Russell warned Adams that men were being enticed to enlist with promises of bounty money. On the following day, Adams protested that no violations of British neutrality had been committed by the Union's representatives in British ports. Russell had no evidence to produce but remained suspicious of Adams' denials.[152] Meanwhile because the growing pool of Federal manpower had become a vital weapon in the war, Confederate Secretary of State Benjamin began to focus on gathering hard evidence of illegal Federal recruitment to present to the British government. Indeed in late 1861, Union Consul Henry Hammond had learned that 'there were southerners in Dublin trying to induce certain officers to take commissions in the army of the rebellionists'.[153] But it was not Confederate but rather that of the Federal side that would be problematic.

On 21 March 1863, the Confederate commercial agent and propagandist in London, Henry Hotze sent Benjamin an article from the Liverpool *Albion* which stated 'that recruiting for the Federal armies is carried on to a great extent in Ireland'. He also hired private detectives to dupe Union agents into violations but the plan failed.[154] Benjamin, however, reacted quickly to the news that 'extensive enlistments' were progressing in Ireland. He assumed that Confederate Commissioner to England,

150 Joyce, 'The American Civil War', 39; Miller, *Emigrants and Exiles*, 364.
151 Ged Martin and Ben Kline, 'Cork and the American Civil War: the Queenstown affair of 1863', *Cork Historical and Archaeological Society*, 89 (January–December 1984), 99; NARA, D/S, DIDS, RG59, M77, 75, Marcy to Buchanan, 28 December 1855.
152 Quoted in Martin and Kline, 'Cork and the American Civil War', 99; John B. Heffernan, 'Ireland's contribution to the navies of the American Civil War, 1861–65', *The Irish Sword*, 3 (1957–8) 81–7, 87.
153 NARA, D/S, USD, 3, 3, T199, Hammond to Seward, 3 December 1861.
154 Ignatius L. Ryan, 'Confederate agents in Ireland', *Historical Records and Studies*, 26 (1936), 47; Cullop, 'An unequal duel', 105; De Leon, *Secret history*, xvi.

James M. Mason, had procured 'the necessary evidence to establish the facts' for Earl Russell. Benjamin and Davis wanted the British government to act against 'the official agents of the United States' promoting enlistment in Ireland and breaching British neutrality. His main objective was, of course, to stem the flow of Irish emigrants to work and fight for the Union.[155] Mason believed that Irishmen with prepaid passages and in receipt of small bounties had left from Liverpool with the aim of joining the Union army or working on railways or on farms. But in order to uncover the 'real purpose' of this emigration, Mason had already engaged J. H. Ashbridge, president of the Southern Independence Association in Liverpool, who was 'entirely to be trusted' to employ agents or detectives to obtain evidence of recruiting. Unfortunately, his network failed to uncover clear-cut evidence to offer to the British government. Mason also intended contacting Dowling in Cork to make inquiries but the former consul was in ill-health at this time.[156] Instead Hotze assumed responsibility for ending Federal recruitment in Ireland. Along with other Confederate officials A. Dudley Mann, James D. Bulloch and southern Democrat, lawyer and politician, Lucius Q. C. Lamar, he was convinced that not only was it widespread in Ireland but throughout Europe and in Canada. Hotze intensified his propaganda drive to counteract Federal efforts and told Benjamin that 'legal evidence can only be procured by going to Ireland and duping the recruiting agents'.[157]

The British administration in Ireland also believed that Union recruiting was taking place in the country. On 24 March 1863, notice was given that Conservative member of parliament Lord Henry Thynne would ask Home Secretary Sir George Grey 'whether his attention has been called to a statement that the Federal Government of America are recruiting largely in Ireland; whether that statement is true; and, if so, whether Her Majesty's Government propose to take any steps to prevent such recruiting'. Under-Secretary for Ireland, Thomas Larcom, investigated and responded that the 'latest reports on this subject' offered no evidence. On 28 March, Sir Robert Peel, Chief Secretary for Ireland, informed the House of Commons that 'no reports' had been received about enlistment of recruits in Ireland for the Federal army, although there had been 'rumours on the subject'.[158] However, in the following

155 James D. Richardson (ed.), *A compilation of the messages and papers of the Confederacy including the diplomatic correspondence, 1861–1865*, 2 vols, 2 (Nashville, 1906), Benjamin to Mason, 29 April 1863, 478–9.
156 *ORUCN*, ii, 3, Mason to Benjamin, 4 June 1863; Ryan, 'Confederate agents in Ireland', 46.
157 Ryan, 'Confederate agents in Ireland', 52.
158 House of Commons debate, 26 March 1863, vol. 169, c. 1930, online at http://hansard.millbanksystems.com/ (accessed 18 November 2008); NLI, Thomas Larcom

weeks and months, Dublin Castle authorities kept a close watch. Police in Queenstown commented that 1,200 men sailed in a two-week period for New York and most were 'strong, active, young men' while some were former militia men from Cork, all of whom planned to enlist upon arrival and collect the bounty of between $250 to $300. A further 800 were booked to leave.[159]

Many were leaving to enlist and many more preparing to depart. On 5 April 1863, Captain J. W. Easoines of the Westmeath Rifles Militia asked Larcom whether the intending emigrants could be prevented. He knew that many men were set to depart from Mullingar and to embark at Cork. He enclosed a police report which indicated that a man named De Lacy was in Mullingar and had been enrolling and engaging men for public works in the US except that he measured the breadth of chest and height of men, 'just as Mullingar Militia recruits' were measured. Moreover, men under 5 ft 6in. in height were rejected and he preferred to take only a proportion of married men.[160] Additional newspaper coverage of federal recruiting under the guise of emigration appeared in the following months in the Dublin *Evening Mail*, *Saunders Newsletter* and *Glasgow Herald*. The *Cork Examiner* report of an American 'having all the airs of a military man' recruiting in Mitchelstown and Charleville in county Cork, was reproduced in the Dublin *Evening Post* and *Freeman's Journal*. P. Wallis an emigration officer in Bruff, county Limerick, reported to Dublin Castle that an American agent was also recruiting at Charleville also. The *Clonmel Chronicle* commented on Federal recruiting at Bansha, county Tipperary, while the *Irish Times* ran with the same story into summer 1863. These reports including a denial in the *Evening Mail* 'on the authority of the United States consul in Dublin that the Federal government are recruiting in Ireland', were collected and noted by Larcom's staff.[161] Larcom concluded that while the Union government had not employed agents or individuals, the force of rumour and encouragement from relatives and friends living in the Union states indirectly contributed to widespread recruitment. However he believed that no proceedings could be taken under the Foreign Enlistment Act.[162]

In an effort to appear neutral and to appease Confederate sympathisers particularly among the wealthier classes, Russell wrote again to Adams on 24 April 1863, with reports of Union recruitment published in the

---

Manuscript (hereafter TLM), Ms. 7585, Enclosure in Bland to Larcom, 25 March 1863; *ibid*., Larcom, 25 March 1863; *ibid*., Peel, 28 March 1863.
159 *Ibid*., Graves to Larcom, confidential, copy of police report, 8 April 1863.
160 *Ibid*., Captain and Adjutant J. W. Easoines, Westmeath Rifles, 5 April 1863.
161 NLI, TLM, Ms. 7585; NAI, CSORP, 1863, Wallis note, 26 May 1863.
162 NLI, TLM, Ms. 7585, Larcom to H. Waddington, 10 April 1863.

Cork Examiner. Over 1,200 emigrants had recently sailed from Queenstown to New York and another 800 were booked to sail on the next vessel and, he stated, most were young men going to join the 'northern army'.[163] Adams denied the accusation which his secretary believed relied 'solely on rumour'. Adams regarded the charges, coming soon after his explicit denials, to be 'discourteous'. Seward agreed and wrote on 9 May that he had observed a remarkable increase of Irish immigrants but not one person has been enlisted, directly or indirectly by any agent or under any authority or with any knowledge of his government. Instead they were seduced by 'military ambition', an 'increase of confidence in the Union cause', increasing wage rates and the 'advantage offered to the poor of every land by the homestead law'.[164]

Emigration continued unabated from Queenstown with Eastman reporting on 2 May 'no less than fifteen hundred persons leaving this port this week for New York'. Despite Adams and Seward's disingenuous interpretation, former Consul Keenan sent Seward other newspaper articles which, like the *Cork Examiner*, reported that enlistment in the Union forces continued apace. The *Ulster Observer*, *Waterford News*, *Galway Vindicator* and *Limerick Recorder* all lamented the departure of young men to enlist in the northern armies.[165] It was clear that as long as emigration remained at high levels, British officials in Ireland would closely monitor the Union consuls.

When Confederate Commissioner Mason returned to health and returned to London from Paris, he instructed Dowling in Queenstown 'to collect evidence, if practicable, in regard to the supposed Federal enlistments in Ireland' so that a protest could be presented to Earl Russell.[166] Dowling was vigilant throughout the summer and later reported that he saw 'an enormous number of people in a floodtide of immigration in merchant-immigrant vessels leave for the Northern States' but he gathered no evidence to support a violation of the Enlistment Act.[167] In the meanwhile, Benjamin was sufficiently convinced by the reports and rumours that he decided in early July to send two or three Irishmen to communicate directly with the people and persuade them of the 'folly and wickedness' of volunteering in the 'savage warfare waged against

---

163 Quoted in Martin and Kline, 'Cork and the American Civil War', 100–1.
164 *PRFA first session of the 38th Congress*, Part 1 (Washington, 1864), Seward to Adams, 9 May 1863; Wallace and Gillespie (eds), *The journal of Benjamin Moran, 1857–65*, ii, 9 April 1863.
165 NARA, D/S, USC, 5, 5, T196, Eastman to Seward, 2 May 1863; *ibid*., Keenan to Seward, 1 May 1863.
166 *ORUCN*, ii, 3, Mason to Benjamin, 12 June 1863, 894.
167 Ryan, 'Confederate agents in Ireland', 53.

us'.[168] One of these men was to be Lieutenant James. L. Capston, a graduate of Trinity College Dublin and resident of Virginia, who had offered his services. Benjamin appointed him as a 'confidential agent' to use 'strictly legitimate, honourable and proper' means to disrupt the work of a 'regular organisation' of Federal agents in Ireland and particularly to tell the people the 'fate of their unhappy countrymen who have already fallen victims to the arts of the Federals', how they would 'be called on to meet Irishmen in battle' and how the Know-Nothing party was 'triumphant in its career' in the north while it was crushed in the south. Capston was to disseminate these views through newspapers, mixing with ordinary individuals and meeting influential people. But he was warned against violating any law.[169]

He left Richmond on 6 July, arrived in London on 2 September, reported to Hotze and travelled on to Dublin that night. He did not meet Mason who had just finished a two-week visit in Ireland. Mason doubted whether Capston would 'make much impression upon the emigrating class' as to 'the true character of the war'. He believed that 'such seems the ignorant and destitute condition of most of that class that the temptation of a little ready money and promise of good wages would lead them to go anywhere'. Mason knew that 'northern emissaries' offered the inducements to the people 'under the guise that they were wanted for work on railroads or as farm hands' but he doubted whether sufficient hard evidence could be obtained for a protest. Nonetheless he offered Capston assistance.[170]

Using his experience and contacts, Capston initiated a series of articles in the *Irish Times*, *Freeman's Journal*, *Morning News* and *Catholic Telegraph* supporting the southern cause. He then moved out of Dublin and worked his way through the countryside, meeting the ordinary classes from within whose ranks, he, Mason and Benjamin believed, came the emigrants flocking to the Union side. He travelled to the west coast, through counties Galway, Limerick and on to Cork. Unfortunately for Capston this great mission was circumscribed from the start by financial restraints as he was allowed only two months' salary with little extra for travelling and printing. Nonetheless he was well received by Roman Catholic parish priests whom he targeted and who deplored, in the words of John Ryan, Catholic Bishop of Limerick, the 'exodus of the people.' He also won support from the *Galway Vindicator* and *Galway Express*. In Queenstown, he met with Dowling who had already made

---

168 Richardson (ed.), *A compilation*, 2, Benjamin to Mason, no. 29, 6 July 1863, 533.
169 ORUCN, ii, 3, Benjamin to Capston, 3 July 1863, 828–9; Ella Lonn, *Foreigners in the Confederacy* (Chapel Hill, 2002), 75–6.
170 ORUCN, ii, 3, Mason to Benjamin, 4 September 1863, 890–1.

an impact by winning support from the *Cork Examiner*, local Catholic clergy and some merchants. Capston distributed notices in boarding houses and accommodation sheltering departing emigrants in the port and throughout the district, publicising Benjamin's warnings about the fate of Irish Catholics in the Federal army and reviving memories of the Know-Nothings.[171]

Dowling and Capston's efforts were strengthened by the arrival of Edwin De Leon in August. As mentioned above, De Leon had a secret service fund of $25,000 for counter-propaganda purposes and West believed that some of it was channelled to newspapers to secure a southern bias in their reporting. Prior to leaving Ireland in late September, Capston met with the Earl of Carlisle, lord lieutenant of Ireland.[172] Despite their best efforts, Dowling, Capston and De Leon failed to stem the departures. They also failed to identify individual Federal recruiters. Confederate defeats at Gettysburg and Vicksburg in July did not end Benjamin's Irish strategy. On 5 September, he wrote a letter of introduction for Father John Bannon to hand to Henry Hotze who had replaced Mason, now based permanently in Paris. In it he explained that Bannon, who was born in Roosky, county Roscommon, in 1829 and was a chaplain to the First Missouri Confederate Brigade, had agreed to become an agent in order to tell Irish people of the' true nature of our struggle', how the South had only 'ever received the Irish emigrant with kindness and hospitality' and that the Federal government would be drafting Irish emigrant labourers from railway works into their army. In addition to going to Ireland, Bannon had offered to visit Rome to secure a papal approval that might lead to diplomatic recognition for the Confederacy from Catholic countries in Europe and secure him a 'welcome among the Catholic clergy and laity of Ireland'. Hotze was instructed to defray Bannon's expenses and afford him assistance to fulfil his mission. Bannon departed from Richmond on 9 September with $1,212 50c. in gold from the secret service fund and carried with him a copy of Benjamin's instructions to Capston and a letter from President Davis to Pope Pius IX.[173]

Having successfully evaded the Union blockade, the *Robert E. Lee* headed for Liverpool where Bannon decided to travel on to Rome. During two interviews with Pope Pius IX, he received 'much

---

171 The above is based on Ryan, 'Confederate agents in Ireland', 63–7; Lonn, *Foreigners*, 76.
172 Cullop, 'An unequal duel', 108.
173 Tucker, *The Confederacy's fighting chaplain*, 2–3; Richardson (ed.), *A compilation*, 2, Benjamin to Hotze, 5 September 1863, 562; *ORUCN*, ii, 3, Benjamin to Bannon, 4 September 1863, 893–5; Phillip Thomas Tucker, 'Confederate Secret Agent in Ireland: Father John B. Bannon and his Irish mission, 1863–1864', *Journal of Confederate History*, 5 (1991), 67–8.

encouragement' for his mission.[174] In early November he arrived in Ireland and stationed himself in Dublin where he stayed with friends initially and then moved to the Angel Hotel from where he could meet farmers and clergy attending the Smithfield market. He also wrote between fifty and sixty letters to the families of deceased Irishmen who had fought in the Missouri Brigade and later met with some of them. Bannon quickly realised, just as Mason had, that the forces behind Irish emigration were less related to the Federal recruiters and had more to do with economic conditions. Thus, from the beginning, he was pessimistic about stemming the tide. Nonetheless, he travelled into the countryside to meet with influential clerics and laymen among them William Smith O'Brien and John Martin, former Young Irelanders who began a letter-writing campaign at his request. Bannon also assisted Martin to prepare editorials for *The Nation* and wrote articles himself under the pen name 'Sacerdos' warning against enlistment in the Federal army. He supplied newspapers with articles from the ichmond *Whig* and the Catholic New York *Freeman's Journal*. Broadsheets, circulars, posters and 2,000 copies of a handbill were distributed across the country, particularly in ports of embarkation such as Queenstown, Galway and around Dublin. With the support of the head of the Catholic Church in Ireland, Archbishop Paul Cullen, 3,000 copies of a six-column broadsheet addressed to the 'Catholic clergy and people of Ireland' were sent directly to clergymen throughout the island and posted on the gates and doors of Catholic churches in Dublin. This was followed by a plea to the 'Young men of Ireland' not to enlist.[175] Bannon and Hotze were convinced that the combination of their work, Pope Pius' criticism of Archbishop Hughes' pro-Union activities as well as increasing newspaper coverage of letters home from disillusioned Union Irish recruits, was effective in reducing emigration to the Union states by two-thirds between December 1863 and May 1864.[176] Against this background of a long-term rise, this decline had little impact and Confederate Commissioner Mann may have deluded himself when he stated in March 1864 that 'there will be a vast diminution in the number of foreign recruits for the Union armies'.[177]

174 Tucker, 'Confederate secret agent', 70. On 9 December Pius IX's published letter addressed the 'Illustrious and Honourable Jefferson, President of the Confederate States of America'. Many southerners interpreted it as the equivalent of recognition and a diplomatic success. Richardson (ed.), *A compilation*, 2, Mann to Benjamin, 14 November 1863, 594; Tucker, Confederate secret agent', 74.
175 Tucker, *The Confederacy's fighting chaplain*, 170–4; Ryan, 'Confederate agents in Ireland', 71; Ryan, 'Out of Ireland', 14; Hernon, *Celts*, 105; Lonn, *Foreigners*, 78.
176 Tucker, *The Confederacy's fighting chaplain*, 177; Cullop, 'An unequal duel', 110.
177 Richardson (ed.), *A compilation*, 2, Mann to Benjamin, 11 March 1864, 628.

Nevertheless, the presence of these Confederate agents in Ireland with the aim of 'checking and turning' Irish emigration away from the northern states, posed challenges for Union consuls on the ground, particularly Eastman in Queenstown a centre of much Confederate support. He identified one agent who had letters of introduction from southern leaders, probably Bannon, as being particularly effective during the winter of 1863–4. Eastman suggested to Secretary Seward that a 'few well known Irish Catholic chaplains be allowed to visit their homes [in Ireland], that they may see and explain to the clergy of this country the true state of affairs in the United States'. The consul was convinced that their southern enemies were doing 'all in their power to turn the opinion of the Irish clergy and people'. Obviously, Seward did not act on Eastman's suggestion but it revealed that the opposing sides saw Ireland with its labour resources as strategically important for the war effort.[178]

Meanwhile, other consuls worked hard to avoid attempts at entrapment and handing evidence of illegal recruitment to Confederate agents. A newspaper notice from a railroad company in Ohio resulted in a 'great number' of eager young men storming West's Dublin consulate but he recognised two police officers out of uniform among the group. One told him that he was 'burning' to join the Union army if he got a free passage but West was equal to the challenge and replied 'If he were equal to ten thousand men, and that a shilling would pay his passage I could not do it; and we had plenty of men at home to fight our battles and put down the rebellion.'[179] West avoided becoming implicated but the USS *Kearsarge* affair drew in Eastman and also provoked memories of impressment.

In November 1863, in Queenstown, Confederate agent Dowling believed he finally had evidence of illegal consular recruiting that could secure a conviction. Two versions of the events emerged from respective Union and Confederate camps. According to Captain John Winslow's deposition, the USS *Kearsarge* arrived in Queenstown on the night of 2 November and disembarked the following day to go to Cork city. When Winslow returned, accompanied by Consul Eastman, he visited British Rear Admiral Jones who referred to a paragraph in a newspaper that the *Kearsarge* had called to Queenstown for the purpose of enlisting men. Winslow told Jones that in his absence in Cork 'many persons had

178 NARA, D/S, USC, 6, 6, T196, Eastman to Seward, 22 January 1864; Joyce, 'The American Civil War', 40–1.
179 NARA, D/S, USG, 1, 1, T570, West to Seward, 15 August 1863. West also suggested that if part of the US territory was named 'New Ireland' and the governorship was given to General Meagher, it would attract many Irish emigrants. *Ibid.*, 28 November 1863.

applied to be shipped' and upon his return to the vessel he ordered 'that no enlistments would be made'. Three nights later, the *Kearsarge* went to sea and on 6 November, Winslow was told that several men had been discovered on board. Investigations revealed that they had concealed themselves in the ship hoping to be enlisted after it went to sea. As the *Kearsarge* was en route to watch the CSS *Florida* off Brest, France, Winslow said it was 'impracticable to return the men immediately'. Neither did he put them ashore at Brest because they would have joined the *Florida*. Instead he returned to Queenstown where he sent sixteen men ashore on 5 December. Winslow's deputy, Lieutenant Commander James Thornton, clarified how the men came to be on board. Three days before departure and while Winslow was absent, 'several men' from Queenstown came on board 'as applicants for enlistment' in the Union navy and Thornton told them that 'if they were physically qualified for enlistment they might remain on board' until Winslow's return when he 'would decide'. After Winslow returned and issued his instructions 'not to enlist them', they were accordingly 'sent out of the ship.' Others found 'in the hold in the carpenter's locker and elsewhere' were also put off the ship in some cases by force while men in rowing boats who surrounded the ship were not allowed on board. Thornton believed that the sixteen were 'securely concealed' with the 'connivance of the crew'. However, his account differed from Winslow's in that he said 'the men were sent out of the ship at Brest ... but pleading destitution they returned and were permitted to remain on board' until set ashore on the pilot boat at Queenstown. They were given uniforms and their names were entered in the ship's books after their return to the vessel at Brest 'for the purposes of their support and comfort, they being, otherwise utterly destitute'.[180]

Prior to the ship returning to Queenstown, Confederate agent Dowling had taken affidavits from witnesses and on 24 November, reported to Mason, Benjamin and James Whiteside, a Conservative Member of Parliament for Trinity College, Dublin and later lord chief justice of Ireland, that once Admiral Jones was informed about the arrival of *Kearsarge*, he ordered it to depart immediately but was ignored. When Winslow left the vessel for Cork, Eastman and Dawson his agent, were seen on board talking with the officers. Soon a rumour spread in Queenstown that Union officers on the *Kearsarge* were enlisting men for the navy. The affidavits showed that the conditions were attractive particularly the pay at $12 per month, and that Patrick Kennedy, Edward Lynch and two companions who went on board were given a physical examination and accepted

---

180 TNA, ADM1/5814 1863, Winslow to Eastman, 7 December 1863 in Winslow to Jones, 7 December 1863; *ibid.*, Thornton to Winslow, 7 December 1863 in Jones to Admiralty, 8 December 1863.

for the naval service as were many other men. Dowling believed that he now had evidence of Federal wrongdoing and it soon found its way into the British and Irish newspapers and to Russell's desk.[181] The Foreign Secretary also learnt about the 'alleged enlistment of British subjects on the *Kearsarge* ship at Queenstown' from F. G. Gardner, commissioner of Customs in Dublin, and from the earl of Donoughmore, Conservative politician and former president of the Board of Trade, who corresponded with Mason. Gardner did not implicate Eastman while Admiral Jones only referred to him in the context of accompanying Winslow at their meeting and providing him with Winslow's account. Nevertheless, on 30 November, Russell wrote to Adams 'to call your attention' to the alleged enlistment of British subjects and specifically that the witness Kennedy saw 'Eastman on the *Kearsarge* in conversation with one of the officers and that Mr Dawson, the agent of the consul was also on board'.[182] Adams brought the matter to Seward's attention on 4 December, and indicated that Eastman 'might be implicated' while his legation secretary, Moran, felt that Winslow's 'skirts are not altogether clear'. However, Moran privately described Russell's note as 'insolent' and believed the charges to be based on 'the most frivolous grounds' consisting of 'nothing but words asserted'. Seward already knew about the incident because on 28 November Russell instructed Lord Lyons, British minister in Washington, to complain to Navy Secretary Gideon Welles about recruiting in Ireland and because Eastman had telegraphed him 'explicitly denying' that he had, 'directly or indirectly, any knowledge of or participation in the enlistment of a British subject'.[183] On 26 December, Seward ordered Adams to 'immediately investigate the charges' against both men and, if proven, to 'dismiss' Eastman from his office and suspend Winslow.[184]

Russell favoured prosecution against the 'enlisted' men 'as soon as sufficient evidence' was collected under the Foreign Enlistment Act.[185]

181 *PRFA*, part 1 (1864), online at http://digicoll.library.wisc.edu (accessed 27 June 2008), Mason to Donoughmore, 23 November 1863, 433; Ryan, 'Confederate agents in Ireland', 53–6; Hernon, *Celts*, 83. For examples of Irish newspaper correspondence see *Cork Examiner*, *Daily Express*, *Evening News*, 3 December 1863.
182 *PRFA*, part 1 (1864), Gardner to Hamilton, 19 November 1863; *ibid.*, Mason to Donoughmore, 23 November 1863; *ibid.*, Donoughmore to Russell, 25 November 1863; *Diplomatic correspondence 1864–1917 papers relating to foreign affairs Great Britain* (hereafter *PFAGB*), part 3 of 4, Russell to Adams, 30 November 1863; TNA, ADM1/5814 1863, Jones to Admiralty, 7, 8 December 1863.
183 Quoted in Martin and Kline, 'Cork and the American Civil War', 102; Wallace and Gillespie (eds), *The journal of Benjamin Moran, 1857–65*, ii, 30 November 1863; *ibid.*, 2 December 1863; *PFAGB*, part 3 of 4, Adams to Seward, 4 December 1863.
184 *PFAGB*, part 3 of 4, Seward to Adams, 26 December 1863; NARA, D/S, DIDS, RG 59, M77, 78, Seward to Adams, 26 December 1863.
185 SPFA, part 1 (1864), Hammond to Waddington, 12 December 1863.

Six of the sixteen were indicted. At their trial in the Cork assizes on 14 March 1864, all six, who did not have legal representation and appeared in Union navy uniform, pleaded guilty, and one of them stated 'we went on board thinking it was no harm', another said 'we went on board to earn a living for ourselves'.[186] The court's decision to acquit was defended by Russell in the House of Lords in reply to a question from Donoughmore. Adams continued to argue that Eastman's presence on board the ship was insufficient to prove that he broke English law while Winslow's orders to prevent enlistment combined with his return of the sixteen stowaways, vindicated him. Adams maintained that Winslow had put their names on the vessel's books 'to make the accounts regular' and they wore Union sailors' uniforms because they had done so 'for some time'. By early April, Russell accepted Adams' denials of guilt largely because Seward had been prepared to remove Eastman and suspend Winslow, if they were guilty. Jones, however, believed that enlistment had taken place on board the *Kearsarge* even though Winslow had told him that 'he did not want any men and only wanted a clerk'.[187] Although the Emigration Board reported in early 1864 that a high proportion of single Irish men emigrated in 1863 to enlist, to get work and to secure high wages in the northern states, no further prosecutions for enlistment were taken.[188] West commented on 9 April, that the British government remained 'greatly exercised … on the subject of phantom federal enlistment in Ireland'. Eastman survived in office until 1869.[189] Both Benjamin and Hotze regarded the British response to the *Kearsarge* incident as further evidence of British bias against the Confederacy[190]

The flow of emigration continued in 1864 even though Bannon and Capston were joined in April by county Monaghan-born Catholic bishop, Patrick N. Lynch of Charleston, South Carolina, and by yet another Confederate agent, Captain James F. Lalor. The latter sailed from Wilmington, South Carolina, sometime after 24 February, reported to Hotze in London before 16 April and then proceeded to Ireland. Despite these efforts, the Confederate government could not prevent either Irish

186 Martin and Kline, 'Cork and the American Civil War', 102–3; *Freeman's Journal*, 16 March 1864.
187 House of Lords debate, 5 April 1864 vol. 174, online at http://hansard.millbanksystems.com/lords/ (accessed 19 November 2008), The Earl of Donoughmore, Earl Russell, col. 448–50; TNA, ADM1/5814 1863, Jones to Admiralty, 7 December 1863.
188 SPFA, part 1 (1864), Murdoch to Sir Frederic Rogers, 23 January 1864; *ibid.*, Rogers to Hammond, 'Correspondence respecting recruitment in Ireland for the military service of the United States', 18 January 1864; *ibid.*, Waddington to Hammond, 2 February 1864 and enclosures.
189 NARA, D/S, USD, 4, 4, T199, West to Seward, 9 April 1864.
190 *ORUCN*, ii, 3, Hotze to Benjamin, 16 January 1864, 1002–3.

emigration or Federal enlistment.[191]

USS *Kearsarge* was not ordered home by Secretary Welles because 'it did not comport with the interests' of his department.[192] Instead it carried on its duties and had a notable victory against the CSS *Alabama* in the English Channel on 19 June. Among the enlisted men discharged from the *Kearsarge* at the end of November were Michael Ahern and James Haley both were later awarded the Medal of Honour.[193] But the *Kearsarge* affair revealed the precarious position of Union consuls in Ireland during 1863 and 1864 who encouraged emigration but avoided prosecution for enlistment.

The consequences of enlistment were soon felt in Ireland and brought additional duties for the Union consuls specifically to ensure that the family of deceased and sometimes living soldiers and sailors, received pay, pension and belongings. Even news of their fate was hard to come by. Most Irish and native-born American volunteers in the New York area joined the Irish Brigade which commenced military action at the first battle of Bull Run on 21 July 1861. After initial successes they retreated back to Washington.[194] A few months later Consul Young in Belfast, writing on behalf of a 'poor widow', requested information from Seward on the fate of her two sons, James and Robert Kane, both soldiers in the 69th New York Volunteer Infantry Regiment, the core regiment of the Irish Brigade.[195] While the brigade quartered around Washington in winter 1861, theatres of war opened up throughout the country. By spring 1862 with stalemate in the east, land and sea-based engagements continued elsewhere. In March 1862, Consul Hammond in Dublin sought information on the 'whereabouts of certain officers born in Ireland in the Federal army', specifically Captain Francis Jameson.[196] Late in October, after the reorganised Irish Brigade fought tenaciously at Malvern Hill (1 July), Second Bull Run (28–30 August) and Antietam (17 September), West asked for an alphabetical list of those killed, wounded or missing by regiment for relatives contacting him.[197]

From the beginning of the war he identified some of the problems in securing monies owed to soldiers and their relatives. In Galway, a

191 *Ibid.*, 6 April 1864, 1087–9; Ryan, 'Confederate agents in Ireland', 85; Lonn, *Foreigners*, 75, fn. 61.
192 *PFAGB*, 3, Adams to Seward, 28 January 1864, Seward to Adams, 7 May 1864; NARA, D/S, DIDS, RG 59, M77, Roll 78, Seward to Adams, 7 May 1864.
193 Marvel, *The Alabama and the Kearsarge*, Appendix 2, Ships' Roster, 273–88.
194 Paul S. Boyer (ed.), *The Oxford companion to United States history* (Oxford, 2001), 130; Ural Bruce, *The Harp*, 42–81.
195 NARA, D/S, USB, 2, 3, T368, Young to Seward, 3 December 1861.
196 *Ibid.*, USD, 3, 3, T199, Hammond to Seward, 19 March 1862.
197 *Ibid.*, USG, 1, 1, T570, West to Seward, 11 October 1862.

US marine, Patrick C. Byrnes, applied to West for a pension in January 1862. But West found the forms impossible to fill in and the procedure which required the written oaths from two physicians to verify the applicant's certificate of health, as expensive and inappropriate. He advised Seward to review the whole process which did not occur. Byrnes though did receive his pension. The extent to which other soldiers' families had come to rely on enlistment monies became obvious as soon as casualties began to build up. By October 1862, West was dealing with 'numerous' callers and he frequently gave relatives 'pecuniary aid'. He followed this by suggesting to Seward that the government directly forward any bounties, compensation, pay and pensions owing to families of deceased sailors or soldiers to US consuls for delivery. He hoped the move would encourage further emigration, ensure honesty in disbursement and of course, increase consular income. Not all applicants for US pensions were in dire need, illustrated by the case of the family of Thomas Scully Persse, son of the former vice consul in Galway, lost in the battlefield some time in 1862. West's annoyance at government delay in contacting relatives intensified particularly after the carnage at the battle of Fredericksburg on 13 December 1862, when 'numerous widowed mothers, wives, sisters, parents' of dead or injured soldiers or sailors flocked to his door in Galway for help.[198] Over in Waterford, Consular Agent Williams transmitted seven claims for the recovery of deceased soldiers' pay, including two from families who had lost relatives at Fredericksburg.[199]

As the 'military momentum' in the eastern theatre remained with the Confederates until the battle of Gettysburg on 2 July 1863, West commented on the 1862 Pension Act which detailed the categories of personnel and sums to be awarded to a range of relatives upon a soldier's partial or total disability and death. Army pensions varied from the $30 per month of lieutenant colonels and other officers of highest rank, to $8 for non-commissioned officers and privates. In the navy those holding rank as commander, lieutenant commander and master received $30 each month and petty officers and others $8.[200] The only category West was concerned about was the lowest; $8 per month would ease the plight of 'many' widows, children, mothers and sisters of men lost 'in our war'.

198 *Ibid.*, West to Seward, 9 January 1862; *ibid.*, 4 March 1862; *ibid.*, West to Seward, 25 October 1862; *ibid.*, 19 December 1862; *ibid.*, 24 March 1863; *ibid.*, Record of Treasury Fees, 1862, 10 January 1863; *ibid.*, West to Seward, 26 May 1862; *ibid.*, 23 January 1863.
199 *Ibid.*, USC, 6, 6, T196, Returns of fees, Waterford, 31 December 1863.
200 Boyer, *The Oxford companion*, 131; A century of lawmaking for a new nation: US congressional documents and debates, 1775–1875, online at http://lcweb2.loc.gov/ (accessed 19 November 2008), *Statutes at Large, 37th Congress, second session*, ch. clxvi, 14 July 1862, 'An act to grant pensions', 566–9.

Claimants would have to establish their right to the pension, bounty or any pay outstanding and he was unhappy that the bounty would not be paid except to those residing in the US, particularly as he believed that it would have funded a passage that would ultimately benefit the Union. He repeated that soldiers' remittances for families in Ireland living far from a town or bank, should be sent directly to consuls who could disburse it.[201] By summer 1863, he had received fifty claims from families requesting pay due to deceased soldiers and sailors. In September, he acknowledged receipt of arrears of pay of £7 2s. 9d. for Mary Regan, a widow. Nevertheless, the delays and difficulties he encountered in securing payments grew encouraging him to describe in great detail the poverty, destitution and evictions he encountered on a daily basis.[202]

His growing experience of the benefits issue led him in April 1864 to ask Seward to consider amending the legislation which only allowed for a bounty to widows and heirs of deceased soldiers and sailors. West asked that since the widow always received the pension, should half the bounty not be paid to any next of kin. He cited the many cases of poor parents who appealed to him for arrears of pay and promised to send another son to replace the 'lost one … that he might kill the rebels'. Though fighting would continue until April, by early 1865 the Confederate cause was lost. For West, authenticating signatures of family members who needed to claim the bounty, pay or pensions was now a regular part of his job and a staple of his fee income. He believed he had prepared and certified more claims than any other consul in Britain or Ireland.[203] Indeed West used this war-related business to argue for his retention in the Dublin post for a further six months, although he was genuinely concerned that dependants would receive due compensation from the US Pension Office. Indeed he was amazed at the 'great ignorance' prevailing among all types of people about the mechanics of claiming, in particular that landlords as justices of the peace, regularly applied on behalf of their tenants enabling them to obtain rent directly. This situation encouraged him to write to the main newspapers in early 1866 to directly convey information to potential applicants.[204]

Despite West's self-proclaimed diligence, he was not alone. It was no different for the Queenstown-based consul who claimed that between

201 NARA, D/S, USG, 1, 1, T570, West to Seward, 7 July 1863; *ibid.*, 18 July 1863.
202 *Ibid.*, USG, 1, 1, T570, West to Seward, Fees, 1863; *ibid.*, West to Seward, 28 September 1863; West to Seward, 18 April 1863; *ibid.*, 23 May 1863.
203 *Ibid.*, USD, 4, 4, T199, West to Seward, 16 April 1864; *ibid.*, West to Seward, 12 May 1865; *ibid.*, 7, 7, T199, West to Fish, 26 June 1869.
204 *Ibid.*, 4, 4, T199, West to Seward, 13 May, 24 June 1865; *ibid.*, 14 January 1866; *ibid.*, 29 July 1865.

1863 and 1868 he went to much 'trouble and expense' to determine the whereabouts of 'thousands' of Irishmen so that relatives could request monies due.[205] Similarly Thomas King in Belfast in 1867 recognised the dependence on US pensions of 'poor, some times very poor' people in his district. Consequently, he proposed charging 25c. and not the $2 fee, as his predecessor did, to authenticate the signature and official character of the magistrate before whom a US pensioner annually appeared to make an oath of his service. Among the reasons given in 1870 by his successor, James Rea, for an increase in the Belfast post's salary was 'the additional duties that have grown out of the late war' specifically 'collecting pensions ... looking after the claims of some two hundred odd illiterate, unfortunate pensioners – male and female ... presenting the claims of others whose names are not yet on the rolls'.[206] It was clear that the 'return tide' of letters and remittances from America, would increasingly include pensions. Between 1 July and 30 September 1865, West handled one hundred claims for soldiers and seamen's pay and effects. By June 1869, he reported that the greatest cause of complaint to him from relatives of deceased soldiers related to the government's decision to pay the bounty only to widows and children. Throughout the 1880s, consuls John Piatt in Queenstown, and George Savage and Samuel Ruby in Belfast, dealt largely with pension queries from Civil War veterans and relatives and friends of enlisted men. Ruby wrote in April 1890, 'my experience has been, that we meet with no class of people who are more exacting or give us more trouble than the pensioners especially the women'. Margaret Johnston complained to the acting commissioner of pensions that she had been charged fifty cents by Consul Agent Rodger in Londonderry, for authenticating her pension vouchers. Although Rodger acted illegally, unaware of a change in the law in June 1888, Ruby explained that 'in view of the annoyance these foreign pensioners give us', his action was 'just and reasonable'.[207]

Changes in the pension legislation in March 1893 provided that from 1 July, no pension would be paid to a non-resident who was not a US citizen except to those who had incurred actual disabilities incurred in

---

205 *Ibid.*, USC, 6, 6, T196, Eastman to Seward, 8 February 1868.
206 *Ibid.*, USB, 5, 5, T368, King to Seward, 10 September 1867; *ibid.*, 6, 6, T368, Rea to Fish, 16 February 1870.
207 NARA, D/S, USD, 4, 4, T199, West to Seward, 21 October 1865; *ibid.*, USC, 10, 10, T196, Piatt to Porter, 19 November 1886; *ibid.*, Piatt to Porter 20 January 1887; *ibid.*, USD, 7, 7, T199, West to Fish, 26 June 1869; *ibid.*, USB, 9, 9, T368, Savage to Porter, 29 July 1887; *ibid.*, 10, 10, T368, Ruby to Wharton, 7 March 1890; *ibid.*, Ruby to Wharton, 25 June 1890; *ibid.*, Rodger to Ruby, 19 April 1890. In April 1886 a rumour circulated in Dublin that even a two-week residence in the US could result in a government pension. *Ibid.*, USD, 9, 9, T199, McCaskill to Porter, 1 April 1886.

the service. It is not clear how many people were affected in Ireland but at least one, a Catherine McGrath, was dropped from the pension roll. Her son was killed during the Civil War and she had survived for almost thirty years on a pension. Her husband had been a US citizen which conferred the same status on her and even though she provided an authenticated signature to the Bureau of Pensions, which was identical to the original version given, she was struck off the roll. She was personally known to Deputy Consul Arthur Piatt in Dublin who immediately wrote on her behalf to have the 'injustice' reversed as he had authenticated her signature which, he said, had changed over time as she was now over eighty years of age, 'had one foot in the grave' and her handwriting was shaky. His newly–appointed superior, Consul Newton Ashby weighed in also, indicating that it was a 'matter of justice and in harmony with the liberal principles of our government' and McGrath was entitled to 'our sympathy.' He indicated that she had seen 'better days' and would have to spend the last months of her life in the poor house if the pension was not restored.[208] Unsurprisingly each successive American war prolonged pension work for consuls and produced queries from Irish people about the fate of relatives who had joined the armed forces. In the first decade of the twentieth century, between eighty and ninety pension vouchers were issued from the Dublin consulate every three months and nearly one hundred US pensioners presented vouchers to the Queenstown consul for certification. Many were widows and mothers, most were feeble and illiterate and of the poorer classes.[209]

There is still some discussion among historians as to the turning point in the Civil War with some seeing the Union victories at Vicksburg in the western theatre in July 1863 and at Gettysburg in the eastern theatre in July 1863 as decisive, while others view the fall of Richmond in 1865 as signalling the end of the Confederacy.[210] The Union consuls noted the effect which the news of northern victories had on local communities, particularly when the tide firmly turned against the Confederate forces. Each quietly welcomed the turnaround by Confederate sympathisers, or to use John Young's words; 'Our secessionist Irish and English merchants never realised a doubt of southern independence until now … They are terribly crest fallen indeed'.[211] Queenstown became more congenial and

---

208 *Ibid.*, USD, 10, 10, T199, Ashby to Uhl, 21 June 1894; *ibid.*, Piat to Sydney S. Willson, US Pension agent, Washington, 14 March 1894; *ibid.*, William Lochran, Commissioner of Pensions to Piatt, 15 May 1894; *ibid.*, Piatt to Lochran, 26 May1894.
209 *Ibid.*, USD, 11, 11, T199, Wilbour to Hill, 25 July 1901; *ibid.*, USC, 12, 12, T196, Gunsaulus to Secretary of State, 16 April 1906.
210 Carroll, *The American presence*, 80.
211 NARA, D/S, USB, 2, 4, T368, Young to Seward, 21 September 1864.

Eastman decided not to move the consulate to Cork even though he was given permission to do so.[212] It was not until a Union victory was almost assured that West reported 'a wonderful change in public opinion' in Dublin in January 1865.[213] It was the same in Britain. When Consul Dudley in Liverpool heard by telegram from Queenstown, news of the capture of President Davis he wrote, 'it has extinguished the last ray of hope for the rebellion'.[214] President Lincoln's death on 16 April which united north and south enhanced the pro-Union sentiment of religious and political leaders as well as the public.[215] West was eager to report two resolutions of sympathy. The first came from 'one of the most influential meetings ever held' in Dublin, attended by Attorney-General Sir Thomas Kane, lord mayor of Dublin Sir John Barrington and the earl of Howth, which unanimously passed the resolution. The second address came from a 'crowded' meeting of working men' at the Dublin Mechanics Institute. West continued 'now all are united their expression of horror of the deed and sympathy for us' and later he reported on a similar resolution passed at a meeting in Galway chaired by the former US Vice Consul and now chairman of the Town Commission, Thomas Moore Persse. West hoped that Seward would gratefully receive all expressions of regret and support from up to now 'hostile' sources to allow 'a restoration to amity'. He did, but also instructed West and the other consuls to distribute anonymously throughout Ireland, thousands of copies of the *Narrative of the sufferings of our prisoners whilst in the hands of the rebels*. Every Catholic bishop and parish priest received a copy while Protestant clergy, magistrates, gentry and nobility received a copy of *America and her army* by Robert Mackenzie which compared 'the cruel and barbarous conduct of our foes with the mild and Christian treatment of their soldiers, when our prisoners'. Seward acknowledged the 'healthy tone' in the Irish press and public and while West prided himself on getting Seward's note published in the 'uniformly and persistently hostile' Dublin *Evening Mail*, he was subsequently rebuked.[216]

If the US consular service entered the Civil War unprepared, it emerged from it in high esteem. Just like consuls elsewhere in the British empire who operated in a pro-Confederate atmosphere, it was a difficult time

212 Ibid., USC, 6, 6, T196, Eastman to Seward, 20 June 1865; ibid., Eastman to Seward, 4 May 1864.
213 Ibid., USD, 4, 4, T199, West to Seward, 7 January 1865.
214 Quoted in Lankford (ed.), *An Irishman in Dixie*, 123, fn. 28.
215 Hernon, 'Irish sympathy', 82.
216 NARA, D/S, USD, 4, 4, T199, West to Seward, 29 April; ibid., 13 May; ibid., 5 June; ibid., 27 May; ibid., 17 June 1865; ibid., West to Seward, 22 July 1865; ibid., West to Seward, 26 August 1865.

for the Irish-based consuls, both professionally and personally. These men were part of a network of a few hundred mostly untrained officials, who were often ostracised at least until a Union victory seemed assured. Yet, they served in challenging conditions with low or no pay and often without much contact or guidance from the State Department.[217] Although the Confederate foreign service network was not equivalent in size, a significant financial and personnel investment was made in Ireland thus providing Union consuls with a further challenge. Union consuls, therefore, helped to defeat the efforts of the Confederate government to build, buy and equip ships. The consistent gathering of intelligence combined with Adams' diplomatic efforts in London, denied the Confederacy these vital resources. Moreover, they successfully ensured that emigration from Ireland to the Union states whether for enlistment or work purposes continued apace during the period despite widespread political and religious opposition, the work of Confederate agents and the possibility of facing charges in British courts for breaching the Foreign Enlistment legislation. Not all consuls remained neutral in relation to the respective American or Irish causes. West became entangled in Irish nationalist issues and could see the many benefits from Irish emigration to the Union states, including the promotion of Irish freedom. However, Union consuls acknowledged that the desperate economic state of Ireland contributed mainly to the ongoing emigration more than their own efforts. For those intent on leaving, the absence of pre-paid passages combined to the widespread opposition and the possibility of facing death on the battlefield did not deter them. Approximately, 332,660 emigrants left Ireland for America during the conflict and approximately 150,000 of Irish origin fought in the Union army and some 30,000 on the Confederate side.[218]

The Civil War revealed the weaknesses in the Union consular system; the absence of training, the lack of support from the State Department where too few clerks supervised the consular section and left consuls on the ground without guidance and non-existent or inadequate salaries. Indeed the long-serving Benjamin Moran in the London legation did not alter his opinion of the Irish consuls whom he described as 'all muffs, and not one is fit for his place', although this view may be partly explained by the huge increase in consular correspondence that he had to deal with during the crisis and his own disdain for consuls.

217 Kennedy, *The American consul*, 140.
218 Hernon, *Celts*, 20; Sam J. Newland, 'Civil War, The' in Glazier, *The encyclopedia*, 153, 155; Ural Bruce, *The harp*, 2; Phillip Thomas Tucker, *Irish Confederates: the Civil War's forgotten soldiers* (Abilene, 2006), 12. These are generally accepted figures but they do not indicate if the men were recently arrived emigrants and second, do not appear to include those who joined the two navies.

Yet, northern interests were well served.[219] The end of the war reduced the consuls' intelligence-gathering activities, although Queenstown remained a telegraph despatch centre into 1866 and Eastman's arrangements which gave special protection to US government mails on board the Cunard and Inman lines and from the vessel to the railway station in Queenstown, were still in place in late 1869.[220] However, the war's legacy remained with Irish-based consuls seeking pensions, bounties and backpay for relatives of deceased soldiers and sailors, information on the whereabouts of missing personnel on both sides and the release of southern prisoners in Union jails.[221] A further consequence of the Civil War was the impetus given to Irish nationalists and the Fenian movement in the following decades which embroiled consuls in Irish domestic affairs, as well as American–British diplomatic relations.

---

219 Kennedy, *The American consul*, p.141; Wallace and Gillespie (eds), *The journal of Benjamin Moran*, ii, 26 February 1862.
220 NARA, D/S, USC, 6, 6, T196, King to Fish, 12 November 1869. During the war with Spain in 1898, Wilbour in Dublin recruited James Armstrong of 30 Lower Pembroke Street, to watch ships in Dublin destined for Spanish ports. Armstrong received £5 from the National Defence Appropriation to bribe a port official, enter the sailors' reading room and to 'treat' sailors for information on port traffic. *Ibid.*, USD, 10, 10, T199, Wilbour to Hill, 1 December 1898; *ibid.*, account from James Armstrong, 18 November 1898.
221 As late as February 1870, Neill in Dublin, personally delivered pension arrears to Eliza O'Brien a pauper in the North Dublin Union and he promised to seek out the widows and orphans of all Civil War Irish soldiers in order to pay them their pensions. NARA, D/S, USD, 8, 8, T199, Neill to Fish, 3 February 1870.

4

'Our Guardian Angel abroad':* American foreign policy and Irish nationalism, 1865–70

A critical feature of post-famine emigration to the United States was identified by Edward Brooks, US Consul in Cork in 1881; departing Irish saw themselves as forced to flee 'from 'hated British rule'.[1] Bringing such sentiments with them augmented the Anglophobia of much of Irish-America, revived the American dimension to the nationalist struggle in Ireland and posed a difficulty in the US–British diplomatic relationship which forced an elucidation by American political élites of their views on the Irish cause.

Organised in 1853 by James Stephens in Ireland and John O'Mahony in the US, the aim of the Irish Republican Brotherhood (IRB) was to supply money and arms to achieve an independent Irish republic. On 10 December 1858, Consul Hugh Keenan in Cork informed US Minister George Dallas in London, about the arrest and imprisonment of IRB members.[2] The outbreak of the American Civil War had postponed the Fenian rebellion in Ireland but when it ended, the American Fenians recognised the value of the wartime experience. Many individuals believed they had changed from being an 'untrained peasant' to becoming a 'disciplined warrior' and, thus, were even better prepared to fight for the cause. Consul William West had reported from Dublin in spring 1864 that Fenians were ready for action which made the British government 'nervous'.[3] However, the movement was weakened by disagreement

---

* NARA, D/S, USD,6, 6, T199, Second series, M. W. Fitzgerald to West, 21 January 1868.
1 *Ibid.*, USC, 8, 8, T196, Brooks to Evarts, 3 March 1881.
2 Wallace and Gillespie (eds), *The journal of Benjamin Moran, 1857–65*, 1, 10 December 1858. See *History Ireland*, 16:6 (November/December 2008) for most recent review of the historiography and debates on the Fenians.
3 Joyce, 'The American Civil War', 40; Comerford, 'Gladstone's first Irish enterprise, 1864–70' in Vaughan (ed.), *A New History of Ireland, v*, 434–5; Gerard Moran, 'The National Brotherhood of St Patrick in Britain in the 1860s', *Irish Studies Review*, 7:3 (1990), 325–36; John Devoy, *Recollections of an Irish rebel. Introduction by Seán Ó Lúing* (Shannon, 1969), 130; Neal Garnham, 'American Civil War' in Connolly

between O'Mahony and Stephens over money and strategy. Additionally Michael Scanlon and William Roberts in Chicago favoured intervention in Canada to provoke an Anglo-American war and not Ireland. Indeed British Consul Edward M. Archibald in New York predicted a Fenian raid into Canada in October 1865 but it did not happen until 1866. Other Fenians worked to win support from sympathetic American politicians who were preparing for House of Representative elections in 1866. It was against this uneasy background that in August 1865, O'Mahony ordered his officers to Ireland and a military intervention was planned for October.[4] Even before they left, many were under surveillance which continued after arrival when several were arrested and more were harassed by Irish Constabulary detectives. Two categories of prisoner emerged: those interned on the Lord Lieutenant's warrant during the suspension of the *Habeas Corpus* Act (1679) and those against whom there was sufficient evidence for a trial.[5] In both cases, the Americans turned to their consul for protection and once again Irish nationalist activity came to the centre of American–British relations. The quiescent issues of citizenship, naturalisation and US government tolerance of anti-British activities on its soil and the related threat to British control of Ireland, were revived.

1865: the 'year of action'[6]

US Minister Charles Francis Adams provided Secretary Seward with a first-hand account of the strength and popularity of Fenianism in Ireland following a visit in August 1865. Adams, like Abbot Lawrence, his predecessor, was struck by 'depopulation' and that one of its effects was 'to leave in the midst of the community a great and festering sore of discontent'. He knew little about the Fenian movement but sufficient that its popularity reflected widespread 'hatred of the English rule' and it was sustained by 'American sympathy'. It had a military structure and aims but, unlike the British government, he did not think it posed a threat to its control of Ireland – 'the disaffected class may be large; but it is poor,

---

(ed.), *The Oxford companion*, 12. R. V. Comerford, *The Fenians in context: Irish politics and society 1848–82* (Dublin, 1985); Comerford, 'Gladstone', 437; NARA, D/S, USD, 4, 4, T199, West to Seward, 26 March 1864.

4 Michael H. Kane, 'American soldiers in Ireland, 1865–67', *The Irish Sword*, 23 (summer 2002), 111; TNA, ADM1/6574 1881, Archibald to Earl Russell, 16 September 1865.

5 Seán McConville, *Irish political prisoners, 1848–1922: theatres of war* (London and New York, 2003), 146, 153.

6 Devoy, *Recollections*, 88.

unarmed, and generally wanting in the elements of moral power'. Essentially, he had identified the weakness of the organisation; the Fenians were not sufficiently organised or armed.[7] Indeed by this stage, regular drilling and marching was taking place but arms were slower to arrive. In 1864 rifles bought in Britain were distributed throughout Ireland but America was expected to provide most of the arms and ammunition particularly as prices dropped after the Civil War. On 2 September 1865, the British Admiralty wrote to Rear Admiral Frederick in Queenstown, warning him that attempts might be made to land arms from America on the south-west coast of Ireland and to provoke Fenian disturbances.[8]

Regardless of Stephens' prediction that conflict would occur in 1865, the government acted first.[9] On the night of 15 September, West reported the 'Fenian bubble was burst by a "coup d'etat" of the government'. Although West's comment was somewhat premature, the police raided the Dublin offices of the Fenian newspaper, the *Irish People* and arrested Fenian organisers including Thomas Clark Luby, John O'Leary and Jeremiah O'Donovan Rossa. Martial law was introduced in Cork city and county which enabled the police to seize all arms found on passengers arriving on transatlantic vessels into Queenstown and to arrest Fenians. Dublin city remained quiet on 16 September but the army was ready for any emergency once the effects of the arrests became known.[10] British naval surveillance off the southern coast led to arms seizures and the arrest of a 'party charged with high treason'. Existing naval and coastguard powers to stop, search and seize vessels, arms, ammunition and men were strengthened by the martial law measures in county Cork if not in other places.[11]

Despite the setbacks, British Consul Archibald in New York reported to Foreign Secretary Russell that Fenian arrangements for the departure of men from Boston and New York and the transmission of arms and ammunitions were being made 'with great secrecy – <u>death is threatened</u> as the penalty for revealing information on this subject'. Thus, he believed the only efficient way of preventing the shipments was through 'diligent watchfulness' by the coastguard and British naval authorities were to look out for 'Fenian sisters' from America who were said to carry

---

7 *PFAGB*, 3, Adams to Seward, 22 September 1865.
8 TNA, ADM1/6574 1881, Admiralty to Frederick, 2 September 1865
9 Comerford, 'Gladstone', 437.
10 NARA, D/S, USD, 4, 4, T199, West to Seward, 30 September 1865; *ibid.*, West to Seward, 16 September 1865; TNA, ADM1/5920 1865, Frederick to Admiralty, 16 September 1865.
11 TNA, ADM1/6574 1881, Note Petty Sessions Court to Admiral Commanding, 18 September 1865; *ibid.*, Confidential copy, opinion of law officers of the Crown, 19 September 1865.

arms concealed in their luggage.[12] Immediately, Lord Wodehouse, Lord Lieutenant of Ireland, requested Admiral Frederick to co-operate with the civil authorities and intercept both the *City of New York* and the *Erin* before Fenian passengers could communicate with the shore and search for arms or any treasonable correspondence. HMS *Blazer*, *Nightingale* and *Hyena* proceeded to the south-west coast and made their headquarters at Crookehaven, county Cork.[13]

In autumn 1865, irrespective of whether or not the returning Irish-Americans who landed in Irish ports, mainly Queenstown and Dublin, possessed revolutionary intentions, many were caught up in the government's pre-emptive action. Most were aware of their rights as native or naturalised citizens, and turned to the resident American consul for help. Among the first who appealed to Consul Edwin Eastman in Queenstown was native-born John McCafferty, a former a captain in the Confederate cavalry, imprisoned in the Cork County jail. Eastman visited him, took a deposition and sent the details to Adams and Seward. Eastman was convinced that McCafferty came to Ireland 'to make war against Great Britain'. He was correct because McCafferty's career as a revolutionary nationalist was just beginning.[14] By 30 September, Eastman believed that Fenian agitation had subsided and any planned rebellion was 'now killed dead by the British government'. The authorities in Queenstown continued to devote attention to the recently arrived passengers, searching for treasonable documents and arresting suspected persons. Eastman complained to the local commander, but with little success.[15]

At the end of September, West in Dublin still reported on the 'insane Fenianism'. But it was the many former American soldiers, 'illegally molested', who commanded his attention. Quickly he identified the revival of a problem with implications beyond a consul's jurisdiction, namely non-recognition under British law of the US naturalisation status of Irish people originally born within the British empire. West received

---

12 *Ibid.*, Archibald to Russell, 16 September 1865; *ibid.*, unsigned enclosure in Archibald to Russell. The Fenian Sisterhood in America was a parallel organisation to the Ladies Committee in Ireland. Rose Novak, '"Keepers of important secrets": the Ladies Committee of the IRB', *History Ireland*, 16:6 (November/December 2008), 28–9; Devoy, *Recollections*, 113.

13 TNA, ADM 1/6574 1881, Dublin Castle to Frederick, 30 September 1865; *ibid.*, 1/5920 1865, Frederick to Admiralty, 16 September 1865; *ibid.*, Instructions to Senior Officers on the Coast of Ireland.

14 NARA, D/S, USC, 6, 6, T196, Eastman to Seward, 24 September 1865; Tucker, *Irish Confederates*, 25; David A. Wilson, 'Swapping Canada for Ireland: the Fenian invasion of 1866', *History Ireland*, 16:6 (November/December 2008), 26–7; Devoy, *Recollections*, 65, 187.

15 NARA, D/S, USC, 6, 6, T196, Eastman to Seward, 30 September 1865; *ibid.*, Eastman to Seward, 24 September 1865.

requests for guidance from American citizens, Captain James Murphy formerly of the 20th Massachusetts Volunteers and former Federal soldier Maurice J. McGrath from Illinois, who were incarcerated in Richmond bridewell in Dublin under the Treason Felony Act. West would not interfere in 'an affair of so much importance' without Minister Adams' approval. Yet, he believed there were no legal grounds for Murphy's detention and he asked Adam's for permission to visit them and attend the preliminary legal proceedings.[16] Much to West's relief, Murphy was released. He could not have known that Murphy's military expertise was in training basic fighting tactics, bayonet exercise and discipline and later he would be heavily implicated in the Clerkenwell prison explosion.[17] The Dublin consul reported almost every day in September 1865 on Fenian activities and was critical of the 'silly and ill-advised movement' and its attempts to entangle 'our government.' In addition to dealing with prisoners, many Americans called to the consulate for money, food and a free passage back to the US. West showed little sympathy for 'adopted' Americans who tried to cause 'revolution'. Yet, his duties forced him to give assistance.[18]

During late September and October, the British consuls in New York, Chicago and Philadelphia reported on the supposed departures of more Fenians who were armed with rifles, side-arms and uniforms. Two issues concerned Archibald in New York; first that the Fenians were buying steam ships and war materials which the US government was selling cheaply and second, that if an Irish 'republican provisional government' was proclaimed, there was a danger that 'privateers' would be 'let loose' from American ports for Ireland. Other information sent to Admiral Frederick in Queenstown suggested that a German vessel, *Rosher Adler*, would land arms and ammunition at or near Chicago for shipment in flour and port barrels to Liverpool and then on to Ireland. In mid-October British vessels were sent to Lough Swilly and the mouth of the river Shannon in addition to patrolling seventeen locations on the southern coastline where 'hostile' landings of men, horses and artillery could take place.[19] When it was rumoured that the US frigate *Niagara* had offloaded

16 Ibid., USD, 4, 4, T199, West to Seward, 20 September 1865; *ibid.*, West to Adams, 30 September 1865, *ibid.*, 16 September 1865; *ibid.*, 19 September 1865.
17 Kane, 'American soldiers in Ireland', 128–9; Devoy, *Recollections*, 237.
18 NARA, D/S, USD, 4, 4, T199, West to Seward, 14 October 1865; *ibid.*, West to Seward, 20 September 1865.
19 TNA, ADM 1/6574 1881, C. E. Kortright to Sir Frederick Bruce, 30 September 1865; *ibid.*, Archibald in Baring Whitehall to Secretary of the Admiralty, 24 October 1865; *ibid.*, Admiralty to Frederick, 15 October 1865; *ibid.*, Admiralty to Frederick, 15 October 1865; *ibid.*, 'Landing places on south west coast of Ireland between Cape Clear and River Shannon', undated.

arms to boats coming from the shore around Ballycotton, county Cork, Foreign Secretary Russell asked Adams for confirmation. Adams denied it but gave the story some legitimacy by stating that the vessel had been ordered to return to the US.[20] Archibald had already told Russell that the US government was 'uneasy' about the 'probable troublesomeness' of Fenianism. But he stressed that the 'importance' of the Irish vote would always mean that Fenian activities would be 'dealt with tenderly' by the US authorities until 'necessity' compelled harsher handling.[21] His view became a constant theme in British diplomatic reporting from the US into the twentieth century and was a source of embarrassment for their American counterparts in London.[22] In early October, Adams seemed relieved to report to Seward that Fenian 'excitement' was subsiding.[23]

The consequences of the crisis for the consuls soon manifested. West began to deal with the 'impudent conduct' of imprisoned Americans and those still at liberty which produced a 'rather delicate affair' for him. After Adams received the official charges against the incarcerated Americans, he presented them to his legal adviser to ascertain if the cases merited official intervention. In turn, West was instructed to exercise discretion when communicating with and advising detained American prisoners and their relatives. Already West had learned that James Murphy was innocent and another who had appealed to him, Lieutenant Colonel John W. Byron, previously of the 88th New York Volunteers, who was visiting his relatives in Clogheen, county Tipperary, when he was removed from his bed by over twenty police, had been released by Lord Lismore, Attorney General, on payment of £200 bail.[24] West accepted Byron's denial of the charge, not knowing that in late 1863 Byron had succeeded James Rorty as recording secretary of the Potomac Circle of the Fenian organisation. Two years later, he was the first of James O'Mahony's American envoys sent to Ireland to report on the military situation and satisfy the American leaders that 'a fight' was possible. Prior to his arrest in 1865, he met with John Devoy at the European Hotel in Bolton Street, Dublin, and then started for Clogheen.[25]

West, unlike Eastman, did not protest to the authorities that prisoners' correspondence were intercepted and read by the Irish Post Office

20 *PFAGB*, 3, Adams to Seward, 27 September 1865, 2 October 1865; Seward to Adams, 31 October 1865.
21 TNA, ADM 1/6574 1881, Archibald to Russell, 16 September 1865.
22 See Whelan, *US foreign policy*.
23 *PFAGB*, 3, Adams to Seward, 5 October 1865.
24 NARA, D/S, USD, 4, 4, T199, West to Seward, 23 September 1865; *ibid.*, 6, 6, T199, First series Fenian correspondence of Dublin consulate (hereafter First series), West to Moran, 9 November 1865.
25 Kane, 'American soldiers in Ireland', 117; Devoy, *Recollections*, 57.

authorities.²⁶ Moreover, he was slow to complain about the arrest of so many Americans because their 'square-toe boots and felt hats' made them conspicuous. It is unlikely that he was absolving the authorities but perhaps was asking Secretary Seward to warn those departing for Ireland. Indeed Devoy acknowledged that the American officers in their distinctive 'squared-toed boots and double-breasted vests' attracted attention and the Fenian leadership warned them to make themselves less conspicuous.²⁷ Meanwhile West visited Maurice McGrath in the Richmond bridewell who was among a group arrested in a boarding house but McGrath maintained that it was only on the basis of association with 'perfect strangers'. Afterwards, the Attorney General told West that he had sufficient grounds for McGrath's detention. Even though West was not sympathetic, he engaged a solicitor for him and used the case to highlight to Seward another unjust practice. If a jury decided he was guilty of treason, McGrath could be convicted on the basis of an informer's evidence and be transported for life. McGrath agreed to return to the US and was eventually released. On 28 October, he left Londonderry on board the SS *Peruvian*. West reminded Seward that though the evidence against McGrath was 'slight', he had suffered one month's imprisonment. Also if McGrath had not compromised and agreed to leave, 'a well founded and serious charge might have been made for such unjust incarcerations of our citizens'.²⁸ Ironically, later on McGrath became involved with the Roberts' faction of the Fenian movement.²⁹ Similarly, Patrick Leonard, formerly lieutenant colonel in the 99th New York National Guard, was arrested at his mother's home in Begrath, county Louth, for possession of a weapon. He was imprisoned for twenty days and then released. West believed there was no evidence to connect him with the attempted rebellion beyond 'being an officer in our army, an Irishman and having arms and military uniform'. Leonard was subjected to 'arbitrary and ... harsh treatment'.³⁰ Again West could not have known that Leonard was a deeply committed Fenian and a personal friend of John O'Mahony.³¹

West was less convinced of the innocence of naturalised Captain Michael O'Boyle formerly of the 69th New York National Guard, who protested against the 'indignity' of imprisonment in Richmond bridewell.

26 NARA, D/S, USD, 4, 4, T199, West to Seward, 23 September 1865; *ibid.*, 6, 6, T199, First series, West to Moran, 9 November 1865.
27 Kane, 'American soldiers in Ireland', 117; Devoy, *Recollections*, 66.
28 NARA, D/S, USD, 4, 4, T199, West to Seward, 22 September 1865; *ibid*, 23 September 1865; *ibid.*, 7 October 1865; *ibid.*, 28 October 1865.
29 Kane, 'American soldiers in Ireland', 127.
30 NARA, D/S, USD, 4, 4, T199, West to Seward, 16 December 1865.
31 Kane, 'American soldiers in Ireland', 125.

When he was committed for trial, West explained to him that American citizens should not be under the 'erroneous impression' that it was in his power or that of the US government, to secure releases for those charged with treason. But O'Boyle's health was poor and West kept an eye on his case, promising Seward that if he suffered from bad treatment in prison he would ask Adams to act.[32] Neither did he get embroiled initially in George Archdeacon's case. He was an agent in Liverpool for the *Irish People*, and was arrested in the sweep-up in Dublin in mid-September. Twice West refused his appeals for help on the ground that he did not have naturalisation papers and the evidence against him seemed stronger because he admitted selling the *Irish People* albeit as one of eighteen newspaper agents in Liverpool. Attorney General Lawson would not recognise either Archdeacon or O'Boyle's citizenship claims. But if both pleaded guilty and threw themselves upon the mercy of the Crown he would favourably consider their cases. West's humanity came to the fore. He met with Archdeacon and discovered him to be a 'poor, old, penitent' man and again appealed for his release. Lawson refused because Archdeacon was an active Fenian in Liverpool and connected with treasonable activities.[33] West advised O'Boyle and Archdeacon to plead guilty at their upcoming trials by the special commission.[34]

In the interim, Archdeacon was released on his own bail of £200. But after his return to Liverpool, he found his business destroyed, his daughter ill having lost her employment because of his arrest and his wife 'vainly struggling against difficulties'.[35] But West's concern for Archdeacon could not overcome his fear of acting inappropriately and it was only upon Adams' instruction that he asked Lawson to discharge Archdeacon's bail thereby permitting him to go to the US. Lawson agreed on condition that Archdeacon not return to Ireland, England or Scotland for three years.[36] O'Boyle was still imprisoned in Kilmainhaim jail and refused to plead guilty because the charge of conspiracy was 'nothing more nor less than trumpery balderdash'. He thanked West for this kindness and effort to have him released and apologised for the trouble he had put him to.

32 Kane, 'American soldiers in Ireland', 131; NARA, D/S, USD, 4, 4, T199, O'Boyle to West, 23 September 1865; *ibid.*, West to O'Boyle, 27 September 1865; *ibid.*, West to Seward, 7 October 1865.
33 NARA, D/S, USD, 4, 4, T199, West to Seward, 7 October 1865; *ibid.*, West to Seward, 28 October 1865; *ibid.*, West to Seward, 4 November 1865; *ibid.*, 6, 6, T199, First series, Lawson to West, 4 January 1866; *ibid.*, West to Lawson, 11 January 1866; *ibid.*, 4, 4, T199, Attorney-General to West, 12 January 1866.
34 NARA, D/S, USD, 6, 6, T199, First series, West to Archdeacon, 15 January 1866.
35 *Ibid.*, Archdeacon to West, 28 February 1866.
36 *Ibid.*, Second series Fenian correspondence of Dublin consulate (hereafter Second series), West to Adams, 31 March 1866; *ibid.*, West to Archdeacon, 9 April 1866; *ibid.*, West to Larcom, 9 April 1866; *ibid.*, Larcom to West, 15 April 1866.

This polite, even deferential tone, appealed to West's sensibilities and he encouraged O'Boyle to change his mind because conviction might lead to a 'convict life in a distant land' for the rest of his life. O'Boyle's attitude was full of 'contradictions, coolness and indiscretions, if not impudence' and West accepted that he was 'far from innocent'.[37]

Even though a rising had not yet taken place in Ireland, the British authorities hoped that the harassment, detention and charging of approximately one hundred Fenians who stood trial for treason and felony by special commission in Dublin beginning on 1 November and Cork on 15 December, would quell the movement's momentum. However, public interest in Fenianism remained at a high pitch not least because James Stephens was sprung from Richmond bridewell on 24 November. Once again Admiral Frederick directed HMS *Liverpool* to intercept all packet ships going west from Cape Clear and search for Stephens who might have been dressed as a Frenchwoman with a child.[38] West described the event as a 'wonderful escape', perhaps revealing his admiration for the audacity of the rescue. The commission continued in Dublin where extensive use was made of the documents removed from the *Irish People* offices and 'American Fenians' figured 'prominently'.[39]

Not all the prisoners presented to the Cork commission required Eastman's assistance as in the case of Charles Holmes O'Riordan, a former captain in the Michigan Light Artillery, who was arrested at Queenstown in September. *The Times* noted that when arrested and searched, he had in his possession a copy of the bye-laws of the Detroit Fenian Brotherhood and that he was the younger brother of a rising barrister on the Munster circuit. He was defended by J. M. Barry and promptly acquitted. The other prisoners also arrested in Queenstown on board vessels recently arrived from the US included John McCafferty, a Confederate captain, and Charles Underwood O'Connell, a Federal captain, who were defended by Isaac Butt, Queen's Counsel. O'Connell, surprised that he had not been released, asked for West's help. West read through the Crown's case against him and indicated that unless O'Connell had new information to offer and because the government believed it would get a conviction under the Treason Felony Act, there was little reason in them meeting.[40] Eastman adopted the same approach because when arrested

37 *Ibid.*, First series, O'Boyle to West, 17 January 1866; *ibid.*, West to O'Boyle, 18 January 1866; *ibid.*, First series, West to Adams, 3 February 1866.
38 TNA, ADM1/5920 1865, Frederick to Secretary of the Admiralty, 26 November 1865; Devoy, *Recollections*, 77–87.
39 NARA, D/S, USD, 4, 4, T199, West to Seward, 2 December 1865; *ibid.*, 6 January 1866; Kane, 'American soldiers in Ireland', 126.
40 Mairead Maume, Patrick Maume, Mary Casey (eds), *The Galtee boy: a Fenian prison narrative. John Sarsfield Casey* (Dublin, 2005), 8; Kane, 'American soldiers

O'Connell had in his possession a revolver and 'treasonable' documents. He was eventually sentenced to ten years' penal servitude. McCafferty was acquitted because he had not committed an overt treasonable act.[41]

Throughout autumn 1865, West and Eastman went to pains to indicate their sympathy for the position of the British government and the authorities in Ireland, accepting that security concerns often predominated over fairness and, therefore, the detention of innocent Americans. On 20 December, Consul John Young in Belfast simply commented 'our consul in Dublin has had some trouble with Fenianism but here very little of that has appeared'.[42] However, even though the 'fenian seditioners' had caused him 'no small trouble and anxiety', West in particular was sensitive to the arbitrary nature of harassment, arrests and detentions of Americans. Ultimately, he recognised that he had to do well by all parties; prisoners, police and his own government.[43] Although Adams described West as 'a conceited, chattering Irishman', his determination to secure fair treatment for the American prisoners proved useful to Adams. In December, Seward instructed his minister to request the British government to investigate the case of Captain John Fanning.[44]

Fanning was a naturalised American, a commissioned officer in the 10th Ohio Volunteer Infantry and had served in the élite 2nd US Cavalry prior to the Civil War. He arrived in Queenstown on 14 September on board the USS *Louisiana* to visit his family and recover his health after his war experiences. On his way to Ballinamore, county Leitrim, he was arrested at Kileshandra, county Cavan, where his baggage was searched and a pistol and ammunition taken. He was handcuffed and incarcerated in Cavan prison for seventeen days without trial, from where he wrote to Seward. Subsequently, he was discharged on bail to stand trial and was ordered to remain in the country. On 25 November, Attorney General Lawson decided not to proceed with the case.[45] Fanning's circumstances aroused American public interest and Seward's intervention because it involved protection of the rights of naturalisation and citizenship and

---

in Ireland', 132; NARA, D/S, USD, 6, 6, T199, First series, O'Connell to West, 8 December 1865; *ibid.*, West to O'Connell, 11 December 1865.

41 *The Times*, 7 October, 16, 18, 26 December 1865; NARA, D/S, USD, 6, 6, T199, Second series, West to US Secretary of State Hamilton Fish, 20 March 1869.

42 NARA, D/S, USB, 4, 4, T368, Young to Seward, 20 December 1865.

43 *Ibid.*, USD, 6, 6, T199, First series, West to Moran, 30 December 1865; *ibid.*, 4, 4, T199, West to Seward, 6 January 1866; *ibid.*, West to Attorney General, 25 December 1865.

44 Quoted in Brian Jenkins, *Fenians and Anglo-American relations during Reconstruction* (Ithaca, 1969), 73; *PFAGB*, part 1, Seward to Adams, 11 December 1865.

45 *PFAGB*, part 1, Fanning to Seward, 11 November 1865; NARA, D/S, USD, 4, 4, T199, Declaration of Captain Fanning, 21 November 1865; *ibid.*, 6, 6, T199, First series, John D. Garde, Crown Solicitor Longford and Cavan to West, 25 November.

went to the core of US sovereignty. West was able to tell Adams that he had already secured Fanning's release. Adams offered his own interpretation of events, namely that during the 'present difficulties' the Irish authorities experienced some difficulty in 'distinguishing between the persons who have come ... from America' and it was impossible to say whether or not they were connected with Fenianism.[46] Adams provided mitigating circumstances for the arrest of innocent men which may be explained by his unwillingness to have the matter develop into a diplomatic incident. Fortunately, West's work had spared Adams having to seek a formal British investigation into Fanning's case. Instead Adams advised the consuls in Ireland 'to secure a proper share of protection for innocent persons' who were American citizens without interfering on behalf of those who had 'justly subjected themselves to suspicion of complicity with treasonable projects'. In other words, given the prevailing circumstances if an American was arrested in Ireland, it was probably his own fault and consuls could be less concerned about them. Adams did not intend dealing any further with the case and thought it 'superfluous' to report further on the matter to Seward because consuls would keep him 'fully advised'.[47] West could not abandon the issue and by early November he had become highly critical of the arrests and imprisonments of 'our citizens' on the 'mere caprice of the constables and without a scintilla of evidence to warrant such arbitrary conduct' but he was determined not to appear as a 'pro-Fenian Consul'. He seemed to be successful. William F. Roantree, who had served in the American Navy and was head of a Fenian circle in Leixlip, county Kildare, described West at his trial in Dublin as the 'pro-English American Consul'. While, John Calvert Stronge, chief magistrate of police, noted that West 'was doing [his] part to smooth the difficulties between the two governments arising from Fenianism' and he was entitled 'to respect and courtesy' from the police.[48]

At the end of 1865, Lawson's principal aim was to induce American officers and soldiers who were 'travelling through the country encouraging this absurd Fenian movement' to leave Ireland for America which, he believed, they had been induced to leave by 'false representations of the state of things in Ireland'. Also the authorities decided that some American prisoners would not be prosecuted and could be released on West's guarantee or assurances that the prisoner would return to

46 *PFAGB*, part 1, Adams to Seward, 28 December 1865.
47 *Ibid.*; quoted in Jenkins, *Fenians and Anglo-American relations*, 73.
48 NARA, D/S, USD, 4, 4, T199, West to Seward, 27 January 1866; *ibid.*, 6, 6, T199, First series, West to Adams, 6 November 1865; *ibid.*, 18 November 1865; *ibid.*, West to Seward, 27 January 1866; Devoy, *Recollections*, 140–4.

America. Lawson emphasised that he was not at all disposed 'to press the laws with severity' against American citizens and he would 'deal in this spirit with any of them who are desirous to return'.[49]

The rising did not occur in 1865, 'the optimum year' and while the arrests, trials, convictions and sentences damaged the Fenians in the long term, it did not seem to be the case at the time. The movement maintained its support and gathered momentum again.[50] In early 1866, West commented the land was full of 'ire, where angry passions rage, and the almost daily discovery of fresh conspiracies, pikes and ammunitions keep up the most intense excitement'.[51] Adams agreed that the trials and sentences of imprisonment in Ireland and penal servitude abroad, had not diminished the 'uneasiness and discontent'. But he was in far off London, while West in Dublin felt that the respective prisoners' 'usually defiant' addresses to the court after being found guilty was not 'manly and prudent' and caused him embarrassment. At the same time, these statements continued to fan the flames of nationalist Ireland's sympathy for Fenians and their cause. Indeed Fenianism became increasingly popular.[52] Of greatest concern to West was that the press and people were linking the US government, 'directly or indirectly', with the Fenian conspiracy against the British government. He correctly noted the prominence of members of the New York National Guard with the Fenian conspiracy. Indeed the 99th NYNG included the former Phoenix Brigade commanded by Colonel John O'Mahony, who had actively recruited Irish-American soldiers into the Fenian Brotherhood.[53] The Dublin *Daily Express* commented on this New York connection also.[54] Despite the arrests and trials, many of the hundreds of demobilised American offices and men who were the 'sinew and muscle' for Fenian plans, remained determined and ready for battle.[55]

1866: the suspension of *habeas corpus*

According to Devoy, Stephens blamed the US leadership difficulties for the inadequate money and arms sent to Ireland which ultimately doomed the rising.[56] These differences created a schism within the movement. The

49 NARA, D/S, USD, 6, 6, T199, First series, Lawson to West, 31 December 1865.
50 McConville, *Irish political prisoners*, 124.
51 NARA, D/S, USD, 4, 4, T199, West to Seward, 14 January 1866.
52 *PFAGB*, 1, Adams to Seward, 18 January 1866; NARA, D/S, USD, 6, 6, T199, First series, West to Adams, 3 February 1866.
53 Kane, 'American soldiers in Ireland', 109.
54 *Daily Express*, 20 January 1866.
55 McConville, *Irish political prisoners*, 125.
56 Devoy, *Recollections*, 90–1.

Irish Times commented that General Thomas Sweeney was preparing to raid Canada not Ireland.⁵⁷ These plans were given further credence by public comment such as that from the *Washington Globe* which criticised the US government for permitting the Fenian preparations for an assault on 'a nation [Canada] with which we are at peace'.⁵⁸ In Ireland, Colonel Thomas J. Kelly, Stephens' chief of staff, buoyed the dispirited Fenians with Stephens' prediction that whether or not aid arrived the 'fight would come off'. The American officers who were still free in Ireland and England, numbering around 150, did not believe that the breach between the leaders in the US would be healed in three or four weeks to allow the rising to go ahead. Some had even returned to the US to side with O'Mahony and others feared for their continued freedom. On 5 February 1866, the *Daily Express* reported further Fenian arrests.⁵⁹ In spite of the obvious weakness in the Fenian organisation, the daily discovery of arms and assaults on police combined with information obtained by the British spy network in the US predicting the arrival of more arms and men, the government took additional precautionary measures. British naval surveillance was intensified along the coastlines and more soldiers arrived.⁶⁰ On 14 February, the Irish authorities estimated that there were approximately 500 Irish-American Fenians in the country. A short while later, martial law was imposed in Dublin county and city followed by the suspension of the *Habeas Corpus* Act on 17 February in order to pre-empt a further attempt at a rising, even though Minister Adams was well informed about the events through the consuls there, he gauged the seriousness of the situation by the fact that parliament met on a Saturday and the necessary measures were rapidly passed. Meanwhile, West reported the arrests of hundreds of people suspected of complicity in the Fenian conspiracy, many of whom were naturalised as well as native-born Americans.⁶¹ Adams acknowledged that the arrests took place without a reason assigned, or time given for deliberation or the production of evidence to show their innocence.⁶² West was in no doubt but that the arbitrary and extreme measure was directed against Americans in order, 'with one fell swoop, to sweep them ... innocent and guilty alike into the gaols of this unfortunate country, without the neces-

---

57 *Irish Times*, 5 February 1866.
58 Quoted in W. S. Neidhardt, 'The American government and the Fenian Brotherhood: a study in mutual political opportunism', *Ontario History*, 64:1 (1972), 32.
59 *Daily Express*, 5 February 1866.
60 TNA, ADM1/6574 1881, Frederick memo, 9 February 1866.
61 NARA, D/S, USD, 6, 6, T199, First series, West to Adams, 18 February 1866; *ibid.*, 4, 4, T199, West to Seward, 20 January 1866.
62 *PFAGB*, 1, Adams to Seward, 22 February 1866.

sity of having to assign any cause for their committal'.[63] Indeed Lord Lieutenant Wodehouse was determined to catch as many Irish-Americans as possible before they learned of the suspension of *habeas corpus* and attempted to escape. Devoy maintained that Fenian sympathisers within the police had warned some who managed to avoid arrest. But thirty-eight men claimed US citizenship among the 150 detained in Dublin on 17 February.[64] In a rare contribution to the Fenian crisis, Consul Young in Belfast felt that the 'indiscriminate sweeping up' of foreigners' was unacceptable particularly when it was simply on the basis of their dress and having money, although he acknowledged the British government's right to punish people engaged in treasonous activity and that the Fenian movement in the US gave the authorities 'just cause' for suspicion of all Americans in Ireland.[65]

One of the first consequences of the February events was that a number of naturalised Americans who were either arrested or liable to arrest appealed to the US consuls for help. During the round-up, the consulate in Dublin was occupied and invaded by Irish-Americans seeking protection on their own behalf and on behalf of imprisoned friends. West used the opportunity to repeat to Adams and Seward all the arguments about the unjustness of the British distinction between native and naturalised American Fenian prisoners. However, on 18 February, he signalled that the government was not disposed to release the prisoners on condition of their returning home, unlike after the September 1865 arrests.[66] Adams advised West to investigate the respective circumstances of each case, and where there were no grounds for imprisonment, to write a polite letter of protest to Under Secretary Larcom and report all cases involving harsh treatment.[67] Adams' own view was not straightforward. On the one hand, he believed that by reversing the 'established principles of English law' and assuming every stranger arrested was guilty until proven innocent, the British government had shown little 'wisdom' and it would be difficult 'to avoid some rather strong notice of this ... in our international relations'. But on the other hand, there was reason to believe that many of the prisoners were 'more or less implicated'. Moreover, he recognised that the Fenians were 'astute enough' to be capable of using the issue to antagonise American–British relations. Caught between adherence to new world values and old world political realities, Adams advised Seward

63 NARA, D/S, USD, 6, 6, T199, First series, West to Adams, 18 February 1866.
64 Jenkins, *Fenians*, 87; Devoy, *Recollections*, 98–9; NARA, D/S, USD, 4, 4, T199, West to Seward, 24 February 1866.
65 NARA, D/S, USB, 4, 4, T368, Young to Seward, 21 February 1866.
66 *Ibid*., USD, 6, 6, T199, First series, West to Adams, 18 February 1866.
67 *PFAGB*, 1, Adams to Seward, 22 February 1866.

that a formal complaint to the London government should be made only as a last resort. In the US, the news of the suspension of *habeas corpus* was a fillip for American Fenians; mass meetings were held throughout the country and their headquarters in New York was thronged with visitors. O'Mahony demanded immediate action by American Fenians, irrespective of their faction and called for more money to buy arms for shipment to Ireland. Seward had other reasons to avoid trouble with Britain; there was his 'fondness' for the Irish, Irish-Americans' contribution during the recent Civil War, the importance of the Irish vote in the reconstruction struggle and the already fractious nature of US–British relations over the Newfoundland fisheries issue. Accordingly Seward had to be careful and in the interim, he supported Adams' suggestion that the best course to meet this 'danger' was 'frankness', and, if possible, the establishment of a 'clear understanding' with the British government to secure the release of innocent persons, while leaving it free to deal with 'unquestionable offenders'.[68] But in March 1866, Adams warned Seward that British politicians were disappointed that the US government was sustaining Fenianism.[69] Adams hoped that his measured policy would lead to releases of the innocent and avoid a diplomatic dispute. The British government was not inclined towards a similar restrained position.

Among the many callers to the Dublin consulate on 19 February looking for West's help, were the relatives of prisoners whose plight touched him. Kate Burke, wife of Colonel Denis F. Burke, told him that she and her husband came to Ireland for the benefit of her health in the previous September. He was arrested at their lodging in 33 Mount Pleasant Square along with Colonel Michael Kirwan and Captain Bernard McDermott. West sympathised with her because her husband was forcibly taken from her without having breached the law. But she expected the US government to have her husband released. Another visitor was Mrs Ellen Scanlan, an American born in Chicago, who came to Ireland to improve her children's health. She was accompanied by a servant, 18-year-old Philadelphia-born, James Smith formerly a sergeant in 65th Illinois Infantry, who was arrested at her lodgings in Phibsboro near Dublin and 'dragged off to gaol without being allowed to eat his breakfast'. The father of Major Thomas M. Holden also reported his 20-year-old son's arrest along with that of Lieutenant Joseph Lawlor, and Captain James Burns who were arrested in the same boarding house. Captain John Dunne was also arrested and a friend of his told West he was ill in prison and requested a physician's certificate to show he was

---

68 *PFAGB*, 1, Adams to Seward, 22 February 1866; Neidhardt, 'The American government', 32–3; Glyndon G. Van Deusen, *William Henry Seward* (New York, 1967), 501.
69 *PFAGB*, 1, Adams to Seward, 2 March 1866.

incapable of enduring prison confinement. West found that prisoners Corporal William Mackay of the 179th New York Infantry and Captain Edward Morley were American born. Burke and Kirwan were members of the Fenian military council and Smith, Holden, Mackay and Morley had Fenian connections. West asked Adams whether he should begin to collect citizenship evidence to support an application for the release of the US-born prisoners. But he warned Adams that 'adopted citizens' would be 'very jealous and dissatisfied' if they heard of a distinction being made between native-born and naturalised Americans. In addition, he feared the Irish-Americans would deliberately obstruct any 'amicable arrangement' which the two governments might agree in order to secure their release. In some respects West's insight proved to be correct. Adams instructed him to write to the attorney general to protest at the arrests and imprisonment of US citizens without 'sworn information against them, or the slightest allegation of their guilt'. He accepted that there might be grounds for suspicion against some of them but many were not guilty of any 'design to subvert the civil order established in this realm'. The US government expected to be shown the evidence for detention and in the interim, hoped that the same rights would be accorded to all US citizens as the British government would expect for its citizens in similar circumstances in America.[70]

During the rest of February 1866, West was busy in Dublin writing daily to Adams and replying to prisoners' appeals for assistance. Some of those in Kilmainhaim jail offered no reason for being in Ireland at the time, while John Horan a citizen of Natick, Massachusetts, was in Ireland for twelve days solely to visit friends in Tipperary. Burke confirmed his wife's reasons for his presence in Ireland and ill health also brought Bernard McDermott and Maurice Fitzharris to Ireland. Young James Smith wanted to manage his brother's property although the latter stated he was there as a servant to Mrs Scanlan. Another prisoner, Hugh Dennedy was in the process of buying 8 Upper Ormond Quay to start a business when he was arrested. John A. Comerford, a former captain in the 3rd Massachusetts Cavalry, was accompanying his father home on a pleasure trip and defied 'any living mortal to prove' that he was a Fenian. Former US officer William McGrath was in Ireland to visit his uncle.[71] On 23 February, West sent out a circular to twelve 'alleged' American

---

70 NARA, D/S, USD, 6, 6, T199, First series, West to Attorney-General, 20 February 1866.
71 NARA, D/S, USD, 6, 6, T199, First series, Horan to West, 21 February 1866; *ibid.*, Burke to Adams, 21 February 1866; *ibid.*, McDermott to West, 24 February 1866; *ibid.*, Fitzharris to West, 6 March 1866; *ibid.*, Smith to West, 22 February 1866; *ibid.*, Dennedy to West, 24 February 1866; *ibid.*, Comerford to West, 24 February 1866; *ibid.*, McGrath to West, 7 March 1866.

citizens incarcerated in prison asking for the evidence of their citizenship before he could act on their behalf.[72] Also he worked to improve their prison conditions and in one week sent three letters to Larcom protesting against the solitary confinement and 'other inconveniences, privations and sufferings' inflicted on US citizens without 'assigning any cause or even alleged criminality against them'.[73] He kept reminding Adams that outside of the prisoners having come from the US or having some connection with the US military, there was not a 'scintilla of evidence of their guilty connection with the Fenian conspiracy'.[74]

By late February, the Dublin prisons which held the most important prisoners were full and in order to relieve the congestion, some men were released on bail for their good behaviour but were liable to rearrest while others were released on condition that they leave for America immediately.[75] West knew of thirty-eight American prisoners, nine of whom were naturalised Americans and the rest native born. But the British government refused him and other US consuls, any claim to represent the naturalised men 'in their native country.' He emphasised to Seward that the majority of the prisoners had served with distinction and held high rank in the Federal army during the Civil War but many had not been in the US long enough to secure evidence of their naturalisation. He wanted to employ a solicitor to take affidavits, sworn before a magistrate. Adams was less interested in protecting the undocumented citizens and in the interim instructed West to seek the releases of those with certificates of citizenship.[76] Larcom confirmed that nine men were US citizens and the rest were considered British. By early March, West had failed to secure the release of any American prisoner nor permission to interview any.[77] At this stage he did not address the issue of their guilt or innocence but simply ensured that their rights to full representation were met. He became even more determined to affect his duties when Larcom suggested that he provide evidence of their innocence of the treasonable offences. West replied that it was the responsibility of the Irish executive to produce proof of guilt and not his. Unlike after the September round-up when Americans were tried on sworn information made against them for the serious crime of treason-felony, in February 1866, most were

72 *Ibid.*, Copy Circular addressed to 12 Alleged American citizens, 23 February 1866.
73 *Ibid.*, West to Seward, 24 February 1866; see *ibid.*, 6, 6, T199.
74 *Ibid.*, West to Adams, 20 February 1866.
75 Devoy, *Recollections*, 112.
76 NARA, D/S, USD, 4, 4, T199, West to Seward, 24 February 1866; *ibid.*, 6, 6, T199, First series, West to Adams, 27 February 1866.
77 *Ibid.*, 4, 4, T199, West to Irish government, 20 February 1866; *ibid.*, Larcom to West, 20 February 1866; *ibid.*, West to Seward, 3 March 1866; *ibid.*, West to Larcom, 21 February 1866.; *ibid.*, West to Seward, 10 March 1866.

'unceremoniously arrested and thrown into prison'. On the question of prison visits, Larcom replied they could visit American citizens only and not British subjects thereby excluding naturalised Americans. But West could correspond with all prisoners which was unsatisfactory because mail was easily intercepted by the authorities.[78]

West began to receive proof of US citizenship from the prisoners themselves and also from friends and family in the US and Ireland including Mrs Kate Burke still resident in Mount Pleasant Square Dublin and Mrs Gleeson in Limerick on behalf of her husband, John H., and his brother, Joseph, both incarcerated in Nenagh jail, county Tipperary. Then West requested the Attorney General and the under secretary to furnish him with information on the charges, permissions to visit and a relaxation of prison conditions. Larcom replied that the two Gleesons and Bernard McDermott were Irish-born subjects of Queen Victoria, were bound by their oath of allegiance to her and would be dealt with accordingly, thus their US citizenship was not recognised.[79] The same response applied to Michael O'Brien and Michael Duffy both in Kilmainhaim jail.[80] Keeping in mind Adams' instructions, he penned a respectful but firm letter to Larcom giving the names of six America-born prisoners – Daniel J. Mykins, James Smith, John A. Comerford, Frank Leslie, William Mackay and Edward Morley incarcerated in Kilmainhaim and Mountjoy prisons – and asking for their release or evidence of their guilt.[81] Larcom replied that Smith and Comerford were born in Ireland and would be charged with treason.[82] Adams was furious at West's action, specifically for making 'positive' promises to the prisoners that American officials could secure their freedom, for not obtaining evidence of guilt before liberation and for using the words 'immediately' and 'forthwith' in the letter to Larcom which looked 'discourteous'. Instead he should have used 'more polite and softened phraseology.' West robustly defended himself declaring he was not the 'diplomatist' and it was him, not Adams, who was refused permission to visit 'our adopted citizens' in prison in the course of his duty. Although he did apologise to Larcom for using the two words, he explained to Seward that if he exceeded his function as a consul, he did

78 Ibid., West to Larcom, 21 February 1866; ibid., 4, 6, T199, First series, West to Adams, 23 February 1866; Larcom to West, 22 February 1866.
79 Ibid., 6, 6, T199, First series, Kirwan to West, 21 February 1866; ibid., J. Ryan to West, 23 February 1866; ibid., 6, 6, T199, First series, West to Adams, 25 February 1866; ibid., 4, 4, T199, Larcom to West, 28 February 1866.
80 Ibid., West to Larcom, 27 February 1866; ibid., 6, 6, T199, First series, Larcom to West, 3 March 1866.
81 Ibid., West to Adams, 6 March 18666; ibid., 4, 4, T199, West to Larcom, 5 March 1866; see ibid., 6, 6, T199.
82 Ibid., 4, 4, T199, Larcom to West, 9 March 1866

so with Adams' approval, while operating in 'a very trying crisis'. Additionally, West felt he had a friendly relationship with Larcom in marked contrast to the coolness of the former lord lieutenant, George Howard.[83]

Meanwhile in Cork, Eastman believed the suspension of *habeas corpus* backed the Fenians into a corner where 'they must either fight or give it up'. He felt they were unprepared and did not expect a revolt. Nevertheless, his services were soon called upon. Cork-born John Dunne arrested on the charge of treasonable conspiracy against the government and held in Cork prison, claimed Eastman's assistance and denied membership of the Fenians. Dunne had enlisted as a private in the 164th New York Infantry, was eventually promoted to regimental quartermaster and was a Fenian. Others followed, including one Kenmare-born, former captain of the 8th New Hampshire Volunteers and Fenian leader, Cornelius Healy, held in Tralee jail, county Kerry, and William Pope held in Clonmel jail, county Tipperary. In all three cases, in addition to visiting them and passing on their depositions to Adams and Seward, he asked Larcom if they were held under any charges and if so, could they be investigated and if not, might they be released. Larcom replied that Pope was born in county Waterford and, therefore, was not a US citizen while Healy had been released on 7 March on condition he leave Ireland.[84] In Belfast, Young seemed surprised when three American prisoners turned to him for aid; John P. Dunne, Edward O'Byrne and Mr Smith, a collecting agent for the American Freedman's Aid Society. However, unlike West and Eastman, he did not think that any further action was needed beyond reporting the information to Seward and Adams.[85] Young, like Adams, was empathetic to the authorities and was embarrassed by the US government's tolerance of Fenian activities. Consequently, while he would do as directed, he would only act on behalf of those American prisoners whom he thought were innocent.[86]

The longer prisoners remained incarcerated, appeals for protection, some abusive, continued to flow directly to West and to Adams. Miss

83 *Ibid.*, 6, 6, T199, First series, West to Adams, 1 March 1866; *ibid.*, West to Larcom, 9 March 1866; *ibid.*, 4, 4, T199, West to Seward, 24 March 1866; *ibid.*, 6, 6, T199, First series, West to Adams, 11 March 1866.
84 *Ibid.*, USC, 6, 6, T196, Eastman to Seward, 25 February 1866; *ibid.*, Deposition, 23 February 1866; *ibid.*, Thomas Larcom to Eastman, 3 March 1866; *ibid.*, Eastman to Larcom, 5 March 1866; Kane, 'American soldiers in Ireland', 123; NARA, D/S, USC, 6, 6, T196, Eastman to Seward, 28 March 1866; *ibid.*, Eastman to Seward, 28 April 1866; *ibid.*, Larcom to Eastman, 7 April 1866.
85 *Ibid.*, USB, 4, 4, T368, Young to Seward, 21 February 1866; Kane, 'American soldiers in Ireland', 120, 131. The Freedman's Aid Society, originally the Fugitive Aid Society, helped fugitive slaves and later developed a fundraising role to establish colleges in the south, online at http://auctr.edu/ (accessed 8 December 2008).
86 NARA, D/S, USB, 4, 4, T368, Young to Seward, 21 February 1866.

Jane Beatty appealed on behalf of her relative, James McDermott, a naturalised American citizen and soldier who came home to Boyle, county Roscommon, to take charge of his widowed sister's business. He was arrested and imprisoned in Roscommon jail, then moved to Kilmainhaim jail and later Mountjoy prison. West asked Larcom to release him, if he was not guilty of any breach of the law. In March, West's handling of this and other cases merited Seward's approval.[87] But the consul was still permitted only to meet with native-born American prisoners in order to verify their statements and could not obtain the reasons for their arrests. Larcom also disputed details of prisoners' identities and refused to discuss individual cases with him.[88] West attempted to find a way of verifying American prisoners' claims to citizenship. After Adams opposed his suggestion to use the services of a solicitor and magistrate because it would be 'secondary evidence', West offered to visit US-born prisoners and obtain their personal information under oath which he could offer to the lord lieutenant as proof of citizenship. He would follow this with a request for liberation 'supposing', of course, that there was no evidence to justify detention. But he argued that liberation could not be conditional on their leaving Ireland even though Michael O'Brien was released from jail on 3 March on condition that he depart. West worked tirelessly to establish the naturalisation credentials of American prisoners and was subjected to their increasingly desperate 'arrogant demands'.[89] He investigated John Comerford's information that his cousin, William Delany who lived in Kells, county Kilkenny, had visited his parents in Lowell, Massachusetts, and could provide an affidavit of his naturalisation. West forwarded this 'conclusive' evidence to Larcom but then had to tell Comerford that he could do more for him because the authorities had evidence of his involvement in the Fenian conspiracy and would continue to be detained. He was disappointed to learn that Frank Leslie in Mountjoy was really Irish-born, Eugene O'Shea, but uncovered that two American prisoners shared the name James Smith.[90]

87 *Ibid.*, USD, 6, 6, T199, Second series, West to Adams, 3 July 1866; referred to in Seward to West, 6 March in *ibid.*, 4, 4, T199, West to Seward, 24 March 1866; *ibid.*, 6, 6, T199, Second series, McDermott to West, 1 May 1866; *ibid.*, 6, 6, T199, Second series, West to Larcom, 9 May 1866; *ibid.*, 6, 6, T199, First series, West to Moran, 4 March 1866.
88 *Ibid.*, 4, 4, T199, Larcom to West, 9, 10 March 1866; *ibid.*, West to Seward, 31 March 1866.
89 *Ibid.*, 6, 6, T199, First series, West to Adams, 6 March 1866; *ibid.*, O'Brien to West, 5 March 1866; *ibid.*, West to Moran, 4 March 1866.
90 *Ibid.*, 4, 4, T199, West to Larcom, 26 March 1866; *ibid.*, West to Larcom, 26 March 1866; *ibid.*, West to Adams, 26 March 1866; *ibid.*, 6, 6, T199, Second series; West to Larcom, 6 April 1866; *ibid.*, 4, 4, T199, Smith to West, undated probably March 1866.

West's dealings with the British authorities belied Adams' description of him as 'timid'. On 9 March, he ratcheted up the atmosphere when he complained to Larcom about being refused permission to visit Mykins, Smith, Comerford, Shea (alias Leslie), Mackay and Morley in Mountjoy prison. Later that day, Larcom told him that the government had evidence of their treasonable activities and queried Smith and Comerford's claims to be native-born. However, he was granted permission to visit Smith and Comerford and native Americans. Larcom admitted that the ban on West's visits was because several prisoners who claimed US citizenship were 'known not to be'.[91] This latter admission combined to his knowledge that charge sheets were being prepared may have motivated West to issue a circular on 15 March to twenty-one naturalised Americans in Dublin prisons indicating that the British government would not recognise their citizenship and, therefore, as US consul he would not be able to 'interfere' for them.[92] By then he had received just six certificates of naturalisations from fifty prisoners in the two Dublin prisons, claiming American citizenship. William McGrath, Hugh Dennedy, Denis Burke, Joseph P. Cleary, John W. Byron, Michael Duffy, James O'Byrnes, Eneas Dougherty, M. Kerwin, John H. Gleeson, Bernard McDermott, Maurice Fitzharris and James Murphy immediately provided detailed statements to support their claim to citizenship, denied involvement with the Fenians and outlined their reasons for being in Ireland.[93] By now, West believed that the detentions were unacceptable. He was scathing of the Attorney General's announcement in the House of Commons on 22 March that he would be willing to entertain any 'reasonable proposition' from those 'foreigners' imprisoned under the Suspension of *Habeas Corpus* Act (Ireland), 1866, who wanted to return 'home'. West argued to Seward that innocent prisoners were entitled to freedom as a right without conditions and he agreed with some prisoners' view that Adams should insist on it. Also he was convinced that '99 out of 100 of our population' would support a firm approach by the US government. Clearly, he was aware of the widespread sympathy in America for the Fenian prisoners, but given his long-standing fear of being replaced as consul, he was determined not to become a scapegoat, if Seward eventually needed one. Throughout the period, he insisted to Seward that he always acted under Adams' instructions.[94]

91 *Ibid.*, 6, 6, T199, First series, Larcom to West, 10 March 1866; *ibid.*, Larcom to West, 9 March 1866.
92 *Ibid.*, West to Adams, 11 March 1866; *ibid.*, West to Adams, 19 March 1866; *ibid.*, 4, 4, T199, Circular, 15 March 1866.
93 See *ibid.*, 6, 6, T199, First series and Second series.
94 *Ibid.*, 4, 4, T199, West to Seward, 31 March 1866; *ibid.*, 6, 6, T199, First series, West to Adams, 8 March 1866; *ibid.*, 5, 5, T199, West to Seward, 2 June 1866.

The wholesale arrests of more than six hundred men, gave an impulse to Fenianism in America which its leaders, in Eugene O'Shea's words, turned every imprisoned American citizen in Ireland into a 'Fenian martyr'. Seward received correspondence from the relatives of prisoners and almost 100,000 people gathered in Jones' Wood in New York, to denounce British policy in Ireland, despite Roman Catholic Archbishop John McCloskey's opposition. A Fenian congress in Pittsburgh criticised Seward for not interceding with the British government and in turn, he pressed Adams for some results.[95] Even though West viewed the events around him as having more 'of a local than international character', on 5 March Adams raised the matter with Foreign Secretary Clarendon. Adams wanted to avoid a 'collision' and proposed the release of the American citizens on the pretext of 'good behaviour or of their quitting the country'. Otherwise, he warned, continued imprisonments intensified popular sympathy for Fenianism in America. Clarendon reiterated his government and law officers' position on the inviolability of allegiance to the country of birth and his government's right to deal as it pleased with its natives.[96] Both sides were entrenched. Although Clarendon feared the matter would serve as a pretext for a 'quarrel' between the two countries, there was no change in policy.[97] In Washington, Seward acknowledged the 'friendly sprit' of the discussions to date but indicated the seriousness of the situation to British Minister Bruce. He then reprised the US government's view for Adams; the US government still adhered to the inviolability of citizenship, British intransigence was giving succour to 'any parties who may wish to disturb the peace of Great Britain either at home or in the provinces' and the 'delay in coming to a reasonable and friendly understanding' was 'unpropitious'.[98] Seward wanted an explicit assurance from the British government that it would abandon the distinction made between native and naturalised American prisoners.

In Ireland, a change of approach was evident. On 19 March, the lord lieutenant would not discuss the detention of 'aliens', albeit those of a 'friendly nation', with West. Any representations on behalf of prisoners were to be addressed by Adams to Clarendon. Although West disliked the 'sophistry' in the description of the naturalised prisoners, he was given permission to visit six native-born citizens for a half-hour in their cells and under the supervision of prison guards. He believed the policy

---

95 Quoted in Jenkins, *Fenians*, 89; NARA, D/S, USD, 6, 6, T199, First series, Leslie to West, 7 March 1866; *ibid.*, West to Adams, 6 March 1866.
96 *Ibid.*, West to Adams, 25 February 1866; *PFAGB*, 1, Adams to Seward, 2 March 1866; *ibid.*, Adams to Seward, 8 March 1866.
97 Quoted Jenkins, *Fenians*, 94.
98 *PFAGB*, 1, Seward to Adams, 26, 31 March 1866.

had changed because there was no conclusive proof of guilt against them.[99] This may also explain Lawson's decision to quietly offer some Irish-American prisoners their freedom on condition that they leave Ireland immediately. It met with a 'No Surrender' response.[100] However, the reality of prison life soon changed this blanket refusal. Throughout the nineteenth century, the Irish prison regime was the subject of debate and reform. Local control persisted until the General Prisons Board was established in 1877 and, therefore, a mixture of solitary confinement, hard labour, military-style discipline and surveillance still characterised the system.[101] Although some prisoners did not have to wear uniforms, they could, if they had funds, obtain food from outside, exercise together and have paper for writing but they were forbidden to talk to each other.[102] For those American citizens committed to prison without trial in 1865 and 1866, this regime and poor physical conditions soon took their toll on some.

Fenians in Cork City jail were held in small cells, flagged and vaulted with a small window. Each cell had an iron bed, a worn mattress of straw, a sheet, a blanket and a chamber pot. Untried men were supposed to have access to an exercise yard for six hours each day.[103] But the Irish-Americans claimed to have had just two hours for exercise and several hours for communication in a common room. In Kilmainhaim jail for six months by late March, Michael O'Boyle described it as 'worse than death'. It was no different in Mountjoy where prisoners and their relatives complained to West about the 'close solitary confinement' for twenty-two hours each day.[104] James Murphy in Mountjoy feared he had 'lost my reason' as a result of the sleeplessness.[105] In April, West asked Inspector General of Prisons, James Corry Connellan, to ease the situation for untried prisoners and expanded further to Larcom on some cases:

> Eneas Doherty has suffered from a pain in his head, and a partial loss of the use of his limbs ... Bernard McDermott has been so ill as not to be able to leave his cell for five weeks past ... Michael Kirwin is also in an extremely

---

99 NARA, D/S, USD, 6, 6, T199, First series, Lord Lieutenant's office, Dublin Castle to West, 19 March 1866; *ibid.*, West to Adams, 20 March 1866.
100 *Ibid.*, West to Adams, 20 March 1866; Funchion, *Irish American voluntary organisations*, 110; NARA, D/S, USD, 4, T199, West to Seward, 31 March 1866.
101 David Rottman, 'Prisons' in Brian Lalor (general ed.), *The encyclopaedia of Ireland* (Dublin, 2003), 896–7; Maume *et al*, *The Galtee boy*, 11–12.
102 McConville, *Irish political prisoners*, 147.
103 Maume *et al*, *The Galtee boy*, 49–50.
104 NARA, D/S, USD, 6, 6, T199, Second series, West to Connellan, 2 April 1866; *ibid.*, O'Boyle to Adams, 29 March 1866; *ibid.*, West to Adams, 21 April 1866.
105 *Ibid.*, Murphy to West, 28 November 1866.

delicate state of health and suffering greatly from rheumatism since his confinement ... John H. Gleeson ... has several attacks of ague ... Denis F. Burke was ... suffering from diarrhoea.[106]

West also appealed to Adams to obtain a relaxation of the rigorous discipline in Mountjoy and Kilmainhaim prisons.[107] Larcom agreed that the medical attendant in Mountjoy would prepare a report on each of the prisoners suffering from bad health. Some 'irregularities' particularly punishment for untried men such as solitary confinement, whitewashing walls and cleaning cells, were stopped. Eventually, prisoners, in Mountjoy at least, were allowed to have food brought in from outside by either friends or the Fenian Ladies Committee. But in spring 1866, each prisoner's case was treated on an individual basis and Larcom reserved the right not to discuss with the 'Consul of a Foreign State' any question regarding naturalised American prisoners.[108] Meanwhile the diplomatic negotiations proceeded in London and Washington attempting to secure what most of the American prisoners ultimately wanted – release.

In early April, the British government set aside its distinction of American citizens' status. However, the cabinet decision was not unanimous and some ministers advocated that the US government prevent Fenians from demonstrating and preparing plans to invade Ireland and Canada. Both Clarendon and Adams agreed that the decision would not be announced publicly as it would be 'seized upon by agitators'.[109] The deal was unacceptable to Seward who wanted the British government to issue a public statement accepting the naturalised status of Americans and the right of his consuls to intervene with the Irish authorities on behalf of all Americans. Clarendon replied that a public statement was unnecessary because West was already writing on behalf of all Americans and releases were taking place.[110] West was not entirely satisfied, as innocent Americans had to agree to certain conditions, particularly to leave Ireland and not return, in order to be freed. He left the matter in Adams' hands who did not take the matter further.[111] Among the earliest prisoners offered conditional release was John A. Comerford who received funds from

---

106 NARA, D/S, USD, 6, 6, T199, Second series, West to Connellan, 2 April 1866; *ibid.*, West to Larcom, 18 April 1866; *ibid.*, West to Adams, 21 April 1866.
107 *Ibid.*, West to Adams, 21 April 1866.
108 *Ibid.*, Larcom to West, 24 April 1866; *ibid.*, McDonagh to West, 29 April 1866; *ibid.*, Larcom to West, 18 May 1866; *ibid.*, West to Moran, 20 October 1866; *ibid.*, West to Adams, 27 July 1867; *ibid.*, West to Adams, 9 September 1867; *ibid.*, McDonagh to West, 29 April 1866; *ibid.*, Larcom to West, 18 May 1866.
109 *PFAGB*, 1, Adams to Seward, 12 April 1866.
110 Jenkins, *Fenians*, 103; Van Deusen, *William Henry Seward*, 502.
111 NARA, D/S, USD, 5, 5, T199, West to Seward, 14 April 1866.

family in the US and was released on 17 April.[112] West expected US natives James Smith, Daniel Mykins and William Makay to be offered the same terms which they would gladly accept but would prefer an unconditional release. West did not expect an immediate mass release and advised naturalised-American prisoners to present a memorial to the authorities seeking release.[113] In these last ten days in April, West drew Larcom's attention to three categories of cases. The first included those where no charge had been made and release on bail could be expected in return for future good conduct as in the case of naturalised-American Dr M. F. Garvin in Kilmainhaim who never participated in politics and whose arrest was a 'mystery.' The second involved those where there was some evidence of association with the Fenian organisation. In these cases a conditional discharge was offered but prisoners would need money to pay bail and the passage ticket to the US. The third category included those where there was no evidence of guilt and prisoners expected to stay in Ireland.[114] West's work reveals the complexity of the situation but it was lost on most Fenian sympathisers and supporters, particularly in the US where the Johnson administration was still under pressure to obtain the release of all American prisoners. Meanwhile its apparent tolerance of other Fenian activities strained the American–British relationship.

President Johnson and Secretary Seward allowed Fenian agitation and organisation due to constitutional constraints and domestic pressures. On the one hand, the government knew that the Fenian leadership was planning to invade Ireland and Canada which violated American neutrality. On the other hand, the Irish vote was considered vital in the 1866 congressional election. Any government action against the Fenians would be perceived not only as an attack on American freedoms but pro-British and might jeopardise the electoral campaigns of Republican candidates in the large urban areas where most Irish-Americans lived. Johnson admitted that he was seeking 'support from any quarter' and would avoid 'if possible, any collision with the popular sentiment of [the] Irish masses'. Moreover, Seward and Edwin Stanton, Secretary of War, were known Irish sympathisers as were Representative Nathaniel Banks, former governor of Massachusetts and Richard Oglesby, governor of

---

112 *Ibid*., 6, 6, T199, Second series, Larcom to West, 13 April 1866; *ibid*., Larcom to West, 13 April 1866; *ibid*., West to Adams, 15 April 1866; *ibid*., West to Comerford, 16 April 1866; *ibid*., West to Larcom, 23 April 1866.
113 *Ibid*., West to Adams, 17 April 1866; *ibid*., West to Thomas Costello, 17 April 1866; *ibid*., West to James Murphy, 15 April 1866.
114 *Ibid*., West to Garvin, 19 April 1866; *ibid*., Garvin to West, 14 April 1866; *ibid*., West to Attorney General, 17 April 1866; *ibid*., West to Costello, 19 April 1866; *ibid*., West to McDonogh, 19 April 1866; *ibid*., West to Smith, 19 April 1866; *ibid*., West to Larcom, 20 April 1866.

Illinois. Within this world of competing forces, the Fenians fully exploited the freedom available to them which did not go unnoticed in British political circles.[115] The Fenian invasion of Ireland in autumn 1865 failed to produce a rising and neither did the incursion into Canada in March 1866. But the John O'Mahony-led wing came to believe that the US government would not interfere in any way with its activities and revealed an unexpected militancy. On 14 April, 300 Fenians attempted to capture the small island of Campobello off the Maine and New Brunswick but it failed. Afterwards, Gideon Welles, Secretary of Navy, wrote that Seward and Stanton remained 'very chary about disturbing the Fenians.'[116]

Meanwhile Americans languished in Irish prisons and caused endless problems for West especially those with strong political convictions and knowledge of their rights as citizens. Eneas Doherty, John W. Byron and Denis F. Burke, all members of the Fenian military council, had not presented evidence of naturalisation and were impatient at their prolonged imprisonment without any apparent prospect of their release. The three adopted the same argument namely that the US government should secure nothing less than their imminent release. Consequently, they demanded an answer as to whether the US government considered them to be American citizens or British subjects.[117] Naturalised Bernard McDermott refused the offer of conditional release until he knew 'what his own government will do for him'.[118] These appeals were representative of many others that West received throughout April. Towards the end of the month, however, he decided that instead of writing to Larcom requesting the liberty for individual Americans, he would send a list of the numerous men still confined in Irish jails (see appendix 4.1) and sent a circular to each of fifty-three American prisoners to inform them of his action. He also reminded Larcom of his promise on 20 February to investigate each of the cases involving 'subjects or citizens of foreign states' who had been arrested with a view to releasing them if the circumstances made it possible. He asked for the results of the investigation also.[119]

By then, the pressure on West was immense and he could not control it at times.[120] But he must have been relieved when nine men; Costello, Smith (James), Smith (George), Dunne, Holden, McLoughlin, Farrell,

115 Neidhardt, 'The American government', 38–9; for example see House of Commons Debate 23 February 1866, vol. 181 col. 994–1014, online at http://hansard.millbanksystems (accessed 9 December 2008).
116 Neidhardt, 'The American government', 35–6.
117 NARA, D/S, USD, 6, 6, T199, Second series, West to Adams, 19 April 1866.
118 *Ibid.*, West to Adams, 21 April 1866.
119 *Ibid.*, West to Larcom, 20 April 1866; *ibid.*, Circular addressed to the above-named prisoners.
120 *Ibid.*, West to Adams, 21 April 1866.

Foy, McDermott, accepted conditional release and agreed to leave for America immediately.[121] By way of contrast he refused to write to Larcom on behalf of Joseph Cleary who was offered a conditional discharge but would take only 'an honourable release'. West advised him to accept the deal because he would not get a better one. The same advice was given to Kate Burke to pass on to her husband, Denis, and also to prisoners Kavanagh and Patrick J. Condon.[122] Neither would he submit a special plea on behalf of Eugene O'Shea alias Frank Leslie, because he had lied to him.[123] He was furious when he learned that Edward Morley and Stephen J. Farrell had misinformed him about their true nationality and that they were naturalised citizens. Not only had they embarrassed him, thrown doubts on their cases but they had no naturalisation papers.[124] It is clear that West was wary of making a mistake because prisoners who had nothing else to do, were quick to complain to Adams and to relatives that he was doing nothing for them. He also knew the two governments disagreed on the question of allegiance and that all his correspondence with the prisoners was intercepted by prison authorities. Neither had he received any reply from Larcom to five despatches he had sent on 19, 20 and 21 April and was pessimistic about further releases.[125] But additional prisoners were offered conditional release and some of the naturalised citizens raised the same question with West: 'If I am no longer a citizen of the US, I will accept the conditions of the government. If, on the other hand, I am still a citizen of the United States, I will abide by the issue of that government.' In other words, they wanted to be directed on which course to take and perhaps some naïvely tried to trap West. His standard reply was: 'I could not advise you to reject any proposition for your release.' On 26 April, he circularised them with what he called 'the old-story'; if they were offered conditional freedom, 'it will be for you to consider whether it be not expedient for you to accept the terms that might be afforded'. However, he took up Larcom's offer to furnish him with information regarding US citizens' status.[126]

121 *Ibid.*
122 *Ibid.*, Cleary to West, 23 April 1866; *ibid.*, West to Cleary, 25 April 1866; *ibid.*, Burke to Mrs Burke, 25 April 1866; *ibid.*, West to Cavanagh, 25 April 1866; *ibid.*, West to Condon, 30 April 1866.
123 *Ibid.*, West to O'Shea 24 April 1866; *ibid.*, West to O'Shea, 10 May 1866.
124 *Ibid.*, West to Morel, 29 May 1866; *ibid.*, West to Farrell 12 May 1866.
125 *Ibid.*, West to Adams, 27 April 1866.
126 *Ibid.*, West to Cavanagh, 25 April 1866; *ibid.*, West to Cleary, 25 April 1866; West to O'Carroll, 25 April 1866; *ibid.*, West to Adams, 27 April 1866; *ibid.*, Circular sent to thirty-three naturalised American citizens, 26 April 1866; Larcom to West, 24 April 1866; *ibid.*, West to Larcom, 25 April 1866; *ibid.*, Larcom to West, 24 April 1866; *ibid.*, Circular to Messrs John. Gleeson, H. G. Gleeson, Michael Kirwin, Aeneas Dougherty, Denis F. Burke, James Smith and William McGrath.

Lord Wodehouse refused to release McGrath and Morley as they were British-born and Mykins because he was 'deeply implicated in the treasonable practices against Her Majesty'. The naturalisation evidence for William Mackay was rejected. But these men were offered conditional bail.[127] There was insufficient evidence to hold them or indeed others, any longer. At the beginning of May, some of the native-born and naturalised in possession of official citizenship certificates and who were not charged with an offense, were also offered conditional release.[128] News of these releases combined with a realisation that the citizenship issue would not 'rupture' Anglo-American relations, influenced many remaining prisoners and their relatives to inundate West with appeals for their respective cases to be considered by the lord lieutenant. West was 'much importuned' by Mrs Ryan, sister of naturalised American, James Bible in Mountjoy, a former US army officer who denied any contact with the Fenians. The recently released Bernard McDermott frequently called on West to secure his brother, James' release from Mountjoy. Upon their release, some of the prisoners called to thank West for his efforts on their behalf, others did not, which he resented. His defensiveness was such that he expected some recently released prisoners to complain about him to Seward. He asked Adams to reassure Seward that he was 'not sleeping on my post or unmindful' of his responsibilities.[129]

Seward's interest in the continued detention of Denis F. Burke in Mountjoy, a member of the Fenian military council, resulted in West's preoccupation with it in May and June. West had corresponded already with Burke and with his wife and he knew that Burke would not accept conditional release. Nevertheless, he reminded Larcom that Burke was 'late a Colonel in the U.S. army ... that his honourable service in the late civil war, and his marriage in America, together with the painful situation of his wife in this country, has interested the government at Washington in his fate'. Unless there were strong grounds for his detention, the lord lieutenant should release him.[130] Larcom acknowledged the US government's interest but it was impossible to release Burke because, he was a 'natural-born subject of the Queen' and he was 'deeply implicated in the Fenian conspiracy'. West dreaded giving Mrs Burke this latest bulletin

127 Ibid., Larcom to West, 4 May 1866; ibid., Larcom to West, 4 May 1866.
128 Ibid., Holden to West, 16 May 1866; ibid., Larcom to West, 19 May 1866; ibid., Larcom to West, 23 May 1866. In late May, naturalised McGuigan, John H. Gleeson, Edward Maguigan, Michael Kirwan, Stephen F. Farrell, James McDermott, Edward Morley, Michael O'Boyle, James Bible, Joseph O'Carrroll, James McDermott were still in prison, despite West's appeals.
129 Ibid., West to Adams, 5 May 1866.
130 Ibid., West to Adams, 11 May 1866; West to Larcom, 10 May 1866.

on her husband's fate and suggested to Adams that the only recourse left was for him was to raise the case directly with the Foreign Secretary in London.[131] On 25 May Adams informed Seward that Burke would not be released because he was 'deeply implicated in the Fenian plot'.[132] Adams' underplaying of the situation was unacceptable to Seward not least because of events in the US. The failure of the Campbello raid left the field clear for the opposing Fenian faction led by William Roberts to organise its excursion across the Niagara River. With a force of almost 1,000 men, the Roberts faction engaged the Canadian military. The *New York Times* wrote on 1 June, 'the Fenian ghost is walking again'. Following a victory over an ill-prepared Canadian volunteer force at Ridgeway between 1 and 2 June, the Fenians retreated knowing of the imminent arrival of regular Canadian forces.[133] After the latter incursion, Fenians were taken on board the USS *Michigan* where they surrendered, were disarmed and sent home. Fenian arms depots were seized along the frontiers where all cargoes were carefully watched. But it was Johnson's unexpected reaction after the event that momentarily halted Fenian activity.

On 5 June, Johnson issued a proclamation ordering the arrest of 'all prominent, leading or conspicuous persons called "Fenians" who ... may be guilty of violations of the neutrality laws of the United States' and all official law agencies were to be used to enforce the law. Although vast quantities of arms were seized but later returned and the men arrested including Roberts, were released in return for a promise not to repeat the offence, the government's reaction bitterly disappointed the Fenians. One Fenian officer stated: 'We have been lured on by the Cabinet, and used for the purpose of Mr. Seward. They encouraged us on this thing. We bought our rifles from your arsenals, and were given to understand that you would not interfere.' When Roberts visited Washington, he described Seward as a 'dirty tool' of the British government. Two further Fenian attempts on 7 June to occupy Pigeon Hill and on 9 June to cross the St Lawrence River, failed and American forces arrested several men.

131 *Ibid.*, Larcom to West, 15 May; *ibid.*, West to Adams, 17 May 1866.
132 See *BDFA*, 1, C, North America, 1837–1914, 3, The Irish problem of immigration, 1848–70 (1986), 'The Fenian Brotherhood; an account of the Irish American revolutionary societies in the United States from 1848 to 1870 by Lord Tenterden' (hereafter 'The Fenian Brotherhood'), Adams to Seward, 25 May 1866; see NARA, D/S, USD, 6, 6, T199; Kane, 'American soldiers in Ireland', 115–16.
133 *New York Times*, 1 June 1866; for further see Jenkins, *Fenians*, 210–82; Leon Ó Broin, 'The Brotherhood' in David Noel Doyle and Owen Dudley Edwards (eds) *America and Ireland, 1776–1976: the American identity and the Irish connection* (Westport, 1980), 117–33; Seán Cronin, 'Fenians and Clan na Gael' in Glazier (ed.), *The encyclopedia*, 317–21.

A few days later, they were released and given free railroad tickets to go home.[134]

Canada's first prime minister, John A. MacDonald, proclaimed that the Irish vote was so powerful in the US that the 'vigilance of Uncle Sam's officials was relaxed, and they winked the other eye as the invaders marched towards Canada'.[135] Neither Canadian nor British political leaders doubted but that the US government's actions had encouraged the Fenians. However, there were wider issues at stake such as temporising America's claims for an indemnity due to Britain's alleged violation of neutrality during the recent Civil War, known as the *Alabama* claims. Adams reported that Johnson's proclamation was well received in London and 'at no time since the revolution has the reputation of the country stood so high in Europe as it does now'. Moreover, Minister Bruce communicated Queen Victoria and her government's thanks to the US authorities 'for the friendly and energetic assistance which they have afforded in defeating a wicked attempt to disturb the peace of Her Majesty's possessions in North America'. Although Clarendon took the opportunity to emphasise that the British government had for some months past observed 'with regret, though without alarm' Fenian activities in the US, he abstained from making any official representation on the subject to the Johnson cabinet.[136] The British government's cautious response to the raids was endorsed by Lord Derby's Conservative government which had toppled the Liberals at the end of June.[137] Even in the following weeks, the British government did not officially object when the Johnson administration reversed its Fenian policy. Johnson purportedly told John O'Neill that he deliberately delayed issuing the proclamation to allow the Fenians to consolidate their position in Canada and the US House of Representatives considered resolutions to repeal the neutrality legislation, release American prisoners in Canada and end the prosecutions against Fenians in American courts.[138]

Although the Fenian threat of invasion on both sides of the Atlantic

---

134 Neidhardt, 'The American government', 39–40; Florence E. Gibson, *The attitude of the New York Irish towards state and national affairs, 1848–1892* (New York, 1951 and 1968), 184; Funchion, *Irish American voluntary organisations*, 111; Cronin, 'Fenians and Clan na Gael', 318; Ó Broin, 'The Brotherhood', 123.
135 Arthur Mitchell, 'The Fenian movement in America', *Éire-Ireland*, 4:4 (1967), 9.
136 Neidhardt, 'The American government', 40–1; Bourne and Watt (general eds.), *BDFA*, 1, C, North America, 1837–1914, 3, The Irish problem of immigration, 1848–70 (1986), 'The Fenian Brotherhood', Clarendon to Bruce, 23 June 1866.
137 Jenkins, *Fenians*, 172, 174.
138 Neidhardt, 'The American government', 42–3. In October, the government ordered the release of Fenian arms and ammunitions seized in June and immediate trials for prisoners.

had subsided, public and political interest in Fenianism remained high. The Irish authorities still refused to release naturalised-Americans Bible, Mykins (whose birthplace was still disputed), James McDermott and Joseph O'Carroll. While Joseph P. Cleary, Thomas Holden, Michael McLoughlin, Thomas Costello and James Smith accepted the conditions and were escorted by police to vessels in Dublin and Queenstown for the transatlantic voyage. Conditional release was offered to Michael Kirwan, D. C. Moynihan and a youth named Costello who rejected it 'scornfully and in terms offensive to ears polite'.[139] The prisoners' 'high and peremptory tone' in their correspondence about release and prison conditions tried West's patience. On 8 June, he circularised twenty-six naturalised prisoners to request their naturalisation papers in order to apply for their releases. By now he was utterly disapproving of the men who had 'come over here to create revolution' while embarrassing their government and he hoped to silence their dissatisfaction by showing them that they were in default.[140] The circular elicited certificates of naturalisation from men he had not heard from previously and many other forms of identification including army papers. Documents were also sent to the London legation which delayed the process of identification. In addition to family and friends providing documents on their behalf, the ubiquitous former US Consul James Cantwell also did so.[141] Cantwell had assumed an important role in the saga. In addition to delivering Eneas Dougherty's certificate, West believed that his house was a 'kind of _rendezvous_ for many of our citizens' particularly prisoners' wives, whom he introduced to the governor of the prisons to secure visiting rights and he had stoked up the 'animus of many of our imprisoned citizens'. West warned all prisoners that the authorities would only accept official certificates of citizenships. By mid-June he hoped that the failed invasion of Canada combined with the certificates he had received, would accelerate releases and end the whole matter. Unsurprisingly, Adams agreed that the US government would be glad 'to rid itself' of the Fenian conspirators.[142] At the end of June, Clarendon recommended to the lord lieutenant, the

---

139 NARA, D/S, USD, 6, 6, T199, Second series, Larcom to West, 31 May 1866; *ibid.*, West to Mykins, 4 June 1866; *ibid.*, West to McDermott, 8 June 1866; *ibid.*, Larcom to West, 7 June 1866; *ibid.*, West to Adams, 4 June 1866; *ibid.*, West to Adams, 5 June 1866; *ibid.*, Larcom to West, 11 June 1866; *ibid.*, West to Adams, 2 June 1866; *ibid.*, Smith to P. J. Murray, Director, Convict Prisons, Dublin Castle, 22 May 1866.
140 *Ibid.*, West to Adams, 15 June 1866; *ibid.*, West circular, 8 June 1866; *ibid.*, West to Adams, 15 June 1866.
141 See NARA, D/S, USD, 6, 6, T199, Second series.
142 *Ibid.*, West to Adams, 22 June 1866; West to O'Brien, 28 June 1866; *ibid.*, West to Adams, 15 June 1866; *ibid.*, Condon to West, 10 June 1866; *ibid.*, West to Adams, 25 June 1866. Underlining in original.

immediate release of the remaining men.[143] However, with the Conservatives now in power, the Fenians faced tougher opponents.[144]

Prisoners' cases were still dealt with on an individual basis but as time elapsed it was proving more difficult to justify detention without proof of guilt even though intelligence suggested involvement in the Fenian movement. On 2 July, native-born Daniel Mykins, believed to be, in Larcom's words, 'one of the most deeply implicated in the Fenian conspiracy', was offered release but only to meet the wishes of the US government. American official interest had become a useful excuse for the Irish authorities.[145] Eight days later, Larcom reported that Morley, Kirwan, McDermott, Condon and Burke were offered conditional release again due to US government interest in their cases but none was considered innocent.[146] Meanwhile other prisoners complained to Adams, Seward and Johnson about the denial of their rights as US citizens, West's 'shameful neglect' of them, and demanded investigations into their cases.[147] After at least four months in prison, many were desperate and the situation was made worse when their correspondence was examined by the prison authorities which delayed communication. Also Maguigan, Hynes, Byrnes and Duffy knew that West was holding passage tickets for them.[148] Another reason further galled them: the circumstances of release.

After the individual prisoner agreed to leave Ireland and not return, he signed the release document and the police escorted him to the port of embarkation. E. Ryan from Waterford witnessed such a scene and demanded that his imprisoned brother not be treated as if he was 'a sheep stealer' or 'convicted pickpocket' but as an 'officer and a gentleman'. West agreed and complained to Adams that these American officers were innocent of any offence and placed in a 'humiliating and disgraceful position' which those only found guilty of the 'worst crimes are punishable with'. He felt it added to the men's impression that their government

143 Jenkins, *Fenians*, 173.
144 Paul Bew, *Ireland* (Oxford, 2007), 258.
145 NARA, D/S, USD, 6, 6, T199, Second series, Larcom to West, 5 July 1866; *ibid.*, Larcom to West, 2 July 1866; *ibid.*, West to Adams, 25 June 1866; *ibid.*, Larcom to West, 25 June 1866; *ibid.*, Larcom to West, 29 June 1866; *ibid.*, West to Bible, 26 June 1866; *ibid.*, West to Kirwan. Neither had he received a naturalisation certificate from Burke despite repeated requests. *Ibid.*
146 *Ibid.*, Larcom to West, 10 July 1866; *ibid.*, Larcom to West, 7 July 1866; *ibid.*, Larcom to West, 6 July 1866; *ibid.*, Larcom to West, 6 July 1866; *ibid.*, Larcom to West, 3 July 1866; *ibid.*, Larcom to West, 5 July 1866.
147 Edward Maguigan intended writing to Seward, Thomas Hynes appealed to President Johnson and O'Boyle wrote to Adams. *Ibid.*, Maguigan to West, 6 July 1866; *ibid.*, Hynes to West, 6 July 1866; *ibid.*, O'Boyle to Adams, 17 July 1866.
148 *Ibid.*, West to Maguigan, 9 July 1866; *ibid.*, West to Hynes, 9 July 1866; *ibid.*, West to Byrnes, 14 July 1866; *ibid.*, West to Duffy, 14 July 1866.

had 'forgotten them as to permit it'.[149] Unsurprisingly, when Condon and Burke were offered conditional release on 4 and 5 July respectively, every aspect of the terms was objectionable to them. Burke was 'deeply humiliated' by his own government. He wanted to stay in Ireland for a short while to organise a loan to pay for his wife's medical treatment and the journey home. Neither would he accept to be guarded by the police 'like a common malefactor' because he had not committed, or had been accused of any crime. Condon would 'sooner find a grave here' than accept the terms which he and Burke believed had been negotiated by West on Seward's instructions. West denied the accusation and was even more incensed because he had learned that Kate Burke had moved from Dublin to the home of a Catholic priest active in the 1848 rising, perhaps John Kenyon in Templederry, county Tipperary, which, in his eyes, enhanced her husband's guilt.[150] West's indignation was tempered, however, after he received an apology from Burke for his offensive letter. Kate Burke had told her husband that West knew nothing about the terms of his release. By 11 July, Burke was anxious to be freed on honourable terms and he respectfully requested West to obtain for him a short delay before he started for the US. The new Lord Lieutenant, James Hamilton, Marquis of Abercorn, would not permit Burke 'to be at liberty for a single day in Ireland'.[151] Finally Burke, Hynes, Duffy, Maguigan, Burns, Dougherty, Moynihan and Mykins accepted the conditions and were set for release from Mountjoy on 3 August. They were to be accompanied by six police constables in uniform carrying arms who would deliver them into the hands of the Londonderry police for embarkation the following day on the SS *Britannia* to New York.[152] Hynes protested to the end telling West 'with my naturalisation papers you may do, I don't care what ... "American citizen" is nothing but an empty sound'. He was even more scathing of Adams, the former 'Know-Nothing', who had showed 'cold indifference to the sufferings of mere Irish'.[153]

West's request for the release of James McDermott and John A. Gleeson was allowed but Larcom emphasised that approval was granted only because of West's intervention and further imprisonment would impair Gleeson's health already damaged by epileptic fits. West passed on the

149 *Ibid.*, Ryan to West, 24 May 1866; *ibid.*, West to Adams, 30 May 1866.
150 *Ibid.*, Burke to West, 8 July 1866; *ibid.*, West to Burke, 10 July 1866; *ibid.*, West to Condon, 12 July 1866; *ibid.*, Condon to West, 10 July 1866; *ibid.*, West to Burke, 6 July 1866; *ibid.*, West to Kate Burke, 6 July 1866;. West to Adams, 10 July 1866.
151 *Ibid.*, Burke to West, 11 July 1866; *ibid.*, West to Larcom, 13 July 1866; *ibid.*, Larcom to West, 16 July 1866.
152 *Ibid.*, West to Adams, 2 August 1866.
153 *Ibid.*, Dougherty to West, 2 August 18666; *ibid.*, Hynes to West, 27 July 1866; *ibid.*, Hynes to West, 1 August 1866.

news to Mrs Gleeson who resided at the same address as Kate Burke did in Templederry, county Tipperary.[154] On 19 July, Eugene O'Shea accepted conditional release. He thanked West for his kind treatment of him and asked for the price of the passage because his 'rich old bachelor' brother in Tralee, county Kerry, had not replied to his letters. O'Shea, Morley and John Horan remained in prison because they could not pay for their passage which was a prerequisite of release. West had no funds for such a purpose and appealed to Adams.[155] On 15 August, seventeen American citizens were in custody in Dublin prisons.[156] O'Boyle was released on 22 August and West believed him to be the last American citizen, although the impecunious three awaited release and seven citizens had no proof of naturalisation. On the same day, West lodged a complaint with Larcom about the manner of release of American prisoners.[157] Byron refused to leave prison because of the escort although the equally fractious O'Boyle did not and even offered West his 'vote and influence' if he ever wanted to run for US president.[158] West described the letter as 'amusing' and 'ridiculous' perhaps reflecting his optimism that the end was in sight. Adams agreed and approved the payment of a travel ticket for Horan. Mary Morley, a relative of Edward Morley, sent £25 from Montreal for his passage. At the end of August, James McDermott was accompanied by a police escort unarmed and in plain clothes, from Mountjoy prison to Queenstown.[159] On 24 September, West, still anticipating an end to his travails, sent Seward the final part of his correspondence with prisoners, their families, the Irish authorities and Adams.[160] By the end of 1866, there were just two American citizens (O'Brien and Byron) arrested in February, still in prison. Described by West as 'voluntary prisoners' they

---

154 *Ibid.*, West to Adams, 27 July 1866; *ibid.*, West to Larcom, 12 July 1866; *ibid.*, Larcom to West, 17 July 1866; *ibid.*, West to Mrs Gleeson, 19 July 1866.
155 *Ibid.*, West to Larcom, 20 July 1866; *ibid.*, O'Shea to West, 20 July 1866; *ibid.*, O'Shea to West, 3 August 1866; *ibid.*, West to O'Shea, 3 August 1866; *ibid.*, Morley to West, 11 August 1866; *ibid.*, West to Morley, 13 August 1866; *ibid.*, Morley to West, 2 August 1866; *ibid.*, West to Morley, 3 August 1866; *ibid.*, Larcom to West, 3 August 1866; *ibid.*, West to Adams, 15 August 1866.
156 These were O'Shea, Morley, Bible, O'Boyle, Gleeson, Cavanagh, Byron, Fitzharris, McGrath, O'Carroll, Costello, Lawler, Hynes, Smith and James McConville who was up until then unknown to West. Thomas O'Brien should have been on the list. *Ibid.*, Larcom to West, 18 August 1866; *ibid.*, McConville to West, 5 August 1866.
157 *Ibid.*, West to Adams, 20 August 1866; *ibid.*, West to Adams, 21 August 1866; West to Adams, 20 August 1866.
158 *Ibid.*, O'Boyle to West, 18 August 1866.
159 *Ibid.*, West to Horan, 27 August 1866; *ibid.*, Morley to West, 27 August 1866; *ibid.*, West to Adams, 27 August 1866; West to Adams, 4 September 1866.
160 *Ibid.*, West to Seward, 10 October 1866.

'obstinately' refused release because of the police escort.¹⁶¹

By way of judging West's performance of his duties in 1865 and 1866, it is useful to examine the role county Antrim-born Consul, John Young, in Belfast. Carroll disputes that Young was removed from his post because he was less attentive to the plight of naturalised American Fenian prisoners in his district.¹⁶² Undoubtedly, Young's infrequent references to Fenianism in his reports are noticeable particularly when compared to those in West and Eastman's dispatches. Between August and December 1865, Young merely commented on the presence of Fenianism but elaborated on how Belfast's prosperity was 'almost unexampled'.¹⁶³ He noted the arrest of three men on 21 February 1866 and his next reference to the political situation does not come until 16 May when he requested a transfer back to a consulate in the US because he was 'tired' of Ireland.¹⁶⁴ In the interim, he found time to deliver a lecture to the First Presbyterian meeting in Newtownards while continuing with his lucrative commercial work.¹⁶⁵ However when Seward became aware of the case of Patrick Hassan, attention turned to Young. Hassan was born in county Londonderry, served as an enlisted soldier in the US 4th Infantry and was arrested in North Queen Street in Belfast in February 1866. Neither Adams nor West knew anything about his case even though it was reported in *The Times* on 23 February. Young's subsequent report on 8 August indicated that he had known about Hassan and other detention cases but he had done nothing because he believed that the US government had decided not to act on behalf of naturalised citizens in Ireland. Adams described the reply as 'extraordinary' and he rebuked Young for not consulting either with the department or the legation. Before the reprimand arrived, Young had resigned. His replacement, Gwyn Heap from Pennsylvania, learned from Dublin Castle that Hassan had been released on 23 July and had left Ireland for America.¹⁶⁶ Young's lack of initiative may be explained by any number of reasons; his personal lack of sympathy with the imprisoned Fenians, too close an alignment with local political élites, the pressure of dealing with commercial business in what was the busiest of port in Ireland or, after five years, he was simply tired of the Belfast post.¹⁶⁷

161 *Ibid.*, West to Adams, 12 December 1866.
162 Carroll, *The American presence*, 83 fn. 53.
163 NARA, D/S, USB, 4, 4, T368, Young to Seward, 20 December 1865.
164 *Ibid.*, Young to Seward, 21 February 1866; *ibid.*, 16 May 1866.
165 *Northern Whig*, 28 March 1866.
166 *PFAGB*, 1, Adams to Seward, 17, 23 August, 29 September 1866; NARA, D/S, USB, 4, 4, T368, Young to Seward, 23 June 1866; *ibid.*, Register of official letters received at the US consulate at Belfast from 10 to 30 September 1866. *The Times*, 23 February 1866.
167 Carroll, *The American presence*, 84.

West was not highly regarded by Adams or Moran not least because he generated so much correspondence requiring their attention, and perhaps because of his previous connection to the National Brotherhood of St Patrick. At times, he worked seven days a week, on Sunday 24 June 1866 he wrote thirty-five letters and between September 1865 and 1866 he wrote 400 letters and dispatches.[168] Also he had decided that it was better to have an epistolary correspondence with prisoners because a conversation could be misunderstood or would perhaps be misrepresented. He employed a second clerk to copy all his correspondence with Adams, the prisoners and authorities and to create an index. The resultant document, 577 pages in length, was sent to Seward to answer any complaints about his conduct particularly to clarify his non-involvement in the conditions of release.[169] This clever move revealed his diligence on behalf of US citizens but also protected him if a case became troublesome. Indeed in summer 1866 as soon as the recently released Patrick J. Condon arrived in New York, he published some of his correspondence with West and Adams to support his complaint to President Johnson about their treatment of him. West asked that the State Department publish the whole of his voluminous correspondence to 'satisfy' the US government and people that he had performed his duty during the late 'crisis' in Ireland. Yet, on 3 November he was instructed by Adams to respond to Condon's accusation of neglect, which he did and then anxiously awaited the outcome. His behaviour was vindicated.[170] Although the Dublin post did not regain full consulate status until June 1867, West's performance eventually merited Adams' approval, Seward's thanks and further public acknowledgement from an unexpected corner.[171] Lord Lieutenant Wodehouse who departed Ireland in July 1866, praised West's conduct and indeed the US government's 'decisive action' on the Fenian invasion of Canada. Wodehouse who was elevated to become the Earl of Kimberley as a reward for deflating the Fenian rising, repeated his compliments in early August during a House of Lords' debate on the second reading of the bill to continue the *Habeas Corpus* Suspension Act. He acknowledged West's 'temperate manner' and 'discretion' when presenting him with the cases of American prisoners. Prime Minister Derby applauded as did others in the house.[172]

168 NARA, D/S, USD, 6, 6, T199, Second series, West to Adams, 25 June 1866; *ibid*., West to Seward, 24 September 1866.
169 *Ibid*., 5, 5, T199, West to Seward, 28 July 1866; *ibid*., 6, 6, T199, First series; *ibid*., Second series, West to Seward, 24 September 1866.
170 *Ibid*., 6, 6, T199, Second series, West to Adams, 27 August 1866; *ibid*., West to Adams, 15 November 1866; *ibid*., West to Adams, 13 December 1866.
171 *Ibid*., West to Adams, 22 June 1866.
172 *Ibid*., 5, 5, T199, West to Seward, 28 July 1866; *The Times*, 6 August 1866; John

Despite the arrests, deportations and trials from February 1866 onwards and the extension of the *Habeas Corpus* Suspension Act in August for another six months, Fenianism remained resilient in Ireland. The movement was also buoyant in the US due, according to the British authorities, to the lenient treatment from the beleaguered Johnson government which had abandoned prosecutions, returned their arms and permitted Fenian mass meetings in return for their votes.[173] It is unclear how influential the 'Fenian vote' actually was on election day in November, because other issues such as President Johnson's refusal to safeguard the civil and political rights of former slaves, his poor personal performance on the hustings, his failure to establish a tribunal to investigate the *Alabama* compensation claims and the reunification of the Republican party all combined to play a part in the Democrats losing control of Congress to the radical Republicans. The Fenians had not delivered the 'Fenian vote' to Johnson and it is unlikely that any one individual could ever have delivered it as a bloc, let alone a divided Fenian leadership. But the British government remained convinced that the 'Irish vote' remained the mainstay of the Fenians and gave them the confidence to make other plans. Roberts favoured another Canadian invasion while James Stephens declared that 1867 would finally see an Irish rising.[174] Once again, Stephens needed American men, arms and ammunitions.

1867: the year of the rising

In November 1866, Eastman noted growing Fenian confidence in his Cork district. During the first two weeks, 800 Americans landed at Queenstown while others appeared in the west of Ireland and in Britain.[175] Admiral Frederick learned that arms and ammunition had also been distributed during the week. His informant Resident Magistrate J. L. Cronin went further to indicate that 'there will be a rising shortly'. Frederick ordered

---

Powell, 'Earl of Kimberley, John Wodehouse', *Oxford dictionary of national biography*, 60 vols, 59 (Oxford, 2004), 923.

173 See *BDFA*, 1, C, North America, 1837–1914, 3, The Irish problem of immigration, 1848–70 (1986), 'The Fenian Brotherhood'. In October 1866, the British government prevented the appointment of Charles Dougherty as US consul to Londonderry due to his Fenian connections. NARA, D/S, USDL, 3, 3, T216, A. B. Wood Consular Bureau, 16 February 1876.

174 The term 'Fenian vote' was used by Church, a New York political activist, after the election. See Jenkins, *Fenians*, 208; Edgar A. Toppin, 'Andrew Johnson 1865–1869' in Urofsky (ed.), *The American presidents*, 193; Van Deusen, *William Henry Seward*, 503; Gibson, *The attitude of the New York Irish*, 191–3; Neidhardt, 'The American government', 43–4.

175 Ó Broin, 'The Brotherhood', 127–8.

his fleet and the Coast Guard ships to be vigilant. The instruction was upgraded a few days later to prevent the 'expected' landing of arms from 'fast ships ... from America'.[176] The nature of the threat was clarified by General Lord Strathcairn, commander of British troops in Ireland, who believed that attempts would be made to blow up ships by means of torpedoes, while James Stephens was expected to arrive with two armed vessels.[177] Despite the preparations, Eastman expected the Fenian attack to fail because of the 40,000 British soldiers in Ireland and their control of the railway system.[178]

At the other end of the country, Gwyn Heap in Belfast saw the government exercising its power and using 'its resources to the fullest extent'. On 12 December, he was critical of the enlarged military and constabulary presence 'at every point', arrests by 'over zealous and ignorant police' and detention of people 'who excite the slightest suspicion'. These measures combined to government control of the railway and telegraph systems and the fleet would prevent a rising but were counterproductive as they increased Fenian support. He expected to hear from imprisoned Americans and promised to use every proper exertion to obtain their release, if they were arrested without charges. A few days later, he reported that most of those detained were Irish men home from America, no charges were made and they were usually soon released.[179] The round-up in Dublin and the western counties immediately produced appeals for consular protection. West sought certificates of naturalisation from Edward Toomey, John O'Grady, Stephen J. Meany, William J. Smith and Patrick Bastible.[180]

The government remained on high alert particularly when the lord lieutenant's office in Dublin Castle learned that a paddle-wheel steamer, the *Star*, had been purchased by the Fenians in New York, was expected to arrive in Ireland with supplies for war some time after 17 December and on 1 January 1867, British forts in Carlisle, Camden, Spike Island in Cork harbour and Haulbowline also in Cork would be attacked to seize

---

176 TNA, ADM1/5963, enclosure in Frederick to Secretary of the Admiralty, 19 November 1866; *ibid.*, 1 December 1866.
177 *Ibid.*, enclosure in Frederick to Secretary of the Admiralty, 12 December 1866; *ibid.*, 1/6574 1881, General memo Frederick, 14 December 1866.
178 NARA, D/S, USC, 6, 6, T196, Eastman to Seward, 24 November 1866.
179 *Ibid.*, USB, 4, 4, T368, Heap to Seward, 5 December 1866; Ó Broin, 'The Brotherhood', 128.
180 O'Brien accepted conditional release on 13 March to get out of 'this god forsaken country'. Adams believed that 'Senator' Meany was a US congressional politician until West informed him that Meany had taken part in the 1848 rising and the police had evidence against him for Fenian activism. NARA, D/S, USD, 6, 6, T199, Second series, Byron to West, 13 March 1867; *ibid.*, West to Adams, 28, 30 January 1867; West to Adams, 18 February 1867.

magazines and arsenals.[181] A rumour circulated also that James Stephens had landed and that one of his captains was in London.[182] At the end of 1866, both land and sea defences were reinforced for the expected rising. But Stephens had secured less than £3,000 in funds and the war materials were less than one-quarter of the minimum 30,000 rifles needed. Stephens attempted to postpone the rising but was overruled and then replaced by Colonel Thomas J. Kelly who was indeed in London by the end of January 1867. Kelly's provisional government decided that the rising should take place in March and continue for three months to arouse sufficient support among the Irish in the US.[183] In preparation, John McCafferty, a former Confederate captain who took the Union oath, decided to raid Chester Castle in England on 11 February to get arms for the rising, then planned to seize the London train for Holyhead and boats in that harbour and then cut the railway and telegraph lines between England and Ireland. The audacious scheme recalled the 1848 Young Ireland plan and the guerrilla strategy of the American Civil War. The British government was well warned of the raid by an informer, former Union Lieutenant John Joseph Corydon, and the men were arrested when they arrived in Ireland. Soon they began to protest their innocence and appealed to the US consuls to secure their release and provide them with passage and rail tickets.[184]

Eastman learned of a 'small insurrection' in county Kerry on 12 February, the original date for the rising. The group, led by Colonel John J. O'Connor, obtained arms from the barracks at Cahirciveen, shot a police courier and set out for Killarney. They captured arms from the Coast Guard's station at Kell's Bay and learned that the rising was postponed to 5 March. The group dispersed but some were later captured. Eastman predicted another attempt even though the British government 'would stamp it out'.[185] Indeed, British troops flooded into Kerry from Limerick, Kildare and Cork. HMS *Gladiator* was despatched to Cahirciveen, while 600 marines were sent from Portsmouth and Plymouth to Queenstown and ten other vessels ordered into Irish waters.[186] Despite

181 TNA, ADM1/5963, enclosure in Frederick to Secretary of the Admiralty, 17 December 1866.
182 NARA, D/S, USB, 4, 4, T368, Heap to Seward, 12 December 1866.
183 Ó Broin, 'The Brotherhood', 126–7.
184 *Ibid.*, 128; Kane, 'American soldiers in Ireland', 126; Devoy, *Recollections*, 186–9; McConville, *Irish political prisoners*, 129.
185 TNA, ADM1/6002, 1867, Fredericks to Admiralty, 15 February 1867; NARA, D/S, USC, 6, 6, T196, Eastman to Seward, 16 February 1867; Ó Broin, 'The Brotherhood', 128–9; Devoy, *Recollections*, 190–1.
186 Devoy, *Recollections*, 191; John De Courcy Ireland, 'A preliminary study on the Fenians and the sea', *Éire–Ireland*, 2:2 (1967), 44.

these measures, on 4 to 5 March all the wires were cut at the Electric and International Telegraph company in Cork except those to Queenstown, Crookhaven and Kinsale and the railway tracks between Cork and Blarney were torn up. Frederick reported a 'rumoured general Fenian rising has taken place in the country and ... the insurgents appear to be heading northward'.[187] Although based in Dublin, West knew that armed bands were causing 'much terror' throughout the southern counties and into parts of Dublin and Drogheda. But the police and military authorities were on the alert, trains were running and telegraph wires in operation to and from all parts of Ireland. He predicted the rising will 'extend rather than diminish'.[188] Similarly, Eastman felt the rising caused great consternation but admitted that it was fully anticipated by the British government and thus, it was a 'miserable failure'. Along with having inside information and being prepared, the British government had dispatched new army recruits untainted by Fenian infiltrators to Ireland. Moreover, bad weather hindered the March rising. Nevertheless, Eastman, like Heap, believed Fenianism would still exist in some form 'as long as Ireland starves' and he was in no doubt that if 20,000 American Civil War veterans arrived with arms and officers, the 'peasantry' would rise again and 'defy the whole power of Great Britain'.[189] Indeed one week later, Frederick expected two armed vessels with 'rebels' from America to land on the Kerry coast. Accordingly he instructed his commanders to keep a 'very sharp look out' and to communicate with the local coastguard.[190]

On 12 April, *Erin's Hope* formerly the *Jacknel*, laden with arms, men and money, left New York and arrived into Sligo off the west coast on 29 May. Commanded by former US Navy Lieutenant and Waterford-born, John F. Kavanagh, it had a crew of nine and thirty-four volunteer soldiers two of whom, Buckley and Nolan, were the informers. After being told by local Fenian Richard O'Sullivan Burke, former Harbour Master in Chicago, that the rising had failed, seven men disembarked and *Erin's Hope* left the port. In the end, Kavanagh put thirty-one of his passengers ashore at Helvick near Dungarvan, county Waterford, where they were immediately arrested and no weapons landed. *Erin's Hope* arrived back in New York on 1 August.[191] All the men who landed were arrested

187 TNA, ADM1/6002, 1867, Fredericks to Admiralty, 6 March 1867.
188 NARA, D/S, USD, 6, 6, T199, Second series, West to Adams, 8 March 1867.
189 *Ibid.*, USC, 6, 6, T196, Eastman to Seward, 7, 14 March 1867; Eastman to Seward, 9 March 1867.
190 TNA, ADM1/6002, 1867, Fredericks to Admiralty, 13 March 1867.
191 Arthur Mitchell, 'The Fenian movement in America', 9–10; de Courcy Ireland, 'A preliminary study', 46–7; McConville, *Irish political prisoners*, 130. TNA, ADM1/5963, Fredericks, 12 June 1867; *ibid.*, 1/6002, George V. Goold 11 June 1867

including former US colonels William J. Nagle and John Warren. Their cases along with that of Augustine E. Costello and others arrested elsewhere, had the potential to revive the naturalisation issue and thereby antagonise the US–British relationship again.[192]

Immediately after the March rising, Conservative politicians were even more convinced that US congressional demagoguery and resolutions kept Fenianism alive in the US and, therefore, in Ireland. Seward, however, warned British Minister Bruce that American sympathy for the Fenian movement and the delay in settling the *Alabama* claims, might lead to a revision of US neutrality laws detrimental to British interests. Seward's threat convinced Bruce that he was 'reckless and dangerous' while Adams was still exasperated at Seward's leniency towards Fenianism. It was against this background that American consuls re-engaged with American Fenian prisoners.[193] In an effort to smother the revolt and warn off other Irish-Americans from coming to Ireland, the government held special commissions to try the captured Fenians.[194]

Heap had already complained to the State Department that he was finding it difficult to gather information about prisoners from the 'cautious authorities' in Belfast.[195] In Cork, Eastman surprisingly wrote on 28 March that no US citizen was involved in 'such a ridiculous abortive affair'.[196] But within a few days he had visited Thomas B. Hennessy, a US citizen born in Eastport, Maine, in Cork jail, taken a deposition, sent an inquiry to Larcom and the details to Adams. Hennessy, a correspondent for the *Boston Journal* working in the office of the *Cork Daily Herald*, denied membership of the Fenians. Hennessy was released on condition he leave Ireland but he had no money and Eastman paid his passage rather than see him return to prison.[197] A more serious case was that of John McLure in Cork jail, arrested on the charge of 'firing on the forces sent to arrest him'. He did not appeal to Eastman for assistance. But his father contacted the State Department and then travelled to Ireland where he met with Eastman. Adams also instructed Eastman

---

    enclosure in Fredericks to Admiralty, 12 June 1867. NARA, D/S, USD, 1790–1906, vol. 6, roll 6, T199, First series, John Adair, Abstract report of the trials of John Warren and Augustine Costello and Octave Fariola, 20 November 1867.
192 Kane, 'American soldiers in Ireland', 129, 134; Devoy, *Recollections*, 236; TNA, ADM1/6002, George V. Goold 11 June 1867 enclosure in Fredericks to Admiralty, 12 June 1867.
193 Jenkins, *Fenians*, 226–7; Van Deusen, *William Henry Seward*, 504, 505.
194 McConville, *Irish political prisoners*, 144.
195 NARA, D/S, USB, 5, 5, T368, Heap to Seward, 22 February 1867.
196 *Ibid.*, USC, 6, 6, T196, Eastman to Seward, 28 March 1867.
197 NARA, D/S, USC, 6, 6, T196, Eastman to Seward, 3 April 1867; *ibid.*, deposition, 23 March 1867; *ibid.*, Eastman to Seward, 18 April 1867.

to appeal for McLure's release on the grounds that he admitted guilt, was only twenty years of age and would leave Ireland immediately and never return. Eastman asked the trial judges for a postponement of the case until a reply was received from Larcom. But the trial for high treason went ahead on 23 May, McLure pleaded guilty and the sentence was reduced from death by execution to penal servitude for life. Larcom assured Eastman that it was McLure's change of plea rather than anything Eastman had done which influenced the final sentencing. Larcom commented at this time: 'We hold Fenianism by the throat as you would a burglar, but the moment you relax, up it springs as strong as ever. The root is in America, in the discontent of a million and a half of people, mourning and brooding over a grievance.'[198]

From March 1867 onwards, West was busier than ever attending to the interests of imprisoned Americans. However, he was able to build on some of the special privileges already accorded to Fenian prisoners and took advantage of the incoherence between the Dublin Castle administration and the Home Office.[199] Unlike the previous year, once West was contacted by a prisoner he requested details from him on the time, place and circumstances of arrest, the purpose of his visit to Ireland, his trade or profession, the reasons, if any, given by the authorities for refusing his release and finally, he made it clear that the individual was considered an alleged US citizen until he provided West with a certificate of naturalisation or proof of birth such as a baptismal certificate or two official affidavits from credible persons in the US. Only after he confirmed citizenship, would West apply for permission to visit the native-born Americans, and bring cases to the lord lieutenant's attention. Once again, he was sympathetic to those arrested on the basis of accent, clothes, association, sharing the same lodging house or 'mere suspicion'.[200] Before, during and after trials, he ordered glasses, pipe, tobacco, reading matter and clothes for one and forwarded money and documents for others in Dublin prisons.[201] But he was more decisive in his behaviour towards prisoners and his dealings with the authorities were more circumspect because, like Adams, he was embarrassed that many of them had been previously arrested, given conditional release and by returning to Ireland and in possession of weapons, had broken that agreement which West had worked so hard to facilitate. Adams advised West not to put himself in a

---

198 Ó Broin, 'The Brotherhood', 121–4.
199 McConville, *Irish political prisoners*, 144.
200 NARA, D/S, USD, 6, 6, T199, Second series, West to Burke, 17 July 1867; *ibid.*, West to Healy, 20 February 1867; *ibid.*, West to Rogers, 21 February 1867; *ibid.*, West to Adams, 22 June 1867.
201 *Ibid.*, 5, 5, T199, West to Seward, 24 April 1867.

position that would afford the slightest opportunity for a 'rebuff' from the authorities who believed that their 'generosity' has been 'abused'.[202] Yet, as the intermediary, West had to be seen to be acting, particularly after he learnt that a Fenian deputation had met with President Johnson and demanded their government's protection for Meany and O'Brien who it was claimed were being maltreated in prison. As far as West was concerned, there was nothing he could do in either case. The food and discipline in Naas jail where Meany was held, was the same as in all other county jails. Similarly, O'Brien was treated the same as an ordinary untried prisoner with the exception that he was exempted from industrial work and given an indulgence of an additional meal of bread and milk which he refused.[203] Adams went so far as to instruct West to apologise to Larcom for O'Brien's discourteous language used in his letter of complaint.[204] Unfortunately, for West an oppressing correspondence quickly developed between himself and American prisoners, their relatives, the authorities and Adams. Most of it consisted of complaints about detention without charge and prison conditions particularly in county prisons, but also in Mountjoy where there was an outbreak of cholera in early 1867. He also had to deal with a continuous stream of visitors to the legation.[205]

Another more problematic case was that of John McCafferty alias 'William Jackson', who led the raid on Chester Castle. Immediately West was on his guard because McCafferty had previously been arrested in Queenstown, asserted his right to be tried before a mixed jury of Irish and native-born Americans and was acquitted for lack of evidence. Also he had complained to Seward about West, Eastman and Adams' handling of his case.[206] West followed his own procedures and requested evidence of citizenship before he could act. McCafferty was astonished when his own affidavit was unacceptable to the Irish authorities.[207] By 8 March, West had accepted the police evidence that McCafferty was a Fenian leader and he would be charged with high treason. McCafferty was among the first of 169 prisoners sent for trial before the special commissions held between 8 April and 19 June. In the interim, his

202 NARA, D/S, USD, 5, 5, T199, West to Seward, 10 August 1867.
203 *Ibid.*, 6, 6, T199, Second series, West to Adams, 8 March 1867; *ibid.*, West to Adams, 4 April 1867. O'Brien accepted the release terms after he was transferred to Naas jail on 23 May 1867 where the discipline was 'barbarous'. *Ibid.*, O'Brien to West, 7 June 1867; *ibid.*, Larcom to West, 27 June 1867.
204 *Ibid.*, West to Larcom, 20 July 1867.
205 *Ibid.*, West to Adams, 4 April 1867; *ibid.*, Adams to Warren, 10 October 1867.
206 *Ibid.*, West to Adams, 25 February 1867.
207 *Ibid.*, West to Jackson, 28 February 1867; *ibid.*, Jackson to West, 3 March 1867; *ibid.*, West to Jackson, 4 March 1867; *ibid.*, Jackson to West, 7 March 1867.

supporters in the US brought the case to Seward's attention.[208] The US government agreed to pay fees for his solicitor, John Lawless, to retain Isaac Butt as his barrister.[209] McCafferty received one of the eight death sentences handed down for high treason. Adams refused to intervene with Foreign Secretary Stanley because it was not 'prudent' to do so.[210] In the ensuing days, the Conservative government received appeals for leniency from public figures, including Roman Catholic Cardinal Paul Cullen. The State Department approved the payment of £20 to pay Butt to submit a writ of error and to engage any other counsel needed.[211] Finally, on 25 May Adams appealed to Stanley for mitigation of the death sentences handed down to McCafferty and another American, Thomas F. Burke, on the grounds that it would have an unfortunate effect on Irish-America's anti-British sympathies and that 'others' thought it a harsh decision. Adams was acutely embarrassed by his position and acknowledged that his intervention might be seen as passing the 'proper limits of international courtesy.'[212] However, three days later, British Minister Bruce reported that President Johnson believed the executions would increase support for Fenianism and he threatened that the US government might not act to prevent any further raids into Canada.[213] The McCafferty writ was refused which Lawless described as 'unprecedented in the circumstances', and insisted that the US government would have to intervene with its British counterpart.[214] Adams requested the British government to take a favourable view of the petitions.[215] Eventually both reprieves were granted, clemency was extended to the six others and all were sentenced to imprisonment for life.[216]

The threat of a Fenian insurrection subsided after March 1867. However, the movement remained forceful because of the publicity arising from the funerals of Richard Stowell in May, William Harbinson

---

208 *Ibid.*, West to Adams, 8 March 1867; *ibid.*, Jackson to West, 7, 22 April 1867; *ibid.*, McCafferty to West, 28 April 1867; *ibid.*, West to McAfferty, 1 May 1867. McConville, *Irish political prisoners*, 130, fn. 66.
209 NARA, D/S, USD, 6, 6, T199, Second series, West to Lawless, 19 May 1867.
210 *Ibid.*, 5, 5, T199, West to Seward, 24 May 1867; *ibid.*, 6, 6, T199, Second series, West to Adams, 19 May 1867; *ibid.*, West to Adams, 27 May 1867. McConville, *Irish political prisoners*, 130, fn. 66.
211 NARA, D/S, USD6, 6, T199, Second series, West to Adams, 27 May 1867.
212 Quoted in Gibson, *The attitudes of the New York Irish*, 198; Comerford, *The Fenians in context*, 145.
213 McConville, *Irish political prisoners*, 130, fn. 67.
214 NARA, D/S, USD, 6, 6, T199, Second series, Lawless to West, 19 June 1867; *ibid.*, Lawless to West, 9 July 1867; *ibid.*, West to Adams, 18 July 1867.
215 *Ibid.*, West to Lawless, 8 July 1867.
216 Quoted in Gibson, *The attitudes of the New York Irish*, 198; Comerford, *The Fenians in context*, 145; McConville, *Irish political prisoners*, 130, fn. 66.

in September and William Kelly in October, the continued imprisonment without charge of Americans, the conditions of release still regarded by American prisoners as 'humiliating to their national pride' and the ongoing trials.[217] None of the men who arrived on the *Erin's Hope* had been in Ireland long enough to commit any crime before their arrests. However, their cases, particularly those of Nagle, Warren and Costello, attracted sufficient public and congressional attention that Seward raised them with Bruce and Adams. West believed that as no arms or documents were found on Nagle, Warren and the others, there was no evidence to show their connection with the Fenian conspiracy, 'on that occasion at least'.[218] Accordingly, a reluctant Adams instructed West on 27 July to look for Nagle's release. Larcom replied that Nagle was one of the leaders of the expedition and he would not be released. Meanwhile Nagle demanded that West and Adams secure his 'liberty' or the evidence of the 'truth of the charges' made against him. He also complained that solitary confinement was seriously affecting his health.[219] In Washington, these detentions were sustaining anti-British agitation in Congress. On 22 August, Minister Bruce cabled Prime Minister Derby 'I think it advisable to release Nagle and Warren'. Adams was instructed to pursue the same course with Foreign Secretary Stanley. But it was West who sought Warren and Costello's releases and a reconsideration of the Nagle decision. He gave explicit assurances that Nagle was not guilty of any hostile act within the British empire. Seward cabled Adams on 11 September 'Urge prompt release of Nagle and Warren ... affair is embarrassing'. Two days later, Adams finally obeyed instructions and contacted Stanley.[220]

The timing of his approach on the matter was inopportune as two American Fenian prisoners, Thomas Kelly and Timothy Deasy, were freed on 11 September in a Fenian attack on the prison van carrying them from the court house in Manchester to the county jail. During the attack, Charles Brett, a police sergeant, was shot dead.[221] The events reduced the possibility of the British government offering conditional releases to the American Fenians incarcerated in Ireland. West still obeyed his instructions and appealed to the authorities on 13 September to have

217 Comerford, *The Fenians in context*, 147; NARA, D/S, USD, 6, 6, T199, Second series, West to Larcom, 12 April 1867.
218 *Ibid.*, West to Adams, 27 July 1867.
219 *Ibid.*, West to Larcom, 27 July 1867; *ibid.*, Larcom to West, 10 August 1867; *ibid.*, Nagle to West, 16 August 1867.
220 Quoted in Gibson, *The attitudes of the New York Irish*, 198; NARA, D/S, USD, 6, 6, T199, Second series, West to Larcom, 24 August 1867; *ibid.*, West to Larcom, 4 September 1867; Jenkins, *Fenians*, 238–40.
221 Neal Garnham, 'Manchester martyrs' in Connolly (ed), *The Oxford companion*, 343.

fourteen untried US citizens transferred to Mountjoy where the regime was less severe. Warren and Nagle were moved thereby reducing from West's perspective, one 'serious and just' reason for their complaints.[222]

Prior to the opening of their trials in Dublin on 25 October, the US government paid for legal counsel for Warren, Nagle and Costello. Solicitor, John Scallan, instructed barristers Constantine Molloy and Denis C. Heron while John Adair, and solicitor, Henry Mills, watched the *Erin's Hope* trials of Lawrence Doyle, Robert Kelly, Patrick Kane, William Nugent, Denis O'Connor and John Rooney. After Nagle's trial opened, Heron and Molloy requested bail for him due to ill health but it was refused.[223] The portents did not look good when on 2 November five men were found guilty for the Manchester raid and two of them, Edward Condon and William O'Brien as American citizens, claimed the protection of their government.[224] The issue of American citizenship soon appeared during the course of the Dublin trials. Charged with treason-felony, Warren was a naturalised American and demanded a jury of which at least half were American citizens. This was opposed by Attorney General Michael Morris, and the court. Warren instructed John Scallan to withdraw from the case and he placed it in the hands of his government.[225] After hearing the evidence against Warren, West expected him to be found guilty but as his trial proceeded, the pressure on the State Department to intervene on behalf of its citizens intensified. In early November, the State Department asked West to transmit the indictment against Warren so that the facts and not what the newspapers reported, could be ascertained.[226] The American involvement was not lost on some observers including the Dublin *Evening Mail* journalists who

222 NARA, D/S, USD, 6, 6, T199, Second series, West to Larcom, 13 September 1867; *ibid.*, West to Adams, 30 September 1867.
223 *Ibid.*, 5, 5, T199, West to Seward, 26 October 1867; *ibid.*, 19 February 1868; *ibid.*, 6, 6, T199, First series, John Adair, Abstract report of the trials of John Warren and Augustine Costello and Octave Fariola, 20 November 1867; *ibid.*, Second series, Nagle to West, 19 October 1867.
224 Condon was sentenced to life in prison and US diplomatic efforts to free him continued into September 1877. O'Brien's naturalisation status did not save him from the death sentence. NARA, D/S, USD, 5, 5, T199, 'The Queen v. *Warren and Nagle*' in West to Seward, 19 February 1868; *ibid.*, Registers of Correspondence of the Department of State, 1870–1906, RG59, M77, 83, Fish to Pierrepont, 8 August 1876; *ibid.*, F. W. Seward, acting secretary, to Pierrepont, 1 June 1877; *ibid.*, Seward to William J. Hoppen, 3 September 1878; Robert Kee, *The green flag: a turbulent history of the Irish national movement* (New York, 1972), 342.
225 NARA, D/S, USD, 6, 6, T199, First series, John Adair, Abstract report of the trials of John Warren and Augustine Costello and Octave Fariola, 20 November 1867; *ibid.*, Second series, West to Adams, 5 November 1867.
226 *Ibid.*, West to Adams, 30 October 1867; *ibid.*, 5, 5, T199, West to Seward, 9 November 1867.

denied the American government the right to any role in internal British affairs.²²⁷ It was a crucial issue for the prisoners as without the protection of American citizenship and possibility of US government intervention, they faced capital punishment, if convicted. On 21 November, two days before the hanging of O'Brien, William O'Meara Allen and Michael Larkin, Democrat William Robertson from New York submitted a resolution to the House of Representatives. He demanded that Adams be charged with 'neglect of duty' towards American citizens and if proven, that he be impeached and withdraw him from London.²²⁸ This did not happen but on the same day, Seward warned Adams that the Warren case was a cause of 'serious concern' to Johnson.²²⁹

West expected the native-born Nagle to be found guilty also but his trial was postponed because he asked for a mixed jury. In the meanwhile, West received State Department authentication of his citizenship and Attorney General Morris decided that Nagle could not be tried for acts committed while he was in the US. Nagle's trial was adjourned to the Sligo spring assizes.²³⁰ Augustine Costello was tried twice. Morris charged that he was a Fenian 'conspirator' active in America and one of an 'armed band, who invaded Ireland in an armed ship fitted out in America'.²³¹ He articulated the anger felt in some circles at the US government for allowing the *Erin's Hope* expedition to be initiated in the first place. The *Irish Times* commented 'no nation worthy of the name could tolerate the interference of another nation'.²³² During the last session of Costello's second trial on 12 November, Heron raised his client's American citizenship inferring that he should not be on trial at all. *Saunders Newsletter* worried that the government would overlook 'the crime in deference to the United States'.²³³ When Lord Chief Justice Baron delivered his sentence he emphasised that 'he who is born under the allegiance of the British crown, cannot by any act of his own, or by the act of any other country or government be absolved from that allegiance'.²³⁴ In other words, native-born status could not be set aside by the US naturalisation process. Neither Warren nor Costello was

227 *Evening Mail*, 12 November 1867.
228 *Irish Times*, 26 November 1867.
229 Jenkins, *Fenians*, 247.
230 NARA, D/S, USD, 6, 6, T199, Second series, West to Adams, 30 October 1867; *ibid.*, 5, 5, T199, West to Seward, 9 November 1867; *ibid.*, 16 December 1867; *ibid.*, 6, 6, T199, Second series, West to Scallan, 13 November 1867; *ibid.*, Adams to West, 15 November 1867; *ibid.*, 'The Queen v. Warren and Nagle' in West to Seward, 19 February 1868.
231 *Ibid.*, First series, John Adair, Abstract report of the trials of John Warren and Augustine Costello and Octave Fariola (hereafter Abstract), 20 November 1867.
232 *Irish Times*, 21 November 1867.
233 *Saunders Newsletter*, 8 November 1867.
234 NARA, D/S, USD, 6, 6, T199, First series, John Adair, Abstract, 20 November 1867.

sentenced to death but respectively received fifteen and twelve years' penal servitude. Fellow American prisoner General William Halpin (not associated with *Erin's Hope*, but captured in Dublin) was sentenced to fifteen years. The convicted men were conveyed on 29 November from Mountjoy to Millbank prison in London.[235] The trials of the remaining *Erin's Hope* prisoners – Nagle, Doyle, Kelly, Kane, Nugent, O'Connor, Rooney, John Fitzsimons, Michael Green – were sent for trial to the spring assizes along with Joseph Lawler, Morgan Burke and Michael O'Brien, the only other citizens whose fate concerned West.[236]

The reaction in America to Baron's pronouncement was swift. Petitions from public meetings, legislative bodies and public societies poured into Congress. All demanded clarification of their government's naturalisation policy. President Johnson addressed the issue in his annual message to Congress on 3 December by proposing that the naturalisation of a foreigner as a citizen of the United States should absolve the recipient from allegiance to the sovereign of his native country.[237] The issue was now firmly on the diplomatic agenda between the US and British governments. Seward proposed a comprehensive review of all outstanding issues between the two countries including boundaries, fisheries and the rights of naturalised Americans in Ireland. As the pressure intensified, Adams became even more disgusted with the situation and repeated his request to be relieved of his duties. He was caught between on the one hand, the need to obey instructions from his government and on the other, personal hostility towards the Fenian cause and antipathy towards Seward's 'theory of Irish patriotism'. He was horrified at the events of the Clerkenwell bombing on 13 December when Fenian attempts to rescue two prisoners from a nearby jail included 'the murder of policemen and blowing up of people with mines and gunpowder'.[238] However, his low-key approach appeared to be vindicated by the Clerkenwell events and amid rumours of another American-inspired invasion of Ireland, as well as attacks on prominent British persons including Queen Victoria, and on public buildings.[239] Throughout December, Rear Admiral Claude Buckle's fleets remained on the alert for suspicious vessels off the southern and western Irish coasts but nothing of importance was reported up to

---

235 *Ibid.*, 5, 5, T199, West to Seward, 29 November 1867; *ibid.*, *Report of the trial of William G. Halpin: treason-felony at the County of Dublin Commission Court, November 1867* (Dublin, 1868) enclosure in West to Seward, 12 September 1868.
236 *Ibid.*, 6, 6, T199, Second series, West to Adams, 22 November 1867; *ibid.*, Larcom to West, 8 January 1868; *ibid.*, Larcom to West, 12 February 1868.
237 *Irish Times*, 6 December 1867.
238 Van Deusen, *William Henry Seward*, 505.
239 Comerford, 'Gladstone's first Irish enterprise', 442.

22 December.²⁴⁰ British fears heightened in January 1868 when a torpedo was found in the house of an American officer and a Fenian head centre in Limerick city which Captain W. Murray of HMS *Frederick William* believed was meant for his ship.²⁴¹ Although news of the deaths and injuries resulting from the Clerkenwell bombing interrupted Irish and Irish-American public protests about the Manchester martyrs and *Erin's Hope* sentences, the movement regained its momentum. Eastman commented in January 1868; 'the Fenian excitement in this part of Ireland has been revived'.²⁴²

As the Irish-American prisoners realised that their trials would proceed thereby prolonging their detention in cold, uncomfortable prisons, West again bore the brunt of their anger.²⁴³ Throughout this period, he was acutely aware of the need to have Adams' approval for his every move. In turn Adams looked to Seward which often delayed West's replies to prisoners making him seem weak and indecisive.²⁴⁴ Gradually, the pressure of work became too much for West who consulted a doctor, appointed John Rainsford as Vice Consul and his clerk, Patrick McCormick, was to devote all his time to Fenian business.²⁴⁵

British naval vessels continued patrolling the Irish coasts on the lookout for Fenian vessels but there was no repeat of *Erin's Hope* or a Fenian rising. Consequently, Adams presented Seward's request for the abandonment of the Nagle and other trials to the Foreign Office, without fear of provoking a diplomatic crisis.²⁴⁶ But his moderated approach failed to reflect the increasing pressure on Seward and Johnson. The New York legislature and House of Representatives demanded protection for American travellers and the immediate discharge of Americans held in British prisons on insufficient evidence. A few weeks later, the House Foreign Affairs Committee chaired by Republican Representative Nathaniel P. Banks, produced a bill 'Concerning the Rights of American Citizens in Foreign States' which included a reprisal clause whereby for every American detained abroad the president was empowered to detain in custody a foreigner. Seward made it clear to Adams that American 'sympathies ... are every day more profoundly moved ... on behalf of Ireland'.²⁴⁷ Adams failed to recognise the complex forces operating at

---

240 TNA, ADM1/6002, 1867, Buckle to Admiralty, 22 December 1867.
241 *Ibid.*, 1/6049, 1868, Murray to Buckle, 25 January 1868.
242 NARA, D/S, USC, 6, 6, T196, Eastman to Seward, 8 January 1868.
243 See *ibid.*, USD, 5, 5, T199; *ibid.*, 6, 6, T199, Second series.
244 *Ibid.*, West to Nagle, 30 November 1867; *ibid.*, Scallan to West, 13 November 1868.
245 *Ibid.*, 5, 5, T199, West to Seward, 22 December 1868.
246 See TNA, ADM1/6049, 1868, Paget to Buckle, 21 January 1868; *ibid.*, Buckle note, 23 January 1868; Jenkins, *Fenians*, 256–7.
247 Jenkins, *Fenians*, 261; Van Deusen, *William Henry Seward*, 506; Gibson, *The*

home; first, there was persistent fear, grounded or not, that there was an Irish vote to be appeased during the upcoming presidential campaign, second, growing sympathy among Americans, previously neutral on Fenianism, for detainees who had not had a fair trial and finally, Johnson's need to garner as much public support as possible in his battles with Congress to prevent his impeachment.[248] Instead, Adams appreciated and accepted the British position of not wishing to negotiate all Anglo-American issues at one time but to discuss each separately and according to British national interests. As the man on the spot, he encountered the continuing anger within British political circles about Irish-American activities that sustained Fenianism. The Earl of Mayo, the Chief Secretary of Ireland, believed that if communication between America and Ireland was cut off for a 'short while', Fenianism would become 'extinct for ever'. Mayo told the House of Commons that between 1 January 1867 and 1 January 1868, 265 were arrested and 96 including all the leaders, had spent a 'great part of their life in America.'[249] Adams hoped that the gradual reduction of Fenian-inspired activity and continuing release of American prisoners in Ireland during February 1868 would quieten the naturalisation lobby at home. But he was misguided. Seward's position on naturalisation hardened further because, as *The Times* commented, it could 'turn the scale in favour' of Johnson.[250]

Between March and May 1868, Adams was spared from directing a rupture in US–British diplomatic relations over the Irish problem as Seward and Johnson's attention was focused on the latter's survival in office. Also Adams prepared for his own departure from London. In the interim, Nagle's trial was postponed twice because of the impossibility of obtaining six 'aliens' in Sligo qualified to serve on the mixed jury. The trials of the other *Erin's Hope* prisoners were adjourned because of the difficulty in getting proof of overt acts committed by them in the US. But West learnt that some of the US prisoners would be released from custody, if funds were forthcoming to pay their passage to the US.[251] In order to expedite the releases and relieve the pressure on the Johnson

---

attitudes of the New York Irish, 200; NARA, D/S, USD, 5, 5, T199, '*The Queen* v. *Warren and Nagle*' in West to Seward, 19 February 1868.

248 *The Times*, 7 December 1867.
249 House of Commons debate, 10 March 1868, 190, 1356, online at http://hansard.millbanksystems.com/ (accessed 23 March 2009).
250 NARA, D/S, USD, 5, 5, T199, West to Seward, 19 February 1868; *The Times*, 'America and England' 18 February 1868. Also Seward had just concluded a naturalisation treaty with other countries and needed to resolve the *Alabama* claims. Gibson, *The attitudes of the New York Irish*, 201; Jenkins, *Fenians*, 264.
251 NARA, D/S, USD, 5, 5, T199, West to Seward, 4 March 1868; *ibid.*, 6, 6, T199, Second series, West to Seward, 13 December 1867.

administration, in early April the State Department began to defray prisoners' expenses. Immediately West drew down $300 from the US Treasury which paid the travel costs and incidental expenses for Burke, Kane, Lawlor, Fitzsimons and Burns who saw themselves as 'liberated' by their government.[252] Later in the month, Nagle, Leonard, O'Connor and Nugent still in Dublin prisons, accused West of doing nothing for them.[253]

In addition to the financial conditions associated with release, the prisoners had to accept police escorts and in some cases, admit guilt. Nugent and O'Connor were the only US prisoners who declined to accept the 'obnoxious' conditions. In the first week in May, Nagle admitted to the insurrectionary purposes of the *Erin's Hope* expedition and along with Leonard, accepted the release conditions. Significantly both would travel to Queenstown without a police escort.[254] In the following days Nugent and O'Connor finally accepted their release terms.[255] On 14 May, a relieved West sent his final correspondence on the Fenian prisoners to Adams.[256] London Legation secretary Moran acknowledged that West had conducted the 'perplexing business' with 'marked patriotism, tact and sound sense' and had 'performed it well'.[257] Seward agreed with him and instructed that the 'gratification' of the department be conveyed to West. Despite this, Secretary Fish refused West's claim for compensation for 'special services'.[258]

In summer and autumn 1868, West reported that Irish political life was marked by 'excitement and flux' largely due to the continued political alignment of Irish Catholics with the Liberals under William Gladstone's leadership. His plan to disestablish the Church of Ireland had, according to Eastman, 'firmly united' these two elements.[259] Indeed, more generally, the Liberal leader's constitutional approach to Ireland's

252 *Ibid.*, West to Adams, 11 April 1868; *ibid.*, 5, 5, T199, West to Seward, 11 April 1868.
253 *Ibid.*, Nugent to West, 24 April 1868.
254 *Ibid.*, Nugent to West, 10 April 1868; *ibid.*, Larcom to West, 8 May 1868; *ibid.*, Larcom to West, 9 May 1868.
255 James Smith was actually the last of the American prisoners to be released on 25 June. US citizens Augustine Costello and John Warren were released under the partial amnesty offered in early 1869.
256 NARA, D/S, USD, 6, 6, T199, Second series, West to Adams, 14 May 1868.
257 *PRFA 1* (Washington, 1869), 1575, 191, 22 April 1868; *ibid.*, Moran to Seward, 22 May 1868.
258 NARA, D/S, USD, 5, 5, T199, comment initialled F. S. [Frederick Seward]; *ibid.*, 8, 8, T199, West to Fish, 25 June 1870.
259 See NARA, D/S, USD, 5, 5, T199; *ibid.*, USC, 1790–1906, T196, Eastman to Seward, 28 April 1868; Comerford, 'Gladstone's first Irish enterprise', 441; Comerford, *The Fenians in context*, 160.

problems had attracted many nationalists away from Fenianism.²⁶⁰ As 'political excitement' raged in Dublin and increased during the general election campaign in late 1868, Thomas King in Belfast, failed to make any comment on political matters perhaps because his time was taken up with commercial work.²⁶¹ West predicted that Irish Catholics would vote for the Liberals and that the Presbyterian vote would split thereby giving Gladstone some seats in Ulster. Gladstone carried 66 of the 105 Irish Members of Parliament which gave him more than half of his House of Commons majority that brought him prime ministerial office on 3 December.²⁶² Expectations were now high that disestablishment was imminent. West wrote that 'the excitement it has caused in this country [is] almost unparalleled in its history'. This significant event for nineteenth-century Ireland took place on 22 July 1869.²⁶³

The Motley–Clarendon Convention signed on 12 May 1870 stated that all American citizens would have the benefit of reciprocal protection throughout the British empire as British subjects would have in the US. It had settled a long-standing, difficulty in American–British relations which were brought to a head by American-inspired Fenian activities. Fenianism continued in its original form until the mid-1880s but never again did the combination of circumstances occur to allow it such prominence in American–British diplomatic affairs. In the years after the American Civil War, several factors allowed the Fenians to influence US domestic politics, at least for a period. These included the condition of American domestic politics, the widespread anti-British feeling and the growth of the Irish vote. Nonetheless, during this time of intense pressure from domestic sources, challenging conditions in Ireland, and with consuls attending to prisoners' problems on a daily basis, neither side formally protested to the other on the Fenian issue and the relationship remained cordial. Fenian hopes of engineering a war between the US and Britain went unfulfilled. Nonetheless, Fenianism remained a constant irritant for both sides though there were always larger priorities which required the status quo to be maintained in the diplomatic relationship. Fenian agitation could never sunder the relationship even though the recast movement tried again in May 1870 and October 1871 to invade

---

260 Loughlin, 'Fenianism', 190.
261 NARA, D/S, USD, 5, 5, T199, West to Seward, 25 July 1868; *ibid.*, See USB, 5, 5, T368.
262 *Ibid.*, USD, 5, 5, T199, West to Seward, 5 December 1868; Comerford, *The Fenians in context*, 161–3; Comerford, 'Gladstone's first Irish enterprise', 442.
263 NARA, D/S, USD, 7, 7, T199, West to Fish, 24 March 1869; Comerford, 'Gladstone's first Irish', 443.

Canada. Despite their anxiety about this threat, neither Ulysses Grant nor Hamilton Fish would tolerate the challenge to their authority or to Fish's hopes for an Anglo-American accord. Although subsequent US presidents still worried about losing the Irish vote and, therefore, appeased Irish-Americans when politically expedient, the American–British relationship predominated. For London, the 'irreconcilable' Fenians in the US and Ireland was a constant source of anxiety.[264]

Between 1865 and 1868, the US consul's role significantly expanded and in these challenging times, some consuls were found wanting but the presence of William West in Dublin where most prisoners were incarcerated, ensured that American citizens' interests were protected. At times West assumed diplomatic skills negotiating between prisoners, their families, their legal representatives, police, prison and civil authorities and his minister in London and the Secretary of State in Washington. Moreover his approach helped establish procedures for approaching the cases of American prisoners such as requiring official certification of citizenship from native and naturalised prisoners, querying the circumstances of arrest and detention with the authorities and requesting humane prison conditions and treatment. At the very least, while the US Secretary of State and his minister in London decided whether to intervene or not with the British authorities, American prisoners in Ireland, whether innocent or guilty, knew they could call on their government's consular official for assistance.

---

264 Allan Nevins, *Hamilton Fish: the inner history of the Grant administration*, ii (New York, 1936), 470.

5

Building the Union, 1865–1913: the immigration process

The ending of the American Civil War brought crisis to Ireland but peace to the US. A sense of calm eventually returned to the US foreign service. More generally reconstruction dominated US politics and society. The slave-owning, southern Democrat Andrew Johnson, worked to protect presidential authority from congressional interference, to preserve the distinctiveness of the southern states against central government encroachment, and to maintain 'white supremacy'. However, his refusal to compromise led to conflict and racial hostility in domestic affairs. His decision to allow William Seward a free hand in foreign affairs saw the purchase of Alaska from Russia and pressured France to leave Mexico. Overall, Johnson's tenure was overshadowed by his eventual impeachment in 1869. His successor, Ulysses Grant, a Civil War hero, was utterly unprepared for his two terms (1869–77) in the highest office and presided over one of the most corrupt administrations in US history. His weak appointments paved the way for the beginning of substantive civil service reform in 1877. A rare foreign policy success was not the naturalisation problem but the settlement of the controversial *Alabama* claims which prevented the outbreak of a war between the US and Britain.[1] Johnson, Grant and their successors struggled with the issues of race, economic recovery and industrial growth. Despite this instability, consuls continued to serve US interests and for those based in northern Europe, to manage the continuous flow of emigrants to the US.

The word 'immigration' is not mentioned in the US Constitution but it allowed for a naturalisation process, permitted immigrants to hold all offices, except that of president and vice president. Early congressional leaders realised that increasing their control over territory required people and, therefore, they encouraged immigration. In 1808 Congress ended the importation of slaves and in 1819 it legislated that immigrants be counted at all ports. Just over forty years later, the Supreme Court ruled that immigration was 'foreign commerce' and could be regulated

---

1 Urofsky (ed.), *The American presidents*, 185–206.

by Congress. But it was not until the ineffectual Page Act in 1875 and the creation of a dedicated bureaucracy in the 1880s, that consistent congressional interest in the issue emerged. At a popular level, however, anti-immigrant movements appeared, particularly during the 1840s, which produced state-level efforts to restrict immigration. The nativism of the Order of the Star Spangled Banner (the Know-Nothings) emerged in the 1850s but was temporarily overcome by immigrants' patriotism during the Civil War.[2]

Pace of emigration

In August 1865, when US Minister Charles Francis Adams visited Ireland, he knew he was following in Abbott Lawrence's footsteps, but he hoped to give Secretary Seward an up-to-date opinion. Adams observed from the condition of the dwellings and land, that 'wretchedness' prevailed in the south and west, and was most striking in counties Cork, Kerry, Galway and Tipperary. But even in these areas, he saw hope for improvement because of depopulation and consequent rise in wage levels. In 1851, Lawrence saw low agricultural wages as a cause of emigration but Adams recorded increases from 4–5$s.$ per week to 6–8$s.$ even though they were still 'painfully small' when compared to American levels. He wondered why more people did not emigrate and remarked that 'the cheapest [steamship] rate is far beyond the reach of the mass of people'. Consequently, those who left 'to cross' were either people with 'small means', or those who obtained assistance from others.[3] This astute analysis was corroborated by evidence from other contemporary State Department sources.

Also in 1865, Consul William West felt that nothing could exceed the 'anxiety' of the Irish people 'to reach our shores'.[4] Table 5.1 indicates a slower but steadier rise in Irish settlement in the US after the 1850s.[5]

Table 5.2 confirms a reduction in the annual pace of emigration between 1865 and 1870. Nonetheless, dealing with this persistent flow of people made West argue for his retention in Dublin and Galway.[6] Similarly Consul Alexander Henderson in Londonderry appealed for a fixed salary because the 'much increased trade for emigration' made his port 'only second' in importance to Queenstown.[7]

2 Roger Daniels and Otis L. Graham, *Debating American immigration 1882–present* (Oxford, 2001), 5–13.
3 *PFAGB*, 3, Adams to Seward, 22 September 1865.
4 NARA, D/S, USD, 4, 4, T199, West to Seward, 11 March 1865.
5 Mageean, 'Emigration from Irish ports', 12.
6 NARA, D/S, USD, 4, 4, T199, West to Seward, 11 March 1865.
7 *Ibid.*, USL, 3, 3, T216, enclosure 'To the Honourable Senate and House representatives of the United States Washington' in Henderson to Seward, 3 March 1866.

Table 5.1 Number of Irish immigrants in the United States, 1820–1940

Period	Number
1820–30	54,338*
1831–40	207,381*
1841–50	822,675
1851–60	989,880
1861–70	690,845
1871–80	449,549
1881–90	626,604
1891–1900	427,301
1901–10	418,995
1911–20	172,490
1921–30	220,591
1931–40	13,167

*Figures for early decades are a rough guide.
Source: Blessing, 'The Irish', table 1, 528; *Commission on emigration*, table 26, 314–16

Table 5.2 Number of overseas emigrants from Ireland to the United States, 1865–70

Year	Number
1865	82,085
1866	86,594
1867	79,571
1868	57,662
1869	66,467
1870	67,891

Source: *Commission on emigration*, table 26, 314–16

By way of contrast, Consul John Young in Belfast, was busy with commercial, rather than emigration, matters because of the city's prosperous economy.[8] But West's message never wavered; Ireland was a country of 'unparalleled poverty' and it had supplied the US 'more than any other' country with people and labour – the 'great elements of wealth and power'.[9] In 1868, Consul Eastman in Queenstown, was in the middle of 'a constant tide of emigration' to the US which was

8 Ibid., USB, 4, 4, T368, Young to Seward, 19 March 1866.
9 Ibid., USD, 4, 4, T199, West to Seward, 12 August 1865.

'fast depopulating' the country. However, he hoped that the upcoming general election would install William Gladstone and the Liberal party in government and bring peace and prosperity to this 'unhappy country', as chapter five indicated. He believed that the Liberal programme to disestablish the Church of Ireland, to alter the legal relationship between landlord and tenant – the 'most difficult and intricate questions' – and to restore an Irish parliament in Dublin would ease Ireland's difficulties including emigration.[10] These expectations were not realised immediately. In early 1869 West noted 'the condition of Ireland is at present in a most disturbed and unsatisfactory state, murders and robbery of arms being not uncommon'.[11] Dublin Castle authorities agreed and were apprehensive that a reorganised Fenian movement and a disgruntled tenant-right movement were adding to the generally uneasy climate.[12]

The departures of the 'very bone and sinew of the land'[13]

The economic pattern identified by consuls had continued to unfold specifically the predominance of agriculture in the west and south and manufacturing in the north. One of the persistent micro trends was that children were now 'reared as potential emigrants'.[14] In 1864, Eastman had reported good wages, a decent harvest and improved prices for crops and stock but all simply afforded people 'the means of reaching the goal of their ambition viz. "emigrating to America"'.[15] Four years later, another strong harvest was expected in the southern counties at least. But unpredictable weather accompanied by excessive rain followed by intensive heat in the region, ended these hopes and emphasised the delicate balance in agriculture. The flight from the land continued. The departures were assisted also by the move from labour intensive tillage to livestock farming and increasing mechanisation. Among the categories of emigrants identified by Eastman were 'younger branches' of the farming population (who were effected also by impartible inheritance), 'mere servants', landowners whose land was too small to farm profitably and political refugees arising from the Fenians' failed attempt at revolt.[16]

Eastman could see few employment opportunities in his southern district. He held little hope that the fishing industry which was 'far from

10 *Ibid.*, USC, 6, 6, T196, Eastman to Seward, 19 November 1868.
11 *Ibid.*, USD, 7, 7, T199, West to Fish, 8 May 1869.
12 Comerford, *The Fenians*, 181.
13 NARA, D/S, USC, 7, 7, T196, Brooks to Hay, 10 August 1880.
14 Fitzpatrick, *Irish emigration*, 29.
15 NARA, D/S, USC, 6, 6, T196, Eastman to Seward, 22 October 1864.
16 *Ibid.*, Eastman to Seward, 19 November 1868.

prosperous', would provide employment. In 1867, 11,008 men and boys were employed around the southern coast and 9,962 in 1868.[17] This pattern, replicated in other parts of the country, was part of a long decline. By the mid-1870s, the number of fishing vessels was reduced by approximately one-third of its 1846 level and the number of men to less than one-quarter.[18] A similar picture was reported in other sectors. Eastman noted the 'total failure of remunerative occupations' in the Cork textile industry where the number of tanneries had decreased in the previous twenty years with 'no hope of a reversal'. 'Scanty' employment was available in the local foundry and metalworks which now focused on fitting and repairing machinery with new machines imported from England and Scotland. Similarly ship building in the Cork Steamship Company was now replaced by only repairing and refuelling vessels, which offered less work. Another staple industry in Cork was provisioning the British forces. This industry had undergone a 'marked revolution' with new preservation processes and when combined to the steam-powered vessels, ships did not have to stock up for their journeys between ports. Consequently, large stores of heavily salted meats particularly beef, were no longer necessary. This once lucrative trade was now 'destroyed' although there was still some employment in providing salted pork. Work in mills, distilleries and breweries had recently expanded but not sufficiently to prevent continued departures. Manufacturing paper had once given 'large employment' in Cork but legislative restrictions now meant it was concentrated in England and Scotland and only two mills operated in county Cork making low-grade paper. As for infrastructure, transportation improved with the expanding railway system in the county and Catholics were availing of education but Eastman believed that so long as there was 'no change' in the economic pattern, departures would continue. While much of his evidence related to Cork city and county and counties Kerry and Waterford, Eastman highlighted the continued dependent nature of Ireland's economic and political system on Britain and the ingrained nature of the emigration process in society.[19]

In the Ulster counties, the so-called 'cotton famine' during the American Civil War stimulated the linen industry with the number of steam-powered looms increasing from 58 in 1850 to more than 17,000 in 1875. Mechanisation also required investment in machinery and buildings. Belfast, Lisburn, Ballymena, Londonderry, Lurgan, Newry and Carrickfergus were centres of manufacturing and provided continuous

17 *Ibid*.
18 Ó Gráda, *Ireland*, 151–2.
19 NARA, D/S, USC, 6, 6, T196, Eastman to Seward, 30 June 1868; *ibid*., Eastman to Seward, 19 November 1868.

employment.[20] In 1867, Consul Heap commented that the 'prosperity' of the linen trade was 'inescapable' but it was experiencing the effects of overproduction and a business depression in the US.[21] Indeed the boom period was followed by difficult years when both exports and production declined and growth was not at the same pace as previously.[22] Yet, at this time the volume of linen exports to the US brought in fees averaging $10,000 annually to the Belfast consulate. Between 1869 and 1873, Consul James Rea regularly requested an increase in his salary, extra allowances to pay for an additional clerk and a move to a 'respectable office' that would uphold American 'national pride' among the commercial classes who were key figures in the thriving Irish–US linen trade.[23] He admired and socialised with these 'merchant princes' and encouraged the emigration of a 'superior class' but had little interest in analysing the condition of the poor.[24] He failed to comment on the relationship between the underdeveloped economy, a declining population, emigration and the warning signs of another imminent crisis. Similarly, the interests of his replacement, businessman James M. Donnan of Petersburg, Virginia, centred on expanding trade links between Ulster and the US by securing a reduction in US import duties on linen goods and developing a direct steamship connection.[25] When Donnan mentioned emigration, he noted in November 1874 that 'it has not been large' from Belfast, in October 1875 it was 'small' and 'very small' in October 1877. He paid little attention to the consequences of the 'unusually severe winter' in 1874–5 for the rural population, yet he reported that it delayed orders being placed for American goods. At the end of 1875, two lines of a four-page report noted that the crops in his district had been 'good', except for potatoes which in certain parts of his district had been a 'partial failure'. Instead it was the signs of improvement in the linen trade which preoccupied him in October 1877 and reflected the specific nature of the predominant economic activity in his district.[26] The gathering clouds over the economy, unnoticed by Belfast consuls, induced the same reaction from

20 Carroll, *The American presence*, 87; Ó Gráda, *Ireland*, 286–9.
21 NARA, D/S, USB, 5, 5, T368, Heap to Seward, 7 May 1867.
22 Ó Gráda, *Ireland*, 290.
23 NARA, D/S, USB, 6, 6, T368, Rea to Fish, 16 February 1870.
24 *Ibid*., Rea to Fish, 14 July 1870.
25 *Ibid*., Donnan to Davis, 5 November 1874; *ibid*., 7, 7, T368, Donnan to Secretary of State, 30 October 1877; *ibid*., 6, 6, T368, Donnan to Davis, 17 May 1873; *ibid*., 7, 7, T368, Donnan to Secretary of State, 12 October 1876; *ibid*., 6, 6, T368, Donnan to Davis, 4 June 1873.
26 *Ibid*., 7, 7, T368, Donnan to Asst. Secretary of State, 5 May 1875; *ibid*., Donnan to Asst. Secretary of State, 1 October 1875; *ibid*., Donnan to Asst. Secretary of State, 2 October 1877.

Edward Neill and then Benjamin Barrows in Dublin.[27]

It was not until 11 April 1878 when the State Department instructed European-based consuls to report on the state of agriculture in their respective districts, that some analysis of the Irish economy was forthcoming. Barrows confirmed the major trends in the economy: 'general dependence' on agriculture rather than industry, a movement from tillage to pastoral farming, reduced employment, increased cost of living, continued migration to England for higher wages and emigration especially from rural areas.[28] It was the increases in the cost of living of about one-sixth during the previous five years that the Rhode Island-born, Lewis Richmond in Queenstown, noted as did Donnan in Belfast who saw that the labouring classes could not 'accumulate anything' as wages were used for 'living'.[29] For Livermore in Londonderry, the local economy was dominated by shirt-making, the manufacture of artificial manures which was 'prosperous' and the curing of bacon and hams. Biannual hiring fairs were held in the city on 15 May and November respectively, which saw girls and boys engaged for farm employment, and girls paid 'nearly as much' as boys for largely the same work. The mills provided 'apparently undiminished' employment, particularly for females who were 'much valued' and could earn 7s. each week. Livermore was based in the main embarkation point for emigrants from counties Donegal, Tyrone and Londonderry but he did not refer to rural distress, except for a comment on the dependence on imported Indian meal, and that potato prices were 'uncertain and fluctuating'.[30] Neither Barrows, Richmond, Donnan or Livermore commented further in 1878 on the deteriorating position of the landless labourer and tenant farmer, tenant demands for rent concessions or evictions. In early October, Donnan was pleased that the flax crop as well as other crops in the Ulster counties were 'very good', although the 'complaint in general is that trade is bad'. Yet, he was astonished at how many new buildings were being built in 'all parts' of Belfast. Clearly, his personal reference points were industry and the Belfast city landscape. In the following months, Donnan, Barrows and Livermore prepared for the visit of former President Ulysses S. Grant in January 1879.[31]

27 See *ibid.*, USD, 8, 8, T199.
28 *Ibid.*, Barrows to Asst. Secretary of State, enclosure, 3 July 1878; *ibid.*, Barrows to Asst. Secretary of State, enclosure, 3 July 1878.
29 *Ibid.*, USC, 7, 7, T196, Richmond to Seward, 27 June 1878.
30 *Ibid.*, USB, 9, 9, T368, Livermore to Secretary of State, 18 May 1878.
31 *Ibid.*, vol. 7 roll 7, T368, Donnan to Asst. Secretary of State, 4 October 1878; John Russell Young, *Around the world with General Grant: a narrative of the visit of General Ulysses S. Grant ex-president of the United States to various countries in Europe, Asia, Africa in 1877, 1878, 1879: to which are added certain conversations with Grant*

The Land War gathered pace from April 1879 onwards, leading to the establishment of the Irish Land League in Mayo on 16 August by Michael Davitt and its integration into the Irish National Land League. The latter was formed on 21 October by Davitt and Charles Stewart Parnell, one of the leaders of the Irish Parliamentary Party. Following a meeting in Cork addressed by Parnell, Consul Richmond noted the 'serious effects' of the land campaign, specifically the demand for 'peasant proprietary', and the possibility of a 'no rent' campaign being used in the 'battle' with landlords. He was anxious about the increased army presence in the countryside and the probable disruption of life.[32] Although he failed to expand on the iniquitous conditions and circumstances experienced by rural tenants, Barrows' response was more revealing. He explained that after the introduction in 1860 of the Landlord and Tenant Law Amendment (Ireland) Act and the Tenant Improvement of Land (Ireland) Act:

> the Irish landlord ... found no trouble in evicting their tenants, either for non-payment of rent or other causes, and as a large majority of Irish tenants occupy their holdings from year to year, the insecurity of their tenure after 1860 became more and more patent. The Act of 1860 in short afforded every facility to landlords for evicting, a practice which Lord Russell [former prime minister] said "had with the attendant evils been the leading cause of agrarian outrage in Ireland".

William Gladstone's Land Act in 1870 legalised the Ulster custom whereby tenants gained customary rights of fair rent, free sale and fixity of tenure, forced landlords to compensate evicted tenants for improvements, except if they had rent arrears, and allowed tenants to borrow two-thirds of the purchase price of their holdings from the government. Barrows, however, believed the act had not 'proven successful', although some landlords had reduced rents by 10 to 25 per cent and the 'best' landlords in Ulster implemented the 'Ulster custom'. He explained that distress was localised and if it existed in 'rugged Connemara or Galway or among the dreary hills of Skibbereen', then the local government boards all over Ireland were 'competent' to deal with a 'calamity should it come'. A 'famine' was not imminent but the League's aims and methods would bring 'agitation'.[33] He failed to note the other causes of

---

connected with American politics and history, 1 (New York, c. 1879), 576–84.
32 NARA, D/S, USC, 7, 7, T196, Richmond to Seward, 10 October 1879.
33 The 1860 act was known also as Deasy's act after the Irish Attorney General Rickard Deasy, and the latter as Cardwell's act after the Irish Chief Secretary Edward Cardwell. NARA, D/S, USD, 8, 8, T199, Barrows to Asst. Secretary of State, enclosure, 27 October 1879; E. D. Steele, *Irish land and British politics* (Cambridge, 1974), 68; NARA, D/S, USD, 8, 8, T199; Barrows to Asst. Secretary of State, enclosure, 27 October 1879; *ibid.*, Barrows to Asst. Secretary of State, 16 December 1879;

rural distress: incessant rain and the loss of crops. Ultimately, Barrows had little sympathy for the plight of the peasant and he was more worried about Parnell's intention to visit America in November to:

> solicit money for the relief of Irish tenants. Money for a starving people is a noble charity – money given a factious tenantry to encourage them to shoot their landlords is another thing, and Mr Parnell's political teaching simply fosters agrarian outrage ... the movement is purely political (in view of an approaching general election). In case of actual famine in certain districts the government is abundantly able to care for its own.[34]

Unusually, he wrote three weeks later noting the 'considerable suffering' in the west and that the poor law relief system was 'totally insufficient'. Perhaps attempting to counteract American newspaper reports, he drew attention to the denunciation of the League by Roman Catholic Archbishop of Dublin, Edward McCabe, in a pastoral letter on 23 November.[35] Barrows faced a dilemma between accurately reporting the rural distress and the emergence of the League but not exaggerating the situation.

Significantly, it was not the politicisation of rural distress or the continuing 'bad weather' that concerned Donnan in Belfast when he first informed the State Department in September 1879 about difficulties with the harvest. Echoing his predecessor's comments during the 1845–51 famine, he focused on the profits which US farmers and grain merchants could make from the situation and mentioned in passing that emigration, 'though not large', had increased in 1879 over previous years.[36] When Livermore in Londonderry noted the failure of the 'potatoes and turnips', he expected the 'peasants' to eat more meat and oats because that crop was in 'good condition'.[37] In Cork, Richmond had not linked the worsening rural situation with continuing departures. However, in early 1880, the 'extraordinary' increase in emigration to the US was of such 'especial notice' that his replacement, Edward Brooks, devoted a ten-page letter to it. He began by quantifying the departures for the US given in table 5.3.

Not only was there an almost sixfold increase in departures in early 1880 but emigrants also used other routes 'across the channel' to get to the US. Brooks reminded his superiors that the emigration season had 'not yet fairly begun'. The emigrants were as a rule, 'young in years,

---

Jonathan Bardon, 'Ulster Custom' in Lalor (ed.) *The encyclopaedia*, 1090; Lindsay Proudfoot, 'Tenant right' in Connolly (ed.), *The Oxford companion*, 538–9.
34 NARA, D/S, USD, 8, 8, T199, Barrows to Asst. Secretary of State, 27 October 1879.
35 *Ibid.*, Barrows to Asst. Secretary of State, 25 November 1879.
36 *Ibid.*, USB, 7, 7, T368, Donnan to Asst. Secretary of State, 3 September 1879.
37 *Ibid.*, 9, 9, T368, Livermore to Secretary of State, 3 October 1879.

Table 5.3 Emigrants from Queenstown, February, March 1879 and 1880

Year	February (entire month)	March (first ten days)	Total
1879	169	154	323
1880	1,270	601	1,871

Source: NARA, D/S, USC, 7, 7, T196, Brooks to Hay, 12 March 1880.

ranging from eighteen to thirty, hale and hearty and are from the more adventurous or public-spirited of the classes known here as labourers and cottiers or peasantry'. The reasons were 'distress among the classes in question, some times called "the famine" and which follows from crop failures and business depression last year … much deprivation and great misery prevails among them'.[38] Brooks may not have known about the New Departure pact between Davitt, Parnell and Irish-American Clan na Gael leader, John Devoy.[39] However, he correctly noted that rural distress in county Mayo had sparked the creation of the Land League in late 1879 and it was extending to southern and northern counties. In places where landowners did not reduce rent; it was not paid and evictions ensued or were attempted with the aid of police and soldiers. In these violent, unstable circumstances, the attraction of emigration increased for many.[40] Meanwhile US consuls became entangled in other aspects of the Land War.

Irish-American money and support for the Irish National Land League was secured by Clan na Gael but the potential benefits of having Parnell visit the US seemed immense. Barrows had already expressed concern about the impact of such a visit on Irish-America and wider US society and that it would be a source of embarrassment for the US government. The visit took place between January and March 1880 and during his sixty-two city tour, Parnell received a rapturous welcome from his exiled compatriots. He addressed the state legislatures in New York, Virginia, Kentucky, Wisconsin and Iowa. He was warmly welcomed by the American Roman Catholic bishops and clergy despite the disapproval of the Vatican and the Irish hierarchy. The high point for Parnell was his address to the US House of Representatives on 2 February 1880, when he attacked the landlord system as the cause of agricultural distress, criticised emigration as a solution and offered his own remedy; 'every

38 *Ibid.*, USC, 7, 7, T196, Brooks to Asst. Secretary of State, 30 January 1880; *ibid.*, Brooks to Hay, 12 March 1880.
39 James Loughlin, 'New Departure' in Connolly (ed.), *The Oxford companion*, 386. Clan na Gael was the successor organisation to the Fenian Brotherhood.
40 NARA, D/S, USC, 7, 7, T196, Brooks to Hay, 12 March 1880.

occupying tenant farmer in Ireland to become the owner of his own farm'. Although the speech contained few appeals for money, two weeks afterwards the Senate instructed Secretary of War George W. McCrary to have a naval vessel loaded with food and other goods and sent to the 'famishing poor of Ireland'. Additionally Parnell's American committee raised in excess of $200,000, US Catholics contributed almost $800,000 and the *New York Herald* Relief Committee Fund donated $100,000 to relieve Irish distress.[41]

On 20 April, USS *Constellation* arrived in Queenstown carrying flour, meat, potatoes and other goods funded by private donors and the *New York Herald* fund. Brooks was proud of the welcome given by the 'official and unofficial classes' in Queenstown, Cork, Dublin and Galway respectively, to the crew and captain. But soon enough, he felt that Irish nationalists were using the public events 'to talk ... politics'. Brooks and Commander Edward Potter of the *Constellation* were careful not to give the impression to the authorities that the expedition represented official American 'discontent' with the British government. Neither did Potter accept any petitions or addresses of a political nature for transmission to his government. Both men tried to counteract the Land Leaguers' view that the act was an official American 'rebuke' to the British government and that the Anglo-American relationship must 'naturally' be 'unfriendly'.[42] The British government indicated its 'high appreciation' of the generous act of 'international comity'.[43] Brook's resistance to attempts to politicise the American humanitarian gesture was motivated by his duty to remain neutral but also by the need to protect US interests at home and abroad. Moreover, his continuing exposure to the political torment throughout the country intensified his apprehension that as:

> the present swollen tide of immigration will be kept up ... the thoughts and longing hopes of thousands of Irishmen are now turned to the United States as a haven of refuge and are fixed thereupon, not only because of the famine, so-called, but by reason of current political agitations which have to a certain extent transferred the discussion of the "Irish Question" to American soil.[44]

Not only did the number of Irish emigrants to the US increase from 30,058 in 1879 to 80,018 in 1880 but they augmented the embittered

41 Michael V. Hazel, 'First link: Parnell's American tour, 1880', *Éire–Ireland*, 15:1 (1980), 6–24; Merle Eugene Curti, *American philanthropy abroad* (Reprint. New Jersey, 1963), 96.
42 NARA, D/S, USC, 7, 7, T196, Brooks to Hay, May 1880.
43 Curti, *American philanthropy*, 96. The Canadian government's donation of $100,000 represented a greater gesture. *Ibid.*, 97.
44 NARA, D/S, USC, 7, 7, T196, Brooks to Hay, 12 March 1880.

anti-British feeling among those who had already left during and after the 1845–51 famine.⁴⁵ American sympathy, but more significantly their money for relief, ensured that the Land War continued throughout the period and Parnell had a 'sizeable war chest' to sustain the organisation, particularly in the upcoming general election, following the dissolution of parliament at the start of March 1880.⁴⁶ Donnan's replacement in Belfast, Lewis Richmond, commented how business was 'temporarily checked' because of the campaign which 'absorbs the attention of all classes'. But following his predecessor's example it was the continued increase in the value of exports from Belfast and Ballymena during March, that merited most notice.⁴⁷

Meanwhile, conditions in the west of Ireland deteriorated. In the absence of sufficient government relief, the Duchess of Marlborough Fund and the Mansion House Relief Fund organised by the Lord Mayor of Dublin, E. Dwyer Gray, were established. In early 1880, when the relief supplies from the Marlborough Fund began to be delivered by the British Navy to remote coastal communities, even Lieutenant Thomas Suckling of the HMS *Goshawk* who considered the 'distress' among the islanders off the coast from Galway to Clifden to be 'exaggerated', described 'distressed' people in Clifden and the islanders on Innisturk, Turbot and Omey to be 'one and all in a very poor way'. On Dursey island and in Baltimore, county Cork, the 'poorest and worst needy' were helped.⁴⁸

After the 1880 election, twenty-seven Parnellite Members of Parliament made Parnell chairman of the Irish Parliamentary Party (IPP) at Westminster and Liberal leader, William Gladstone, returned to office in June. Irish hopes of a settlement to the ongoing Land War were revived. Brooks confirmed that 'distress, debt and eviction' persisted and contrasted the delay in government intervention with its readiness to use military and police force in evictions. His sympathy for tenants was tempered though by his criticism of their consumption of porter and spirits as if they were the 'necessities of existence'.⁴⁹ Whereas Richmond located in Belfast, believed that Ulster's 'active and industrious' population whose lives displayed 'thrift, industry, enterprise' contributed in late 1880 to a 'revival of prosperity' with an 'abundant harvest' gathered

45 *Commission on emigration*, table 26, 314–16.
46 Hazel, 'First link', 22.
47 NARA, D/S, USB, 7, 7, T368, Donnan to Hay, 18 February 1880; *ibid.*, Richmond to Hay, 1 April 1880.
48 TNA, ADM1/6536 1880, R. A. Dowell to Secretary of Admiralty, 27 January 1880; *ibid.*, 16 February 1880; *ibid.*, Suckling to Admiral Dowell, 17 February 1880; *ibid.*, Suckling to Dowell, 24 February 1880; Suckling to Dowell, 30 July 1880.
49 NARA, D/S, USC, 7, 7, T196, Brooks to Hay, 10 August 1880.

and linen manufacturers expecting a 'most prosperous business'.⁵⁰ The crisis did not affect the Belfast area to the same extent. Commanders of British vessels patrolling the southern and western coasts, confirmed the continuing popularity of the Land League, the raging Land War and distress. Lieutenant J. Rendell of HMS *Orwell* wrote on 25 October that they had brought some RIC men to Castletown Bere, county Cork, to police a Land League meeting. A few weeks later Lieutenant Suckling on HMS *Goshawk* described much bitterness and ill feeling on Arranmore island, county Donegal, between Protestants and Catholics while people who would not join the Land League were 'almost entirely "tabooed" by the others'. Rendell concluded that the country is 'very unsettled' and there were agrarian outrages reported nearly every day; hayricks burned, cattle mutilated and men threatened.⁵¹

Events in Ireland had overtaken Gladstone's approach. Once in office, he established a commission of inquiry into the working of the 1870 land legislation under the chairmanship of Irish nobleman, Frederick Ponsonby, Earl of Bessborough. But when Parliament reconvened on 7 January 1881, US Minister James Russell Lowell wrote:

> Seldom has a session of Parliament begun under more critical circumstances. The abnormal condition of Ireland and the question of what remedy should be sought for it have deeply divided an embittered public opinion. Not only has the law been rendered powerless and order disturbed (both of them things almost superstitiously sacred in England), but the sensitive nerve of property has been rudely touched. The opposition have clamoured for coercion, but while they have persisted in this it is clear that a change has been gradually going on in their opinion as to how great a concession would be needful.⁵²

A few days later the Bessborough Commission supported changes to land legislation and the minority Richmond Commission favoured fair rent, free sale and fixity of tenure (the Ulster custom), namely the Land League's demands.⁵³ Lowell felt that any 'cure' would fail to meet 'the overweening expectations' and 'inconsiderate temper' of the Irish people. This belief in the existence of a weak Irish character, noted above, was not out place for the Bostonian intellectual. As early as 1848, he associ-

---

50 *Ibid.*, USB, 7, 7, T368, Richmond to Hay, 6 July 1880; *ibid.*, Richmond to Hay, 25 October 1880.
51 See Vaughan, 'Ireland *c.* 1870' in Vaughan (ed.), *A New History of Ireland* v, 5, 781, for a discussion on prosperity in parts of Ulster. TNA, ADM1/6536 1880, Rendell report, 25 October 1880 in Dowell to Admiralty, 26 October 1880; *ibid.*, Suckling to Hamilton, 10 December 1880; *ibid.*, ADM1/6573 1881, Salter to Hamilton, 2 February 1881; *ibid.*
52 Willson, *America's ambassadors*, 377–9.
53 Alan O'Day, *Irish home rule, 1867–1921* (Manchester, 1998), 69.

ated the Irish with 'thriftlessness, superstition and dirt'. As US minister he believed the popularity of the land movement resulted more from bullying and intimidation than politicisation and sympathy with the cause. Significantly, however, with the IPP now ensconced in Westminster, he recognised that the land movement encompassed political and agrarian issues. However, it was 'folly' for the IPP to expect the government to ever 'peaceably consent' to Irish independence but they could expect 'thorough reform' of the land laws and a 'certain amount of local self-government'.[54] Lowell viewed the situation in Ireland as 'critical' and Secretary of State William Evarts agreed. The latter hoped in January 1881 that Gladstone would pursue a 'wise and a statesmanlike' policy.[55] Unfortunately, rural agitation intensified. In February, coercive legislation was introduced. Brooks finally referred to the presence of 'famine' and he could see that it was the poorer classes who were hit hardest, particularly those living on poorer land along the western seaboard. The Land League 'with its ... all-pervading influence for good and evil' was the main cause of this 'deplorable situation'. Yet, he recognised the dilemma; the League derived its power and authority from the 'masses' while 'land owners, land lords, land agents, capitalists, conservative middle men' supported an undemocratic government. Within this *'imperium in imperio'*, it was the Land League which was 'at present more powerful'. Both Lowell and Brooks were appalled by the Coercion Act which ran counter to their belief in democracy, equality and freedom.[56] After the suspension of the *Habeas Corpus* Act, the 'revolution against landlordism', to use Brooks' words, gathered pace. American funds reinforced tenant resistance to eviction and imprisoned American citizens appealed to their consuls and politicians for protection.[57] Secretary of State James G. Blaine instructed

54 Willson, *America's ambassadors*, 377–9.
55 NARA, RG 59, DIDS, M77, 85, Evarts to Lowell, 20 January 1881.
56 A 'government within another'. NARA, D/S, USC, 8, 8, T196, Brooks to Hay, 3 March 1881; TNA, ADM1/6664 1884, Confidential memo. no. 1 referred to in memoranda on Irish stations and transfer of command, 16 April 1883; Allan Nevins, *Henry White: thirty years of American diplomacy* (New York, 1930), 53. White was a member of the London legation staff at this time.
57 NARA, D/S, USC, 8, 8, T196, Brooks to Hay, 3 March 1881. Early 1881 also saw the United Irishmen of America launch a bombing campaign in England while Clan na Gael planned a similar strategy for London in 1883–5. A further American dimension to the Land War lay in the reduced demand for American products occasioned by business stagnation. On the other hand, Brooks identified that Irish industries and agriculture suffered because of competition from American imports. R. Vincent Comerford, 'Land War' in Connolly (ed.), *The Oxford companion*, 300–1; S. J. Connolly, 'Coercion acts' in Connolly (ed.), *The Oxford companion*, 101–2; Comerford, *The Fenians*, 240–3; NARA, D/S, USC, 8, 8, T196, Brooks to Hitt, 24 August 1881; *ibid.*, Brooks to Hay, 3 March 1881.

the consuls first, to investigate each case and second, if charges were not levelled against individuals, Lowell was to intervene with the Foreign Office. Lowell resisted acting on the instruction because he wanted the law to take its course.[58] In April, rumours abounded that British gunboats and vessels along the west coast would be attacked by American 'adventurers' using dynamite and caused 'some amount of anxiety' within the Admiralty in Ireland. Once again, the expected 'rising' did not materialise.[59]

Brooks accepted that so long as 'hated British rule' continued, emigration was inevitable and that most emigrants would be from the tenant class. In early August, he wrote that the 'tide of emigration' to the US 'still continues'.[60] Some mistakenly believed that it stopped during the Land War except for those on prepaid passages.[61] But Fr James Nugent obtained funds for departures through a public appeal in 1880, the *New York Herald* Relief Committee funded the Fermanagh Relief Association to help 100 people to leave and the Duchess of Marlborough Relief Committee provided £2,600 to assist emigration from congested areas.[62] These and other private efforts facilitated departures while guidance from local clergy was influential also. During these years, individual Catholic clergy in the poorer parts came around to seeing emigration as a solution to the destitution and distress they encountered on a daily basis.

By the end of August 1881, the much-promised Land Act had been introduced and included fair rent to be assessed by arbitration, fixity of tenure while rent was paid and freedom for the tenant to sell his occupancy at the best market price. However, it did not cover tenants in arrears of rent.[63] Brooks in Queenstown, commented that the legislation 'did not promise an abatement of unrest and agitation'. Although he welcomed the Land League's scheme to encourage domestic industrial manufacturing, he also felt the Irish people were not 'naturally given' to mechanical or manufacturing pursuits. But Livermore was of the opinion that 'new forms of industry' would remedy the discontent in his northern

---

58 Owen Dudley Edwards, 'American diplomats and Irish coercion, 1880–1883', *Journal of American Studies*, 1:2 (October 1967), 217; Allan Nevins, *Henry White*, 53.
59 TNA, ADM1/6664 1884, Confidential memo. no. 1 referred to in memoranda on Irish stations and transfer of command, 16 April 1883.
60 NARA, D/S, USC, 8, 8, T196, Brooks to Hay, 3 March 1881; *ibid.*, Brooks to Hitt, 4 August 1881.
61 Miller, *Emigrants and exiles*, 491. Brooks believed in 1880 that 50 per cent of passengers from Queenstown had prepaid tickets from the US and the others paid for their own passage. NARA, D/S, USC, 7, 7, T196, Brooks to Hay, 12 March 1880.
62 Gerard Moran, *Sending out Ireland's poor: assisted emigration to North America in the nineteenth century* (Dublin, 2004), 172.
63 D. G. Boyce, *The Irish question and British politics 1868–1986* (London, 1988), 26.

Table 5.4 Number of overseas emigrants from Ireland to the United States of America, 1875–85

Year	Number
1875	31,433
1876	16,432
1877	13,991
1878	18,602
1879	30,058
1880	83,018
1881	67,339
1882	68,300
1883	82,849
1884	59,204
1885	50,657

Source: *Commission on emigration*, table 26, 314–16

district. Brooks remained convinced that Ireland would continue an 'agricultural or grazing country' and, therefore, it was 'among the certainties of the future that this exodus will continue for several years to come'.[64] Table 5.4 confirms this view.

While tenants in arrears of rent awaited legislation, the Land League was proscribed and Parnell and other leaders were arrested. Disorder, violence and tenant resistance intensified throughout much of the countryside. Parnell promptly announced a 'no rent manifesto' which called for the withholding of all rents. Livermore in Londonderry, commented that 'discontent would seem to be of a chronic nature'. It was not until early 1882 when American prisoners began to be released and negotiations were initiated between Gladstone and the imprisoned Parnell, that an end to the Land War seemed possible. Parnell agreed to secure a restoration of order in return for an end to coercion, his liberty and legislation dealing with tenants in arrear.[65] However, the Phoenix Park murders on 6 May when the newly appointed Lord Lieutenant, Lord Frederick Cavendish, and his Under Secretary, Thomas H. Burke, were killed by a secret republican organisation, the Invincibles, produced further coercive

---

64 NARA, D/S, USC, 8, 8, T196, Brooks to Hitt, 24 August 1881; *ibid.*, USB, 9, 9, T368, Livermore to Hitt, 10 October 1881. Arthur Wood's correspondence between August 1881 and January 1884 did not refer to the Land War. See NARA, D/S, USB, 8, 8, T368.
65 Comerford, *The Fenians*, 240–3.

measures.⁶⁶ At the end of October, recently arrived John Piatt reported from Queenstown that 'some progress in the direction of peace and prosperity has been made within the last few months ... agrarian outrages though still of occasional occurrence, are rarer now than at the beginning of the year'. But this did not mean an improvement in the condition of the poorer classes. After reading the government's general report based on the 1881 census, Piatt commented 'what a hard struggle for existence must be the lot of the farm people in many of the more remote districts of the island'.⁶⁷

By the early 1880s, consuls were aware that the reasons for emigrating originated in America as well as in Ireland. The lure of 'free land' following from the introduction of the Homestead acts in 1863 was a powerful draw. At that time, William West was convinced that the Irish would make the 'most desirable settlers' in the southern and western states and distributed thousands of copies of a pamphlet on the Homestead and other laws to emigrants leaving Dublin port. He also requested the State Department to forward information on 'our new unproductive and wild lands in the Great West' and suggested that each US state legislature should publish a statement of its 'free' lands and its employment needs. He regarded the *Facts for emigrants to California: a circular issued to workingmen* from the California Labour Exchange in San Francisco, to be 'valuable and badly needed' in Ireland.⁶⁸ A further part of West's campaign was to have official, reliable information about conditions in the US disseminated

---

66 The Invincibles were extremists from Fenian backgrounds. Secretary of State Frelinghuysen was appalled by the act and moved from 'questioning the wisdom of British legislation to ... a strong distaste for the administration and administrators of law and order within Ireland itself'. The detentions of *New York Star* journalist, Stephen J. Meaney, and Henry George, author of *Progress and poverty* and *Irish World* correspondent, provoked State Department action. In Washington, British Minister Sackville West was astonished by the 'outburst of intense feeling' against all things British but identified congressional opposition as the reason for government action. However, by the end of 1882, the arrests issue had slipped down the US–British diplomatic agenda, now dominated by Canadian fishing rights. Also US Minister Lowell succumbed to the 'spell of London'. Dudley Edwards, 'American diplomats', 221–9. Frelinghuysen's letter to Lord Granville on 25 April 1882 encapsulates the evolution of his hostility towards British policy in Ireland. BDFA (1986–95), 1, C, North America, 1837–1914, 9, Expansion and rapprochement, 1877–1888 (1987), Frelinghuysen to Lowell, 22 September 1882; Quoted in Willson, *Friendly Relations*, 248; Willson, *America's ambassadors*, 383.
67 NARA, D/S, USC, 8, 8, T196, Piatt to Davis, 31 October 1882; *ibid.*, 15 December 1882.
68 NARA, D/S, USD, 7, 7, T199, West to Seward, 12 February 1869; *ibid.*, 4, 4, T199, West to Seward, 21 October 1865; *ibid.*, 5, 5, T199, West to Seward, 11 July 1868; *ibid.*, 7, 7, T199, West to Fish, 14 May 1869; 7, 7, T199, West to Fish, 6 July 1869.

through the newspapers.⁶⁹ Although newspapers carried notices of forthcoming sailings, West failed to get any editor to publish a short abstract of the Homestead legislation and only two newspapers reported on the publication of a report by Joseph Wilson, US Land Commissioner, on all the occupied and unoccupied land in the states and territories in the US.⁷⁰ The *Munster News* concluded that while Arizona was the only part that offered land 'least desirable for emigrations', America offered 'equal security, fair play and freedom'. Yet, they wondered why emigrants should prefer to go to America.⁷¹ In mid-1869, after the publication of the annual report of the Commissioners of Emigration of the State of New York, the *Irish Times* welcomed the continued decline in Irish emigration to the US but wanted the government to 'offer as strong inducements to her children to remain, as America can promise to induce them to depart'.⁷² Despite these anti-emigrant anxieties, which were also shared by nationalist leaders, the attraction of America's new lands persisted. Consul James Rea in Belfast asked for a new map showing the new states west of Missouri and Iowa because 'many' persons constantly called to his office looking for geographical information.⁷³ West went so far as to suggest that the government employ an agent in Dublin to supervise the printing and advertising of circulars and maps of the individual states and to send information to the intending emigrant.⁷⁴ This did not occur but departures continued.

By the turbulent early 1880s, Arthur B. Wood, former chief of the US Consular Bureau, was amazed that people turned to his Belfast consulate for every 'feasible sort of enquiry, advice and assistance' about emigration to the US.⁷⁵ Brooks and his staff in Queenstown, who witnessed a short-lived decline in the numbers emigrating during summer 1881, dealt with many queries about life in the US. He wanted official information demonstrating that the labourer in America enjoyed 'a greater variety of

69 Miller, *Ireland and Irish America*, 93.
70 David Fitzpatrick, 'Emigration, 1801–70' in Vaughan (ed.), *A New History*, 583; NARA, D/S, USD, 7, 7, T199, West to Fish, 6 July 1869; *ibid.*, West to Fish, 7 July 1869. Rev. Dr John Hall, pastor of the Presbyterian Church, Fifth Avenue, New York, lectured on 'America' to a packed Rotunda Hall on 5 July 1869. It was reported in three newspapers; *Evening Mail*, 6 July 1869; *Irish Times*, 6 July 1869; *Freeman's Journal*, 6 July 1869; NARA, D/S, USD, 7, 7, T199, West to Fish, 6 July 1869.
71 *Munster Express*, 3 February 1869.
72 *Irish Times*, 8 July 1869.
73 The Fenian organ, *Irish People*, criticised emigration as an 'act of betrayal'. William O'Brien, 'Imagining Catholic Ireland: the nationalist press and the creation of national identity, 1843–1870' (PhD dissertation, University of Limerick, 2007), 123; NARA, D/S, USB, 5, 5, T368, Rea to Fish, 18 December 1869.
74 *Ibid.*, USD, 7, 7, T199, West to Fish, 6 July 1869.
75 *Ibid.*, USB, 7, 7, T368, Wood to Bancroft, 10 July 1881.

food ... cheap clothing ... cheaper than ... here'.[76] In August 1881 and again in February 1882, Livermore in Londonderry who witnessed the 'largest emigration' for many years, asked for a newer map of America's territories because of the 'numerous enquiries' made to him for information. In March 1882, he requested a copy of the *Statistics of the population of the United States by counties and minor civil divisions* so that intending emigrants would have the information of the 'immense changes' that have occurred in the US in a short time and that 'baffle common observation'.[77] Within a few years, Savage in Belfast believed that the 'highly coloured' publications from American railroad companies, state commissioners of emigration as well as various steamship companies which noted the availability of employment in the 'great west', were highly effective in stimulating and encouraging emigration.[78] Perhaps the information obtained in the consulate was regarded as more reliable than that obtained elsewhere.

F. L. Dingley, a State Department official, who toured west European countries in 1890, identified another reason why consuls should provide accurate and, if possible, official information namely to dispel the lure of other places, particularly Britain's colonies.[79] From the early nineteenth century onwards, governments and landlords had assisted aspirant, voluntary and involuntary emigrants to depart for British North America, Australia and the Cape of Good Hope.[80] Irish-based consuls began to comment on it in the 1860s when fares to Australia, New Zealand and Manitoba became cheap, the journey quicker and, as noted previously, inducements were offered by colonial governments. West was greatly concerned at the welcome given to Thomas D'Arcy McGee, the minister for Agriculture, Immigration and Statistics in the Canadian legislative assembly when he arrived in Dublin. The former Young Irelander and Fenian, now an advocate for British-American nationality, was the Canadian delegate to the International Exhibition in Dublin in May 1865. One speech he delivered in his boyhood town of Wexford titled 'My twenty years of Irish life in America', was regarded by West as an attempt 'to disparage our country, and prove that Irishmen had no fair play [in the US] and were treated there as an inferior race'.[81] A few months later,

76 *Ibid.*, USC, 8, 8, T196, Brooks to Hitt, 4 August 1881.
77 *Ibid.*, USB, 9, 9, T368, Livermore to Davis, 3 October 1884; *ibid.*, Livermore to Secretary of State, 4 August 1881; *ibid.*, Livermore to Davis, 5 February 1882; *ibid.*, Livermore to Davis, 24 March 1882.
78 *Ibid.*, 10, 10, T368, Savage to Rives, 4 October 1888.
79 Dingley, 'European immigration', 308–9.
80 Fitzpatrick, 'Emigration', 589–91.
81 NARA, D/S, USD, 4, 4, T199, West to Seward, 20 May 1865; *Evening Mail*, 16 May 1865.

Building the Union, 1865–1913: the immigration process 229

West forwarded a newspaper article titled 'Progress of Canada' to the State Department with a warning in a cover note not to 'rest too confident' with the 'excessive flow of emigration to our shores or become lax in efforts to stimulate it by every means in our power ... Canada is evidently gaining on us in proportion to her population'.[82] A few years later, it was the work of the Brazilian Emigration Office, its *Emigrants' guide to Brazil* and assisted passage scheme encouraging 'immigrants of agricultural families and the useful trades', which West brought to Seward's attention.[83] Irrespective of the purpose of assisted emigration or success rates, some consuls worried about competition.[84]

Of course, the consular office was not the only or indeed, the most important, channel through which information about 'free' land, plentiful work and the possibility to own one's home and prosper, could be obtained.[85] In Queenstown, John Piatt identified perhaps the most important channel: 'numerous members of the emigrant's family, relatives, neighbours or friends have, as generally happens, gone there before them'.[86] Similarly, Livermore located in the northern port of Londonderry, commented:

> The Irish are distinguished for love of their kindred and that love has hitherto acted as a check to the obvious motives that induce them to leave their homes. On the other hand, it has been the case that emigrants who have been any degree fortunate in their new homes, have largely contributed to aid their relatives to follow them.[87]

After thirty years of mass emigration, Livermore exaggerated those family bonds that checked emigration, but the presence of a relative or friend in the US had become a powerful magnet acting in three ways. First, there was the prepaid passage sent home to assist others to leave, a trend evident since 1815.[88] Brooks in Dublin believed in March 1880 that family and friends in the US provided half of those emigrating at this time with the necessary funds.[89] Most who left from Londonderry with

82 NARA, D/S, USD, 4, 4, T199, West to Seward, 12 August 1865.
83 *Ibid.*, 7, 7, T199, West to Seward, 12 February 1869.
84 Dingley, 'European immigration', 308–9.
85 See Miller, *Emigrants and exiles*; Kirby Miller, 'Paddy's paradox: emigration to America in Irish imagination and rhetoric' in Dirk Hoerder, Horst Rössler (eds), *Distant magnets: expectations and realities in the immigrant experience, 1840–1930* (New York, 1993), 264–94; Kerby Miller and Bruce D. Bolling, 'Golden streets, bitter tears: the Irish image of America during the era of mass migration', *Journal of American Ethnic History* 10:1 and 2 (autumn 1990–winter 1991), 16–36.
86 NARA, D/S, USC, 9, 9, T196, enclosure in Piatt to Davis, 20 July 1884.
87 *Ibid.*, USB, 9, 9, T368, Livermore to Brooks, 31 July 1883.
88 Miller, *Emigrants and exiles*, 271.
89 NARA, D/S, USD, 7, 7, T199, Brooks to Hay, 12 March 1880.

'little or no property', had prepaid tickets also funded from the US. Livermore estimated that between 1881 and 1886 approximately £1 million was remitted from the US to the United Kingdom in prepaid passages.[90] Even though Schrier and Fitzpatrick's work suggests this was probably inflated, the consul's general impression was accurate.[91] The 'stream of gold' penetrated most parts of Ireland funding many departures.[92] Second, as Savage in Belfast identified in late 1888, it was not just the prepaid steamship ticket which influenced the decision to go, but so also did news of a relative or friend's achievement.[93] Letters from America brought not just money or a passage but also news of achievements. Consuls, however, could judge also the extent of this stateside success. Many complained that much of their time was devoted to administering powers of attorney to individuals seeking to claim, collect or sell property inherited from deceased relatives in the US and indeed Ireland.[94] This work expanded and eventually the State Department permitted consuls to advertise in order to locate relatives.[95] The final aspect of the pre-existing contact which constantly merited consular comment was the returned American. West reported on American soldiers returning to Ireland after the American Civil War whether to fight for the Fenians or simply to visit friends and family. He detailed cases where three men each possessed £120, £30 and $2,000 respectively. Although the money was stolen from each man, an impression would have been created within the local community.[96] Piatt was convinced in 1884:

> The personal visits to this country of Irish Americans, who come here to spend a few months after having been some years in the United States – persons who may have left Ireland originally in poor circumstances and are now eventually in good credit and prosperous ... these have a great influence upon the minds of those with whom they come in contact and lead many of them also to emigrate.[97]

In other words, the presence of the returned American also transmitted messages to the intending emigrant.[98] Irrespective of the reality of that returnee's American life and that few Irish emigrants to the US returned

90 Ibid., USB, 9, 9, T368, Livermore to Porter, 26 May 1886.
91 Arnold Schrier, *Ireland and the American emigration* (Chester Springs, 1997), 103–28; Fitzpatrick, 'Emigration', 601.
92 Quoted in Fitzpatrick, 'Emigration', 601.
93 NARA, D/S, USB, 10, 10, T368, Savage to Rives, 4 October 1888.
94 Schrier, *Ireland and the American emigration*, 43; see for example, NARA, D/S, USB, 8, 8, T368 and USB, 10, 10, T368, Ruby to Wharton, 7 March 1890.
95 Ibid., USD, 11, 11, T199, Piatt to Hill, 5 November 1900.
96 Ibid., 4, 4, T199, West to Seward, 14 October 1865.
97 Ibid., USC, 9, 9, T196, enclosure in Piatt to Davis, 20 July 1884.
98 See the work of Miller, Bolling and Nevins in the bibliography for further.

home during this period, some who did were often well dressed and exuded prosperity. In addition to observing the phenomenon, consuls came across evidence of this in an unusual way; the death of a US citizen in their district meant that consuls dealt with the deceased's personal effects. On 27 July 1887, Daniel Conway, aged 60 years of 216 east 66th Street, New York city where he kept a livery stable, died suddenly of heart disease on board the Inman steamship *City of Chicago* in Queenstown. He had just boarded having visited his family. Among his effects was a small American valise with clothes including two pairs of woollen pants, one woollen waistcoat, three linen shirts, one linen waistcoat, one new frieze overcoat, a Catholic prayer book, rosary beads, scapulars, medals, books about poems and another entitled *Miracles at Knock* and a stone from Knock. His carpet bag contained more clothes but he also had a draft for the Bank of Ireland in Longford drawn on the Bank of England for £30 ($146), English gold worth £14 10s. ($70 56c.), English silver to the value of 18s. 6d. ($4 50c.) and, of course, his return ticket for £12 ($58 40c). The total value of his possessions was $336 65c. This wealthy, returned emigrant had arrived in Queenstown on the *City of Rome* six weeks earlier, and travelled to his native Drumlish, county Longford, then went on a pilgrimage to the Catholic shrine in Knock, county Mayo. Eight years earlier, fifteen people claimed to have seen a silent apparition of the Virgin Mary, St Joseph and St John.[99] Other returnees who came to consular attention, had similar trappings denoting wealth and success which for some, reinforced the notion of America as a place of opportunity.[100] This consular commentary further reinforces Schrier's view that pre-existing contacts were a key factor in the decision-making process and Fitzpatrick's that the model of chain emigration became predominant during these decades.[101]

Consuls arriving in Ireland during the 1880s continued to provide an outsider's view of the momentous internal events. The combination of the 1881 Land Act and the 1882 Arrears Act had taken the momentum out of the Land War. Indeed Lieutenant Raymond Bulings of HMS *Orwell*, after another visit to the islands in Blacksod bay and the townland of Belmullet in county Mayo, in September 1882, was struck that tenants avoided eviction by paying under the arrears bill which he felt, showed that they were 'thoroughly alive to the benefits to be derived from the act'.[102] In January 1883, Piatt in Queenstown, saw himself in

---

99 NARA, D/S, USC, 10, 10, T196, Piatt to Porter, 30 July 1887; *Cork Daily Herald*, 28 July 1887; Martin Clancy, 'Knock Shrine' in Lalor (ed.), *The encyclopaedia*, 598.
100 See NARA, D/S, USD, 10, 10, T199; *ibid.*, USC, 12, 12, T196; *ibid.*, USD, 11, 11, T199.
101 Schrier, *Ireland and the American emigration*, 103; Fitzpatrick, 'Emigration', 602.
102 TNA, ADM1/6615 1882, Bulings to Morant, 23 September 1882.

the middle of 'political upheaval' and a 'state of ferment'. By March, however, he commented on the general reduction in agrarian violence and crime because tenants were benefitting from better rent and tenure conditions. He hoped that they would feel more secure in the future and become 'enterprising and prosperous'.[103] But his optimism did not last long. Agriculture offered little particularly to those in the west. Alarmed at reports about the extent of the misery, on 25 February US Consul General in London, Edwin A. Merritt, instructed consular officials in Ireland to comment on whether the accounts of distress were correct or exaggerated and the prospects for improvement. He also asked whether the British government, guardians of the poor law unions or associations were sending paupers to the US.[104]

Four consuls and Consular Agent William Eccles in Sligo admitted the presence of distress but that it was not exceptional and reports were exaggerated. In the western agricultural parts of the country, the situation of poorer people was 'miserable' and 'abject poverty' prevailed but Merritt concluded it 'has been the same for years' and was the 'normal condition' of life. Thus, he dismissed talk of 'starvation point'. Instead he believed that the boards of guardians exaggerated the conditions in order to have poor rates supplemented by additional government assistance. Disappointingly for him, his officials saw no real prospect of improvement because government policy was directed at funding the workhouse and emigration, and not employment. The long-term picture was not encouraging either. Drawing on the comments of George Trevelyn, the Chief Secretary, about the predominance of uneconomic small-to-medium farms, poor land, low agricultural prices and foreign competition, Merritt forecast that the farmer and tenant would be in 'still lower depths of poverty' in the future. From every point of view, the Irish situation seemed hopeless to the American officials and all agreed that it would act as a 'powerful stimulus' to emigration.[105] Not only were the indebted classes leaving but so also were the 'vigorous and industrious class of small farmers' and the consuls agreed that most went to the United States – 'our country being the easiest and cheapest to reach'.[106]

The consuls' replies were not surprising given the crisis situation in early 1883. However, their reports confirmed new phenomena; first,

---

103 NARA, D/S, USC, 9, 9, T196, Piatt to Davis, 16 January 1883.
104 USPRFR, December 4, 1883, online at http://digicoll.library.wisc.edu (accessed 27 June 2008), E. A. Merritt, 'Irish distress and emigration', 21 March 1883.
105 *Ibid*. NARA, D/S, USC, 9, 9, T196, Piatt to Davis, 19 January 1883; *ibid*., Piatt to Davis, 15, 20 September 1883.
106 Miller, *Emigrants and exiles*, 393. NARA, D/S, USC, 9, 9, T196, Piatt to Davis, 30 October 1883; *ibid*., enclosure in Piatt to Davis, 20 July 1884.

emigration was a permanent feature of Irish life for men and women, second, the experience of the earlier emigrant both in the US and upon return, was influential in the aspirant emigrant's decision-making process and finally, there was an increasingly prominent reason for leaving – the desire for personal improvement. Livermore, *in situ* in Londonderry since 1870, believed that improved domestic and personal comfort which were previously regarded as 'objects of irrational desire' were now among the 'reasonable necessities of life'. He noted that in the Ulster countryside a 'diet of potatoes, and a cabin of one room and a floor of clay shared between the family and their animals, have ceased to be satisfactory'.[107] In other words, even when good weather conditions prevailed and land agitation infrequent, emigration continued although at a lower rate, as table 5.6 shows. Most who left from Londonderry and Moville, county Donegal, were of 'good repute, good health and having force and intelligence to labour' and it was 'a very uncommon thing to find a young man or young woman who does not write well'.[108] Within twelve months of his arrival in Queenstown, Piatt accepted that the 'exodus' of people had become permanent and the majority were still the 'young, robust and fairly well-to-do of the class of small farmers' along with labourers and unemployed tradesmen from urban areas.[109] Woods commented that irrespective of the relatively prosperous status of the Scottish-Irish worker in Belfast, the 'more ambitious emigrate'.[110] Not only was emigration to the US an informed decision, it had become a rite of passage for most young Irish people and fulfilled personal as well as material needs.[111] Hoping to improve oneself applied as much to women as to men. Piatt provided the following statistics in table 5.5.[112]

The almost balanced gender ratio that characterised the Irish exodus in the years after the 1845–51 famine is noticeable in these returns: male or female they simply 'had to go'.[113] Nolan suggests that in a society characterised by late marriages, many women emigrated to find spouses and start a family while Diner argues that many left to improve themselves. More recently Miller maintains that young women sought 'love

---

107 *Ibid.*, USB, 9, 9, T368, Livermore to Davis, 31 July 1883.
108 *Ibid.*, USB, 9, 9, T368, Livermore to Porter, 26 May 1886.
109 *Ibid.*, USC, 9, 9, T196, Piatt to Davis, 12 November 1884; *ibid.*, Piatt to Porter, enclosure in 15 July 1885.
110 *Ibid.*, USB, 9, 9, T368, Woods to Davis, 29 November 1884.
111 Miller, *Emigrants and exiles*, 415.
112 Piatt drew his figures from the Board of Trade which indicated that 28,359 left Queenstown in the year ended 30 September 1885 compared to 29,850 for the previous year.
113 Miller, *Emigrants and exiles*, 491.

Table 5.5 Number of emigrants who embarked at Queenstown for the United States during the twelve months ended 30 September 1882–5

Period	Males	Females	Total
1882–3	20,697	20,452	41,149
1883–4	14,404	15,446	29,850
1884–5	13,269	15,090	28,359
1885–6	19,926	19,457	39,386

Note: figures include children
Source: NARA, D/S, USC, 9, 9, T196, enclosure in Piatt to Porter, 31 October 1885; *ibid.*, Piatt to Davis, 12 November 1884; *ibid.*, Piatt to Davis, 31 October 1883; *ibid.*, Piatt to Rives, 31 January 1889

and liberty'.[114] Among women who were employed in Belfast linen mills in 1884, Woods found:

> a strong desire to escape from their occupation ... of bettering their condition. There is a feeling that this is impracticable while they remain here and they say that once in a mill there is no way for them but to continue. Many of the younger men emigrate ... it is not an easy undertaking for a young woman. If not aided – as they are in some measure – by relatives in America or elsewhere ... it is difficult to save from their wages even the small sum necessary for their passage. With the middle-aged and the older, the desire to leave leads to no result; they are tied to the wheel.[115]

Although, there was no analysis of how America would improve their lives, State Department official, F. L. Dingley, after surveying western European countries and studying emigration from Europe to the US, concluded that the 'phenomenon' of the 'increase in the swarm of young women' to the US was due to 'its sense of fair play to woman to give her an independent career'.[116] This should not suggest a selfishness but instead, as Miller suggests, that modernising forces such as commercialisation and anglicisation engendered in many a desire for 'self-improvement' as

114 J. J. Lee, 'Introduction: interpreting Irish America' in Lee and Casey (eds), *Making the Irish American*, 29–30; Hasia R. Diner, *Erin's daughters in America: Irish emigrant women in the nineteenth century* (Baltimore, 1983); Janet R. Nolan, *Ourselves alone: women's emigration from Ireland, 1885–1920* (Lexington, 1989); Dianne M. Hotten-Sommers, 'Relinquishing and reclaiming independence: Irish domestic servants, American middle-class mistresses, and assimilation, 1850–1920' in Kevin Kenny (ed.), *New directions in Irish-American History* (Wisconsin, 2003); Miller, *Ireland and Irish America*, 326.
115 NARA, D/S, USB, 9, 9, T368, Woods to Davis, 29 November 1884.
116 F. L. Dingley, *European emigration: studies in Europe of emigration moving out of Europe, especially that flowing to the United States* (Washington, 1890), 380.

well as fulfilling traditional matrimonial needs.[117] Consuls still continued to notice that family and domestic ties were always a reason not to leave but rarely sufficient to prevent it from happening. Indeed many were going to newly created family units and 90 per cent of Irish emigrant voyages to the US were prepaid mostly by family members already established there.[118] Despite the predominance of women emigrants and the emergence of additional motives for departure, economic reasons for emigrating still prevailed for most.

Against the background of the return of eighty-six nationalist members of parliament in the 1885 general election and the introduction and defeat of the first Home Rule bill in 1886, the continuation of tenant misery and evictions resulted in the revival of the Land War. From 1886 until 1890, the Irish National League organised the plan of campaign which demanded lower rents from landlords and if not granted, then rents were withheld. But it was not totally successful due to organised landlord and government opposition.[119] Piatt commented on a 'large increase' in emigration to the US during 1887 which is confirmed in table 5.6.

Table 5.6 Number of overseas emigrants from Ireland to United States, 1886–90

Year	Number
1886	52,858
1887	69,084
1888	66,306
1889	57,897
1890	52,110

Source: *Commission on emigration*, table 26, 314–16

Piatt accepted a *Cork Herald* report that 9,236 left from Queenstown during April compared to less than half the number in the previous year and indicated that the majority appeared to be 'young men and women, well clothed and well provided for', hoping to begin 'a new life in their adopted country'. He acknowledged nationalist leaders 'regret' about the departures.[120]

117 Ibid., 429; Miller, *Ireland and Irish America*, 326.
118 Dingley, 'European immigration', 286–7.
119 James Loughlin, 'Plan of campaign' in Connolly (ed.), *The Oxford companion*, 444; Nevins, *Henry White*, 78; Charles Callan Tansill, *The foreign policy of Thomas F. Bayard, 1885–1897* (New York, 1940), xxxvi–xxxix.
120 NARA, D/S, USC, 10, 10, T196, Piatt to Porter, 2 May 1887.

During 1887, the ongoing Land War in the south and west combined to continuing poor economic and social conditions heightened public animosity towards the government which in turn made political settlement of the home rule issue impossible. Piatt was critical that 'coercion' had become law again through Arthur Balfour's Criminal Law and Procedure Act but he recognised a decline in 'agrarian and associated outrages'. Government supporters promoted a similar line but nationalist leaders believed the calmer conditions resulted from the widespread hopes in Parnell's constitutional campaign in Westminster. Piatt, however, was astute enough to see other consequences flowing from the coercion legislation; it broadened 'the breech' between 'people', specifically Catholics, and the 'government' rather than developing a 'unity of feeling and confidence' between them and when combined to agricultural failure with its 'evils and hardships', intensified emigration in 1886, 1887 and 1888.[121] Savage extrapolated from the official emigration statistics that between 1883 and 1887, 76.5 per cent of emigrants left for the US but 84.2 per cent did so in 1887 and 85 per cent in 1888. Assistant Secretary George L. Rives took note.[122]

As immigration numbers climbed, the US Congress strengthened entry restrictions (see below). State Department officials tried to analyse the reasons for continued European immigration. Piatt reported that excessive rain hampered growth during spring and summer 1888 and crop yields were less than average while the unstable political situation remained unchanged. Savage based in Belfast commented on the 'alarmed' reaction of landlords, employers and newspapers to the 'large and unnatural exodus'. The young and able-bodied men and women 'go to the United States simply for the purpose of bettering their condition, and have no intention in returning to permanently reside in this country'. Like his predecessors, he emphasised that Ulster emigrants were more valuable to the US government than other Irish settlers because of their 'thrift and industry' and they were 'free and voluntary'. All emigrants, however, were considered better informed than earlier generations because of access to information from American railroad companies, state commissioners of emigration, the various steamship companies and, of course, letters. A final advantage was that some Irish male emigrants were better prepared for 'the responsibilities of American citizenship' because of the introduction of the Representation of the People Act in 1884.[123]

The plan of campaign phase of the Land War initiated in 1886, lost

121 NARA, D/S, USC, 10, 10, T196, Piatt to Rives, 15 March 1888.
122 *Ibid.*, USC, 10, 10, T196, Piatt to Rives, 31 January 1889.
123 *Ibid.*, USB, 10, 10, T368, Savage to Rives, 4 October 1888.

Table 5.7 Number of overseas emigrants from Ireland to the United States, 1891–1914

Year	Number
1891	53,438
1892	48,966
1893	49,122
1894	39,597
1895	52,047
1896	39,952
1897	32,822
1898	30,878
1899	38,631
1900	41,848
1901	35,535
1902	37,991
1903	39,554
1904	52,788
1905	44,356
1906	45,417
1907	54,306
1908	31,518
1909	36,611
1910	41,019
1911	36,613
1912	31,967
1913	32,320
1914	24,138

Source: *Commission on emigration*, table 26, 314–16

its momentum over the following years due to the government policy of constructive unionism and the continuation of constitutional nationalism, although Parnell died in 1891 and the House of Lords rejected the second Home Rule bill in 1893.[124] Using the tactics of coercion and conciliation, successive Conservative governments attempted to deal with the Irish problem by tackling the economic causes while also

---

124 *Ibid.*, USD, 10, 10, T199, Reid to Wharton, 1 February 1893; *ibid.*, Reid to Kaye, Assistant Under-Secretary to the Lord Lieutenant, 23 January 1893; *Freeman's Journal*, 11 November 1892; Ciara Breathnach, *The Congested Districts Board of Ireland, 1891–1923: poverty and development in the west of Ireland* (Dublin, 2005), 11.

appeasing the growing unionist opposition to home rule. Piatt noted that tenant ownership was extended by the Purchase of Land (Ireland) Act in 1891 (the Balfour Act). It established the Congested Districts Board with extensive powers to alleviate congestion in impoverished areas.[125] Table 5.7 indicates that emigration continued.

Piatt's successors in Queenstown, Henry Kress and Lucien Walker, knew little about Ireland and instead immersed themselves in the bureaucracy associated with the increasing immigration regulations (see below). Walker was surprised that he was in the port from where 'almost the entire emigration' departed for the US.[126] By 1896 Walker's health had failed and after two absences, he resigned in May 1897. He did not forward any substantial reports on the state of Ireland and nor did Alex Reid or Newton Ashby in Dublin. Within two years of his arrival in 1893, Ashby was determined to secure a leave of absence to visit 'places of interest' in Europe and to return to Iowa on business and family matters.[127] In Belfast, Samuel Ruby found consular work onerous while James Taney and William Touvelle commented on the industrial and manufacturing activities in the district.[128] In March 1894, Taney, however, successfully opposed the appointment of a consular agent to Moville to service the passengers of the Allan Steamship Line and save it money. It was, of course, in Taney's interest that the competent and experienced Consular Agent Rodger who did not want to move from Londonderry to Moville, not be given any reason to resign.[129] Taney's reliance on Rodger was such that three years later, he supported his claim for the continuation of a monthly allowance of $50 for this 'painstaking, deserving officer'.[130] Touvelle from Ohio assumed office in September 1897 but was not interested in Rodger's problems or emigration generally. In early 1904, he went on leave of absence and died later in the year.[131]

Throughout the 1890s, the number of emigrants leaving for the US gradually declined (see table 5.7) but there were intermittent cessations also. The general depression in the US in 1893–4 when instability in bullion, security and stock markets caused bank, business and railway company failures, unemployment rose to over 20 per cent and agricultural prices declined[132] In July, agents operating for the American, Cunard,

125 NARA, D/S, USC, 1790–1906, 10, 10, T196, Piatt to Wharton, 20 November 1889; R. V. Comerford, 'Land Acts' in Connolly (ed.), *The Oxford Companion*, 295.
126 NARA, D/S, USC, 11, 11, T196, Walker, to Quincy, 13 November 1893.
127 *Ibid.*, USD, 10, 10, T199, Ashby to Uhl, 4 June 1895.
128 See *ibid.*, USB, 10, 10, T368.
129 *Ibid.*, USB, 10, 10, T368, Taney to Uhl, 12 March 1894.
130 *Ibid.*, USB, 11, 11, T368, Taney to Rockhill, 8 March 1897.
131 *Ibid.*, USB, 11, 11, T368, Read Touvelle to Department of State, 12 November 1904.
132 Thompson, *Cassell's dictionary*, 122; Robert M. Goldman, 'Stephen Grover Cleve-

Building the Union, 1865–1913: the immigration process

White Star, Anchor and Allan State lines all reported to Taney that more 'steerage passengers [are] coming this way than there are going to the States'. But they expected that once 'business assumes its normal condition', the usual levels of emigration would return. Rodger confirmed from Londonderry a reduction in departures because of the 'depressed state of business' in the US. He expected a recovery when 'business revives' and the small farmers having sold their crops 'had some money to take them out'.[133] Neither did the Anglo-American crisis over Venezuela in 1896 and the outbreak of the Spanish–American war two years later substantially affect departures. Instead consuls commented on the local reaction to both events and stressed their efforts to protect America's blockade in the case of the latter.[134]

By the beginning of the new century, the Queenstown consulate still acted as a bureau of information for emigrants, and much consular time was taken up with meeting intending emigrants and answering queries about the US.[135] Staff in the Dublin consulate answered inquiries about life in frontier states.[136] Consular officials also provided information about the US armed forces. Continuing in the long tradition of Irish participation in wars which the US engaged in and against a background of expanding US involvement in world affairs under President Theodore Roosevelt, 'dozens' of young men called to the Dublin consular office in 1905 and 1906 to inquire about enlistment regulations.[137] Samuel S. Knabenshue who started work in Belfast on 1 March 1905, recognised that the 'regular' emigration of young men and women who formed the 'bulk of the outgo' was a permanent 'drain' on society and that otherwise there would be a 'steady progressive increase of population'.[138] In the same period, no emigrants for the US embarked from the Dublin district except for the 481 who left from Galway (located within the Dublin

land' in Uroksky (ed.), *The American presidents*, 240–2.
133 NARA, D/S, USB, 10, 10, T368, Taney to Uhl, 30 July 1894.
134 *Ibid.*, USD, 10, 10, T199, Wilbour to Gridler, 7 February 1898; *ibid.*, 'Oliver Bond Young Men's Club, '98 Branch' resolution; *ibid.*, '98 Centenary Committee' resolution; *ibid.*, USC, 11, 11, T196, 'Copy of Resolution passed in committee of the whole council this 18 day of February 1898' in Walker to Day, 19 February 1898; *ibid.*, USD, 10, 10, T199, Wilbour to Day, 22 April 1898; *ibid.*, Wilbour to Moore, 20 July 1898; *ibid.*, Wilbour to Hill, 1 December 1898; *ibid.*, 11, 11, T199, Wilbour to Hill, 3 January 1899; Thompson, *Cassells' dictionary*, 387–8.; *Irish Times*, 31 May 1901. NARA, D/S, USD, 1790–1906, 11, 11, T199, Wilbour to Hill, 31 May 1901.
135 *Ibid.*, USC, 12, 12, T196, Gunsaulus to Loomis, 14 April 1906.
136 *Ibid.*, USD, 11, 11, T199, Moe to Asst. Secretary of State, 9 January 1906.
137 *Ibid.*
138 *Ibid.*, USB, 11, 11, T368, Knabenshue to Bacon, 25 July 1905; *ibid.*, Knabenshue to Loomis, 24 November 1905; *ibid.*, Knabenshue to Loomis, 29 August 1905.

consul's jurisdiction).[139] Most of the departures were still from Queenstown where successive consuls were amazed at two permanent features; the numbers leaving and the growing return tide.[140]

More than one-half of the departures from Londonderry in 1905 were American citizens returning to the US and less than one-half were emigrants.[141] Between 1899 and 1930, few Irish returned in comparison to other ethnic groups but those who did still epitomised prosperity for some. However, Joshua Wilbour in Dublin identified a counter-trend among returnees. He had 'constant calls' from stranded Americans, mostly of Irish descent. Some found it impossible to obtain employment and could not raise the 'means to get away'. They turned to him or were sent to him by local police or authorities. Although Wilbour was not officially obliged to assist them and many were 'often very disagreeable to deal with', he often did so out of a sense of duty.[142]

After many years of mass emigration from Europe, the congressional Committee on Immigration had commissioned Dingley's investigation. His comprehensive account of European emigrants' motives was based on special reports from US consuls and his own observations. It placed a century of Irish immigration within a wider context.[143] The major reasons why Europeans left for America related to conditions in both the sending and receiving country. America was seen still seen to offer an escape route from poverty and religious persecution, leaving was officially and unofficially encouraged and assisted, it promised adventure, personal fulfilment and a potentially lucrative lifestyle, while others were following family members along well-worn paths. Despite Dingley's view that socially, industrially, physically and even morally, each emigrating European race was doing America 'a great service', there were 'evils' attached to the movement which required government restrictions.[144]

Implementing the legislation

Prior to 1882, individual states operated their own immigration policies. But in that year, federal control of immigration began in earnest with the passage of the Chinese Exclusion Act and the first general immigra-

---

139 *Ibid.*, USD, 11, 11, T199, Piatt to Bacon, 1 December 1905.
140 *Ibid.*, USC, 12, 12, T196, Swiney to Loomis, 19 November 1903.
141 *Ibid.*, USB, 11, 11, T368, Rodger to Bacon, 14 November 1905.
142 See Mark Wyman, *Round-trip to America: the immigrants return to Europe, 1880–1930* (London, 1993) 78; NARA, D/S, USD, 11, 11, T199, Wilbour to Hill, 7 November 1901.
143 Dingley, 'European immigration', 274–8.
144 *Ibid.*, 311.

tion act. The latter was largely concerned with inspection of passengers, accurate reporting of cargoes of goods and passengers and penalising shipowners by a fine or bond to cover the expenses of dealing with diseased and destitute emigrants.[145] Transatlantic shipping lines operating out of a port in Britain or Ireland were also subject to British passenger legislation. In these locations, a government emigration officer, a revenue officer and a medical officer implemented the legislation relating to minimum standards for the physical condition of the vessel, the numbers of passengers and the space and provisions for them. The consul had no defined role in regard to emigration. Some publicised state regulations, particularly with shipmasters and brokers who could be fined for non-compliance, while others warned the State Department about the departure of any undesirable immigrants such as those who were destitute, paupers, physically or mentally unfit, criminals and politically embittered. Destitute people were unwanted on two grounds; they could be carriers of diseases such as cholera, typhus and smallpox and they might become a public liability.

The first half of the nineteenth century saw several outbreaks of epidemic diseases in Ireland beginning with typhus, followed by cholera. Both were exacerbated by the 1845–51 famine which was accompanied by other diseases. Medical ignorance and inadequate government measures resulted in thousands of deaths. However, the second half of the century was characterised by a greater understanding of the causes of and remedies for epidemic diseases and consequently, its reduction. Unsurprisingly many who emigrated brought diseases with them despite the medical examinations required by the British passenger legislation.[146] Precautionary measures enacted by the US Congress in spring 1847 largely prevented the arrival of the 'Irish-borne fever epidemic'. But the link between Irish immigrants and disease was made and 'copper-fasten[ed] the American image of the Irish as a dirty, disease-carrying race'. The Irish were blamed for the outbreak of cholera in many western cities in the late 1840s and early 1850s.[147]

In the post-famine years, the first consular mention of the disease came in February 1867 when Eastman reported that cholera was present in the

---

145 Daniels and Graham, *Debating American emigration*, 8, 13. Although the federal government encouraged immigration with the 1864 act during the Civil War, this period ended on 4 March 1868 when the act was repealed. *Reports of the Immigration Commission*. 39 of 41 vols. (New York, 1970), 22, 24–8. Also called the Dillingham Commission after its chairman, there are major deficiencies in its conclusions. However, it is a useful compilation of immigration legislation.
146 Hugh Fenning, O.P. 'The cholera epidemic in Ireland, 1832–3: priests, ministers, doctors', *Archivum Hibernicum*, 57 (2003), 77–125; Robins, *The Miasma*, 32, 187.
147 Robins, *The Miasma*, 150, 153, 180–8.

Queenstown district but not in the form of an epidemic. But the presence of cholera and its transfer to the US was more serious because there were about 1,000 emigrants per week leaving Queenstown for New York. He warned the authorities 'to keep a good look out' as the sailing season approached. Although there were fourteen fatalities, the disease had disappeared by early April 1867 but continued to strike periodically during the rest of the century.[148] Secretary of State Seward responded by instructing consuls to issue all vessels bound for New York with a bill of health.[149] Despite immediate compliance by the Inman, National and Cunard ships that called into Queenstown, the measure was not effective because in the absence of having the document, Guion vessels were not turned back at New York. Despite complaints from Eastman to Seward and his successor in Queenstown, Thomas King, to Secretary Fish and the chief medical officer in New York, the 'reprehensible' conduct continued in early 1870. King concluded that captains deliberately ignored the regulation 'as long as they can do so with impunity'.[150] A destructive outbreak of smallpox during 1871–2 in Dublin and Belfast raised consular concern also. In the last two days of November 1871, James Rea in the northern city noted that there were 'alarming numbers' of victims in all social classes. But he failed to indicate whether it affected his work or more likely, Livermore's in Londonderry.[151] In 1879, the State Department required consuls to make regular sanitary reports to the US National Board of Health 'to prevent the introduction and spread of contagious diseases' into the country. Consuls were to certify the health of all passengers and crews and give the ship a certificate that it had cleared from a port free from contagious diseases or illness and that bedding and other household goods had been properly fumigated. The instructions were unclear and were often ignored which resulted in unsuitable immigrants arriving and others denied entry and sent home without money and sometimes separated from family members.[152] Consul Edward Brooks in Queenstown seemed almost proud to pronounce in October 1881:

> of the large numbers of immigrants from Ireland to the United States, very few leave these shores suffering from disease. Of the more than 100,000

---

148 NARA, D/S, USC, 6, 6, T196, Eastman to Seward, 14 February 1867; *Ibid.*, 11 April 1867; Robins, *The Miasma*, 204.
149 NARA, D/S, USC, 6, 6, T196, Eastman to Seward, 18 August 1868.
150 *Ibid.*, USC, 6, 6, T196, Eastman to Seward, 10 September 1868; *ibid.*, 7, 7, T196, King to Fish, 25 January 1870.
151 *Ibid.*, USB, 6, 6, T368, Rea to Davis, 29 November 1871.
152 *PRFA December 1, 1879*, FW Seward, 24 June 1879; quoted in Kennedy, *The American consul*, 213.

Building the Union, 1865–1913: the immigration process 243

who have sailed from this port since I have been at the consulate [January 1880] not one has died at sea and the general health of the entire number has been the occasion of frequent remark by every one who may have had reason to look in the subject.[153]

This improvement had little to do with him and resulted from better dietary, living and personal hygiene conditions, expanded sanitary services and improved reporting and prevention within communities.[154] Typhus began to recede although there were still minor outbreaks. Vice Consul Dawson commented on its occurrence in Queenstown in 1882 and encountered the limits of consular authority when trying to ensure that emigrants or transit passengers did not carry it to the US. The agents of the respective steamers refused to present him with bills of health received from the US consul in Liverpool and to have embarking passengers medically examined in Queenstown. Despite the agents' negligence, the State Department did not declare Queenstown an 'infected port' during this period of the fever.[155] By October 1882, John Piatt described the sanitary condition of the port as 'good' and 'few cases' of sickness had been found among emigrants embarking there by the medical officer of the port.[156] Fortunately for Piatt, intending emigrants leaving British and Irish ports were inspected by medical officers appointed by the British Board of Trade. Thus, he confidently reported in 1883, that 'few cases of serious sickness' were found by the medical examiner among the emigrants leaving from Queenstown.[157]

The disappearance of cholera from Ireland took longer.[158] In 1884, US consuls were instructed to be vigilant for its 'appearance' in their ports and, if it appeared, to immediately cable the Department.[159] This urgency arose from its reappearance in Egypt and fears of it spreading to Europe.[160] Piatt worried because vessels occasionally called into Queenstown from Mediterranean ports. Cholera entered Europe in 1888 and continued westward but Queenstown was reported to be in 'good health' in March.[161] Once again the Belfast consular district seemed immune from outbreaks; Consul Ruby reported 'this is a very healthy locality'.[162]

153 NARA, D/S, USC, 8, 8, T196, Brooks to Hitt, 24 October 1881.
154 Robins, *The Miasma*, 203, 231.
155 NARA, D/S, USC, 8, 8, T196, Dawson to Davis, 3 May 1882.
156 *Ibid.*, Piatt to Davis, 31 October 1882.
157 *Ibid.*, USC, 8, 8, T196, Piatt to Davis, 31 October 1883.
158 Robins, *The Miasma*, 204.
159 NARA, D/S, USC, 9, 9, T196, Piatt to Porter, 21 May 1885.
160 Robins, *The Miasma*, 226.
161 NARA, D/S, USC, 9, 9, T196, Piatt to Porter, 31 October 1885; *ibid.*, 10, 10, T196, Piatt to Rives, 15 March 1888.
162 *Ibid.*, USB, 10, 10, T368, Ruby to Wharton, 19 August 1889.

By 1890, Piatt had not reported cases of contagious diseases for 'several years'.[163] Nonetheless, following his tour of western Europe, Dingley confirmed 'we shall continue to have more to fear from cholera than from all others combined'. He was concerned that the westward advance of cholera would be renewed in 1891 and suggested that certain precautions be taken immediately to halt its arrival in the US especially the disinfection of rags, whether in the 'hold of the ship or on the backs of emigrants' before ships from Europe were allowed to land either cargoes or emigrants.[164] When Ruby in Belfast received the subsequent instruction he hurried to Londonderry to assist Consular Agent Rodger in the 'protection of our country from the threatened cholera epidemic'. Three to four ships per week left Londonderry for the US with an average of 500 passengers. The officials visited the Allan steamship, *State of California*, in the port, inspected it minutely and were pleased with the sanitary arrangements and their reception from the agent, master, surgeon and crew of the vessel. However, Ruby seemed more concerned to ensure that in the event of an epidemic, he and Rodger would be fully compensated for the extra work that might accrue in Londonderry. Ruby disliked the fumes of the disinfecting room and issuing bills of health. The State Department opposed his requests but Ruby persisted because he knew that Rodger could earn more 'cutting bog' and as he was not an American citizen, he could not be expected to do this 'urgent' work 'from purely patriotic motives'. Rodger continued with the work for a while longer but Ruby insisted he receive compensation particularly as the shipping companies had raised the price of a steerage passage. On 20 June 1893, W. E. Frazier recommended to Assistant Secretary Quincy that $50 per month be allowed to Rodger in addition to his fees for the enforcement of the quarantine and immigration laws at Londonderry.[165]

During the rest of the summer months in 1893, the State Department sent out regular circulars emphasising the importance of disinfection. The work assumed even greater seriousness after vessels carrying immigrants from Mediterranean ports infected with cholera, arrived in the

---

163 Dingley, 'European immigration', 285.
164 *Ibid.*, 292. The 1891 legislation made it the responsibility of the shipping companies to note the name, nationality, last residence and destination of each passenger carried for the use of the newly created inspection officers upon arrival in the US port.
165 NARA, D/S, USB, 10, 10, T368, Ruby to Gresham, 26 April 1893; *Derry Standard*, 20 April 1893; NARA, D/S, USB, 10, 10, T368, Ruby to Quincy, 5 June 1893; *ibid.*, W. E. Frasier to Quincy, 20 June 1893; *ibid.*, Taney to Quincy, 10 June 1893. The compensation was allowed but the Belfast office lost the services of a messenger and it was ended after nine months. *Ibid.*, Rodger to Taney, 12 June 1894; *ibid*. Rodger to Taney, 25 April 1895.

Mississippi River Quarantine Station.¹⁶⁶ Later in September, Taney was quick to inform the department that there was no truth in the rumour of a death from cholera in Belfast. But he sent a second letter on the same day indicating that cholera had appeared in England and that there was a possibility of the 'germs of disease being contained in some of the bedding of many of the steerage passengers' leaving Londonderry for the US. He instructed Rodger when he was checking and labelling luggage, to ensure that nothing carried the disease and to send a circular to the steam ship agents in Londonderry to advise intending emigrants not to bring any used bedding with them as it would be confiscated by officials upon arrival in the US.¹⁶⁷ Rodger did not allow any luggage on board the tender at Londonderry until he had inspected it and placed one of his stamped inspection labels on each article. The work became particularly onerous during the emigration season and sometimes he spent eight hours on the quay inspecting luggage.¹⁶⁸ The importance of quarantine work was emphasised a few months later when Taney reported that *The Volunteer*, recently arrived in Belfast Lough from Antwerp was in quarantine. Dr Stanley Coates, the medical officer for Belfast port, confirmed that there was a fatal case of cholera on board and after it was cleaned, disinfected and new clothes issued to the crew, it was declared clear of the disease and permitted to anchor in the port to discharge its cargo of sulphur.¹⁶⁹

The quarantine regulations had little relevance for the work of the Dublin-based consuls because transatlantic ships did not stop there for passengers. But emigrants still passed through the city en route to English ports to pick up a passage westwards. Consequently, in November 1893 Ashby provided a full report on one of the by then rare cases of typhus in Dublin.¹⁷⁰ Notwithstanding this, Assistant Secretary of State W. E. Fairn hoped that 'the quarantine laws may be modified this year, if there is no cholera'.¹⁷¹ There was no cholera outbreak in Ireland in 1893.¹⁷² But

---

166 *Ibid.*, USC, 11, 11, T196, Kress to Quincy, 8 July 1893; *ibid.*, Walker to Quincy, 11 September 1893.
167 *Ibid.*, USB, 10, 10, T368, Taney to Quincy, 6 September 1893; *ibid.*, Taney to Quincy, 6 September 1893; *ibid.*, Taney to Uhl, 18 June 1894.
168 *Ibid.*, USB, 10, 10, T368, Taney to Uhl, 18 June 1894; *ibid.*, Rodger to Taney, 12 June 1894; *ibid*. Rodger to Taney, 25 April 1895.
169 *Ibid.*, USB, 10, 10, T368, Taney to Uhl, 17 September 1894; *Belfast Newsletter*, 12, 13, 17 September 1894.
170 NARA, D/S, USD, 10, 10, T199, Ashby to Asst. Secretary of State, 27 November 1893. Cecil Piatt the Queenstown vice consul, contracted typhus in Glasgow but recovered from it. *Ibid.*, USC, 12, 12, T196, Swiney to Hill, 2 September 1901.
171 *Ibid.*, USD, 10, 10, T199, W. E. Fairn to Strobel, undated.
172 Robins, *The Miasma*, 241.

quarantine laws continued to be flouted by ships captains, particularly in ports without a full consular official. Consular Agent Mackenzie in Limerick commented in 1895 that shipbrokers knew the regulations but 'simply laugh at them'.[173] By the turn of the century, the occurrence of large-scale epidemic disease such as cholera and typhus, was rare. Consul Swiney reassured Assistant Secretary Hill that the 'typhus fever has been entirely stamped out' in Cork city and locality.[174] Although tuberculosis was not yet seen as an infectious disease, Knanbenshue in Belfast commented on its 'ravages' in August 1905 and again in 1906 when over 11,000 people died annually but he did not link it to emigration.[175]

From the 1870s onwards, consular vigilance for infectious diseases in their respective districts intensified not only because of the fears for the safety of US public health but also because of the destitute and pauper component of Irish emigration. Fitzpatrick and Moran have outlined the various schemes in place from the 1820s onwards directed at ridding the country of the unwanted labouring and impoverished classes and other undesirables.[176] Consequently, the activities of the British government, churches, poor law unions, societies, philanthropic organisations, landlords and individuals who encouraged, and sometimes, financed, destitute emigrants to the US, merited consular attention. It was not just the destitute among the immigrant cohort that concerned American officials and public including Irish-Americans, but the pauper element whose expenses were paid under government schemes. During and after the 1845–51 famine, when it seemed to American local legislatures particularly in the east, that the British government, was 'shovelling out paupers' to the US, immigration controls were introduced whereby agents and shipowners were required to pay for paupers' support.[177] But these regulations were not enforced at this time. Indeed, Eastman in Queenstown, reported in August 1865 that John Sealy, chairman of the Tralee Poor Law Union, had informed a meeting that it was not illegal to transport paupers to the US.[178] One of the reasons for the increase in emigration

173 NARA, D/S, USD, 10, 10, T199, Ashby to Uhl, 18 October 1895.
174 Robins, *The Miasma*, 241; NARA, D/S, USC, 12, 12, T196, Swiney to Hill, 29 January 1901.
175 *Ibid.*, USB, 11, 11, T368, Knanbenshue to Loomis, 29 August 1905; *ibid.*, Knanbenshue to Bacon, 9 August 1906.
176 Fitzpatrick, *Irish emigration 1801–1921*, 13–26; See Moran, *Sending out Ireland's poor* for an in depth examination of the topic.
177 The phrase was also used in the context of assisted emigration from English parishes. See Gary Howells, '"On account of their disreputable character": Parish-assisted emigration from rural England, 1834–1860', *History*, 88:292 (October 2003), 587–605; Robins, *The Miasma*, 181; Moran, *Sending out*, 209.
178 NARA, D/S, USC, 6, 6, T196, Eastman to Seward, 30 August 1865.

in 1869 over 1868 was considered by West to be that the guardians of poor law unions in Dublin encouraged emigration 'to rid themselves of the burden of their young and able-bodied inmates' thus relieving the ratepayers of a heavy tax which was increasing with pauperism and had become 'almost intolerable'.[179] Among Edward Neill's first consular duties in 1870 was to visit the North Dublin Union Alms House (with 2,084 inmates) on 2 February to deliver Civil War pension arrears of £89 1s. 9d. to Eliza O'Brien which gave him a first-hand experience of pauperism.[180] This heightened consular sensitivity towards a link between emigration and pauperism became an unofficial requirement of consular work. In January 1872, both the State Department and the Superintendent of Emigration in New York warned consuls to prevent the shipment of Irish pauper children.[181] Three years later, Livermore in Londonderry noted the presence of 'pauperism of a debased sort' in his district but he maintained that the poor were not 'comparatively many' and conditions were 'manifestly improving'. Neither did he refer to them as possible emigrants.[182] But paupers continued to arrive, particularly in the 1879–81 period, provoking opposition.[183] In June 1881, the New York Superintendent of the Poor, called for a reform of the immigration system which permitted European paupers to enter the US freely.[184]

Against this background, Secretary of State James Blaine learnt that Dublin authorities contemplated shipping twenty-five 'incorrigible paupers' in Irish work houses to New York. He instructed Acting Consul John Shaw in Dublin to investigate and 'if true, notify authorities that they will be returned.' Shaw met with Benjamin Banks, Secretary of the Local Government Board, which controlled the poor law union system, who was not aware that any of the unions were contemplating such a course. He promised to 'take care so objectionable a measure should not be carried into effect'. Subsequently, the Board confirmed that neither the North nor the South Dublin Unions contemplated 'taking such a step'.[185] On this issue, American opprobrium was matched by British

179 Ibid., USD, 7, 7, T199, West to Fish, 24 April 1869.
180 Ibid., 8, 8, T199, Neill to Fish, 3 February 1870. *Freeman's Journal*, 3 February 1870.
181 NARA, D/S, Registers of Correspondence of the Department of State, 1870–1906, M17, 11, State Department, 2 January 1872; ibid., M77, roll 82, Superintendent of Immigration, New York, 5 January 1872.
182 NARA, D/S, USL, 3, 3, T216, Livermore to Secretary of State, 7 October 1875.
183 Gerard Moran, 'Shovelling out the poor': assisted emigration from Ireland from the great famine to the fall of Parnell' in Patrick J. Duffy (ed.), *To and from Ireland: planned migration schemes c. 1600–2000* (Dublin, 2004), 146–7.
184 Moran, *Sending out Ireland's poor*, 209.
185 NARA, D/S, USD, 9, 9, T199, Shaw to Hitt, 1 July 1881; ibid., Banks to Shaw, 5 July 1881.

realism driven by the Gladstone government's need to find a solution to Ireland's problems. In 1881, assisted emigration was recommended by the Royal Commission on the Depressed Conditions of the Agricultural Interests whose members were convinced that a 'properly organised' and 'voluntary' scheme would relieve congestion.[186] Government aid became available to support the private emigrant work of individuals such as James Hack Tuke and Vere Foster, clergymen, poor law guardians, landlords and potential emigrants. The 1882 Arrears of Rent Act included £100,000 for state-aided emigration to North America, specifically to New York, Boston, Quebec and Halifax, and the Australasia and South African colonies. Forty-two poor law unions located along the western seaboard were to be aided to co-operate with the Local Government Board's emigration committee. The government also provided the Tuke Committee with £26,445 in grant-aid towards its scheme operating in Clifden and Oughterard in county Galway and Newport and Belmullet in county Mayo. By 1883, government support for emigration was established and enhanced further with the inclusion of £100,000 (later reduced to £50,000) for emigration in the 1883 Tramways and Public Companies Act.[187] Unsurprisingly, among the other questions that Consul General Merritt asked the Irish-based consuls to report on in February 1883 was 'whether the government, the guardians of the poor, or associations are engaged in sending paupers' to the US.[188]

On the other side of the Atlantic, the efforts of the New York legislature to secure federal legislation and its refusal to continue paying for the upkeep of the Castle Garden immigrant facility, forced Congress in 1882 to introduce immigration legislation and immigration bureaucracy thereby making the Secretary of the Treasury responsible for the state-level immigration framework. In addition to imposing a head tax of 50c. on each foreign passenger to defray the costs of caring for immigrants, foreign convicts, except those convicted of political offenses, lunatics, idiots, and persons likely to become public charges were not permitted to land.[189] Many Irish-Americans supported this legislation and abhorred

186 Quoted in Moran, *Sending out Ireland's poor*, 168–9. The commission was known also as the Richmond commission.
187 Moran, *Sending out Ireland's poor*, 175, 176, 177, 178; 'Emigration. 45 and 46 Victoria Cap. 47. Rules prescribed by the Lord Lieutenant in relation to the emigration of poor persons under the 18th, 19th, 20th and 21st sections of the Arrears of Rent (Ireland) Act, 1882. section vii, x.'
188 Merritt, 'Irish distress and emigration', 21 March 1883.
189 *Reports of the Immigration Commission*, 39, 31–2. The Page act, 1875, required that 'Oriental Persons' be processed at the port of embarkation by US consuls to prevent the arrival of contract labour and prostitutes. The act was considered ineffective and the Alien Contract law was introduced in 1885 to replace it. 'The Page Act of

the pauper immigrant even though the Irish formed the greater part of the pauper population in some places. In April 1883, Massachusetts Governor Benjamin F. Butler stated that despite his compassion for the assisted immigrants, if he had the authority he would stop their arrival. Butler refused to recognise 'the right' of the British government to deport 'all its paupers to our shores, as if we though not a penal colony ... [but] a pauper colony of the empire'. He demanded that President Arthur use his diplomatic power to stop 'paupers' being 'dumped' in the US. A few months later, the Chicago lawyer, Alexander Sullivan, President of the Irish National League of America, and his colleagues, met with Arthur to demand the stricter enforcement of restrictions on pauper entry because it damaged the image of the American-Irish.[190]

These types of concerns which coincided with information that government-funded pauper emigration schemes operated along the western seaboard, influenced the US immigration authorities to detain all workhouse inmates arriving from Britain or Ireland. The action also represented a lack of understanding about the schemes. Tuke and Nugent's selection criteria meant that families involved in agriculture, with children over twelve years of age and where at least one spoke English, were favoured but single men and women were also chosen. Moreover, while all had to be destitute, they need not be workhouse inmates or destitute. Successful applicants were given passages, clothes and accommodation in workhouses prior to departure but not all were residents. These latter distinctions were lost on American officials in the US and Ireland and the wider American public who equated poor law recipients and workhouse residents with pauperism.[191]

Throughout 1883, Tuke's assisted emigration scheme worked 'cordially' with British government approval and funds. Naval and coastguard vessels conveyed emigrants from the poor districts in the west to ports of departure.[192] Rear Admiral Hamilton reported the extent of their work in the spring, as set out in Table 5.8.

When Wood in Belfast learnt of the departure on Saturday, 9 June 1883, from Larne of ninety-two emigrants funded by the Carrick-on-Shannon Union, with the 'scantiest means for support on their arrival' in the US, he encouraged his superiors to investigate this obvious case

    1875', online at http://w3.uchastings.edu (accessed 6 January 2009); James P. Walsh, 'American-Irish: West and East', *Éire–Ireland*, 6:2 (1971), 31; Samuel P. Orth, 'The Alien Contract Labor Law', *Political Science Quarterly*, 22:1 (March 1907), 49–60; NARA, D/S, USB, 8, 8, T368, Savage to Porter, 2 June 1886.
190 Moran, *Sending out Ireland's poor*, 210–11.
191 *Ibid.*, 175, 176, 177, 178.
192 TNA, ADM1/6664 1884, lord lieutenant to Hamilton, 8 March 1883.

Table 5.8 Number of emigrants embarked form Ireland by the aid of HMS *Barberer, Britomart, Seahorse, Orwell*, 20 March–20 May 1883

Date	Place from	Men	Women	Children	Total
12, 20 May	Galway	145	174	141	460
12, 20 May	Galway	218	199	96	513
20 March, 15, 21, 27 April	Clew bay	477	521	733	1,731
4, 11, 19 May 5, 19 May	Kenmare	126	149	201	476
		966	1,043	1,171	3,180

Source: TNA, ADM1/6664 1884, Hamilton

of government-funded emigration.[193] In late June, sixteen emigrants from the Tralee, Milford and Cahirciveen unions in county Kerry, were turned back in New York because they possessed no means of supporting themselves and some were single women with children.[194] On 27 June, each consul was ordered to examine 'government emigration or exportation of people', the class of persons involved, whether it was wholly voluntary, the reasons for leaving and the condition of the emigrants whether pauper, criminal or otherwise.[195] Consular Agent William J. Eccles based in Sligo, less than fifty miles from Carrick-on-Shannon, visited the workhouse where he met Abraham O'Connor, clerk of the Union, who supervised the selection of the emigrants and their journey to Larne. The latter emphatically denied 'the exportation of paupers' and that 'no person of bad character or belonging to the criminal classes' was selected. His evidence was backed by a transcript from the union records which showed the sums of money given to each emigrant. O'Connor emphasised that coercion was not used to induce the people to emigrate nor was any inducement held out to them to choose the US as their destination. On the other hand, Eccles learned privately from a prominent merchant and a poor law guardian, that twelve or thirteen were paupers. He believed that the guiding principle was to send those who would be 'likely to remain a tax on the ratepayers' if they did not emigrate, although O'Connor denied this. Barrows in Dublin accepted Eccles' version and that the clerk's report was 'reliable'. He directed Eccles and

193 NARA, D/S, USB, 8, 8, T368, Wood to Asst. Secretary of State, 11 June 1883; *Northern Whig*, 11 June 1883.
194 Merritt, 'Irish distress and emigration', 21 March 1883; Moran, *Sending out Ireland's poor*, 210–11; Funchion, *Irish American voluntary organisation*, 195.
195 NARA, D/S, USC, 9, 9, T196, Piatt to Davis, 12 July 1883.

Consular Agent John Tinsly in Limerick to notify the respective boards of guardians in their districts against 'the shipment of pauper emigrants' to the US and cautioned them that such emigrants would certainly be returned by the US authorities 'probably at the expense of the senders'. Later in July, O'Connor confirmed to Barrows that the emigrants from Carrick-on-Shannon were principally small farmers who had sold land and, therefore, possessed money in addition to the government grant and that five women who travelled alone and might appear to be workhouse paupers, were not, as all had family in the US.[196] In other words, these women, like others, used the workhouse for a short stay during a time of crisis. The clerk attempted to educate the US consuls and presumably the US authorities, about the operation of the poor law system and the emigration scheme. Barrows accepted O'Connor's argument and advised his superiors that if Irish emigrants were questioned they would deny having any means but most 'paupers ... possessed ... funds sufficient to raise him above that term'.[197] The US authorities might not have to deal with paupers, but they would have to deal with liars.

The detailed nature of Piatt and Livermore's reports underlined their comprehension of their government's concern. Both men confirmed the role of the British government through the Arrears Act and the involvement of Poor Law unions and the Local Government Board in selecting and assisting 'poor persons' to emigrate. But guardians were 'leading men' interested only in the relief of the poor. Emigration whether assisted or otherwise was, in Piatt's words:

> long ... regarded ... as the most practical means of alleviating, if not, relieving the condition of extreme poverty and distress in which a large percentage of the agricultural population in the west of Ireland live – a condition which has been aggravated during the last two or three years by the failure of crops, with the numerous evictions, [and] loss of employment.

The emigrants were small farmers and labourers 'willing to work if they had the opportunity' and while some received outdoor relief or had been driven into 'the arms of the work house or poor house', they were 'respectable' also. Like their colleagues, these consuls tried to reveal the complexity of the problem and identified the selection criteria employed and that each was met. In other words, families were favoured and each emigrant had to have relatives already in the US and Canada.

196 *Ibid.*, USD, 9, 9, T199, Barrows to Davis, 24 July 1883; *ibid.*, Eccles to Barrows, 18 July 1883; O'Connor to Eccles, 13 July 1883; *ibid.*, USC, 9, 9, T196, O'Connor to Piatt, 21 July 1883 and enclosure; NARA, D/S, USD, 9, 9, T199, Eccles to Shaw, 18 July 1883; *ibid.*, Barrows to O'Connor, 19 July 1883; *ibid.*, O'Connor to Barrows, 21 July 1883.
197 *Ibid.*, USD, 9, 9, T199, Barrows to Davis, 24 July 1883.

Additionally, each emigrant was 'eager to go', was given a suit of clothing, put into the care of an agent on board ship and upon arrival the agent would give them a landing allowance and direct them to their destination and employment. Livermore was convinced that these emigrants were 'persons of good character, health and constitution' and he expected them to do 'well'. Indeed one of his contacts indicated that the board of guardians would have preferred that a more 'needy and less valuable class' should be exported. Although admitting that this careful selection procedure might have been contravened at times by other unions, Piatt felt that the return of emigrants from the three county Kerry unions by the New York commissioners of Emigration in late June, had a 'salutary effect' in Ireland. The Local Government Board launched a sworn inquiry into the Cahirciveen Union's scheme which had sent out long-term paupers and publicised that the proportion of paupers to other state-aided emigrants was 1 to 511. Even then Piatt emphasised that, like in the US, many were only 'temporary paupers that is to say persons driven by utter improbability of getting employment and food ... many of them may be industrious, vigorous and virtuous people'.[198] While stopping short of completing abrogating the Union's responsibility, his attempt here to humanise the emigrant and give a comparative context offered his superiors a more nuanced view of the situation.

Other corroborative evidence of the difficult situation faced by the government came from Piatt's correspondence with the private philanthropist Vere Foster of Belfast who had assisted approximately 18,000 females aged between 18 and 21 years to emigrate since 1847. Foster indicated that nineteen out of every twenty girls he chose to go to the US were not paupers because each emigrant did not receive the full cost of the journey from him but was required to find the balance themselves. Foster's personal credentials were outlined; his father was secretary of the British legation in Washington and from 1803 to 1812 was minister. Piatt had a 'good' opinion of Foster's scheme and he may have hoped Foster's own experience, respectability and praise of the British government's 'beneficent intention' might have diluted Washington's disapproval. Although James Hack Tuke did not respond to Piatt's letter, his scheme was funded by private and government aid. It had assisted over 5,300 emigrants from the congested districts of the west of Ireland and each applicant who wished to go to the US required a letter from friends willing to receive them. Each emigrant was supplied with an outfit and money for the journey. Piatt exonerated both Foster and Tuke from any

---

198 *Ibid.*, USC, 9, 9, T196, Piatt to Davis, 25 July 1883; *ibid.*, Local Government Board to Piatt, 21 July 1883; *ibid.*, USB, 9, 9, T368, Livermore to Davis, 31 July 1883; *ibid.*, USC, 9, 9, T196, USC, 9, 9, T196, Piatt to Davis, 25 July 1883.

role in the case of one emigrant returned by New York authorities whose passage had been paid by his county Limerick landlord who was owed two and a half year's rent from him. Piatt's analysis of the three sources of official sponsorship – Poor Law guardians, Foster and Tuke – signalled to his superiors that, unlike others, these schemes had worthy aims and discriminated in their selection of candidates for assistance.[199] Moreover, as he was based in Queenstown from where the majority of the assisted emigrants departed, Piatt observed that most 'presented a good appearance', seemed to be 'vigorous and able-bodied', from the 'small farming class' and looked to have sufficient 'means with them to begin life' in the US. Nonetheless he alerted the department to information received from a US citizen and former Civil War soldier, John Minahan, who believed that 'everybody and anybody dependent on poor house relief were exported to America as a means to save the landlords' pocket'. After visiting Tralee, Listowel, Ballybunion and Dingle workhouses in county Kerry, Minahan learned that the guardians intended applying for more government funds to send out further emigrants who would otherwise become a 'burden on our country'.[200]

By late 1884, Piatt believed that one of the reasons for the reduced numbers emigrating from his port – 29,850 for the year ended 31 September 1884 compared to 41,149 for the previous year – was the growing tendency to discourage state-aided schemes due to the 'action of our Commissioners in returning so many pauper class'.[201] However, Wood in Belfast reported that while emigration from his district was 'very small comparatively', those who passed through his port to Liverpool and Larne were mostly from the west and north-west and were 'part of the "assisted class"'.[202] The State Department remained under political pressure from American and Irish-American groups to prevent the arrival of impoverished emigrants either assisted or unassisted. A further circular on 27 December 1884 instructed consuls in Ireland to

199 *Ibid.*, USC, 9, 9, T196, Piatt to Davis, 25 July 1883; *ibid.*, Foster to Piatt, 18 July 1883; *ibid.*, *Cork Constitution*, 25 July 1883; *ibid.*, *The Nation*, 19 July 1883. Piatt's admiration contrasted with F. L. Dingley's suspicion and opposition to assisted emigration schemes for poor Jews. He was sympathetic that they did not have 'a country' but they were 'miserably' poor, mainly 'socialist', and had different culinary and religious practices which inhibited integration. Dingley, 'European immigration, 279, 280–7, 291.
200 NARA, D/S, USC, 9, 9, T196, Piatt to Davis, 25 July 1883; *ibid.*, Minahan to Piatt, 1 July 1883. The clerk of the Waterford union, confirmed to Consular agent W. H. Farrell that no pauper emigration had taken place from the district and state-aided schemes were confined to the western seaboard counties. *Ibid.*, Ferrell to Piatt, 24 July 1883.
201 *Ibid.*, USC, 9, 9, T196, Piatt to Davis, 12 November 1884.
202 *Ibid.*, USB, 9, 9, T368, Woods to Davis, 29 November 1884.

watch out for the departure of 'pauper or indigent' emigrants.[203] Two years later, in reply to another State Department demand for information on the character of Irish emigration, George Savage in Belfast believed that government-assisted emigration had ended and Vere Foster's scheme was operating in a limited way.[204] Livermore reported in May 1886 that government funds for emigration were 'exhausted and no aid is being furnished from any general source' or from 'private funds'.[205] Piatt kept a watchful eye on the government schemes. He reported in 1887 that while Tralee Poor Law guardians discontinued their scheme because its work was 'misrepresented', an emigration committee was formed to take the names of families who were anxious to leave for the US to find work which would 'enable them to live industrious and honourable lives, and in comparative comfort'. Piatt reiterated that 'considerable caution' was taken in the selection process.[206] Savage reported the absence of 'assisted emigration' from his district in late 1888.[207] When Dingley visited Ireland as part of his western Europe tour at this time, he learned from Piatt that 'occasionally' Poor Law guardians still financed first, 'worthy young girls reared and trained in the work houses' to emigrate as servant girls and second, children of 'tender years from workhouses' sent to US convents. Moreover, he learnt that on the occasion of recent strikes in Dublin and Cork, trade unions assisted many striking workers to emigrate. But he was convinced that a state-aided scheme was not operating. Dingley acknowledged the permanence of the Irish transatlantic movement and even seemed to accept that assisted emigration might increase again because 'Ireland yet remains the saddest land in Europe'.[208] Estimates of the number of assisted emigrants vary. Savage believed that at least 10,000 emigrants were assisted to leave by Poor Law guardians in 1883, 1884 and spring 1885. Contemporary estimates suggest that between 1881 and 1885 the unions paid passages for 7,500 pauper emigrants including workhouse inmates. Another commentator estimates that during the 1880s private and state-aided schemes funded the departures of approximately 50,000 from Ireland.[209]

In 1892 against the background of a restrictionist climate in Congress

203 Ibid., USC, 9, 9, T196, Piatt to Davis, 23 January 1885.
204 Ibid., USB, 9, 9, T368, Savage to Porter, 2 June 1886.
205 Ibid., Livermore to Porter, 26 May 1886.
206 *Cork Constitution*, 9 June 1887; Moran, *Sending out Ireland's poor*, 179; NARA, D/S, USC, 10, 10, T196, Piatt to Porter, 6 June 1887. In 1889, Belmullet union applied for funds to aid the departure of 550 people.
207 NARA, D/S, USB, 10, 10, T368, Savage to Rives, 4 October 1888.
208 Dingley, 'European immigration', 284–7.
209 NARA, D/S, USB, 10, 10, T368, Savage to Rives, 4 October 1888; Miller, *Emigrants and exiles*, 401; Moran, *Sending out Ireland's poor*, 179.

Building the Union, 1865–1913: the immigration process

and industrial depression, both Republicans and Democratic parties in their national conventions adopted policies supporting further limits on immigration. In 1893 and 1894, Congress debated greater consular involvement in the process. Legislation already restricted criminals and paupers but a more rigid scheme was demanded by some politicians who argued that there was no reason why immigrants should travel thousands of miles to determine whether he or she was admissible or not. It would be far better for the emigrant to know before embarking. No agreement was reached on whether Treasury agents or consuls should conduct the inspections. The 1893 Act, however, tightened the recording of immigrants which affected consular work. Upon arrival in the US, each captain and surgeon of a vessel carrying immigrants had to deliver an official list of all passengers to the officials. The lists had to be signed by the US consul at the port of departure who had to issue a sworn statement indicating that after a personal examination of all the passengers, no persons excluded by US laws were on the vessel. In other words, each ship required a consular bill of health and each passenger an inspection card.[210]

Henry Kress recently arrived in Queenstown, and Piatt now in Dublin, posted the new regulations on the wall of their respective consulates while the latter sent a copy to Consular Agent Richard Hogan in Limerick.[211] Kress was surprised by the extent of his emigration duties particularly that he had to work on Sundays when two transatlantic vessels were in the port. Additionally when vessels anchored two miles from the dock, he had to travel further. Within a few weeks of arriving, the 'tide of emigration' was 'so great', he hired an extra clerk to help him with office work and inspections when there were two vessels in the harbour on the same day.[212] By early May 1893, he reported that the new regulations were not delaying the departure of vessels or causing any 'friction of any kind'. Indeed, he said, enforcing the Act had not affected the 'numbers emigrating' from Queenstown at all. One month later, he stated that no emigrant had objected to the medical inspection and just eight people had failed it. A local physician, Dr Edmond Seymour Bricknell was appointed as US sanitary inspector to conduct the inspections which took place in the inspection and quarantine room in the consulate.[213] Kress' successor,

---

210 *Reports of the Immigration Commission, 39*, 43.
211 NARA, D/S, USD, 10, 10, T199, Piatt to Quincy, 3 April 1893; *ibid.*, USC, 11, 11, T196, Kress to Assistant Secretary of State, 31 March 1893.
212 *Ibid.*, USC, 11, 11, T196, Kress to Quincy, 15 April 1893; *ibid.*, Kress to Quincy, 6 May 1893; *ibid.*, Kress to Quincy, 2 June 1893.
213 *Ibid.*, Kress to Quincy, 6 May 1893; *ibid.*, Walker to Uhl, 5 January 1894; *ibid.*, Kress to Quincy, 3 June 1893.

Lucien J. Walker, seemed surprised that 'many thousands of emigrants pass through ... room 3' each week and also that out-of-hours work had become normal. Consul General Collins approved the appointment of Fred Piatt as deputy consul.[214] Rodger in Londonderry still operated on his own and his work was considerably more arduous than ever before because he performed his duties in Londonderry port where the passengers boarded and disembarked from tenders and sometimes at Moville further out in the Lough Foyle coast where the transatlantic ships docked. Frequently, ships were delayed by fogs and storms and arrived late into Moville which meant that he endured lengthy stays of up to twenty-five hours on the tender waiting for ship.[215] One challenger for his job, Hugh O'Dougherty, a local solicitor, withdrew his application because the duties were so demanding.[216]

The consul's increasingly prominent role in implementing immigration regulations sometimes brought him into direct contact with proscribed individuals. In June 1893, Michael Foster was released by Resident Magistrate Vesa Fitzgerald on condition that he left immediately for the US on a prepaid White Star line ticket. Foster presented himself to Kress in Queenstown to secure his inspection card which was refused.[217] Five years later, the State Department instructed Touvelle in Belfast to investigate a newspaper report that young convicted criminals were being sent to the US by Belfast courts. Touvelle discovered that Henry Cargo and two associates were convicted of breaking, entering and stealing and they were imprisoned but not exported.[218] On the other hand, the exclusion of contract labourers caused few problems for the consuls not least because the 1885 Act exempted skilled workmen, personal or domestic servants and did not prohibit any individual from assisting any member of his or her family or any relative or personal friend from emigrating to the US for settlement.[219] However, Consul Savage believed that testimony given to the House of Representatives special committee investigating immigration which accused Barbour Brothers of importing labourers from their mill at Lisburn, county Antrim, to work in their mill at Paterson, New Jersey, was accurate and that the practice was widespread in his

214 *Ibid.*, Walker to State Department, 1 December 1899; *ibid.*, 'Plan of the United States consulate offices at Queenstown' in Walker to Quincy, 12 October 1893; *ibid.*, Walker to Quincy, 13 November 1893..
215 *Ibid.*, USB, 11, 11, T368, Rodger to Taney, 13 March 1897.
216 *Ibid.*, O'Dougherty to Touvelle, 14 February 1903.
217 *Ibid.*, USC, 11, 11, T196, Kress to Quincy, 15 June 1893.
218 *Ibid.*, USB, 11, 11, T368, Touvelle to Day, 15 April 1898.
219 'The Page Act of 1875', online at http://w3.uchastings.edu/ (accessed 6 January 2009); Samuel P. Orth, 'The Alien Contract Labor Law', *Political Science Quarterly*, 22:1 (March 1907), 49–60.

Belfast district.²²⁰ But Dingley could not find any evidence in Ireland of syndicates offering prepaid passages to individuals who would then work for them in the US at reduced rates.²²¹

During the economic depression in the 1890s, anti-immigrant feeling intensified and further reasons for excluding peoples were identified. The Immigration Restriction League, established by Harvard graduates in 1894 focused its campaign on inserting literacy tests for immigrants into the legislation.²²² In September 1896, the Irish Local Government Board asked Ashby in Dublin whether the immigration of illiterate emigrants was prohibited now and if so, could they have a copy of the act. Ashby did not know and requested clarification from the State Department.²²³ In fact Congress had passed a bill compelling immigrants to be literate but President Cleveland vetoed it in 1897 as 'unAmerican' and he emphasised that the 'stupendous growth' of the nation had been 'largely due to the assimilation and thrift of millions of sturdy and patriotic adopted citizens'.²²⁴ If introduced, the requirement would have been less onerous for Irish immigrants because educational advancements led to high literacy rates. The 1911 Irish census indicated that 88 per cent of individuals over the age of five years were able to read.²²⁵ Indeed Dingley commented that the majority of the emigrants out of Queenstown could read and write.²²⁶ The literacy issue remained a controversial political matter as Congress passed laws and presidential vetoes reversed them.²²⁷

The US Congress maintained its hostile approach to immigration throughout the period. Officials and politicians became even more convinced that the best way to reach the immigrant was 'before he has touched the ship that is pointing towards these shores'.²²⁸ Consuls located in Germany, Switzerland, England, Scotland and Ireland suggested that:

> the intending emigrant be required to give notice to the nearest consular office of his intention to emigrate, upon which our consular officials shall institute inquiries regarding his fitness for American life, his character

---

220 Daniels and Graham, *Debating American emigration*, 100; NARA, D/S, USB, 10, 10, T368, Savage to Rives, 4 October 1888.
221 Dingley, 'European immigration', 287.
222 Daniels and Graham, *Debating American emigration*, 14.
223 NARA, D/S, USD, 10, 10, T199, Piatt to Rockhill, 8 September 1896.
224 Daniels and Graham, *Debating American emigration*, 14.
225 John Logan, 'Literacy' in Connolly (ed.), *The Oxford companion*, 319; Hamilton Andrews Hill, *Memoir of Abbott Lawrence*, 'Condition of Ireland' (Boston, 1883), 226.
226 Dingley, 'European immigration', 286.
227 In 1917 it became an entry requirement when Congress overrode Woodrow Wilson's veto. Daniels and Graham, *Debating American emigration*, 14.
228 Dingley, 'European immigration', 293.

especially. If the inquiry was satisfactory, the consul shall issue certificates ... to the emigrant ... and to the collector of the port where the immigrant will disembark, none being allowed without a certificate.

The consul would exclude prepaid emigrants, impose a $1 head tax on each and collect proof of the emigrant's 'moral fitness for American citizenship'. Dingley regarded the suggestions as 'hasty, sweeping and ill digested' because 'foreigners helped us to American independence' and there was a 'degree of race-harmony'. The consuls' restrictions would refuse entry to the 'good foreigner' and damage economic growth.[229] However, the substance of the consuls' suggestions was in line with congressional and public opinion.

The surge in immigrant numbers between 1903 and 1907 intensified demands for more restrictive legislation resulting in the 1903, 1907 and 1910 immigration acts.[230] Little had changed for 77-year-old Pat Rodger who still attended at the embarkation of passengers and accompanied by a medical officer, he inspected each emigrant as he or she came on board the tender at the wharf at Londonderry. Each emigrant was issued with an inspection card and each piece of baggage was inspected and a label pasted on it. If the baggage came from a 'disease-infected district', it had to be disinfected again under consular inspection and a disinfection card placed on it. He then proceeded on the tender to Moville and after boarding the vessel and satisfying himself as to its sanitary condition and the health of the passengers and crew, he gave the purser, or other officer in charge of the ship, a supplemental bill of health which was attached to the bill of health given by the consular officer at the original port of sailing and an inspection card for each emigrant. The ship was then allowed to proceed. Just one emigrant was rejected in 1905, a sick child in a family of five, but who subsequently recovered and travelled one week later.[231] The Consul in Dublin had little or no work associated with immigration legislation, except to oversee consular work in Galway. By 1905 the system in place involved Consular Agent Tennant who accompanied Dr R. J. Kinead when he examined emigrants on board the tender on the way to the ship. No emigrant was rejected in 1904–5 although one woman was refused admission to the US because she was pregnant.[232] At Queenstown, Consul Swiney was overwhelmed by the emigration work and secured the services of a deputy consul, Cecil Piatt, who resigned in 1902 because of insufficient remuneration.[233]

229 Dingley, 'European immigration', 293–9, 312.
230 *Reports of the Immigration Commission*, 39, 56.
231 NARA, D/S, USB, 11, 11, T368, Rodger to Bacon, 14 November 1905.
232 *Ibid.*, USD, 11, 11, T199, Piatt to Bacon, 1 December 1905.
233 *Ibid.*, D/S, USC, 12, 12, T196, Swiney to Loomis, 1 May 1903.

Building the Union, 1865–1913: the immigration process

Swiney and his successor in 1906, Edwin N. Gunsaulus, worked many seven-day weeks to deal with the transatlantic traffic. The latter found the work 'arduous and exacting' and believed the work merited a salary of $4,000 per annum and not $2,000.[234] By the turn of the century, it was the immigration and quarantine work that gave the Cork consulate its distinctive character and ranked it among the most important of the US consular posts in Europe.

Consuls located in ports without a significant transatlantic passenger trade, paid little attention to the ongoing wave of departures of peoples from their respective districts. Consuls in Belfast embedded themselves within the local commercial community and reported on manufacturing while consuls in Dublin frequently reported on political issues. The men in the emigrant ports were on the spot, saw the flow of emigrants and increasingly had to engage with them. They did not provide a national perspective on emigration but concentrated on their own district. Yet, collectively, their views offer another insight into the mass emigration movement to the US during and after the 1845–51 famine. Individual consuls were not always sympathetic to the emigrant which arose from personal animosities and local influences, but also reflected American public and political disquiet. At times their views on the emigrant fed into stereotypes of the nature and personality of the Irish Catholic and Ulster-Scots Protestant emigrant but all identified that British government policy forced many to depart. Nevertheless, by the 1880s, consular reports from emigrant European countries provided American politicians with a wider context to the incessant flow of peoples and contributed to the strengthening political desire to restrict and regulate immigration into the US. But the consuls in Ireland accepted the permanence of chain migration and none offered any reason to the US government to restrict Irish immigration. Instead most emphasised how Irish immigration enhanced US society.

The consul's responsibilities and workload increasingly made him a key person and the consulate an intelligence and information office. On the eve of the First World War, newly arrived consuls expressed astonishment at the voluminous unofficial correspondence received from America and within Ireland. The consul was consulted on all possible subjects with an American dimension. To use Consul Barrows words, 'all have faith that the representative is a certain and sure source of light as great as their profound belief in the Great Republic over the sea'.[235] So

---

234 *Ibid.*, USC, 12, 12, T196, Swiney to Loomis, 28 May 1903; *ibid.*, Gunsaulus to Loomis, 14 April 1906.
235 *Ibid.*, USD, 9, 9, T199, Barrows to Porter, 4 November 1885.

great was this responsibility that Third Secretary Herbert Peirce believed the consuls in emigration ports should receive more compensation than those at the 'mere shipping points of merchandise' or at manufacturing towns.[236] This did not happen but the consul and consulate's role in the immigration process meant that they had become another link in the chain connecting the two countries.

---

236 *Ibid.*, USC, 12, 12, T196, Gunsaulus to Loomis, 14 April 1906.

6

Conclusion

Assessing the extent and nature of consular activity in Ireland in the period 1790 to 1913 begins by critically considering their correspondence with the State Department and then examining their impact on the people they served. An examination of consular reports must include the study of the consul's personality, personal proclivities and his predetermined notions, including a certain American worldview.[1] These factors are present in the Irish context. William Knox was dogged by ill health, deeply felt the isolation of his post, but was consumed by the need to make money for himself. Others followed him and were equally disappointed at poor remuneration, the absence of salary and later, when all Irish-based consulships were salaried, the inadequate pay levels, particularly in Belfast where the fees were significant. Although this recurring theme of disappointment led some consuls to engage in corruption such as Hugh Keenan, others did not. During the American Civil War, Union consuls Dr John Young and the former ship captain, Edwin Eastman, sufficiently managed the personal and political opposition directed at them, to uphold their government's interests. Eastman's zeal combined with the strategic location of his southern post motivated him to extend his consular role into the intelligence area. William West's personal and professional dedication during the Fenian crisis stands out also as another example where character influenced performance. Although fearful for his position, West railed against the suspension of *habeas corpus* and subsequent arrests and incarcerations without evidence and went to great lengths to ensure fairness of treatment for American prisoners. Some prisoners were discourteous towards him and unappreciative of his efforts. But he walked a tightrope between, on the one hand, the Irish civil, military and police authorities and, on the other, the interests of his government, the duties of his post and personal sympathy for the nationalists. During difficult circumstances which forced him to assume diplomatic functions, he developed a good working relationship with the

1 Kark, *American consuls*, 295–7.

authorities and tried to behave properly, despite slight ridicule from US Minister Adams and his secretary, Moran.

Undoubtedly Wexford-born West was motivated by his compassion for the poverty-stricken, poorer classes, a sentiment which had brought him into the nationalist movement but also influenced his support for emigration to the US. However, consuls and indeed ministers, based elsewhere in Ireland and Britain, distinguished between the emigrant classes. Beginning in the 1850s officials such as Abbott Lawrence, Nathaniel Hawthorne, Benjamin Moran, Charles Francis Adams, John Young and Arthur Wood projected a prejudiced, American establishment view of the Irish emigrant whereby the Irish Catholic and Ulster-Scots Protestant immigrant possessed opposing innate characteristics. However, the liberal instincts of the poet John Piatt made his reporting about emigration particularly sensitive and nuanced. These contrasting consular traditions emerged also in relation to wider political developments. As Irish nationalism developed from the radicalism of the 1790s, through O'Connellism, the Young Ireland, Fenian, tenant rights and home rule movements and then hardened into diametrically opposed nationalist and unionist camps, consular involvement depended on the individual official's level of engagement and the extent of the American dimension. Thus, when the latter was minimal for example during the 1845–51 famine, the consuls accepted the status quo while the absence of a consul general and a minister in Ireland during the Fenian-inspired upheavals revealed the variety of their human and political responses. Similarly, during the era of mass migration although many identified a link between British policies in Ireland, continuing political and social upheaval and mass emigration, none suggested US government intervention with its British counterpart. Yet, neither did any consul recommend to the State Department that Irish immigration be restricted. Likewise, it was the need to maintain the strong commercial relationship between the northeast of Ireland and the US which saw consuls in that locality accurately identify for their superiors that opposition to London's home rule legislation was natural for some Irishmen. However, the outbreak of wars or disputes involving either or both the US and Britain stretching from the revolutionary period to the Civil War and the Spanish–American War, could provoke consular comment. Criticism of British policy emerged when principles core to American nationhood were threatened such as non-recognition of US naturalised citizenship and excessive sympathy for America's enemies.

Despite the often irregular and subjective nature of the reporting, many consuls actively gathered information, sent reports to Washington on economic, social and political matters and when directed, affected policy directives. Moreover, many consuls tried to be analytical about the information forwarded to Washington. Like consuls elsewhere, they admitted that obtaining reliable information and statistical data about trade and commerce was often hard to get from official sources and private merchants. Although as the century went on, the regular publication by central government of census material and reports from parliamentary investigations into national problems combined with regular publications by local authorities on commercial and emigration traffic in and out of their jurisdictions, gave consuls a solid basis for their own observations. They pointed out also that enclosed newspaper and journal articles often lacked credibility and represented specific political biases. Nonetheless, few consuls ever visited beyond their own base and if they experienced an event or conditions first-hand, few presented themselves as an expert on Irish affairs.

The effectiveness of consular activity, therefore, can only be measured by examining the consul's imprint on the district he attended to. Until the end of the nineteenth century, American political leaders were more concerned with state-building, the national project and regional affairs than with global affairs. Nonetheless, the State Department was determined to secure representation where ever possible which contributed, along with patronage, to the development of a haphazard, amateur service in Ireland as elsewhere. Yet, at the most basic level of engagement, consuls in Ireland always saw themselves representing the new republic and upholding its core values. Some consuls demanded fair and equal treatment for distressed seamen, ship's captains, ship owners and later American prisoners, which often meant unpleasant visits to hospitals, hostels, workhouses, prisons, gaols, courts and negotiating with local officials. In turn as the century wore on, American citizens became aware of their rights in foreign countries and were quick to turn to the local American consul for help and also to complain him to the State Department or newspapers, if he disappointed them. The consul's willingness to act on behalf of the needy citizen and engage with the civil, judicial and military authorities can be seen, therefore, as an extension of the growing confidence of the American nation.

Concurrently, successive American governments' political interest in Ireland must be placed within the wider context of the American–British relationship. Although described as 'special' by Winston Churchill in 1946, others date this characterisation to the Anglo-American Arbitration Treaty in 1897, while radical Irish-Americans believed the Motley–Clarendon Naturalisation Treaty in 1870 was a sell-out by the US government and that from an early stage most American ministers sent to St James' Court became anglicised in behaviour and conduct and in Ambassador John Hay's words, 'slaves of England'.² So, while the American government's political relationship with Ireland seemed non-existent, except through the imperial framework, Irish nationalists both in Ireland and in the US accorded American governments, congresses, politicians and voting public, political responsibility in Irish affairs. They regarded the presence or absence of American political will at executive level to intervene with the British government on their behalf, as a test of their 'special' relationship. More often than not, it did not materialise. Nevertheless, nationalists' hope for American salvation was sustained by their belief in the presence of substantial interest in some quarters of the executive and in the power of the 'Irish vote'. As representatives of official America in Ireland, the consuls' role, therefore, was to deal with the consequences when unofficial America responded to the call for intervention. During the second half of the nineteenth century, when supplies of either American men or money or arms or munitions came to Ireland and roused official attention, the consul, although often critical of Irish-America's involvement, acted as a link between the respective American, Irish and British authorities and at the very least, illustrated that American officialdom would intervene with the British government but only on behalf of its citizens. Rarely did the consul assert his privileged status further than the local level.

The second area where consular work reveals a further dimension to official America's interest in Ireland was the consolidation of support for American foreign policy activities and countering sympathy for the enemy. Along with operating as intelligence officers, they engaged in propaganda work during the War of 1812, the American Civil War in 1861–5, the Venezuelan crisis in 1897 and the Spanish–American War in 1898. During the 1890s crisis, when US relations with Britain reached an all-time low, Consul Taney passed on 'friendly' resolutions from the Belfast Chamber of Commerce to support US policy on Venezuela. In 1898, Consuls Wilbour in Dublin and Walker in Cork transmitted resolutions of sympathy from 1798 commemoration committees to the State Department on the loss of the USS *Maine* in Havana harbour on 15 February which catapulted the US into the war with Spain over the independence of the former Spanish colonies of Cuba, Puerto Rico, Guam and the Philippines. After the Treaty of Paris was signed between the US and Spain in December, Consul Wilbour continued to monitor the Irish reaction to the continuing legacy of the war.³ Ironically, by the end of the

---

2 Quoted in Beckles Willson, *America's ambassadors to England (1785–1928). A narrative of Anglo-American diplomatic relations* (London, 1928) 420.
3 NARA, D/S, USB, 9, 9, T368, Taney toRockhilll, 25 June 1896; *ibid.*, USD, 10, 10, T199, Wilbour to Gridler, 7 February 1898; *ibid.*, 'Oliver Bond Young Men's Club,

Conclusion

nineteenth century when home rule seemed imminent, the Dublin-based consuls began to echo William Knox's view in 1790, that they occupied 'a unique position' in the service because they were stationed in the 'Metropolis' where the US consul occupied the preeminent rank among foreign dignitaries at the Viceregal court and other official functions, one far above his status in the US foreign service.[4] Repeating these sentiments in 1901, Wilbour now saw the consul 'necessarily thrust into a position of prominence' in the capital city.[5] Despite this symbolic distinction, there was no direct political relationship between the United States and Ireland. Instead it was indirect through the minister in London or personal through non-official channels. However, the economic counterpart was more tangible.

It was measurable in terms of the numbers of ships arriving into ports from the US and leaving for American ports, the tonnage of cargo and its composition. During the earliest decades of the relationship when most consuls were merchants trading the Atlantic routes, the merchant families such as the Lukes, Wilsons, Englishs, Harveys, Corscadens and Persees recognised the enormous potential of America's markets for Irish goods and produce. The Act of Union among other factors, put paid to these hopes and instead it was American expectations that began to predominate. Ireland was always viewed as a source of raw materials for American manufacturing and as a market for its goods. After the 1880s, consular efforts to ferret out opportunities for both became intensive not least because of congressional pressure. From this time onwards, the pattern of American economic growth highlighted the long decline in the Irish economy. Undoubtedly, the industries located in and around Belfast, the commercial capital of Ireland, represented a continuous, important and lucrative link between the US and Ireland. Meanwhile American products such as wheat, oil, tobacco and timber established a foothold in the Irish economy which typified the reality of the uneven transatlantic economic relationship into the twentieth century.

The main beneficiaries of the consular presence were the emigrant and returning American citizens. It was this human link which Consul Gunsaulus writing from Queenstown in 1906, believed underpinned the 'intimate relations' between the US and Ireland.[6] As the nineteenth

---

'98 Branch' resolution; *ibid.*, "98 Centenary Committee' resolution; *ibid.*, USC, 11, 11, T196, 'Copy of Resolution passed in committee of the whole council this 18th day of February 1898' in Walker to Day, 19 February 1898; *ibid.*, USD, 10, 10, T199, Wilbour to Day, 22 April 1898; *ibid.*, USD, 11, 11, T199, Wilbour to Hill, 31 May 1901.

4 *Ibid.*, USD, 9, 9, T199, Barrows to Porter, 4 November 1885.
5 *Ibid.*, USD, 11, 11, T199, Wilbour to Hill, 7 November 1901.
6 *Ibid.*, USC, 12, 12, T196, Gunsaulus to secretary of State, 14 April 1906.

century wore on and the emigrant tide from Ireland grew, the consul represented America, providing civil, legal and administrative, and particularly, notarial services to the departees, the resident citizens and later the returnees. His practical duties such as issuing pensions, pursuing inheritance matters and implementing immigration and quarantine regulations expanded and gave substance to America's official presence. The consul was identified as a font of information and advice on all manner of matters relating to America. That the consul in Ireland represented America for so many was evidenced also in the regular flow of complaints to the State Department when it was believed that a consul was overcharging for a service or did not fulfil a specific request to the complainant's satisfaction or more usually, benefit. So although there were few other examples of the effectiveness or calibre of the men who represented the US in Ireland during the period 1790 to 1913 and while they have generally been tarred with the same brush of criticism as others in the consular service, there was some contemporaneous admiration and praise for them. In 1899, the *Consular Journal and Great Britain* commented that the work of other nations' consuls was 'certainly superior to that done by our consular officers abroad'. The French *La Revue diplomatique* identified that American consuls 'have the art of putting life and initiative into a career where other people rest upon routine and immobility'.[7]

At the turn of the nineteenth century, official America's interest in Ireland was peripheral to its relationship with Britain, its formal impact can be identified in the consul's work imposing immigration regulations, handling the return tide and monitoring the economic links. Yet, much to the chagrin of many consuls and later ministers and ambassadors in Dublin, American public and official sympathy for the Irish nationalist cause never completely disappeared which resulted in the continuing centrality of the Irish question to their work.

In conclusion, a great deal of official America's interest in Ireland was standard and not exceptional. However, the picture presented in this study of consular activity reveals the complexity of America's evolution into statehood, as well as Ireland's. It suggests that the consular presence strengthened the bond between the US and Ireland, offered another continuous form of contact, emphasised the two-way nature of the relationship and, at the very least, offers an outsider's view on Irish affairs from before the Act of Union to the eve of the First World War.

---

7 Mattox, *The twilight*, 121.

Appendix 1.1

US consular officers in Ireland, 1790–1913

Belfast (consulate)

James Holmes	1796–1815
William Phelps	1815
James Luke	1815–20
Samuel Luke	1820–30
Thomas W. Gilpin	1830–42
James Shaw	1842–5
Thomas W. Gilpin	1845–7
Thomas McClure	1848
James McDowell	1848–9
John C. O'Neill	1853–4
John Higgins	1854–8
James McAdam	1854
James J. Higgins	1856, 1858
James Arrott	1858
Theodore Frean	1859–61
John Young	1861–6
Gwynne Harris Heap	1866, 1867
Thomas K. King	1867–9
James M. Donnan	1873–80
Lewis Richmond	1880–1
Arthur B. Wood	1881–5
George W Savage	1885–9
Samuel Ruby	1889–93
James B. Taney	1893–7
Malcolm T. Brice	1895 December
Louis Mantell	1897 (deputy)
W. W. Touvelle	1897–1902
Edward Harvey	1902–4 (deputy)
Samuel S. Knabenshue	1905–9
Hunter Sharp	1914–20

Vice consuls

John M. Savage	1885–9
Claude T Ruby	1895

Malcolm T. Brice	1897–8
Arthur R. Touvelle	1904
Edward Harvey	1906
Hugh H. Watson	1914

Cork/Cove/Cobh/Queenstown (consulate)

John Church	1797–1815
Michael Hogan	1815–17
Jacob Mark	1817–26
Reuben Harvey	1827–36
John Murphy	1836–49
Alfred Mitchell	1849–53
John Higgins	1853–4
Hugh Keenan	1854–9
Robert Dowling	1859–61
Patrick J. Devine	1861–2
Edwin G. Eastman	1862–9
E. D. Neill	1869–70 (acting consul)
William H. Townsend	1870–5
Lewis Richmond	1875–80
Edward P. Brooks	1880–2
George Dawson	1881 (acting)
John J. Piatt	1882–93
Henry J. Kress	1893
Lucien J. Walker	1893–7
Daniel Swiney	1897–1905
Edwin N. Gunsaulus	1905–6
George E. Chamberlin	1910–14

Vice consuls

Nicholas George Seymour	1834–49
George Dawson	1871–80 (acting, deputy and vice)
Robert Seymour,	1886–92
James William Scott	1889
Arthur Donn Piatt	1892
James W. Scott	1897

Dublin (consulate)

William Knox	1790–3
Joseph Wilson	1794–1809
Thomas English	1809–26
Isaac English	('pro tem')
Thomas Wilson	1826–47
Hugh Keenan	1847–50
James Foy	1850–3
M. L. Lynch	1853–4
Michael Lynch	1853–4 (agent)
Robert L. Longhead	1854–5
Hugh Keenan	1854–5
James Arrott	1855–8
Michael Lynch	1855–8
Samuel W. Talbott	1859–61
Henry B. Hammond	1861–2
Edward Neill	1869–71
Wilson King	1872–6
Benjamin H. Barrows	1876–81
J. L. McCaskill	1885–9
Alexander J. Reid	1889–93
Wilbur Allan Reid	1890–3 (deputy)
John J. Piatt	1893
Newton B. Ashby	1893–8
Joshua Wilbour	1898–1902
Rufus Waterman,	1902–4
Arthur K. Moe	1904–9
Edward Adams	1909–19

Vice consuls

William B. West	1863–7 (vice consul)
John Rainsford	1871
W. L. Barrington	1871–2
John Shaw	1872–84
Archibald McKenzie	1884–6
Stephen M. MacKenzie	1886–93
Arthur Donn Piatt	1893

Londonderry/Derry (consulate/consular agency)

Thomas Davenport	1830–3 (vice consul)
Thomas Harvey	1833–44 (vice consul)
James Corscaden	1834–42
James McHenry	1842–5
James Cairns	1844–55 (vice consul)
James McDowell	1845 (declined appointment)
Robert Loughead	1845–54
James Corscaden	1853–62 (agent)
James R. Smith, Jr.	1856–8
James Corscaden	1857–8 (agent)
Alexander Henderson	1858–61
James Corscaden	1861–2
Thomas McGunn	1861 (refused *exequatur*)
Alexander Henderson	1862–3
James Corscaden	1863–71 (vice consul)
Charles Dougherty	1866 (not confirmed by Senate)
Felix Agmis	1867 (refused appointment)
Robert C. Mack	1869 (resigned)
D. H. Batchelder	1870 (resigned)
Arthur Livermore	1870–86
P. T. Rodger	1888–*c.* 1905 (agent)
Philip O'Hagan	1908–20 (agent)

Athlone (consular agency)

John Burgess	1888–1906
P. B. Treacy	(interim)

Ballina (consular agency)

Robert Adam Kerr	1900–2

Ballymena (consular agency)

William Young	1843–5 (vice consul)
Francis Skelly	1845 to unknown (vice consul)
George Ballentine	1871–1901 (agent)
Wilson McKeown	1901–08 (agent)

Crookhaven (consular agency)

Isaac Arthur — unknown to 1862

Galway (consulate/consular agency)

Thomas M. Persse	1832–44
Michael Kennedy	1844–7
Thomas M. Persse	1847–50
John Duffy	1853–5
Valentine Hilmes	1855
Samuel W. Talbott	1856–9
Thomas M. Persse	1860–1
William B. West	1861–9
Robert A. Tennant	1901–38 (agent)

Kingstown (Dùn Laoghaire) (consular agency)

Michael Murphy — 1857–unknown

Limerick (consular agency)

Michael Robert Ryan	1843–68, 1873–d. 1874
John Richard Tinsly	1874–90
Richard Hogan	1890–d. 1894
George P Mackenzie	1894
Edward Ludlow	acting 1895
George Paul Mackenzie	1896–September 1896
Edward Ludlow	1896–1906

Lurgan (consular agency)

Frederick W. Magahan — 1882–1908

Newry

Alexander F. Little	1842–4 (vice consul)
William R. Glenny	1844–8 (vice consul)
Charles Day	1848–52 (vice consul)
I. E. Carraher	1861–unknown (vice consul)

Sligo (consular agency)

James Harper	1847–71 (vice consul)
William J. Eccles	1871–84
John Tighe	1884–90

Waterford (consular agency)

Thomas Evans	1835
Benjamin Moore	1864–d. 1879
William Farrell	1880–98

Wexford (consular agency)

Francis Harper	1832–59
Thomas Rowntree	1861–8
Jaspar Walsh	1868–unknown

Appendix 4.1

Table of prisoners claiming to be American citizens, 20 April 1866 (following September 1865 round–up)[*]

Number	Name	Prison
1.	Denis F. Burke	Mountjoy prison[1]
2	Michael Kerwin	ditto
3.	Bernard McDermott	ditto
4.	Daniel J. Mykins	ditto
5.	James Smith	ditto
6.	Frank Leslie (alias Eugene O'Shea)	ditto
7.	Edward Maguigan	ditto
8.	James Burns	ditto
9.	Michael Duffy	ditto
10.	James Bible	ditto
11.	Eneas Doherty	ditto
12.	Maurice Fitzharris	ditto
13.	J. H. O'Brien	ditto
14.	Joseph P. Clery	ditto
15.	Thomas M. Costello	ditto
16.	J. O'Carroll	ditto
17.	Andrew J. Byrne	ditto
18.	William McGrath	ditto
19.	Hugh Dennedy	ditto
20.	Francis N. Kavanagh	ditto
21.	Edward Morley	ditto
22.	William Makay	ditto
23.	Patrick J. Condon	ditto
24.	O'Gorman Barry	ditto
25.	John Dunne	ditto
26.	John Sullivan	ditto
27.	James Murphy	ditto
28.	James Murphy	ditto
29.	John W. Byron	ditto

Appendix 4.1

Number	Name	Prison
30.	John H. Gleeson	Nenagh prison
31.	Joseph Gleeson	ditto
32.	William Quade	Mountjoy prison[1]
33.	Joseph H. Lawler	ditto
34.	James McDermott	ditto
35.	James Smith	ditto
36.	John A. Comerford	ditto
37.	Daniel C. Moynihan	ditto
38.	James E. McDermott	ditto
39.	George Smith	ditto
40.	Thomas J. Hynes	ditto
41.	Corporal McKay	ditto
42.	Thomas Hynes	ditto
43.	Michael O'Boyle	Kilmainhaim gaol[1,2]
44.	John Horan	ditto
45.	Thomas M. Holden	ditto
46.	Michael Fay	ditto
47.	M. F. Garvin M.D.	ditto
48.	Patrick Hart	Sligo gaol[2]
49.	Michael McLoughlin	ditto
50.	James O'Byrne	Wicklow gaol[2]
51.	Michael O'Brien	Tipperary bridewell
52.	Stephen F. Farrell	Roscommon gaol[2]
53.	William Smith	Clonmel gaol[2]
54.	George Archdeacon	Mountjoy prison

* N.B. All the above may not have been and probably were not in prison on 20 April 1866, the names of about ten were subsequently added by West.
1 Mountjoy prison, Kilmainhaim gaol were located in Dublin city.
2 'Gaol' is a historical spelling of 'jail'.

Source: NARA, S/D, Despatches from US consuls in Dublin, 1790–1906, vol. 6, roll 6, T199, Second series, enclosure in Larcom to West, 20 April 1866.

Bibliography

Primary sources

Ireland

Friends Historical Library, Dublin
'1809–1912, Journal of Margaret Boyle Harvey, 1786–1832'.

National Archives of Ireland, Dublin
Chief Secretary's Office
Registered Papers.

National Library of Ireland, Dublin
Thomas Larcom Papers.

National Maritime Museum

United Kingdom

The National Archives, London,
Admiralty.

National Maritime Museum, Greenwich, London
Caird Library Manuscripts Department
Milne, Sir Alexander, 1st Bt., Admiral of the Fleet, 1806–1896, Collection.

United States

Library of Congress, Washington D.C.
Manuscripts Division
Wilbur Carr Papers.
Thomas Jefferson Papers.
James K. Polk Presidential Papers.

National Archives and Records Administration, Maryland,
General Records of the Department of State, Record Group 59.
Despatches from US consuls in Dublin, 1790–1906, vol. 1, roll 1–, T199.

Despatches from US consuls in Belfast, 1798–1906, vol. 1, roll 1–, T368.
Despatches from US consuls in Cork, 1800–1906, vol. 1, roll 1–, T196.
Despatches from US consuls in Galway, 1834–1863, vol. 1, roll 1, T570.
Despatches from US consuls in Londonderry, 1798–1906, vol. 1, roll 1, T216.
Diplomatic Instructions of the Department of State, 1801 to 1906, M77.
Inspector's Report Foreign Service Personnel, 1908, 1909, 1910.
Ballymena
Belfast
Dublin
Galway
Limerick
Londonderry
Lurgan
Queenstown
Waterford

New York Historical Society, New York,
Gilder Lehrman Institute for American History
Henry Knox Papers.

Sanford Historical Society, Florida
Henry S Sanford Papers.
Edwin G. Eastman Papers.

Yale University Library, New Haven
Manuscripts and Archives Division
Piatt Family Papers.

Printed Primary Sources
American state papers, 1, foreign relations, documents, legislative and the executive of the congress of the United States, III (Washington, 1832).
American state papers, foreign relations, documents legislative and the executive of the congress of the United States from the first session to the session of the 23rd congress inclusive, 3 March 1789 to 3 March 1823, class 1, vol. 1, Washington, 8 December 1790 (Washington, 1833).
'An act to regulate the diplomatic and consular systems of the United States' in *The American almanac and repository of useful knowledge for the year 1857* (Boston, 1856), 147–9.
Commission on emigration and other population problems, 1948–1954 reports (Dublin, 1954).
Diplomatic correspondence 1864–1917 papers relating to foreign affairs Great Britain, part 3 of 4 (Washington, 1918).
Official records of the Union and Confederate navies in the War of the Rebellion, series ii–volume 3 of 30 (Washington, 1922, reprinted 1987).
Papers relating to foreign affairs accompanying the annual message of the president, 1783–89, vol. 2 (Washington, 1837).
Papers relating to foreign affairs accompanying the annual message of the president to the first session of the 38th Congress, Part 1 (Washington, 1864).

Papers relating to foreign affairs accompanying the annual message of the President to the third Session fortieth Congress. Part 1 of 4 (Washington, 1869).
Papers relating to foreign affairs accompanying the annual message of the president to the third session, fortieth Congress. December 1, 1879 (Washington, 1880).
Reports of the Immigration Commission (New York, 1970).
Report of the trial of William G. Halpin: treason-Felony at the County of Dublin Commission Court. November 1867 (Dublin, 1868).
United States, official register (Washington, 1833).

Directories

Dublin Directory, 1827.
Pigot and Co.'s City of Dublin and Hibernian Provincial Directory 1824.
Pigot and Co.'s Directory, 1824. Cork City. Co. Cork.
Thom's Directory 1848, 1849, 1862, 1869.

Newspapers

Belfast Telegraph
Cork Constitution
Cork Daily Herald
Cork Weekly News
Daily Express
Derry Standard
Dublin Evening Post
Evening Mail
Evening News
Freeman's Journal
Irish Times
Munster Express
Nation
New York Times
Northern Whig
Saunders Newsletter
The Times
Weekly News

Secondary sources

Abbot, W. W. (ed.), Dorothy Twohig (Associate ed.), *The papers of George Washington. Presidential series. 3 June–September 1789*, 52 vols, five series (Charlottesville, 1989).

Armstrong-Ingram, R. Jackson, 'Early Irish Bahá'is: issues of religious, cultural and national identity', Research notes in Shakai, Babi and Bah'iá studies, 2:4 (July 1998), online at www.h-net.org/~bahai/notes/vol2/irish.htm (accessed 2 September 2008).

Baker, George E. (ed.), *The life of William H. Seward with selections of his works* (New York, 1855).
Bardon, Jonathan, 'Ulster Custom' in Lalor (ed.) *The encyclopaedia of Ireland*, 1090.
Barnes, William and John Heath Morgan, *The foreign service of the United States: origins, development and functions* (Washington, 1961).
Barton, Peter, 'The first blockade runner and "Another Alabama": some Tees and Hartlepool ships that worried the Union', *The Mariner's Mirror Journal of the Society for Nautical Research*, 81:1 (February 1995), 45–65.
Bemis, Samuel Flagg (ed.), *The American secretaries of state and their diplomacy*, 18 vols, 7 (New York, 1927).
——, *The diplomacy of the American Revolution* (Bloomington and London, 1957).
Bew, Paul, *Ireland* (Oxford, 2007).
Bielenberg, Andy, *Cork's industrial revolution: development or decline?* (Cork, 1991).
Biscegelia, Louis R., 'The Fenian funeral of Terence Bellew McManus', *Éire-Ireland*, 14:3 (1979), 45–64.
Blackett, R. J. M., *Divided hearts: Britain and the American Civil War* (Baton Rouge, 2001).
Blessing, Patrick J., 'The Irish' in Thernstrom (ed.), *The Harvard encyclopedia*, 524–45.
Bourke, Edward J., *Shipwrecks of the Irish coast, volume 2, 932–1997*, 3 vols, 2 (Dublin, 1998).
Bourne, K., and D. C. Watt (general eds), *British documents on foreign affairs*, 25 vols (Bethesda, 1986–95).
Boyce, D. G., *The Irish question and British politics 1868–1986* (London, 1988).
Bowyer, Paul S., *The Oxford companion to United States History* (Oxford, 2001).
Breathnach, Ciara, *The Congested Districts Board of Ireland, 1891–1923: poverty and development in the west of Ireland* (Dublin, 2005).
Bric, Maurice, 'The United Irishmen, international republicanism and the definition of the polity in the United States of America, 1791–1800' in *Proceedings of the Royal Irish Academy*, 104c (2004), 81–106.
——, *Ireland, Philadelphia and the reinvention of America, 1760–1800* (Dublin, 2008).
Brooks, Noah, *Henry Knox: a soldier of the revolution* (New York, 1900).
Brown, Stuart Gerry (ed.), *The autobiography of James Monroe* (Syracuse, 1959).
Brown, Thomas N., 'The origins and character of Irish-American nationalism', *The Review of Politics*, 18:3 (1956), 327–58.
Bruce, Susannah Ural, *The harp and the eagle: Irish-American volunteers and the Union army, 1861–1865* (New York, 2006).
Bulletin of the American Geographical Society, 36:12 (1904), 777–8.
Bulloch, James D., *The Secret Service of the Confederate states in Europe or, how the Confederate cruisers were equipped* (New York, 2001 edition).
Burke, Kieran, 'A history of Cork city, 1700–1900', online at www.corkpastandpresent.ie/history/history.shtml (accessed on 31 July 2008).

Burstein, Andrew, 'Thomas Jefferson' in Melvin I. Urofsky (ed.), *The American presidents* (New York and London, 2000), 31–48.
Business History, 23:3 (November 1981)
Calkin, Homer L., 'American influence in Ireland, 1760 to 1800', *Pennsylvania Magazine of History and Biography*, 71 (April 1947), 103–20.
Callahan, North, *Henry Knox: General Washington's general* (New York, 1958).
Carr, Willbur, 'The American consular service', *American Journal of International Law*, 1:4 (October 1907), 891–913.
Carroll, Francis M., *The American presence in Ulster: a diplomatic history, 1796–1996* (Washington, 2005).
Chambers, George, 'The early years of American consular representation in Belfast', *Familia: Ulster Genealogical Review*, 12 (1966), 1–13.
Clancy, Martin, 'Knock Shrine' in Lalor (ed.), *The encyclopaedia of Ireland*, 598.
Clarfield, Gerard H., *Timothy Pickering and American diplomacy, 1795–1800* (Columbia, 1969).
Clark, Ronald W., *Benjamin Franklin: a biography* (New York, 1983).
Cohen, Sheldon Samuel, *British supporters of the American Revolution, 1775–1783: The role of the 'middling-level' activists* (Suffolk, 2004).
Collins, Timothy, *Transatlantic triumph and heroic failure. The Galway line* (Cork, 2002).
Comerford, R. Vincent, *The Fenians in context: Irish politics and society 1848–82* (Dublin, 1985).
——, 'Churchmen, tenants and independent opposition, 1850–56' in Vaughan (ed.), *A new history of Ireland, v*, 396–414.
——, 'Gladstone's first Irish enterprise, 1864–70' in Vaughan (ed.), *A new history of Ireland, v*, 431–50.
——, 'Land War' in Connolly (ed.), *The Oxford companion*, 300–1.
Connolly, S. J. (ed.), *The Oxford companion to Irish history* (Oxford, 1998).
——, 'Coercion acts' in Connolly (ed.), *The Oxford companion*, 101–2.
——, 'Franchise' in Connolly (ed.), *The Oxford companion*, 206.
——, 'Free trade agitation' in Connolly (ed.), *The Oxford companion*, 208.
——, 'United Irishmen, Society of' in Connolly (ed.), *The Oxford companion*, 567.
Cooke, Sholto, *The maiden city and the western ocean: a history of the shipping trade between North America in the nineteenth century* (Dublin, 1950).
Art Cosgrove (ed.), *Dublin through the ages* (Dublin, 1988).
Crapol, Edward P., 'Coming to terms with empire: the historiography of late-nineteenth-century American foreign relations', *Diplomatic History*, 16:4 (autumn 1992), 573–97.
Crawford, E. Margaret, 'Great Famine' in Connolly (ed.), *The Oxford companion*, 228.
Cronin, Seán, 'Fenians and Clan na Gael' in Glazier (ed.), *The encyclopedia of the Irish in America*, 317–21.
Crook, D. P., *The North, the South and the powers, 1861–65* (New York, 1974).
Cross, Jack L. (ed.), *London Mission: the first critical years* (East Lansing, 1968).
Cullen, L. M., *An economic history of Ireland since 1660* (London, 1972).

Cullop, Charles P., 'An unequal duel: Union recruiting in Ireland, 1863–1864', *Journal of Civil War History*, 13:2 (1967), 101–113.
Curti, Merle Eugene, *American philanthropy abroad* (Reprint, New Jersey, 1963).
K. D., 'The press gang in Dublin, 1790', *The Irish Sword*, 2 (1954–6), 363–6.
Dallas, George Mifflin, *A series of letters from London written during the years 1856, '57, '58, '59 and '60* (Philadelphia, 1869).
Daniels, Roger and Otis L. Graham, *Debating American Immigration 1882–present* (Oxford, 2001).
D'Arcy, Fergus, 'An age of distress and reform: 1800 to 1860' in Cosgrove (ed.), *Dublin through the ages*, 93–112.
Davies, A. C., 'The First Irish Industrial Exhibition: Cork, 1852', *Irish Economic and Social History*, 2 (1975), 46–59.
——, 'Roofing Belfast and Dublin 1896–8: American penetration of the Irish market for Welsh slate', *Irish Economic and Social History*, 4 (1977), 26–35.
Davis, William C. (ed.), *Edwin De Leon, Secret history of Confederate diplomacy abroad* (Lawrence, 2003).
deKay, James Tertius, *The rebel raiders: the astonishing history of the Confederacy's secret navy* (New York, 2002).
De Santis, Hugh and Waldo Heinrichs, 'The Department of State and American foreign policy' in Zara Steiner (ed.), *The Times survey of foreign ministries of the world* (Westport, 1982), 576.
Devoy, John, *Recollections of an Irish rebel: introduction by Seán Ó Lúing* (Shannon, 1969).
Diner, Hasia R., *Erin's Daughters in America: Irish emigrant women in the nineteenth century* (Baltimore and London, 1983).
Dingley, F. L., *European emigration: studies in Europe of emigration moving out of Europe, especially that flowing to the United States* (Washington, 1890).
Donovan, Kathleen, 'Good Old Pat: An Irish-American stereotype in decline', *Éire–Ireland*, 15:1 (Fall 1980), 6–14.
Dowler, Clare, 'John James Piatt, Representative figure of a momentous period', *Ohio Archaeological and Historical Quarterly*, 45 (January 1936), 1–26.
Doyle, David Noel, *Ireland, Irishmen and Revolutionary America* (Dublin and Cork, 1981).
——, 'The Irish in North America, 1775–1845' in Lee and Casey (eds), *Making the Irish American*, 171–212.
——, 'The Remaking of Irish America, 1845–1880' in Lee and Casey (eds), *Making the Irish American*, 213–54.
Eaton, Clement, *A history of the Southern Confederacy* (New York, 1954).
Edwards, Owen Dudley, 'American diplomats and Irish coercion, 1880–1883', *Journal of American Studies*, 1:2 (October 1967), 213–32.
Eid, Leroy V., '*Puck* and the Irish: "the one American idea"', *Éire–Ireland*, 11:2 (1976), 18–35.
Fenning, Hugh, O. P., 'The cholera epidemic in Ireland, 1832–3: priests, ministers, doctors', *Archivum Hibernicum*, 57 (2003), 77–125.
Findling, John E., *Dictionary of American diplomatic history* (Westport, 1980).
——, 'Johnson, Reverdy' in Findling, *Dictionary*, 251.

Bibliography

Fitzpatrick, David, *Irish emigration 1801–1921. Studies in Irish Economic and Social History 1* (Dundalk, 1984).
——, 'Emigration, 1801–70' in Vaughan (ed.), *A new history of Ireland, v*, 662–22.
——, 'Emigration: 1801–1921' in Glazier (ed.), *The encyclopedia of the Irish in America*, 254–62.
Foster, Kevin J., 'The diplomats who sank a fleet: the Confederacy's undelivered European fleet and the Union consular service', *Prologue. Quarterly of the National Archives and Records Administration* 33:3 (autumn 2001), 181–93.
Forsythe, W., C. Breen, C. Gallagher, R. McConkey, 'Historic storms and shipwrecks in Ireland: a preliminary survey of severe synoptic conditions as a causal factor in underwater archaeology', *International Journal of Nautical Archaeology*, 29:2 (2000), 247–59.
Frank, Lucy, 'Transatlantic crossings: mapping the Antebellum South in Sarah Piatt's European poetry', online at www.uclan.ac.uk/amatas/english/05november14.htm (accessed 20 August 2008).
Gale, Robert L., 'Piatt, John, James' in *American national biography*, 24 vols, 17 (Oxford, 1999), 463–5.
Garnham, Neal, 'Manchester martyrs' in Connolly (ed.), *The Oxford companion*, 343.
——, 'American Civil War' in Connolly (ed.), *The Oxford companion*, 12.
Gerhardt, Michael J., *The federal appointments process: a constitutional and historical analysis* (Durham and London, 2000).
Gibson, Florence E., *The attitude of the New York Irish towards state and national affairs, 1848–1892* (New York, 1951 and 1968).
Giunta, Mary A. (contributing ed.), 'The diplomacy of the American Revolution' in Robert L Beisner (ed.) *American Foreign Relations since 1600: a guide to literature*, 2 vols, 1 (Santa Barbara, 2003), 142–76.
Glazier, Michael (ed.), *The encyclopedia of the Irish in America* (Notre Dame, 1999).
Gleeson, David T., *The Irish in the South, 1815–1877* (Chapel Hill and London, 2001).
Goldman, Robert M., 'Stephen Grover Cleveland' in Urofsky (ed.), *The American presidents*, 234–46.
Gray, Peter, 'Meagher, Thomas Francis' in Connolly (ed.), *The Oxford companion*, 353.
——, 'Rebellion of 1848' in Connolly (ed.), *The Oxford companion*, 473–4.
——, 'Young Ireland' in Connolly (ed.), *The Oxford companion*, 602–03.
Gribbon, H. D., 'Economic and social history, 1850–1921' in Vaughan (ed.), *A new history of Ireland vi*, 260–356.
Haly, Lt. R. S., *Reasons for abolishing impressment* (London, 1822).
Hamilton, Holman, *Zachary Taylor: soldier in the White House* (Connecticut, 1966).
Hamilton, Stanislaus Murray, *The writings of James Monroe including a collection of his public and private papers and correspondence now for the first time printed*, 7 vols (New York, 1899–1903).

Hatton, Helen E., *The largest amount of good: Quaker relief in Ireland 1654–1921* (Montreal, 1993).

Hazel, Michael V., 'First link: Parnell's American tour, 1880', *Éire–Ireland*, 15:1 (1980), 6–24.

Heffernan, John B., 'Ireland's contribution to the navies of the American Civil War, 1861–65', *The Irish Sword*, 3 (1957–8), 81–7.

Heller, Deane and David, *Paths of Diplomacy. America's secretaries of state* (Philadelphia and New York, 1967).

Hernon, Joseph M., 'Irish sympathy for the southern confederacy', *Éire–Ireland*, 2:3 (1967), 72–85.

Hewitt, Martin, 'The itinerant emigration lecturer: James Brown's lecture tour of Britain and Ireland, 1861–2', *British Journal of Canadian Studies*, 10:1 (1995), 103–19.

Hill, Hamilton Andrews, *Memoir of Abbott Lawrence*, 'Condition of Ireland' (Boston, 1884).

History Ireland, 16:6 (November/December 2008).

Hotten-Sommers, Dianne M., 'Relinquishing and reclaiming independence: Irish domestic servants, American middle-class mistresses, and assimilation, 1850–1920', *Éire–Ireland*, 36:1–2 (2001), 185–201.

——, 'Relinquishing and reclaiming independence: Irish domestic servants, American middle-class mistresses, and assimilation, 1850–1920' in Kenny (ed.), *New directions*, 227–42.

Howells, Gary, '"On account of their disreputable character": parish-assisted emigration from rural England, 1834–1860', *History*, 88:292 (October 2003), 587–605.

Hull, Raymona E., *Nathaniel Hawthorne: the English experience, 1853–64* (Pittsburgh, 1980).

Hunt, Gaillard, 'The history of the Department of State', *American Journal of International Law* (January and April 1907), 867–90.

Ickringall, S. J. S., 'American Revolution' in Connolly (ed.), *The Oxford companion*, 13.

Ireland, John de Courcy, 'A preliminary study on the Fenians and the sea', *Éire–Ireland*, 2 (1967), 36–54.

——, 'The Confederate States Navy, 1861–5: The Irish contribution', *Mariner's Mirror. Journal of the Society for Nautical Research*, 66 (1980), 259–63.

——, *Wreck and rescue on the east coast of Ireland* (Dun Laoighaire, 1983).

——, *Ireland and the Irish in maritime history* (Glendale Press, Dun Laoighaire, 1986).

Ireland, John de Courcy, *Wreck and rescue on the east coast of Ireland* (Dun Laoighaire, 1983).

——, *Ireland and the Irish in maritime history* (Glendale Press, Dun Laoighaire, 1986).

——, 'A preliminary study on the Fenians and the sea', *Éire–Ireland*, 2 (1967), 36–54.

——, 'The Confederate States Navy, 1861–5: The Irish contribution', *Mariner's Mirror. Journal of the Society for Nautical Research*, 66 (1980), 259–63.

Jenkins, Brian, *Fenians and Anglo-American relations during Reconstruction* (Ithaca, 1969).
Johnson, Paul, *A history of the American people* (New York, 1997).
Jones, Chester Lloyd, *The consular service of the United States: its history and activities*, Publications of the University of Pennsylvania Series in Political Economy and Public Law, 18 (Philadelphia, 1906).
Joyce, Toby, 'The American Civil War and Irish nationalism', *History Ireland*, 4:2 (summer 1996), 36–41.
Kane, Michael H., 'American soldiers in Ireland, 1865–67', *The Irish Sword*, 23:91 (summer 2002), 103–40.
Kark, Ruth, *American consuls in the Holy Land 1832–1914* (Detroit, 1994).
Kee, Robert, *The green flag: a turbulent history of the Irish national movement* (New York, 1972).
Kelly, James, *Sir Edward Newenham, M.P., 1713–1814: defender of the Protestant Constitution* (Dublin, 2003).
Kelly, Joseph J., 'Philadelphia' in Glazier (ed.), *The encyclopedia of the Irish in America*, 768–74.
Kennedy, Charles Stuart, *The American consul: a history of the United States consular service, 1776–1914* (Westport, 1990).
Kennedy, Liam, Paul S. Ell, E. M. Crawford, L. A. Clarkson, *Mapping the great famine* (Dublin, 1999).
Kennedy, Liam, 'The cost of living in Ireland, 1698–1998' in David Dickson and Cormac Ó Gráda (eds), *Refiguring Ireland: essays in honour of L. M. Cullen* (Dublin, 2003), 249–76.
Kevin Kenny (ed.), *New directions in Irish-American History* (Wisconsin, 2003).
Kinealy, Christine, *A death-dealing famine: the great hunger in Ireland* (London, 1997).
King, Charles R. (ed.), *The life and correspondence of Rufus King: comprising his letters, private and official, his public documents and his speeches*, 6 vols (New York, 1895).
Kverndal, Roald, *Seamen's missions: their origins and early growth* (Pasadena, 1986).
LaFeber, Walter, *The American age, United States foreign policy at home and abroad since 1750*, 2 vols (London, 1989).
Lalor, Brian (ed.), *The encyclopaedia of Ireland* (Dublin, 2003).
Langley, Lester D., Thomas David Schoonover, *The banana men: American mercenaries and entrepreneurs in Central America, 1880–1930* (Lexington, 1995).
Lankford, Nelson D., *An Irishman in Dixie: Thomas Conolly's diary of the fall of the Confederacy* (Columbia, 1988).
Larkin, Emmet, *The consolidation of the Roman Catholic Church in Ireland 1860–1870* (Chapel Hill and London, 1987).
Lee, J. J., and Marion Casey (eds), *Making the Irish American: history and heritage of the Irish in North America* (New York, 2006).
——, 'Introduction. Interpreting Irish America' in Lee and Casey (eds), *Making the Irish American*, 1–62.
Loughlin, James, 'New departure' in Connolly (ed.), *The Oxford companion*, 386.

——, 'Plan of campaign' in Connolly (ed.), *The Oxford companion*, 444.
Logan, John, 'Literacy' in Connolly (ed.), *The Oxford companion*, 319.
Lonn, Ella, *Foreigners in the Confederacy* (Chapel Hill, 2002).
Lyman, Robert, Howard Gerrard, *Iraq 1941: the Battles for Basra, Habbaniya, Fallujah and Baghdad* (Botley, 2006).
MacCarthy, C. J. F., 'The American prisoners at Kinsale', *Journal of the Cork Historical and Archaeological Society*, 94 (January–December 1989), 46–51.
MacDonagh, Oliver, 'Ideas and institutions, 1830–45' in Vaughan (ed.), *A new history of Ireland, v*, 193–217.
MacRaild, Donald M., 'Crossing migrant frontiers: comparative reflections on Irish migrants in Britain and the United States during the nineteenth century', *Immigrants and Minorities*, 18:2–3 (1999), 40–70.
McConville, Seán, *Irish political prisoners, 1848–1922: theatres of war* (London and New York, 2003).
McDowell, R. B., *Ireland in the age of imperialism and revolution, 1760–1801* (Oxford, 1979).
McGuckin, John J., 'Sergeant Edward McGuckin: an Irish casualty in the American Civil War', *Familia Ulster Genealogical Review*, 16 (November 2000), 61–78.
Magee, Owen, '"God save Ireland" Manchester Martyr demonstrations in Dublin, 1867–1916', *Éire-Ireland*, 36:3–4 (2001), 39–66.
Mageean, Deirdre M., 'Emigration from Irish ports', *Journal of American Ethnic History*, 13:1 (1993), 6–30.
Martin, Ged and Ben Kline, 'Cork and the American Civil War: the Queenstown affair of 1863', *Cork Historical and Archaeological Society*, 89 (January–December 1984), 99–107.
Mattox, Henry E., *The twilight of amateur diplomacy: the American foreign service and its senior officers in the 1890s* (Kent, 1989).
Maume, Mairead, Patrick Maume, Mary Casey (eds), *The Galtee boy: a fenian prison narrative, John Sarsfield Casey* (Dublin, 2005).
Mays, James O'Donald, *Mr Hawthorne goes to England: the adventures of a reluctant consul* (New Forest Leaves, 1983).
Merli, Frank J., *The Alabama, British neutrality and the American Civil War* (Bloomington and Indianapolis, 2004).
Miller, Kerby A., *Ireland and Irish America culture, class and transatlantic migration* (Dublin, 2008).
——, *Emigrants and exiles: Ireland and the Irish exodus to north America* (Oxford, 1985).
——, and Arnold Schrier, Bruce D. Bolling, David N. Doyle (eds), *Irish immigrants in the Land of Canaan: letters and memoirs from Colonial and Revolutionary America, 1675–1815* (Oxford, 2003).
——, 'Paddy's paradox: emigration to America in Irish imagination and rhetoric' in Dirk Hoerder, Horst Rössler (eds), *Distant magnets: expectations and realities in the immigrant experience, 1840–1930* (New York, 1993), 264–94.
——, and Bruce D. Bolling. 'Golden Streets, Bitter Tears: the Irish image of America during the era of Mass Migration', *Journal of American Ethnic History* 10:1 and 2 (autumn 1990–winter 1991), 16–36.

Mitchell, Arthur, 'The National Brotherhood of St Patrick in Britain in the 1860s', *Irish Studies Review*, 7:3 (1990), 325–36.
Moran, Gerard, *Sending out Ireland's poor: assisted emigration to North America in the nineteenth century* (Dublin, 2004).
——, 'The Fenian movement in America', *Éire–Ireland*, 2:4 (1967), 6–10.
——, 'Shovelling out the poor': assisted emigration from Ireland from the great famine to the fall of Parnell' in Patrick J. Duffy (ed.), *To and from Ireland: panned migration schemes c. 1600–2000* (Dublin, 2004), 137–54.
Morley, Vincent, *Irish opinion and the American revolution, 1760–1783* (Cambridge, 2002).
Morris, Anne Cary (ed.), *The diary and letters of Gouverneur Morris: minister of the United States to France; member of the constitutional convention*, 2 vols (New York, 1888).
Murphy, Maureen, 'Asenath Nicholson and the famine in Ireland' in Maryann Gialanella Valiulis and Mary O'Dowd (eds), *Women and Irish history* (Dublin, 1997), 109–24.
Neidhardt, W. S., 'The American government and the Fenian Brotherhood: a study in mutual political opportunism', *Ontario History*, 64:1 (1972), 27–44.
Nevins, Allan, *Henry White: thirty years of American diplomacy* (New York, 1930).
——, Nevins, *Hamilton Fish: the inner history of the Grant administration*, 2 vols, (New York, 1936).
Newland, Sam J., 'Civil War, the' in Glazier (ed.), *The encyclopedia of the Irish in America*, 153–7.
Nielsen, Kenneth E. 'The Irish language in New York, 1850–1900' in Ronald H. Bayor and Timothy J. Meagher (eds), *The New York Irish* (Baltimore, 1996), 252–74.
Nolan, Janet R., *Ourselves alone: women's emigration from Ireland, 1885–1920* (Lexington, 1989).
Nolan, Paddy, 'Four shipwrecks on west Clare coasts', *The Other Clare*, 32 (June 2008), 50–5.
Novak, Rose, '"Keepers of important secrets": the Ladies Committee of the IRB', *History Ireland*, 16:6 (November/December 2008), 28–9.
Ó Broin, Leon, 'The Brotherhood' in David Noel Doyle and Owen Dudley Edwards (eds) *America and Ireland, 1776–1976. The American identity and the Irish connection* (Westport, 1980), 117–33.
O'Day, Alan, *Irish home rule, 1867–1921* (Manchester, 1998).
O'Flaherty, Patrick, 'James Huston, a forgotten Irish-American patriot', *The Irish Sword*, 11 (1973–4), 39–47.
Ó Gráda, Cormac, *Ireland: a new economic history, 1780–1939* (Oxford, 1994).
——, 'Poverty, population and agriculture, 1801–45' in Vaughan (ed.), *A new history of Ireland, v,* 108–36.
——, 'Industry and Communications, 1801–1845' in Vaughan (ed.), *A new history of Ireland, v,* 137–57.
Ó Snodaigh, Pádraig, 'Benjamin Franklin in Ireland', *Ulster Local Studies*, 7:1 (1981), 8–11.

Orth, Samuel P., 'The Alien Contract Labor Law', *Political Science Quarterly*, 22:1 (March 1907), 49–60.
Owsley, Harriet Chappell, 'Henry Shelton Sanford and Federal surveillance abroad, 1861–1865', *The Mississippi Valley Historical Review*, 48:2 (September 1961), 211–28 online at www.jstor.org/stable/1902512 (accessed 19 August 2008).
Pethica, James L., and James C. Roy (eds), *"To the land of the free from this island of slaves". Henry Stratford Persse's Letters from Galway to America, 1821–1832. Irish Narratives* (Cork, 1998).
Pinckney, Charles Colesworth, *Life of General Thomas Pinckney* (Boston and New York, 1895).
Plischke, Elmer, *United States diplomats and their missions: a profile of American diplomatic emissaries since 1778* (Washington, D.C., 1875).
Powell, John, 'Earl of Kimberley, John Wodehouse', *Oxford dictionary of national biography*, 60 vols, 59 (Oxford, New York, 2004), 923.
Powell, J. H. (ed.), *Richard Rush: republican diplomat, 1780–1859* (Pennsylvania, 1942).
Proudfoot, Lindsay, 'Tenant right' in Connolly (ed.), *The Oxford companion*, 538–9.
Quaife, Milo Milton (ed.), *The diary of James K. Polk during his presidency, 1845 to 1849*, 4 vols (Chicago, 1910).
Rakestraw, Donald A., 'Book Review. Raising the Alabama from the "Merli Archive"', *Diplomatic History*, 30:4 (September 2006), 771–4.
Reilly, Eileen, 'Modern Ireland: an introduction survey' in Lee and Casey, *Making the Irish American*, 63–150.
Richardson, James D. (ed.), *A compilation of the messages and papers of the Confederacy including the diplomatic correspondence, 1861–1865*, 2 vols (Nashville, 1906).
Robins, Joseph, *Custom House People* (Dublin, 1993).
——, *The Miasma: epidemic and panic in nineteenth century Ireland* (Dublin, 1995).
Rottman, David, 'Prisons' in Lalor (ed.), *The encyclopaedia of Ireland*, 896–7.
Ryan, Ignatius L., 'Confederate agents in Ireland', *Historical Records and Studies*, 26 (1936), 40–91.
Ryan, Thomas J., 'Out of Ireland into the Union army: the battle over Irish emigration', *The Irish Sword*, 23:91 (summer 2002), 7–22.
Sanderlin, Walter S., 'Galway as a transatlantic port in the nineteenth century', *Éire–Ireland*, 5:3 (1970) 15–31.
Sarbaugh, Timothy J., 'Charity begins at home'. The United States government and Irish famine relief, 1845–9', *History Ireland*, 4:2 (summer 1996), 31–5.
Schrier, Arnold, *Ireland and the American Emigration* (Chester Springs, 1997).
Schuyler, Eugene, *American diplomacy and the furtherance of commerce* (London, 1886).
Serpell, David R., 'American consular activities in Egypt 1849–3', *The Journal of Modern History*, 10:3 (September 1938), 344–63.
Siggins, Brian, *Images of Ireland: the Great White Fair. The Herbert Park*

Exhibition of 1907 (Dublin, 2007).
Sofka, James R., 'The Jeffersonian idea of national security: commerce, the Atlantic balance of power, and the Barbary war, 1786–1805', *Diplomatic History*, 21:4 (1997), 519–44.
Steiner, Zara, 'Introduction' in Zara Steiner (ed.), *The Times survey of foreign ministries of the world* (Westport, 1982), 22–4.
Stuart, Graham H., *The department of state: a history of its organisation, procedure and personnel* (New York, 1949).
Tansill, Charles Callan, *The foreign policy of Thomas F. Bayard, 1885–1897* (New York, 1940).
Taylor, Alan, 'Fenimore Cooper's America', *History Today*, 46:2 (February 1996), 21–7.
Temperley, Howard, *Britain and America since independence* (New York, 2002).
'The Page Act of 1875', online at http://w3.uchastings.edu/wingate/pageact.htm (accessed 6 January 2009).
'The Sailors' Home, Dublin', *Nautical Magazine* (1888), 140–1.
The Sarah M. B. Piatt Collection: guide and inventory catalogue of inventory, Ohio State University, online at http://library.osu.edu/sites/rarebooks/finding/piatt.php (accessed 20 August 2008).
Thernstrom, Stephan (ed.), *The Harvard encyclopedia of American ethnic history* (Cambridge, 1980).
Thompson, Peter, *Cassell's dictionary of modern American history* (London, 2000).
Toppin, Edgar A., 'Andrew Johnson 1865–1869' in Urofsky (ed.), *The American presidents*, 197–206.
——, '(Hiram) Ulysses Simpson Grant, 1869–1877' in Urofsky (ed.), *The American presidents*, 197–207.
——, 'Andrew Johnson, 1865–1869; in Urofsky (ed.), *The American presidents*, 185–97.
Truxes, Thomas A., *Irish-American trade, 1660–1783* (Cambridge, 1988).
Twohig, Dorothy, 'George Washington' in Urofsky (ed.), *The American presidents*, 1–18.
Tucker, Phillip Thomas, *The Confederacy's fighting chaplain: Father John B. Bannon* (Tuscaloosa and London, 1992).
——, *Irish Confederates: the Civil War's forgotten soldiers* (Abilene, 2006).
——, 'Confederate Secret Agent in Ireland: Father John B. Bannon and his Irish mission, 1863–1864', *Journal of Confederate History*, 5 (1991), 55–85.
Urofsky, Melvin I. (ed.), *The American Presidents* (New York and London, 2000).
Van Deusen, Glyndon G., *William Henry Seward* (New York, 1967).
Vance, Nathaniel, *Irish literature since 1800* (New York and London, 2002).
Vaughan, W. E. (ed.) *A new history of Ireland v. Ireland under the union, I, 1801–70*, 9 vols, 5 (Oxford, 1989).
——, (ed.), *A new history of Ireland vi. Ireland under the union, II 1870–1921*, 9 vols, 6 (Oxford, 1996).
——, 'Ireland c. 1870' in Vaughan (ed.), *A new history of Ireland v*, 726–800.

Wallace, Sarah Agnes and Francis Elma Gillespie (eds), *The journal of Benjamin Moran, 1857–65*, 2 vols (Chicago, 1948).
Walch, Timothy, 'Meagher, Thomas Francis' in Glazier (ed.), *The encyclopedia of the Irish in America*, 601–2.
Walsh, James P., 'American–Irish: West and East', *Éire–Ireland*, 6:2 (1971), 25–32.
Warden, D. B. *On the origin, nature, progress and influence of consular establishments* (Paris, 1813).
Werking, Richard Hume, *The Master Architects: building the United States foreign service 1890–1930* (Lexington, 1977).
Whelan, Bernadette, *Ireland and the Marshall Plan 1947–57* (Dublin, 2000).
——, *US foreign policy and Ireland, 1913–29: from empire to independence* (Dublin, 2006).
White, John E., *Peter Tait: a remarkable story* (Little Norton, 2005).
White, Laura A., 'The United States in the 1850s as seen by British consuls', *Mississippi Valley Historical Review*, 19:4 (March 1933), 509–36.
Wiche, Glen N., *Dispatches from Bermuda: the civil war letters of Charles Maxwell Allen, United States Consul at Bermuda, 1861–88* (Kent, 2008).
Willson, Beckles, *America's ambassadors to England (1785–1928): a narrative of Anglo-American diplomatic relations* (London, 1928).
——, Willson, *Friendly Relations: a narrative of Britain's ministers and ambassadors to America (1791–1930)* (Boston, 1934).
Wilson, David A., *United Irishmen, United States: immigrant radicals in the early Republic* (Dublin, 1998).
——, 'Swapping Canada for Ireland: the Fenian invasion of 1866', *History Ireland*, 16:6 (November/December 2008), 22–7.
Wyman, Mark, *Round-trip to America: the immigrants return to Europe, 1880–1930* (Ithaca/London, 1993).
Young, John Russell, *Around the world with General Grant: a narrative of the visit of General Ulysses S. Grant ex-president of the United States to various countries in Europe, Asia, Africa in 1877, 1878, 1879: to which are added certain conversations with Grant connected with American politics and history*, 2 vols (New York, c. 1879).
Ziegler, Philip, 'Introduction' in Richard Rush, *Century lives and letters: a residence at the Court of London* (London and Melbourne, 1987).
Zimmerman, James Fulton, *Impressment of American seamen* (New York, 1925).

Unpublished theses

O'Brien, William George, 'Imagining Catholic Ireland: the nationalist press and the creation of national identity, 1843–1870' (PhD dissertation, University of Limerick, 2007).

Index

Note: 'n.' after a page reference indicates the number of a note on that page

Abercorn, Earl of 189
Adams, Charles Francis
   American Civil War 105–56
   Fenianism 158–207, 262
   in Ireland 211
Adams, John 1, 3, 7, 59
Adams, John Quincy 9, 10, 92, 105
Adela 114, 115
Alabama
   CSS 108, 109, 110, 113, 116, 149,
   claims 186, 193, 197, 210
Aldrich, Thomas Bailey 45
Allan Line Steamship Co. 46, 47, 238
America
   colonies xi
   Continental Congress 10
   Federalist Convention 54
   and Ireland xiii
   patriots xii
   revolution xii 57
   seamen 10
   trade 6
   War Office 4
   War of Independence 7, 10
   see also United States
American Civil War xiv, 10, 33, 35,
   37, 39, 79, 85, 98, 100, 105–56,
   157, 173, 186, 195, 210, 214,
   230, 247, 261, 262, 264
Archibald, Edward 158, 159, 161,
   162
Arrott, Elizabeth 32

James 27, 31, 32, 33, 34, 67, 99
Arthur, Chester 42, 249
Arthur, Isaac 35, 36, 113
Ashby, Newton B. 103, 153, 238,
   245, 257
Ashenhurst, John Talbot 3, 5
Aspinwell, Thomas 10
Atalanta, HMS 60
At the holy well 45
Athlone, Co. Westmeath 126, 47, 47
Atlantic Royal Mail Steam Naviga-
   tion Co. (Galway Line) 98, 109

Balfour, Arthur 236, 238
Ballymena, Co. Antrim 46, 21, 21
Bancroft, George 23, 73, 78, 79
Bannon, John 143–4, 145, 148
Baron, Lord Chief Justice 203, 204
Barrington, Jonah 154
Barrows, Benjamin H. 41, 42, 216,
   217, 217–18, 250–1, 259
Bedford, Duke of 90
Belfast xi
   American Civil War 106, 109, 112,
   113
   chamber of commerce 6, 264
   consul in xi, 6, 7, 10, 16, 18, 18,
   19, 20, 27, 28, 31, 32
   cost of living 216
   desertion 64
   disease 242, 246
   economy 218, 221–2

emigration 82, 215, 218, 228, 230, 233–4, 236, 253
famine 78, 81
fees 16, 21, 22, 29, 31, 36, 32, 49, 78
Fenians 194, 197
impressment 57, 58, 60
pensions 152
salary 29, 31, 45, 46
trade 20, 22, 41, 72, 78, 85–104, 215
Belgium
agent in 25, 36
Antwerp 34
minister 36, 105
Belisarius 60
Benjamin, Judah P. 111, 132, 138–9, 141–2, 148
Bigelow, John 105, 133, 134
Blaine, James G. 223–4, 247
Bristol, England
consul in 2, 38
trade 86
Britain
American Civil War 106–55
American revolution xii
Anglo-American relations 39, 54, 55, 79, 82, 92, 93, 157, 171, 178, 181–6, 197, 202, 206, 208–9, 239, 263–4
Arrears of Rent Ireland Act (1882) 231
coercion measures 223, 236
Conservative party 73, 186, 188, 197, 200, 237
empire 33
famine 221
Fenianism 159–62, 204–5
Foreign Enlistment Act (1819) 108, 132, 140, 141, 147
and France 55, 59
government 12, 60n.28, 73, 203
Habeas Corpus Act (1679) 158, 169, 171, 175
home rule 235, 237
impressment 55–62

Irish famine (1845–51) 73–4
land war 222
Liberal party 73, 186, 207–8
Merchant Shipping Act (1854) 69
Navigation acts 86, 88, 90
Passenger acts 83, 130, 241
Reciprocity Agreement (1830) 93
Suspension of the *Habeas Corpus* Act (Ireland) (1866) 177, 192, 193, 223,
trade 85–103
Trafalgar 59
Treason Felony Act (1848) 161, 165
see also England
Britain
Admiralty 159, 224
Foreign Office 38, 224
Home Office 38, 198
Navy 7, 91, 224, 231
Brooks, Edward 43, 64, 157, 218–21, 223, 224, 224, 229, 242–3
Brown, James 126–7
Bruce, Frederick 178, 186, 197, 200, 201
Brutus 80
Buchanan, James 22, 23, 32, 33, 34, 37, 62, 73, 74, 77, 97, 98
Buckle, Claude 204
Bulloch, James Dunwoody 107–9
Burgess, John 47
Butt, Isaac 165, 200

Campbell, Robert 105
Canada
and America 61
famine 75, 78, 97n.220
Fenians 158, 180–2, 185–7, 193, 200, 208
immigration 127–8, 228–9
Cantwell, James 37, 38, 39, 40, 187
Capston, James L. 142–3, 148
Caroline A. Simpson 33
Carraher, James 19
Carlisle, Earl of 143, 175
Cass, Lewis 33, 63

Index

Chasseaud, Jasper 15
Chesapeake, USS 59, 60, 90
Church, James B. 7, 8
   John 7, 28, 55, 59, 61–2, 90, 91, 92
Churchill, Winston 263
Clan na Gael 219, 257n.223
Clarendon, Earl of 178, 180, 186, 187
Clark, Henry 59
   James 59
Clay, Henry 9, 75
Clayton, John 23, 24, 79
Cleveland, Grover 42, 43, 45, 48, 49, 257
Cole, Christopher Bolton 18
Confederate States of America 105–56
   officials 106, 111, 138, 139, 145, 148
   ports 113, 114, 116, 117
   recognition 107
Conolly, Thomas 122–3
Constellation, USS 220
Cooper, James Fennimore 43
Cork 2
   Blackrock 10
   consul in 4, 6, 7, 10, 16, 17, 18, 19, 23, 24, 25, 26, 27, 28, 35, 36, 37, 38, 55, 106, 264
   disease 243, 244, 246
   economy 213–14
   emigration 50, 82, 84, 131, 141, 211–69
   famine (1845–51) 72, 75–6
   fees 26, 29, 34, 43, 44, 50, 76
   Fenianism 159–207
   impressment 57, 59, 61
   pensions 151–2
   sailors 63, 64
   salary 29, 34, 45
   trade 7, 8, 72, 76, 84–104
   see also American Civil War; *Kearsarge*, USS
Cork Examiner 26, 111, 119, 140, 141
Corscaden, James 16, 19, 28, 96, 265
Cove *see* Cork

Cridler, Thomas 47
Crittenden, John J. 74
Crittenden, Thomas 66
Crookhaven, Co. Cork 35, 36
Cullen, Paul 144, 200
Culver, Henry S. 50

Dallas, George 8n.28, 33, 74, 157
Davis, Jefferson 106, 111, 123, 139
Davitt, Michael 217, 219
Dawson, George 243
Dayton, William L. 105
De Leon, Edwin 111, 132–3, 143
Derby, Lord 186, 192
Devine, Patrick J. 35, 36, 63, 106, 108, 113, 115–16, 134
Devoy, John 162, 163, 168, 169, 170, 219
Dingley, F. L. 228, 234, 240, 244, 254, 257, 258
D'Olier, James 14, 88
Donegal 85
   Ballyshannon 85
   Killybegs 85
   Lifford 79
   Moville 46
   Rathmelton 76
Donnan, James 215, 218
Dowling, Robert 34, 84, 105, 119, 141–3, 145
Dragoon, HMS 79
Drogheda, Co. Louth 19
Dublin 14, 19, 26, 31, 32, 34, 36, 85, 88–9, 144, 264
   American Civil War, 134–6, 154
   Castle 32, 64, 69, 140, 198, 213
   consul and vice consul in 3, 4, 5, 8, 9, 10, 13, 23, 27, 28, 31, 32, 37, 41, 44, 45, 49, 50, 145
   Custom House 60, 85, 86
   embassy xi
   emigration 82, 83, 137, 245
   fees, 29, 31, 239, 258
   Fenianism 159–209
   immigrants 240
   impressment 56, 60, 61

legation xi
Metropolitan Police 38
Port Authority 65
salary 29, 31, 33, 40, 45
smallpox 242
trade 60, 77, 84, 93–4, 99–101
Dudley, Thomas 63, 106, 108, 113, 123, 133, 154
Duffy, John 112n.33, 97
Dundalk, Co. Louth 66, 19

Eagle 116–17
Eastman, Edwin George 36, 40, 41, 99, 207
American Civil War 117–23, 145–9, 154, 156, 261
cholera 241–2
economy 213–14
election 213
emigration 130, 141, 212–13
Fenianism 160, 175, 193, 196, 197, 198, 205
Eccles, William 46, 232, 250
EJ 63
Eliza 88
Ella 63
Emmet, Robert 89
rising (1803) 89
England 1, 10, 13, 22, 32
see also Britain
English family 10, 11, 265
Isaac 9
John 8, 91
Thomas 8, 9, 60, 61, 90, 91
Erin's Hope 196–7, 201, 202, 203–07
Evans, Thomas 16
Evarts, William 223
Everett, Edward 21

Farrell, Matthew 47
William 47
Fenian (Irish Republican Brotherhood) xiv, 39, 136, 261, 262
Fenianism 157–209

Sisterhood 159–60, 180
Fillmore, Millard 24, 104
Fish, Hamilton 40, 42, 208
Florida 41
CSS *Florida* 113, 118–19, 146
Forsythe, John 11, 15, 18
Foster, John 87
Foster, Vere 248, 252, 253, 254
Foy, James 24, 66, 83
France xiii, 1, 6, 32
agent 25, 26, 56
and America 54
consul general 105
government 12, 14
Marseilles 34
minister 105
revolution
(1789) 54
(1848) 78
Franklin, Benjamin 2, 33
Frean, Theodore 32, 37, 105, 114
Frederick, Charles 159, 160, 161, 165, 193–4, 196
Freeman's Journal 125, 126, 128

Gallatin, Albert 9
Galway 80–1
American Civil War 130, 134, 154
consul in 16, 27, 28, 46, 80, 84, 106
deserters 64
fees 29, 30, 33, 36, 47
emigration 80, 130, 134, 137, 239
packet station 97–8
pensions 149–50
salary 29, 33
trade 95, 101
Garfield, James 42, 44, 45
Garrick, William 79, 80
George A. Hopley 70
George III (1738-1820) 5
Gillespy, Edward 61
Gilpin, Henry 18
Thomas 16, 18, 20, 72–85, 95, 96
Gladstone, William 207–8, 221, 222, 223, 225, 248

Index

disestablishment (1869) 208
Land Act (1870) 217
Grant, Ulysses 40, 41, 42, 208–9, 210, 216
Gunsaulus, Edwin 259, 265–6

Haly, Standish 62
Hamilton, Alexander 4
Hamilton, Rear Admiral 249
Hammit, Alexander 10
Hammond, Henry 27, 28, 35, 36, 38
    American Civil War 106, 112–13 115–17, 128–9, 132–7
Harper, Fleming 17
    James 17, 64, 72
Harper, Frances 19
Harrison, William Henry 20, 44
Harte, Francis Bret 44
Harvey, Edward 10
    family 10, 11, 265
    Jacob 10
    Reuben 10, 11, 18, 94
Hawthorne, Nathaniel 30, 43, 64, 262
Hay, John 45, 264
Hayes, Rutherford 42, 43
Heap, Gwyn 11n.41, 191, 194, 197, 215
Helberg, Franz A. 67
Henderson, Alexander 31, 84, 105, 137, 211
Herald 114
Heyn, Gustavus 19
Higgins, James Joseph 31
Higgins, John 19, 25, 26, 27, 28, 31, 32, 99
Hobart, Robert 56–7, 87
Hogan, Michael 8
Holmes, James 6, 10, 58, 61, 62, 85, 88, 89, 91, 98, 99
Holmes, Oliver Wendell 45
Hotze, Henry 138, 139, 144, 148
Howells, William Dean 43
Hughes, John 132, 133, 144

Indian Empire 98

Ireland
    Act of Union (1800) 31, 32, 88, 112, 265, 266
    and American Revolution xii-iv
    Americans arrested in 78–9, 158–208, 223–4
    banking 23, 43
    Chancery (court of) 23
    chief secretary 32, 38, 40
    cholera 80
    coercion 223, 226
    communication 70
    Congested Districts Board 238
    cost of living 13, 15, 32, 216
    Customs Board 65
    economy 99, 129, 213–19, 232, 265
    elections 208, 235
    emigration xii, xv, 46, 50, 55, 60, 70–1, 72, 74, 77, 80, 82, 85, 124–48, 210–60, 262
    epidemic 241–6
    famine xiv, 17, 71–85, 217, 219, 223
    Fenianism 159–207
    General Prisons Board 179
    House of Commons 87, 89
    impressment 55–62
    insurrection (1798) xii
    land legislation (1860) (1870) (1881) 217, 222, 224, 231
    land war 217–22, 225, 231, 235–7
    lighthouses 65, 70
    lord lieutenant 32
    New Departure 219
    parliament 2, 13
    Post Office 163
    religion 50, 219, 231, 236, 259, 262
    shipwrecks 65–70
    trade 6, 16, 20, 22, 55, 72–104, 215
    Ulster custom 217, 222
    US relief 220, 221, 223, 224
Irish National Land League (Land

League) 217, 219, 220, 222–5, 235
Irish Parliamentary Party 217, 221, 222
Irish Times 45, 111, 169, 203, 227
Irving, Washington 43

Jackson, Andrew 2, 9, 10, 18, 44
Jackson, John M. 121
Jacob, Robert 11, 17
James 1 (1603–25) 4
Jamestown, USS 75
Jay, John, 2–3, 11, 17
  Treaty 57–8
Jefferson, Thomas 2, 3, 4, 5, 11, 13, 14, 54, 57, 59, 60, 86
John Bright 67
Johnson, Andrew 181, 185, 188, 193, 199, 205, 206, 207, 210
Jones, Lewis 117–19, 145–6
Juliette 76

Kane, Thomas 154
Kearsarge, USS 145–9
Keenan, Hugh 22, 23, 24, 25, 26, 27, 34, 62, 69, 70, 77, 78, 79, 83, 84, 116, 117, 125, 137, 157, 261,
  James 8n.25
  Thomas 22, 23
Keim, De Benneville Randolph 40, 41, 42
King, Rufus 17, 58, 59
King, Thomas R. 41, 152, 242
Kingstown, Co. Dublin 19, 69, 117
Kinsale, Co. Cork 10
Knabenshue, Paul 50, 51
  Samuel 50, 51, 100, 239, 246
Knox, Henry 4, 5, 13, 56
  John 4
  Mary 4
  William (father) 4
  William (son and consul) 4, 5, 6, 12, 13, 14, 15, 56–7, 69, 85–8, 261, 265
Kress, Henry 238, 255

Larcom, Thomas 38, 99–100, 139–40, 170, 173–7, 180, 182–4, 188, 198
Larne, Co. Antrim 44, 259, 253
Lawrence, Abbot 81–2, 97, 104, 158–9, 211, 262
Lawson, James 164, 166, 167–8, 179
Lee, Robert E. 123
Leeds, Duke of 56
Leopard, HMS 59
Limerick
  agent in 4, 6, 16, 18, 34, 80
  American Civil War 120–1
  emigration 82, 246, 253
  fees 46
  Fenians 205
  trade 85–104
Lincoln, Abraham 37, 43, 85, *see also* American Civil War
Lismore, Lord 162
Livermore, Arthur 42, 43, 67–8, 100, 216, 218, 224–5, 228, 229, 233, 247, 251
Liverpool, England 80
  American Civil War 106–9, 113, 114, 139
  consul in 15, 20, 30, 38, 43, 56, 63, 64, 66, 106
  emigrants 82, 129, 253
  Fenians 164
  trade 20, 86, 93, 94, 96
  Underwriters' Association 8, 17
Livingston, Edward 14, 15, 16, 17, 19
Lloyd's Shipping Co. 19, 65, 70
Lodge, Henry Cabot 47
London, England xii, 5, 10, 13
  consul in 2, 10, 11
  consul general 43, 232
  impressment 57, 62
  legation 38, 43, 55
  minister in xiii, 1, 8n.28, 13, 16, 21, 23, 33, 44, 84, 105
  season 32
  trade 86

Index

Londonderry (Derry) 4
  consul 16, 17, 18, 21, 28, 37, 42, 43, 44, 106
  desertion 64
  downgrading 45
  economy 46, 216, 218, 224
  emigration 72, 82, 129, 211, 229–30, 233, 238–40, 244–5, 247, 256
  famine 72, 76, 79–80
  fees 16, 21, 29, 31, 44, 76
  pension 152
  salary 29
  shipwrecks 67
  trade 63, 76, 84–104
Longfellow, Henry 45
Loughead, Robert 17, 63
  famine 72–3, 77, 79–80
Lowell, John Russell 43, 44, 222–3
Luby, Thomas Clark 159
Lucian Victoria 121
Luke, Campbell 7
  family 265
  Joseph 7
  Samuel 7
  William 7
Lurgan, Co. Armagh 46, 47, 101
Lynch, Michael 27
Lyons, Lord 112, 147

MacBride, Robert 64
MacDonald, John A. 186
Mackenzie, George 246
McCabe, Edward 218
McCandless
  James 67
  Samuel 67
McCormick, Hugh 41
McDowell, James 64, 77–8, 81, 96
McFarland, James 117
McGee, Thomas d'Arcy 127, 228
McGunn, Thomas 37, 105
McHenry, James 17, 20, 44, 96
McKinley, William 49
McLane, Louis 14, 16, 18, 92, 93, 95
McLure, Thomas 81, 97

Macedonian, USS 75
Madison, James 7, 8, 17, 32, 59, 61, 90, 91
Maghan, Frederick 47
Malcolmson, David, 114–15
Mann, A. Dudley 106, 132, 144
Marcy, William L. 19, 25, 26, 30, 31, 32, 33, 67
Mark, Jacob 8, 11
Marshall, John 59
Martin, John 39
Mason, James M. 111, 112, 117, 139, 141, 142
Massachusetts 10
  immigration 84, 249
Maury, James 13, 56
Mayo, Earl of 206
Meagher, General Thomas Francis 37, 112, 138
  Irish Brigade 37, 138, 149
Merritt, Edwin A. 232, 248
Mexico, Mazallan 33
  Mexican–American war (1846–8) 24, 74
Minahan, John 253
Mitchell, Alfred 18, 24, 27, 80
Mobile 66
Moe, Alfred K. 49, 50, 102
Monroe, James 6, 9, 10, 59, 89, 90, 91
Moran, Benjamin 27, 33, 36, 37, 39, 55, 63, 262
  American Civil War 109, 111, 118, 123, 133, 147, 155
Morgan, John T. 48
Morris, Michael 203
Morris, Gouverneur 56
Morse, Freeman H. 3, 110
Motley–Clarendon Convention (1870) 208, 263
Murphy, John 11, 16, 17, 18, 23, 24, 25, 27, 63
  famine (1845–51) 72, 75, 76, 80
Murphy, Michael 19

National Brotherhood of St Patrick 39, 134–6, 192

Neill, Edward W. 40, 216, 247
Nelson, Horatio 59
Newenham, Edward 2
Newport, John 90
Newry, Co. Down 19, 20, 47, 85–104
New York 4, 7, 8, 9, 10, 16, 24, 31, 33, 39, 40
   draft riots 138
   emigration, 82, 83, 130, 131, 227, 247, 248, 250, 252
   Fenians 158, 171, 178, 205
   National Guard 163, 168
Northern Ireland 22
Nugent, James 224, 249

O'Brien, William Smith 112, 144
O'Donovan Rossa, Jeremiah 159
O'Hagan, Philip 46
O'Leary, John 159
O'Mahony, John 136, 157, 158, 162
O'Neill, John C. 66
Oxnard 63

Palmerston, Lord 75, 79, 81, 107
Paris, Treaty of (1783) 1, 56
Parnell, Charles Stewart 217, 218, 219–20, 221, 225, 236, 237
Peel, Robert 73, 104, 139
Pennsylvania, US 22, 24
   Hospital for the Insane 14
   Philadelphia 6, 7, 8, 10, 14, 16, 18, 31, 44, 88
   Pittsburgh 22, 31
Persse, Thomas Moore 16, 9n.33, 80–1, 95, 97, 106, 150, 154, 265
Peterhoff 116
Phelps, William 6, 91
Phoenix Park murders 225
Piatt, Arthur Donn 50, 153
   Cecil 258
   Fred 256
   Sarah Morgan 45
Piatt, John James 44, 45, 68, 152, 262
   emigration 226, 229–55
Pickering, Timothy 6, 58, 88

Pierce, Franklin 24, 25, 43
Pinckney, Thomas 57
Pitt, William 56
Pius IX (1792-1898) 143–4
Poe, Edgar Allan 44
Polk, James 23, 74, 75, 79, 104
Pollacky, Ignatius 110
Poor Law unions 251, 253
   Cahirciveen 250, 252
   Carrick-on-Shannon 46, 249, 250, 251
   Limerick 251
   Milford 250
   New Ross 68
   North Dublin 247
   Sligo 73, 232
   South Dublin 247
   Tralee 246, 250, 254
Porter, James D. 43
Portland, Duke of 90
Portrush, Co. Antrim 70
Portugal 2, 3, 14
Pridy, John 57

Queenstown *see* Cork

Randall, Paul R. 5
Rea, James 152, 227, 242
Reasons for abolishing impressment 62
Reddington, Thomas 78
Reid, Alex 238
Religious Society of Friends (Quakers) 10, 11, 18, 74, 75, 76
Richmond, Lewis 100, 216, 217, 218, 221–2
Rives, George L. 46, 236
Robert Kelly 69
Roberts, William 158, 185, 193
Roche, James 39, 128, 134–5
Rodger, Pat 46, 152, 238, 239, 244, 256, 258
Roosevelt, Theodore 49, 239
Rowntree, Thomas W. 19
Ruby, Samuel 22, 152, 238, 243, 244
Rush, Richard 62

Russell, Earl 38, 104, 107, 138, 140, 147–8, 159, 162
Russia 1, 14, 88
Ryan, Daniel 38
Ryan, Michael Robert 10n.38, 18, 120-1

St John, New Brunswick 16, 50
St John's Island (Prince Edward Island) 60
Sanford, Henry Shelton 36, 41, 105, 110, 122, 132
Sautee 68
Savage, George W. 46, 48, 101, 152, 228, 230, 236, 236, 254, 256
Scotland 1, 2, 22, 32, 47
  Glasgow, 34, 41, 44, 46, 47, 82, 113, 116
  Presbyterians 4
Scott, George 26, 95
Seymour, C. and W.D. Co. 18, 24, 119
  Nicholas 18, 24, 25, 26, 27, 34, 35, 113
Seward, Frederick 115
  American Civil War 105–54
  William 27, 35, 36, 39, 64, 210
  emigration 131, 133, 242
  Fenianism 158–207
Shamrock newspaper 61
Shaw, James 20, 21, 96
Shaw, John 41, 247
Simpson, Captain 33
Sinn Féin 102
Skelly, Francis 21, 96
Slidell, John 111, 112
Sligo 16, 17, 19, 46, 47, 72, 76, 85
Smith, James R. 28, 30, 31, 34, 63, 70
Smith, Robert 8
Snow Alfred D. 68
Sorle, Captain 27
Stanley, Edward 200, 201
South Pacific 28
Spain xiii, 1, 2, 3, 14, 44, 54, 264
  Spanish-American war (1898) xiii, 239, 262, 264

Spencer, John C. 20, 96
Staines, Edward 43
Stanley, Foreign Secretary 200, 201
Stanton, Edwin M. 133, 181
Stephens, James 136, 157, 158, 159, 193, 194, 195
Stephens, Philip 57
Strathcairn, Lord 194
Strobel, Daniel 14
Swiney, Daniel 246, 258

Tait, Peter 120
Talbot, Samuel 19, 27, 28, 33, 34, 37, 40, 84, 97–8, 99, 100, 106, 112
Taney, James 22, 102, 238, 245, 264
Tarbox, J. H. 66
Taylor, Zachary 24, 104
Tennant, Robert Allen 47
Tertius 67
The Clara 69
The foreigner's book of American knowledge 128
The Squire, HMS 57
The usurper: an historical tragedy 44
Tighe, John 46
Tinsly, John 251
Touvelle, William 238, 256
Townsend, William H. 67
Townshend, Lord 60
Trent affair 111, 112
Trevelyn, Charles 73, 232
Tucker, Beverly 35, 106
Tucker, R.H. 67
Tuke, James Hack 248, 252, 253
Tuscarora, USS 108, 109
Tyler, John 18, 21, 44
Tynan, Katharine 45

United Irishmen, Society of 6, 59, 61, 87
United States (Army)
  recruitment 132–50, 239
United States (Navy) 167
  Civil War 115
  impressment 55–62

United States (State Department) 8, 10, 11, 12, 15, 16, 18, 20, 23, 24, 26, 28, 33, 34, 40, 41, 42, 45, 46, 47, 55, 67, 68, 70, 77, 202, 207, 216, 263
  Consular Bureau 47, 48, 67
  immigration 228, 234, 236, 242, 243, 244–5, 247, 253–4, 256
United States (Treasury Department) 22, 29, 35, 40, 43, 45, 248
United States
  citizenship 6, 11, 16, 17, 18, 19, 24, 46, 55–62, 78–9, 167, 172, 178, 203
  consular legislation (1792) 12, 14, (1855 and 1856) 20, 22, 28, 29, 31, 33, 34, 35, (1895) 48, 49, (1906), 49, 50
  Democratic–Republican 3
  Democratic party 17, 23, 24, 45, 48, 49, 75, 79, 80, 105, 193
  economy 2, 103, 215, 257, 265
  Embargo Act (1807) 90
  Executive 62
  Federalists 2, 54
  Fenianism 157–209
  foreign policy xi–xv, 54, 55, 74, 79, 82, 157, 181, 197, 208–10, 239, 263–4
  Homestead Acts (1864) 128, 131, 226, 227
  House of Representatives 28, 45, 58, 59, 131, 158, 203, 219–20
  H. R. Committee on Commerce 20
  immigrants 70–1, 82, 83, 124–47, 210–60
  impressment 55–62
  Irish famine (1845–51) 71–85
  Irish in 17, 24, 37, 44, 58, 74, 78, 124, 248
  Know-Nothing party 110, 124, 142, 143, 189, 211
  Naturalisation Act (1802), 17
  Non-Intercourse Act (1809) 90
  Page Act (1875) 211
  pensions 71, 132, 149–53
  Republican party 37, 40, 49, 105, 193
  revolution xii, 3
  Scottish–Irish culture 6
  seamen 28, 62–8
  Senate 11, 48, 58
  ship wrecks 62–70
  'spoils system' xiv, 9, 10, 12, 45
  trade 16, 19, 20, 48, 55, 85–104
  Washington DC 41, 42, 43
  Whig 20, 23, 24, 44
  see also Parnell
Upshur, Abel 17, 18, 21

Van Buren, Martin 14, 16, 93
Victoria, Queen 174, 186

Walker, Lucien 238, 256, 264
Wall, William 49
Waller, Thomas 43
Walsh, Jasper W. 19
Wandering Jew 26
War of 1812 xiii, 8, 32, 55, 91, 264
Washington, George 2, 3, 4, 5, 6, 10, 13
Washington, Horace Lee 49, 101
Waterford 68
  American Civil War 114, 117, 126
  consular agent in 16, 17, 18, 34, 47, 80
  famine 71
  fees 46
  Passage West 34, 36
  pensions 150
  Portlaw 114
  trade 85, 101
Webber, James 13,14
Webster, Daniel 24, 96, 97
Weed, Thurlow 132
Welles, Gideon 122, 147, 149, 182
Wellington, Duke of 93
West, William 28, 37, 38, 39, 40, 64, 67, 84–5, 104, 213
  American Civil War 106–54
  emigration 130, 134, 211, 226–7
  Fenianism 157–209, 261

Index

pensions 149–51
Westmoreland, Earl of 85
Wexford 37, 66, 228
   agent 19
   Arthurstown 68
   coast 67
   famine 71
Wicklow
   Arklow 67
   Arklow Bank 66, 69
   Marine Society 67
Wilbour, Joshua 240, 264
Wilson family 11, 265
   Joseph 60, 89, 90, 92, 93
   Thomas 9, 10, 15, 22
   famine (1845–51) 71–85
Williams, Josiah 10n.38, 18, 150

Winslow, John 145–6
Wodehouse, Lord (Earl of Kimberley) 160, 170, 184, 192
Wood, Arthur B. 45, 46, 48, 67, 227, 233, 234, 249–50, 253, 262
Woodbury, Levi 15

Young Ireland movement 37, 38, 39, 112, 127, 144, 228, 262
   rebellion (1848) 39, 78, 79, 189
   The Nation 144
Young, John 19, 37, 262
   American Civil War 106, 109–22, 128, 153, 261
   emigration 130
   Fenians 166, 170, 175, 191
   pensions 149

EU authorised representative for GPSR:
Easy Access System Europe, Mustamäe tee 50,
10621 Tallinn, Estonia
gpsr.requests@easproject.com

www.ingramcontent.com/pod-product-compliance
Ingram Content Group UK Ltd.
Pitfield, Milton Keynes, MK11 3LW, UK
UKHW042017140426
5217IPUK00015B/1226